STORIES

MY FATHER TOLD ME

STORIES
MY FATHER TOLD ME
NOTES FROM "THE LYONS DEN"

JEFFREY LYONS

FOREWORD BY CHARLES OSGOOD

ABBEVILLE PRESS

New York   London

FRONT COVER: *see page 234.*

BACK COVER, TOP: see *page 13.*

BACK COVER, BOTTOM: *My father and Orson Welles.*

PP. 2–3: *My father on his beloved terrace overlooking New York's Central Park, circa 1966.*

EDITOR: Walton Rawls
PRODUCTION EDITOR: Michaelann Millrood
COPYEDITOR: Ashley Benning
DESIGNER: Misha Beletsky
PRODUCTION MANAGER: Louise Kurtz

First edition
10 9 8 7 6 5 4 3 2 1

Library of Congress Cataloging-in-Publication Data

Lyons, Jeffrey.
  Stories my father told me : notes from "The Lyons Den" / Jeffrey Lyons.
— 1st ed.
    p. cm.
  ISBN 978-0-7892-1102-6 (hardback)
  1. Celebrities—Anecdotes. 2. Celebrities—Interviews. 3.
Biography—20th century—Anecdotes. 4. Lyons, Leonard, 1906-1976.
—Anecdotes. I. New York post. II. Title.
  CT120.L96 2011
  920.71—dc22
                        2010048256

For bulk and premium sales and for text adoption procedures, write to Customer Service Manager, Abbeville Press, 137 Varick Street, New York, NY 10013, or call 1-800-ARTBOOK.

Visit Abbeville Press online at www.abbeville.com.

PHOTOGRAPHY CREDITS
All photographs are from the Lyons family archive, with the exception of the following:
Cover and page 234: Sam Shaw; pages 2–3: Ben Martin; pages 10–11: Sam Shaw; page 13: Daniel Grossi; page 16: Bill Mark; page 49: *Look* magazine; page 52: Dunman Photos; page 55: *Look* magazine; page 106: Bill Mark; page 137: Gustave W. Gale; page 149: Libsohn-Ehrenberg; page 153: Jay Seymour, Gary Wagner Associates; page 94: Ben Martin; page 235: Sam Shaw; page 251: Bill Mark; page 252: Otto Rothschild; pages 266–67: Horace Sutton; page 280: Agenzia Pieriuggi; page 294: Lawrence Schiller, Credit Alskog, Inc.; pages 296, 301, 305, 309, 310, 313, 315, 317, 319, 321, 322, 324, and 326: *Reel Talk*

This is a testament to my father's life's work.

This is also for my wife Judy, our son Ben, and daughter Hannah, the three most important people in my life. If nothing else, they put up with my eccentricities and my foibles; I don't deserve them.

My parents holding hands during a night out at the Stork Club circa 1940.

How the paper promoted the column in the 1930s, just outside the Post building.

CONTENTS

With Stork Club owner Sherman Billingsley and Sir
Alexander Fleming, discoverer of penicillin, circa 1950.

FOREWORD

By Charles Osgood

In 1999 my *CBS Sunday Morning* TV program marked the 100th anniversary of the birth of Ernest Hemingway with a broadcast from Finca Vigía, the Havana home where the great writer lived for twenty years. When I got home to New York, a neighbor in my apartment building told me he especially enjoyed that show because he'd been to Finca Vigía with his father to visit with Hemingway, and that Papa (Hemingway) himself had taught him to shoot. How many people do you know who could say that?

That neighbor is Jeffrey Lyons, the gifted writer, critic, television commentator, and author of this book. Jeffrey's father was the incomparable Leonard Lyons, who over a span of forty years between 1934 and 1974 wrote a column called "The Lyons Den" which was published in the *New York Post* and in 105 other newspapers around the world. These columns contained fascinating anecdotes about movie stars, Broadway performers, ballplayers, comics, singers, songwriters, painters, poets, politicians, presidents, dictators, restaurateurs, all sorts of people. Leonard Lyons disliked the word "celebrity." He used to say that if his sister in Brooklyn became newsworthy he'd write about her. And when she did, he did.

Leonard Lyons was a lawyer by training. He got the job as columnist beating out five hundred other applicants after writing for the English page of the *Jewish Daily Forward*. "The Lyons Den" was decidedly *not* a gossip column. Lyons did not write about who was "running around," as George Burns used to put it, with whom, who was cheating or being cheated on, or who was arrested again for drunk driving or drug possession. You might find that sort of thing in Walter Winchell's or Earl Wilson's column, but never in "The Lyon's Den." Jeffrey's father believed, as do I, that good journalism does not require that you keep your fangs bared or your claws unsheathed. Lions might do that but not Lyons. It was not his objective to embarrass the people he wrote about or destroy their reputations. Like Charles Kuralt, Leonard Lyons genuinely admired the people he wrote about. And knowing this they would open up to him and tell him the colorful stories that were his bread and butter, and that the readers loved.

Jeffrey tells me that unlike the other big columnists, his father had no "leg man" to gather information for him. He made daily and nightly rounds of New York watering holes himself for all those years. He didn't drink with the in crowd; in fact he was a teetotaler. If he saw another columnist in a restaurant he would leave because he wanted all the stories in his column to be exclusive. In those days the word meant something.

In the 12,479 columns Lyons turned out, over those four decades more than one thousand people were named, including some of the most famous people in the world, many of whom would became his friends. It seemed to Jeffrey and his three brothers that their father knew everybody who was anybody. What their father taught them was that everybody *is* somebody. Imagine what it must have been like for them growing up with parents like theirs. Former New York Mayor Lindsay said in his eulogy of Leonard Lyons: "In a business of sharks, he was a prince."

I never met Leonard Lyons. But my neighbor Jeffrey and his brother Doug obviously inherited some of his friend-making and storytelling gifts. Jeffrey is the only person I know whose telephone is answered by Joe DiMaggio.

My father and his pride of Lyons, circa 1950. I am in the grey suit, and neither my younger brother Douglas nor I have quite mastered the correct position of our feet.

INTRODUCTION

One day when I was in fifth grade, the members of my class were asked to stand in turn and tell what their fathers did for a living. (Back then, there were few working mothers.) I remember hearing: "lawyer," "doctor," "investment banker," "painter," "musician." Then came my turn, and I said: "Columnist." No one seemed to know what that meant, so I said: "My father writes about all *your* fathers."

My father Leonard Lyons wrote "The Lyons Den" column in the *New York Post* and was syndicated in over 100 newspapers around the world from 1934 to 1974. His anecdotal style of writing flourished in the Golden Age of the Broadway column. Whereas others dealt in scandal, gossip, and rumor, he thus stood alone, enjoying a special place in his craft.

"The Lyons Den" became an American journalism institution and a "must-read" for millions. It was our family's key to the world. My father knew *everyone*! Stroll down Madison Avenue on a Saturday afternoon perusing the art galleries with him, and everyone knew him or recognized him or had an item for him. Our home movies, for example, had the usual scenes of my family sledding down snowy hills in Central Park, tossing a football or baseball, and long-dead relatives mugging for the silent camera. But those color films also showed us with family friends: Marc Chagall, Marilyn Monroe, Ernest Hemingway, Edna Ferber, Moss Hart, Adlai Stevenson, Sir Alfred Hitchcock, Cary Grant, Charlie Chaplin, Orson Welles, Sophia Loren, and Frank Sinatra. Oh, and a few others, too: Danny Kaye, Thornton Wilder, José Ferrer, George Bernard Shaw, and Laurence Olivier.

It's a safe bet that most of my classmates didn't have such family friends. Nor did they say goodnight to their fathers at 7 a.m.; most fathers would return from work just before dinnertime. Mine, however, worked from midday until dawn. He spent every night out on the town—not gallivanting or drinking (he was, as they used to say, a teetotaler) but gathering stories for his next column. We thought playing baseball across the street in Central Park with Paddy Chayefsky on Saturdays and Sundays, as well as showing Richard Burton how to bunt, was normal. We thought a phone call from Hemingway or a late-night call from Milton Berle or a holiday gift from J. Edgar Hoover was normal.

One night, Norman Mailer called, seeking legal advice from my father, a practicing lawyer before he became a columnist. Mailer had just stabbed his wife.

Didn't *everyone's* parents get invited to the White House or attend Broadway openings and movie premieres? Didn't *every* family have Nobel Prize winner Dr. Ralph Bunche, composer Harold Arlen, and Phil Silvers sit at their seder table every Passover? Didn't *every* high school football player get to kick field goals at the New York Giants training camp? Or tour Spain with the famous matador Antonio Ordoñez? Didn't *other* kids know Joe DiMaggio on a first-name basis or get a phone call from Marilyn Monroe on their sixteenth birthday? It never occurred to me that there was anything unusual about such an upbringing. Looking back, it wasn't just unusual. It was amazing!

In his tribute the day after my father died in 1976, Clyde Haberman of the *New York Post* wrote that my father "knew personally more names than probably anyone in any country." He quoted my father saying he understood "the appetites of newspaper readers for the kings and stars and villains."

"Lyons made the world's famous familiar to the average subway straphanger," and, saying his was anything but a gossip column, "there was more news to be made looking at people across nightclub tables than through the keyholes of bedroom doors. He expanded the column from mere show business chatter to include the professional activities of notables in politics, literature, and diplomacy.

"Carl Sandburg, our greatest historian, called him 'America's foremost anecdotist.' He reveled in ironic, sentimental, sometimes dramatic human stories about very important persons, from Broadway to the White House. For four decades 'The Lyons Den' was an institution and will be invaluable to historians seeking behind-the-scenes glimpses of that long era."

It was an amazing life he led, going from a poor boy born in a Lower East Side tenement in New York (who twice ran away from Fresh Air summer camp because he missed the city!) to a dinner guest of the Trumans on their last night in the White House; from the son of a Romanian tailor who died young, leaving his widow to sell cigarettes individually at a candy stand (who later learned to read English so she could enjoy her son's column in the newspaper) to invited guest at the Monaco wedding of Princess Grace and Prince Rainier. From a night-school graduate of the City College of New York to having tea at 10 Downing Street with Churchill. He traveled from winning the Spanish prize pin at P.S. 160 to wearing it on his lapel at a white tie dinner at the Kennedy White House, where the invitation had read: "Decorations will be worn." It was quite a journey.

If only I'd had that tribute to read to my classmates so long ago!

This is a book about some of the most amazing people of my father's time and ours: authors, actors, politicians, musicians, and athletes mostly. Stars who've risen to the apex of their professions telling you things you never knew about them.

Along with his brother Al, my father went to the High School of Commerce, then

*Leonard Lyons hard at work in the 1940s (judging
from the lapels and the typewriter).*

to the City College of New York, where he studied accounting; then he finished second in the first graduating class of St. John's Law School, before being admitted to the New York Bar in 1929.

But journalism would become his eventual calling. While practicing law, he began contributing items to columnists and wrote a column under his original name, Leonard Sucher, for the Sunday English page of the famed *Jewish Daily Forward*, a newspaper that still exists. The column was called "East of Broadway," a reference to the Lower East Side where thousands of immigrant Jews from Eastern Europe were clustered at that time. But he kept contributing items to the more established columnists of the day and built up a scrapbook.

Then in 1934, the *New York Post* announced a contest to find its own Broadway columnist to rival Walter Winchell, who'd created the genre in the *Daily Mirror*. My father entered, showed his bulging scrapbook, and beat out 500 other applicants to win a job at the *Post*—the oldest continually published newspaper in America, founded by Alexander Hamilton in 1801.

Starting on May 20, 1934, he would write six columns a week for forty years to the day. It was in the age of New York's so-called "café society." Soon after he'd assumed his new job, his editor told him on a Friday that come Monday he'd have a new name. "Lyons" was chosen to be the alliterative counterpart of Winchell's.

But unlike his rivals, never once did he use the word "celebrity." He abhorred it. He said he'd write about his sister Rosie in Brooklyn if she did something newsworthy, as well as presidents and movie and Broadway stars, politicians, scientists, athletes, soldiers, and statesmen. They had to make news.

Early in December 1955, our family appeared on Edward R. Murrow's famous *Person to Person* show. My father proudly

pointed east out our living room window on Central Park West to indicate the part of town where he was born. Then he showed the nation a book inscribed to him from President Eisenhower, who called my father "a *real* writer."

"So now," he proudly said, "if anyone doubts it, I can call myself a writer by proclamation of the President of the United States."

One night in 1952, my father sat in Sardi's restaurant with famed actress Ethel Barrymore, great aunt of today's star Drew Barrymore. She overheard someone at a nearby table referring to "the Barrymore Theater." "Excuse me," said this member of America's greatest acting family: "That's 'The *Ethel* Barrymore' Theater!"

The next night, my parents gave a party at our home in her honor. My brothers and I were sent to bed at our usual hour. But I awoke to the chatter of the guests in our living room, walked in, and surveyed the landscape: All grown-ups I didn't recognize. Then in the corner I spotted someone I adored. In a room full of bigger names than his, he stood by himself, too shy to mingle. I walked past the other guests, tugged at his jacket, looked up, and said: "Mr. DiMaggio, you're the best guest here!"

Twenty-three years later at an Old Timers' Day at Shea Stadium, DiMaggio in his famed number "5" Yankee uniform spotted me, recognizing me from television (can you imagine!), beckoned me over, and said: "Jeffrey, do you remember that night?" I nodded, of course. "Would you still say that about me?"

Oh, among the other guests—the "nobodies" I bypassed to get to him that night at our home—were Edward G. Robinson, Ernest Hemingway, Marlene Dietrich, Judy Garland, and Adlai E. Stevenson. Lightweights.

It was an incredible grind for my father, six days a week; each day there was a full

A common custom in the 'fifties, my parents rarely flew on the same plane, much less a private plane, but apparently did so arriving at the Grossinger airport in 1951.

Baseball was and still is a very important part of the Lyons family. Here, in 1949, are the four youngest team owners in baseball history. We owned exactly one share of the New York Giants. That's Douglas, today an author and criminal defense attorney, nearly biting the hand that feeds him.

OPPOSITE:
My mother with Denton True "Cy" Young in February 1951, at Toots Shor's. That right arm holding my mother's hand won 511 games, a baseball record which will never be broken.

1,000-word column to fill with exclusive, firsthand copy. To do that, he'd cover a dozen Manhattan restaurants where notables lunched. An actress told the *New York Times*: "He goes where the wind blows, darting from table to table, with his eyes always moving on to the next promising group."

Two hours or so later, he'd have enough material for a rough draft of the next day's column. He took the subway down to the *Post*, then on West Street in Lower Manhattan. He'd write his column, hand it in to the city desk, then come home on the subway. Sometimes, he'd notice someone sitting next to him reading his column. Just before his stop, at Eighty-First Street and Central Park West, he'd delight in saying: "That guy writes a helluva column, doesn't he?" and exit the train just as the reader did a double take.

After a quick nap (he could sleep soundly through any piano practice), or pitching for batting practice, or tossing a football to his four sons across the street in Central Park, his evening would begin. While most of his competitors (who'd handed in the final version of their own columns that afternoon) were now relaxing at home, he'd go out again to gather later stories.

The city was alive in those mostly pre-television days, buzzing with excitement every night. He'd walk into Toots Shor's on West Fifty-Second Street and sit with Jackie Gleason or Mickey Mantle, meet the Duke and Duchess of Windsor down the block at the posh "21," have tea with Marlene Dietrich at the Russian Tea Room, or sit with Richard Burton and Elizabeth Taylor at Downey's. All in one night! Every night! Six nights a week!

This was decades before pagers or cell phones, but if we had to reach my father, we knew he'd always be at Sardi's, the famed theatrical restaurant, around 11:30, in the middle of his rounds. His photograph still adorns a wall in tribute.

Nightclubs like El Morocco, the Stork Club, the Little Club, and in earlier times Jack White's 18 Club and other iconic places of that era, were all in full swing.

He'd come home around 1 a.m., and for several hours would painstakingly write the stories he'd just gathered, then dictate them—no email then—to the night city editor down at the *Post*, working what was in those days called "the lobster shift," updating his column to make it fresher than his competitors'. Then for an hour just after dawn, he'd work on a magazine article. About that time, my brothers and I would awaken, sometimes getting a capsule summary of what happened around town the night before, then losing to him in a quick game of checkers before my father retired.

He wrote an astonishing 12,479 columns, each 1,000 words long. The only day he missed was the day his mother died. One or two had been "evergreen" columns he'd run while traveling overseas, or on rare occasions one was written by a guest. His columns provide a history of a glorious time in America and wherever he traveled.

My parents took many inaugural flights, as airlines were continually expanding their international routes in those days at the dawn of the jet age; Egypt, South America, Australia were all on his beat.

Sunday nights, a Western Union messenger would pick up the column to deliver to the *Post*, and for a year or so it was a teenager named Edward Albee. That's why in his masterpiece drama, *Who's Afraid of Virginia Woolf?*, the quarreling couple learns of the death of their imaginary child by way of a Western Union messenger.

"I printed that first!" my father would often beam when he'd see his stories purloined by others days later. He was trained as a lawyer and accountant, but he was born to be a journalist; for him, a "scoop," getting a story first, was the ultimate prize.

In his time there were no faxes, nor emails, word processors, Internet, computers, laptops, cell phones, and until the mid-'sixties, no electric typewriters. He worked on a boxy Underwood typewriter and carried on trips clunky portables with rickety keys. Every day, his secretary annotated every story on index cards, differentiating between one-time-only news items and "evergreen" anecdotes for future reference. More than 100,000 people were mentioned in the column; some only once; others, like the ones in this book, turned up repeatedly over the years. It's their stories I've culled to present a window into that incredible era.

Overseas, he was with the First Army Press Corps in 1945. There he visited Hitler's mountain headquarters in Berchtesgaden, Bavaria, to examine the remains of the infamous "Eagle's Nest," where a Jewish boy from the Lower East Side made it a point to urinate on the huge, ugly concrete swastikas outside. We have the movies to prove it!

He was on the set of *The Bridge on the River Kwai* in 1957, in what was then Ceylon, and

*At a charity golf tournament on June 3, 1950. My
father actually beat Jim Thorpe, the greatest athlete of
the first half of the twentieth century. Thorpe used only
a putter and a driver.*

accepted an invitation from his friend producer Sam Spiegel to push the plunger that blew up the famous replica of the bridge.

My parents attended a seder in Nasser's Egypt, which was then closed to Jewish visitors; my mother covered Queen Elizabeth's coronation for the column, and he and Truman Capote were the "Group Historians" on a 1955 tour of post-Stalinist Russia by a *Porgy and Bess* troupe.

Back in New York, making his nightly rounds, he'd go "table-hopping," seeing a star or writer he knew or who knew him—working the room, his notebook always at the ready. If he spotted a competitor, he'd leave, fearing his stories would thus not be exclusive.

Other columnists of that day, like Ed Sullivan, Hy Gardner, Jack O'Brien, Bob Sylvester, Lee Mortimer, "Cholly Knickerbocker," and of course his greatest rival, Walter Winchell, used "leg men." Those were assistants and press agents who fed the columnists stories mentioning their clients, or

the restaurants or nightclubs they handled. By contrast, nearly all of my father's stories were either firsthand or double-checked for veracity. Over the years he used several secretaries, including Anita Summer, who worked diligently for him for the last quarter-century or so of the column, as her predecessors had done.

My father went to the High School of Commerce where today's Lincoln Center stands. Though undersized, he turned out for football. The first day of practice, he was lined up in a tackling drill opposite a huge youth named "Henry." That boy's high school nickname was, ironically, "Babe." Ironic because his full name was Henry Louis Gehrig. One tackle from the future "Iron Horse" of the Yankees, and my father headed off to the swimming team. But first Gehrig taught him how to drop-kick the watermelon-shaped ball of that era. It was a skill my father passed on to me forty years later when I was a kicker in college and high school.

In my four decades on TV and radio as a movie and theater critic and interviewer, I've come to know scores of actors of my era and many from my father's. But these are different times. With a very few exceptions, my acquaintances have been professional. Only a handful have become close personal friends. It's just a different world today.

In my father's time, many larger-than-life people became members of our extended family. In December 1952 we were house guests in Cuba at the home of Mary and Ernest Hemingway, who taught me how to fire a rifle. Orson Welles was one of my father's closest friends, as his youngest daughter Beatrice is one of mine today. My brother Warren lived with Ira and Lee Gershwin in California; composer Harold Arlen, UN Undersecretary General and Nobel Peace Prize winner Dr. Ralph Bunche, songwriter and show director Abe Burrows, and comedian Phil Silvers and their wives were regulars at family seders; there was nothing like having the traditional Passover songs played on our living room piano by the man who wrote "The Girl with the Three Blue Eyes," or by Arlen, who wrote "Somewhere Over the Rainbow." Playwrights Clifford Odets and Sidney Kingsley and Supreme Court Justice William O. Douglas were godfathers to my brothers and me. Joe DiMaggio and fellow Hall of Famer Bob Feller attended my bar mitzvah.

This book includes several of my interviews as well. You'll see these current stars in a whole new light, as they reveal things they told my father and me and no one else. You'll feel you're seated across a table at a New York nightspot "back in the day" or are sitting on my set in the studio waiting for the stage manager's cue as interviewees recall incidents in their lives that usually don't appear in biographies or film books.

There's a difference in style. My father's encounters were more social: chats over lunch or coffee—he was a teetotaler (as am I)—or conversations in our home or on trips together. In most cases, I met stars for interviews on my sets at WNBC and, earlier, at WPIX. In my interviews, usually limited to twenty minutes or so, I covered their entire careers; on the other hand, my father's chats were akin to reunions between long-separated friends, relationships sometimes spanning decades.

Often, he'd take one of his sons on his rounds with him. Other times, photographer Henri Cartier-Bresson, astronaut Scott Carpenter, Viktor Sukhodrev (Khrushchev's interpreter), Brendan Behan, Paddy Chayefsky, and former Postmaster General then NBA Commissioner Larry O'Brien accompanied him on his rounds. But most nights, he had no idea whom to expect, beyond those he already knew happened to be in town.

My interviews, by contrast, came after days, sometimes weeks of preparation from my vast clipping file and extensive cinema-book library and movie collection. With my father, actors were always at ease. I had to put them at ease, early in the interview, by showing them that I was well prepared.

In my father's day, newspapers and radio, and only later television, were the primary forms of communication. Today there is a media explosion, and actors are more guarded. Say or do something you wish you hadn't, and if the interviewer isn't trustworthy or professional, it can flash across the world instantaneously. But both his stories and my interviews present a snapshot of times in which the most creative and talented people flourished.

Shortly before illness forced him to end the column on May 20, 1974, my father received a citation "for Distinguished and Exceptional Service" from New York Mayor John V. Lindsay, noting his "courage in the protection of the sources of newspapermen and his service to his native city of New York."

On September 10, 2006, my father's 100th birthday, New York Mayor Michael Bloomberg proclaimed: "No one did more to promote New York's deserved reputation as a capital of glamour and culture." He added that "a century after his birth, the legacy of Leonard Lyons lives on. The names on the marquee may have changed, but the memory of Leonard Lyons remains a guiding light in New York City's cultural community."

These interviews and anecdotes span seventy-five years, and have been condensed and combined to present full pictures of their subjects. Our son Ben Lyons has continued the family tradition, reviewing movies in "The Lyons Den" segment and conducting interviews for the E! television network on *E! News*. Somewhere, somehow, my father is smiling down on him, and his sister Hannah, a natural-foods chef; and his parents could not be prouder.

ACKNOWLEDGMENTS

This book wouldn't have been possible without the support and help of Bob Abrams, the president and publisher of Abbeville Press, and the best captain I ever played with. No other teammate in high school and college so inspired by deeds more than words the way he did. Also to his incredible staff, including Susan Costello, Misha Beletsky, and Michaelann Millrood. Without them, this book would not have the incredible look they've conceived.

My thanks to Edie and Meta Shaw for giving me permission to use the photos taken by their talented father, Sam Shaw, Marilyn Monroe's official photographer.

The encouragement of my wife Judy was crucial. She patiently listened to my favorite stories, and made suggestions with a critical eye to the text. So did my brothers Douglas and Warren; the former helped in the editing, the latter contributed his vast knowledge of Broadway history.

Walton Rawls was my patient editor. Emails flew back and forth as he moved the text around, urged me to expand in some areas and delete in others. He was invaluable.

And thank you to Karen Gantz, my literary agent, for her confidence in me.

Thanks too to my old friend Kirk Douglas for his comments which appear on the flaps, and to Robert Osborne, the superb host of the most enjoyable cable network of them all, TCM.

I first heard Charles Osgood on the Armed Forces Radio in Spain in 1961 and have been a fan ever since. I listen to him twenty times a week, almost without fail. He honored me by writing this book's Foreword.

To all the restaurant and nightclub owners of my father's era, thank you for making him feel welcome every night, allowing him to table-hop and to gather stories and thousands of exclusive anecdotes on newsworthy luminaries about whom this book is written.

And to my father for taking my brothers and me along on so many of the nights around town, when we had the privilege of meeting some of the most amazing people of his time. For thirty of the forty years of "The Lyons Den," we were the beneficiaries of the incredible tireless work of my father. His legacy of journalistic decency endures in the way his son and mine have conducted our careers in the same field and have lived by his tenets. He and my mother gave us an incredible life, filled with culture, music, sports, theater, movies, travel, a love of learning, and respect for all.

'30s

With J. Edgar Hoover at the FBI Headquarters, November 29, 1935. Despite their friendship, Hoover kept a file on my father, as he did on many friends and foes alike.

The Lyons Den

By LEONARD LYONS

When my father wrote his first column for the *New York Post* on May 20, 1934, he was a skinny, nervous young man of twenty-seven, winner of a contest for the job, then assigned to cover the most exciting city in the world, teeming with nightlife, despite the Depression.

Vaudeville, the world of touring variety shows, was just about dead, after New York's Palace Theater, once its mecca for live entertainment, had switched over to talking pictures, then about seven years old.

Vaudeville might've been in its last throes, but it had been the spawning ground for countless comedians and actors who then switched to the theater and radio, by then enormously popular. President Roosevelt had given the first of his "fireside chats" the year before, and Americans were glued to their bulky sets every evening.

Phil Silvers, Red Buttons, Eddie Cantor, Al Jolson, Sophie Tucker, Olsen and Johnson, and others had honed their comedic talents in burlesque.

New York nightlife received a great boost once Prohibition, a terrible idea, was repealed by Congress with the Eighteenth Amendment in 1933. The age of the speakeasies was done.

My mother's uncle, Izzy Einstein, gained a measure of fame during Prohibition, teamed with Mo Smith as the era's most successful federal agents, making nearly 5,000 arrests of violators of the Volstead Act—Prohibition—from 1920 to 1925. They would be portrayed by, respectively, Jackie Gleason and Art Carney in a made-for-TV movie in 1985, which Jackie Cooper, a child star of the 'thirties, directed.

Nightclubs like the posh Stork Club and the Latin Quarter (a former church converted into a nightclub by Lou Walters, father of Barbara) were filled with famous faces every night.

On Broadway, shows like *Porgy and Bess, Jumbo, On Your Toes, Babes in Arms,* and *The Boys from Syracuse* were big hits. It was the time of the Federal Theater, Orson Welles's *Mercury Theater of the Air,* The Group Theater, and writers like Clifford Odets, Robert E. Sherwood, S. N. Behrman, Lillian Hellman, and Sidney Kingsley. (Full disclosure: My godfather.)

New York was *the* newspaper town; long-gone papers like the *Daily Mirror, The World, The Telegram, PM, The Sun,* and *The Brooklyn Eagle* were flourishing, along with the *New York Times, The Herald Tribune,* and *The Journal-American.*

It was into that world that my father, who'd already written a column called "East of Broadway" for the English-language page of the *Jewish Daily Forward* ("Stop the presses! Hold the back page!"), began his career as a Broadway columnist.

IRVING BERLIN

In May 1988, I did a long series for CBS radio commemorating Irving Berlin's centenary. I'd found an old interview he did with my mother, dubbed over from a wire recorder. In his slight, high-pitched voice, he spoke of how his father had been a rabbi in Russia, how he came to America, and how he went on to write nearly 1,000 songs, including "God Bless America," "Easter Parade," "Alexander's Ragtime Band," "White Christmas," and "Cheek to Cheek."

Berlin's talent, seemingly indigenous to America, began not with a "breeze through the trees" nor a "wail of some frail," but in Russia as a boy. During World War II he brought his troupe from *This Is the Army* to London, hoping the Soviet ambassador would invite them to his native country, if only to see his name billed as: "HOMETOWN BOY MAKES GOOD."

The first time Berlin's name appeared in print was the day after Queen Victoria's granddaughter, the Marchioness of Milford Haven, was taken on a tour of the Bowery in Lower Manhattan. In one saloon she was served by a singing waiter. The host of the party was Prince Louis of Battenberg, who later changed his Germanic name to Mountbatten, the English equivalent.

Their guide was Herbert Bayard Swope, the famed executive editor of the New York *World*. The prince offered the poor waiter a tip, which the young man declined. Swope printed that story, and Berlin's debut as a singer was news. Swope recalled, "Irving was a terrible waiter and an awful singer, too."

Years later, when the prince's widow dined with Berlin in London, that story was told at the table. As they began to chat, the daughter, seated at the far end of the table, inquired what they were talking about.

"We're talking about your father, dear. He and Mr. Berlin were old friends."

It was once said of Berlin's singing voice, which can be heard in the movie version of *This Is the Army,* "You have to hug him to hear him."

Berlin later acknowledged that assessment. Nevertheless, when he gave a performance of his songs at a Hawaiian leper colony, he had the stage moved closer to the lepers to make sure they'd hear him. He told an audience of ASCAP members (The American Society of Composers, Artists, and Publishers), "I caught cold yesterday. I thought it would improve my singing voice."

One night in Lindy's, then one of New York's most famous restaurants, Berlin was sitting with the great playwright Clifford Odets and director/playwright Moss Hart. Each was listing his favorite shows. Odets chose his flop play *Paradise Lost,* which ran a scant seventy-three performances. Hart chose *The Fabulous Invalid,* his collaboration with George S. Kaufman. That one ran just sixty-eight performances. Berlin chose *As Thousands Cheer,* which ran 400 performances—nearly a year, "and made lots and lots of money!"

Berlin was surely the most prolific songwriter of modern times. One producer, however, protested that Berlin was giving him songs that must be coming from his trunk; i.e., songs that, like "God Bless America," had been sitting around for decades.

"Don't you have anything 'fresh?'" asked the producer.

"Fresh?" replied Berlin. "What am I, a baker?"

For Franklin D. Roosevelt's inauguration gala in 1941, Berlin brought the orchestrations for "God Bless America" to the National Symphony conductor who said he couldn't decipher even one portion. Berlin replied: "Then I'm sunk, because I can't read music."

Astonishingly, he never could. His specially designed piano (now in the Smithsonian) was able to transpose any song to the simplest of keys, C Major, with a crank of a knob. Berlin played only the black keys, the sharps and flats.

Oscar Levant, the brilliant but dour pianist/actor/raconteur, said of the unending tributes honoring Berlin: "I know of no man who needs them less but deserves them more."

Berlin once took a train from New York to California and sat with a recording company executive who proposed an album of Berlin favorites. He asked Berlin to choose his six favorite songs.

Two days and 3,000 miles later, Berlin told him: "I can't choose six of my favorite songs I've written. It's like choosing a favorite child."

Richard Rogers's wife Dorothy was once in a New York taxi and heard "The Girl That I Marry" playing on the radio. "My husband wrote that," she proudly told the cab driver.

Hours later under the dryer at the beauty parlor she suddenly said aloud: "Dick didn't write that song. Irving Berlin did."

After he achieved worldwide success as a songwriter, Berlin frequently visited the old Bowery haunts where he began his career. One evening he spent time with one of the old men at a mission. The old man asked Berlin to play "White Christmas." Just then some tourists arrived, led by a guide who delivered a talk about the history of the Bowery and about the bar where Berlin had been a singing waiter.

"As a matter of fact," said the guide pointing proudly, "that's Berlin right there at the organ!"

The tourists stared skeptically at the organist, moved on, and one told the guide with a sneer: "We may be from out of town, but you don't expect us to believe *that* do you?"

Late in his life, Berlin took up painting and became quite devoted to it. His friend, photographer Sam Shaw (who took some of the most famous photos of Marilyn Monroe), said: "Irving, those paintings are good. They're really good. Why don't you put them on display?"

"I'm not ready to exhibit my paintings," Berlin replied. "They're not really good until I hear people say: 'I'm not sure Irving Berlin painted them.'"

In July 1949 during the run-through of the Broadway musical *Miss Liberty*, for which Berlin wrote the songs, he went to the New Amsterdam Theater to sit in. At the entrance to the building he met Mae West, and both went into the elevator together. When it started its ascent, Berlin said: "It seems to be climbing more quickly now than it did in the early days, when I used to go up to see Flo Ziegfeld."

"No, Irving, the elevator was no slower back then. It's just that in those days we were younger—and more anxious," West replied.

During another rehearsal of *Miss Liberty*, Eddie Albert, the star, mispronounced one word in a song. "OK, so I made a mistake," he said to Robert E. Sherwood, the FDR speechwriter and author of the libretto. "Even Roosevelt makes mistakes."

"Yes," replied Sherwood, "But never with an Irving Berlin lyric."

Berlin was incredibly prolific. He wrote campaign songs for Al Smith's presidential run in 1928, and penned "I Like Ike" even before Eisenhower had declared his candidacy in 1952. It was a song Berlin put in his show *Call Me Madam*. Eisenhower attended the opening night and was the only one in the audience who didn't applaud.

GEORGE BURNS

On October 9, 1984, during an interview I had with George Burns, he told me a joke. Suddenly he stopped, just as he was approaching the punch line, and said: "I told those jokes to your father. Do you have children? I'll tell these jokes to them, too."

He was ninety-four at the time. I was amazed at his ability to remember names and places from decades earlier. I reminded him that he often performed in vaudeville with acts like "Swain's Cats and Rats," "Madame Burkhart and her Cockatoos," and "Powers' Elephants."

As soon as I mentioned those acts, from the Stone Age of modern American show business, he asked: "What do you think the finish to Swain's Cats and Rats was? A racetrack! Right there on the stage! The cats would run around the track, and the mice were the jockeys. Never saw anything like it!

"Teddy Roosevelt was President. And Madame Burkhart's cockatoos spelled out 'Roosevelt' at the finish with an American flag waving. Applause, applause. Everyone loved it. But not the manager. Somebody named Weinberger. So one day he told them to spell out his name instead, and he said if they could do that they could stay three more days. So Madame Burkhart rehearsed those cockatoos for days and days, and finally they spelled out 'Weinberger,' and the audience booed, so they had to put back 'Roosevelt.'"

Burns got his start training shy, clumsy, immigrant Polish men, some literally just off the boat, how to dance. "We were in a Polish neighborhood, and they learned quickly how to do a waltz, fox-trot, and a two-step, all for five dollars.

"But they could only dance with *me*! So I'd have to go with them to dances, and some of them danced too close. So I quit."

In those days, Burns was eager for any sort of work, and one day his agent told him there was a call for a dog act. So Burns found two strays, led them onstage, and let them do what they wished, while he and his partner did a dance routine.

Burns married Gracie Allen, and they became enormous radio stars, making occasional movies, and transitioned into television in the 1950s. Burns lived to be 100, and he made frequent appearances on *The Tonight Show*, singing long-forgotten songs and telling stories of the old days.

His screen career was resurrected in movies like *Oh, God!* and *The Sunshine Boys*, replacing his dear friend Jack Benny, who had died. He won the Oscar for Best Supporting Actor. His was one of the longest careers in show business, spanning vaudeville, radio, movies, and modern television.

In 1939, Burns and Allen were introduced to Albert Einstein who, they were told, was unfamiliar with their work on radio. So Gracie decided to ask him just one question: "Tell me something," she said. "Is mathematics really on the level?"

In April of that year, an IRS auditor questioned a large deduction Burns and Allen had made for one of Gracie's gowns. "My wife also has an evening gown, and she didn't pay so much money for hers," the auditor said.

"The difference," Burns replied patiently, "is that my wife gets laughs."

Before he met Allen, Burns smoked José Hermosa cigars, so he named his dance partner at the time "Hermosa José." "But to give you an idea what a great act it was," he remembered, "our opening number was 'La Zarina,' which is a mazurka, a Russian dance. And we were wearing Spanish clothes. Naturally, right after the first dance, they cancelled us."

One night in 1950, Burns was in New York and lunched at Toots Shor's restaurant. A woman, suspecting Burns was wearing a toupee, kept staring at him. Finally he'd had enough. He turned to her, nodded politely, then lifted the rug off his head and said to her: "Yes, it is!"

When he and Allen debuted their first TV show, they rehearsed thoroughly. "That way," he told me, "it looked unrehearsed."

Burns was once asked about Judy Garland's success. "When she was signed by Louis B. Mayer at MGM for $5,000 a week," he said, "she was just ten years old. I could've had that kind of success with a contract like that, too," he said, "but the only trouble is, when I was ten—so was Louis B. Mayer!"

Burns was a mainstay at the famed comedians' table at the Hillcrest Country Club in Beverly Hills each afternoon. Someone at the next table surveyed them and looked over Burns, Jack Benny, Groucho Marx, George Jessel, Eddie Cantor, and Lou Holtz, and asked who was the oldest.

"Oh Eddie Cantor is," replied Burns. "Because Cantor's hair is the darkest."

In *Oh, God!* Burns played the title role without makeup. "We're about the same age," he explained, "but we were brought up in different neighborhoods."

I asked Burns to tell me about the time he became a Presbyterian.

"Well, we were four kids on the Lower East Side of New York on Rivington Street," he recalled, going back to his old neighborhood. "And there was a Presbyterian church there, and they had a talent contest sponsored by a department store. And we had a singing group called 'The Peewee Quartet.' And we won first prize. Each of us got an Ingersoll watch, which cost about 65 cents apiece.

"And I ran home and told my mother, who was hanging the wash, that I didn't want to be a Jew anymore. 'I've been a Jew for seven years, and never got anything. I've been a Presbyterian one day and got this watch.'

"My mother said, 'First help me with the wash, then you can be a Presbyterian.'

So I did and the watch fell into a bucket of water and stopped running, so I became a Jew again."

When Burns was fourteen in 1910, he brought home an "older woman."

"Oh, that was Gertha DeFore," he recalled seventy-four years later. "She was sixteen and had a beauty mark; in those days that meant you were a streetwalker. And not just any beauty mark; hers had little hearts around it. And I brought her home and said: 'Mama, I want you to meet my sweetheart.'

"And my mother looked at Gertha and looked at me and said to Gertha: 'Do you speak Jewish?' (i.e., Yiddish). And when Gertha said no, my mother turned to me and said in Yiddish: *'Gay mandrea,'* which means 'Go to Hell!' And then she turned to Gertha and said: 'I just told my son what a charming girl you are.'"

Burns loved talking about his show business origins, and I reminded him about "The Three Smoothies," a long-forgotten act.

"When Gracie and I were on radio," he recalled, "we were offered a kid singer who'd just left Tommy Dorsey's band, and we were offered him for $250 a week. But I was also offered this harmony act, also for $250. Well look, I'm a businessman, right? Am I going to take just one young, unknown singer for $250 a week when I can get *three* people for the same money? Of course not. So I took 'The Three Smoothies,' and I didn't make a mistake. You know how big they are today. By the way, whatever happened to that kid singer—Frank Sinatra?"

Though born Nathan Birnbaum, George Burns used many names in his long career. One was "Willie Delight." Another vaudeville hopeful, after printing up a thousand name cards, gave up show business to remain a cab driver. "He had 920 cards left," said Burns, "so he sold them to me for $2. So I changed my name to 'Willie Delight' until I used them up. Then I chose some other name."

Burns had four brothers and seven sisters, but an older brother—also named George—was the provider. "So we all changed our names to 'George,' and when our mother called out 'George,' nobody turned around. Not me, not Izzie, not Morris, not Sammy. Not even George."

CHARLIE CHAPLIN

In 1971, I covered my first Academy Awards, the year Charlie Chaplin, the first mega-star in the movies, made a dignified return to Hollywood to receive an honorary Oscar. Unlike the other journalists, I was in the auditorium, not in the adjoining press area, so I could feel the crowd go absolutely silent until, in his soft, gentle voice, he finished his remarks. Then thunderous applause, years overdue, burst out.

Attorney General James P. McGranery, otherwise lost to history, had revoked Chaplin's reentry visa while the Chaplins were on a ship en route to Europe for a holiday in 1952. It was due to Chaplin's supposed Communist sympathies, part of the Red Scare hysteria during the McCarthy era. Unfortunately, McGranery had died

Words of wisdom from Sir Charlie Chaplin at the Stork Club circa 1950.

nine years before and didn't see the tribute at the Oscars.

Late in 1938, Chaplin met with Gertrude Stein, the great writer. He told her about his movie *Modern Times*, relating the complete story in all its details. Stein listened carefully. Finally when he'd finished, all she said was: "Oh. It's a comedy."

Two years later, "The Lyons Den" reported that one of Albert Einstein's prized possessions was an autographed photo of Chaplin presented to him after a meeting in which Chaplin questioned Einstein about the Theory of Relativity, Einstein suggested that it would impossible to try to explain it.

"It would be the same as if I were to ask you to do some acting for me now," said Einstein. "You couldn't." Nevertheless, for the next hour, Chaplin talked, argued, and extolled about complex mathematical theories, until the confused Einstein, having to rebut some of what Chaplin was saying, was left exhausted.

The next morning, a messenger brought Einstein a picture of Chaplin on which was inscribed: "To a great mathematician. I hope you enjoyed my acting."

In October 1940, the infamous German-American Bund, a pro-Nazi group, was at its height. Chaplin wanted to visit a theater located in its base in Yorkville, also known as Germantown, on Manhattan's Upper East Side. "I want to go there, just to see how much I hate 'em," he insisted to his friend, writer-director Garson Kanin. But Kanin convinced him it would be dangerous if someone recognized him. Instead, they headed to Rockefeller Center where Chaplin enthralled a crowd by reciting a six-minute speech as a mock Hitler in *The Great Dictator*.

Chaplin was the most famous man of his time. A little-known incident is an example of how difficult that could be. It was 1924 and Chaplin was miserable. Reporters had been covering his divorce proceedings with Mildred Harris Chaplin, and he grew weary of the constant hounding. So one night he jumped into a taxi and asked the driver to cruise around Central Park so he could find some peace and temporary privacy. An hour of aimless riding followed.

Finally the driver looked into the rearview mirror and said: "I know who you are, Mr. Chaplin. What's wrong? How can I help?"

Chaplin confided his woes and his desire to avoid photographers for just one night.

"So why not come to my place and sleep there?" the driver suggested. "Our two kids can double up and you can have the extra bed."

So the most famous man in the world spent the night in welcomed obscurity at 761 Trinity Avenue, the Bronx, New York.

In April 1942, Chaplin invited some friends to his home, including the great English actor Charles Laughton, best known as Captain Bligh in *Mutiny on the Bounty*. All evening, they debated politics, economics, and world affairs. Every few minutes, Laughton would shake his head, marveling at Chaplin's knowledge of any subject, and say: "You're the greatest, Charlie."

Finally, Chaplin asked: "You keep saying that. 'The greatest *what*?'"

"The greatest comedian," came the reply.

One scene in Chaplin's *Limelight* showed the audience hissing the clown portrayed by Chaplin, who also wrote and directed the movie. At an early screening, Chaplin didn't think the audience in the movie had hissed him convincingly, so he dubbed in his own hissing—of himself!

After the first preview of *Limelight*, Chaplin spoke to the audience about his youth and his first idol, a music hall juggler named Paul Cinquevalli. He taught the young Chaplin a lesson. Cinquevalli had studied a difficult trick, and for seven years tried to perfect it. He practiced it four hours a day. Finally he mastered it, but when he performed it, he got no applause.

"He told me he made it look too easy," said Chaplin. "He told me first to learn to make it look impossible. Learn to fail a few times convincingly. Then when you get it right, they'll love you."

During their time, Chaplin and Orson Welles were among the few filmmakers in Hollywood who wrote, produced, and starred in their own films. Chaplin was a shrewd businessman who earned millions. Welles cared little about his own money and thus accumulated but a pittance. Welles once gave Chaplin an idea for a movie. Chaplin liked it and told his business manager to ask Welles how much he wanted for it.

"Nothing," said the trusting Welles. "We're friends. It's a gift." But Chaplin insisted on paying. Welles offered to sell the idea for $10,000. "Offer him $7,500," Chaplin told his office.

Eventually, Chaplin made *Monsieur Verdoux*, based on an idea different from Welles's. Although he'd promised Welles screen credit anyway, Chaplin said: "Oh, additional names would just clutter up the screen." But the day after the movie opened and received some unfavorable reviews, Chaplin added the screen credit of Welles's name.

On July 15, 1957, Chaplin invited Dylan Thomas to his home for lunch. Chaplin quickly dominated the conversation. Thomas finally complained, saying, "Mr. Chaplin, I came here to talk *to* you, not have you talk *at* me." Chaplin ignored him. Thomas finally got Chaplin's attention when, after Chaplin had talked another half hour, Thomas turned his glass of champagne upside down on Chaplin's rug.

Chaplin bought his first studio on Sunset Boulevard in 1916 and made his historic comedies there. On the day he moved in, he walked with his famous tramp shoes over the still-wet cement, leaving permanent imprints that would be known all over the world. He even signed them. But years later, the property was sold to a TV network. The first thing the new owners did was to rip up the famous footprints.

When he was a young, unknown performer, Chaplin got his first chance to be noticed onstage. He was an understudy but went on one night, pushing a cart across the stage while the two stars of the comedy bit worked up nearer the audience. All he was required to do was to call out: "Fish!" Suddenly the stars heard the audience howling at something going on behind them.

It was Chaplin, who extended the thirty-second bit to eight minutes by improvising. He tripped, pretending the cart was too heavy with fish to push. Then he pretended to be injured. He sniffed at the wares, as if unsure what was in the cart. Then after several vain attempts to utter a sound, he called out: "Fish!" and got the biggest laugh of the show. He was fired the next day.

When he sold his interest in Pathé Comedies, Chaplin got his first million dollars. He was given a check, but instead of depositing it right away kept it for two days. He'd frequently toss it into the air in exultation for anyone to see. When asked why he didn't take it directly to the bank, he replied: "What? And miss all this fun?"

In May 1960, Chaplin showed off his vast Swiss house in Vevey and its treasures to a guest. The mansion was large enough for servants and seven children, several governesses and chauffeurs for the three cars, an Alfa-Romeo, a Peugeot, and a Bentley.

"And yet," he sighed, "in America, they call me a Communist."

In January 1962, the British government announced it wanted to confer a knighthood on Chaplin. At first, however, he refused it, explaining that "audiences would find it impossible to accept the mustached little forlorn tramp if they knew he really was 'Sir Charles.'" He then was asked about future projects and said he was considering starring in biographies about Napoleon and Eisenhower. "But I'm too tall for one, too short for the other."

Chaplin once told my father about dealing with a publisher and questioning a clause in their contract. But the publisher, in a condescending tone said: "You're suspicious because you're accustomed to the movie business. This is quite different."

"I agree," replied Chaplin. "Quite different. There are far more crooks in publishing." Then he stormed out.

In March 1966, Chaplin met someone he hadn't seen in fifty-three years. "I had a bit role in your first film, *Tillie's Punctured Romance*, in 1914," said the man, hoping somehow Chaplin would remember him. "I was one of the kids you gave candy to and patted on the head in one scene," he continued.

"Ahh yes, I remember," replied Chaplin. "That was 'exposition.'" The man was Milton Berle.

When it was announced that his wife would have their eighth child, Chaplin explained his large family: "It began when someone told me that the best way to raise an only child is to give birth to another one."

His son Sydney was an actor of some note who revealed that his father always thought him a college graduate. In reality, however, Sydney had dropped out of high school at sixteen after playing hooky at the beach. This lasted two years before he enlisted in the Army and fought in World War II. Then he turned to acting. He said his father was never the wiser.

Sophia Loren starred with Sydney Chaplin in *A Countess from Hong Kong*, which the elder Chaplin directed in 1967. "We got along superbly on the set," she recalled. "Besides, how could anyone argue with a man who invented the business we're all in?"

TY COBB

I remember meeting Ty Cobb at a game in Yankee Stadium, several years before he died in July 1961. I knew that during his playing days he was despised by opponents and teammates alike. He ran the bases with spikes flying, and reportedly carried a Confederate flag and a gun most of his adult life. There is also the story of his attacking an armless and legless heckler in the stands.

After the sixth game of the 1955 World Series, Cobb was in the Yankee dressing room. Reporters surrounded him, trying to get his reaction to the game. "The Yankees," Cobb began, "always win the big one. There's something special about being a Yankee. When you put on a Yankee uniform, it adds something to your dimension as a player, an intangible."

Just then Yankee pitcher Tom Morgan tapped Cobb on the shoulder, and without recognizing the greatest player of baseball's "Dead Ball era" and the man who still holds the career lifetime batting average of .367, said: "Move over, Mac. You're crowding the front of my locker."

One night my oldest brother George made nightclub and restaurant rounds with my father, as all three of my brothers and I occasionally did. At Toots Shor's restaurant, there sat Cobb. My father introduced him to George, who knew more about baseball than anyone I've ever known.

Cobb was holding a glass of whiskey in his hand and noticed a puzzled look on my brother George's face. "Look at this drink," he told the boy. "It's Scotch. I never touched a drop of whiskey nor smoked a cigarette until I was thirty-eight. And you mustn't either. You must give your body a chance to develop. After you're thirty-eight, it won't matter."

In everything he did, Cobb wanted to be the best. He was surely the richest man to play the game, having invested in two small companies about 1909: Atlanta-based Coca-Cola and General Motors back when GM was a budding corporate giant. When his playing days were over in 1928, Cobb managed the Tigers and used a practice sliding pit to compete with his young players in what was, in those days, called a "broad jumping" (now long jumping) contest.

A young player, who'd been a decathlon champion, once outjumped him by three feet. Two weeks later, Cobb ordered a rematch and won. They tried again and again, and Cobb kept winning. He'd taken lessons from the track coach at a nearby college, just to beat that rookie.

As a player, Cobb didn't admire many competitors. But he did like "Dizzy" Dean, the aptly named Cardinal and Cub Hall of Famer, whose career began two years after Cobb retired. Cobb said Dean came into the Tiger locker room before the opening game of the 1934 World Series and, one-by-one, recited the weaknesses of each opposing player and told everyone how he'd pitch to them. Dean then pitched a complete game victory.

Cobb recalled taunting Lefty Grove in an effort to trick him into giving him a fat pitch to hit.

"I don't need a bat to hit you," Cobb yelled at Grove. "I'll ram the ball down your throat if you give me a straight fast one." Grove did, and Cobb got a base hit.

Like every player, Cobb had an embarrassing moment or two on the diamond. One of the worst was in a game after he singled and stole second base.

"I swear I saw Eddie Collins return the ball to the pitcher," he said. So he took a long lead off the base. Collins then approached him with one hand behind his back.

"Mr. Cobb," said Collins, "Guess what I have?"

It was the ball, of course, and Collins tagged out one of baseball's greatest base runners.

Gene Fowler, the famed writer, once described Cobb as one of the worst drivers he'd ever seen. "He loves to turn around while driving and tell you how he stole home from second base," Fowler explained.

GARY COOPER

Preceding John Wayne by just a few years as the personification of the American movie hero, Gary Cooper had already made some sixty movies, many of them silent films, by the time my father began writing "The Lyons Den" in 1934. Cooper was one of those stars of the Golden Age of Hollywood who didn't come East too often, so I was surprised to find anecdotes about him in my father's column. But he must've come through town now and then, where they probably met at the Stork Club.

Cooper described New York as "a great town for carrying groceries."

John Ringling North of the famous circus productions said Cooper told him he was interested in speaking to the circus's sixty Bengal Lancers. He asked them detailed questions, amazing them with his knowledge, until he explained that he'd appeared in *Lives of a Bengal Lancer*.

When Cooper was spotted shopping at the women's nightgown counter at Macy's in 1939, he was soon surrounded. By 500 women!

After it was announced that he would star in the movie version of *For Whom the Bell Tolls*, his good friend Ernest Hemingway, who wrote the classic novel, recalled Cooper's fine performance in Hemingway's *A Farewell to Arms,* and the one and only fan letter he ever wrote to the actor.

Cooper's trademark was his propensity for saying only a few words, the most famous of which was, "Yup." Helen Hayes, who starred with him in *A Farewell to Arms,* met Cooper's mother on the set and asked her if, as a boy, he was uncommunicative. "I once saw him looking out the window at the rain," recalled Mrs. Cooper. "I asked him what he was thinking. 'Nothing,' he said. And he's been like that ever since."

After Gregory Peck, who'd just done *The Gunfighter,* turned down the part, Cooper accepted the lead role in *High Noon* and won the Oscar for best actor. Composer Dmitri Tiompkin, who won an Oscar for writing the famous theme song, said that when he took the assignment and learned that Cooper was the star, he thought all he'd have to do was put music to the word "Yup."

Producer Sam Goldwyn recalled that of all the movie people he'd ever employed, Cooper always gave the impression of being the deepest thinker, since he was usually silent. Once, just before he went to a state dinner at the Roosevelt White House, Cooper stopped off at the home of a Washington notable and appeared to be steeped in thought. "What are you thinking," asked another guest, Supreme Court Justice William O. Douglas, expecting words of wisdom. "Only this," came the reply. "Where the hell can I get a drink?"

Clifford Odets, probably the greatest American playwright of the 1930s, wrote the screenplay for *The General Died at Dawn,* in which Cooper starred. Cooper lifted the hefty screenplay and said simply: "A lotta words. But I'll learn 'em."

My father once shared that after he appeared in *For Whom the Bell Tolls* with Cooper, veteran character actor Akim Tamiroff refused to work in another movie with the star. "Nobody noticed me," he explained. In fact he said he went to see the movie and found himself looking only at Cooper.

The great playwright Robert E. Sherwood heard someone call out "Hello, Bob" at New York's posh "21" club. The near-sighted Sherwood had forgotten his glasses and couldn't quite make out the tall man who'd greeted him. So he said: "Oh, hello, Gary," explaining later that "No man is insulted by being mistaken for Gary Cooper."

When production was about to begin on Cooper's famous movie *Sergeant York,* about the World War I hero, the studio had to obtain consent from notables being portrayed on the screen. Secretary of State Cordell Hull and General John J. Pershing quickly consented. The last one to grant a release was "Oscar of the Waldorf," the hotel's maitre d'.

At a movie premiere, Phil Silvers sat next to a woman who spotted Cooper and tried to get his attention. "Just whinny like a horse," the comic advised.

Cooper flew to the Utah desert to visit his friend John Wayne filming *The Conqueror*. He saw the scene in which Wayne, as Genghis Khan, galloped across the desert pursued by a horde of Tartar warriors. "At last, here's a picture where I couldn't play your role," said Cooper. "There's no way to say 'Yup' in Mongolian."

Still, at one point, Cooper grew tired of Westerns and ordered his agent to "get me anything you can to get me out of a ten-gallon hat." In *Friendly Persuasion*, Dorothy McGuire played his wife. "When I read the script," she recalled, "I had to make sure Coop was kissing me, not his horse."

Cooper once described where his mini-malist style came from: "Acting embarrassed me. It was painful for me to make a gesture that was broader than the absolute minimum."

Like many stars during World War II, Cooper made U S O tours to meet and greet the troops. In New Guinea in April 1944, several soldiers shouted for him to recite Lou Gehrig's farewell speech that he did in *Pride of the Yankees*. "It's been several years," replied Cooper, "but I'll try. Give me a minute or two." He wrote out the famous speech, and delivered it flawlessly.

Then he added: "Gehrig was a simple man, with simple standards. When the time came, he responded with typical American courage. I suppose that's the way all of you are, simple men whose courage will win this war for our nation." Cooper had left the states not knowing how he could entertain the troops other than by showing up and shaking hands.

Now he knew. He recited the speech for the remainder of his tour, always to thunderous applause.

NOËL COWARD

When you think of British sophistication and urbane wit, no one outdid Sir Noël Coward, the writer, composer, playwright, and actor. I first met Coward in the South of France in the summer of 1958, when my parents took my younger brother Douglas and me to the home of W. Somerset Maugham, where Coward was a guest. I remember a long discussion I had with Coward, defending bullfighting, which, despite my feelings, is of course indefensible from a non-Spanish perspective.

Now, all these years later, I can't believe the patience that great man had with me, a precocious thirteen-year-old. Did I *really* debate Sir Noël Coward at that age—or any age, for that matter?!

When Coward returned to London from one of his frequent visits to New York, he said: "New York is a marvelous place to live." Then he threw up his hands in despair, adding: "But to visit?"

When a member of the audience saw Coward after he'd attended Coward's play *Set to Music* in a Boston tryout, the playwright said: "I think I'd better write a new finish to that." The theatergoer agreed, saying: "I think you'd better." That was the unofficial first decision made by the theatergoer, Felix Frankfurter, after being named a Justice of the Supreme Court of the United States.

In October 1937, Coward, who liked to send gag telegrams under the signature of others, encountered a Western Union operator who was paying strict adherence to the rules. She wouldn't let him sign: "Mayor Fiorello La Guardia" to a telegram. "OK, just sign it 'Noël Coward,'" he sighed.

But the operator wouldn't believe it was Coward, who then had to keep talking until he finally convinced the operator he was indeed who he said he was.

"Oh in that case," said the operator, "it'll be OK to sign your telegram 'Mayor La Guardia.'"

It wouldn't be until 1969 that Coward would be knighted. But even as far back as 1938, he envisioned such an honor. After he was passed over that year, he was asked by a reporter if it's true that "98 percent of those knighted are morons."

"My dear chap," replied Coward, "I have never heard that figure set so low."

Soon after that, my father, who loved introducing people from different worlds who'd never otherwise meet, brought someone to meet Coward. It was "Two Ton" Tony Galento, the Newark bartender who'd floored Joe Louis in their title fight a few weeks before.

"Nice to meet you, Mr. Galento," said Coward, in his crisp, upper crust British accent.

Taking note of Coward's obvious sophistication, Galento, thinking he had to say something highfalutin, said: "Oh, Howdy Doody."

Coward said he made his money "by the sweat of my high brow," and explained why he first came to New York in May, 1940. He had been in Paris, just before the German invasion, but quickly left town. Not because the invasion was imminent, but because "I had a sudden craving for the peanut butter sandwiches I used to get here in New York at a lunch wagon on Lexington Avenue. So here I am."

"I prefer sailing to New York on a French ship," he proclaimed. "They don't have that silly rule, 'Women and children first.'"

But he wasn't in love with everything French. When, for example, his play *Present Laughter* flopped on the Parisian stage, he said: "Frenchmen must not understand French. My French was too perfect. The Paris critics looked upon me as just another French actor."

There was once a "Noël Coward imitations" contest held in New York, and playwright/director Garson Kanin, a friend of Coward's, won. But as he reached for the prize, Coward, who'd been in the audience, arose and announced he was entering the contest. He ascended the stage, then recited the complicated lyrics to a song he'd written twenty-five years earlier—something no other contestant would even attempt, and won.

Coward had this advice for actors: "Just go out and do it. The 'how to' books are usually written by those who went out and did it, then spent their later years boring everyone by writing how to do it."

In October 1944, Coward toured all the British fronts to entertain the troops. Officers he met insisted upon making the introductory speech, and invariably each would conclude by asking the troops to sing: "For He's a Jolly Good Fellow."

Backstage, Coward and his accompanist always anticipated the song and joined in, but one time, their timing was off by a few seconds, and before the introduction was finished the troops heard prematurely over the loudspeaker the voices of Coward and his accompanist singing lustily: "For We Are Jolly Good Fellows."

In August 1947, Coward was praised for his performance in *Present Laughter* and said: "It's no surprise, really. I wrote it about myself . . . *for* myself."

Back in London in September 1947, Coward received an invitation to a party from Beatrice Lillie, the comedienne/actress. His RSVP read: "Mr. Noël Coward regrets exceedingly that he can attend the dreary party given by Miss Beatrice Lillie."

One day, Coward took Lillie to visit Teddington-on-Thames and told her it was the finest spa in the world. "I owe a lot to this place," he said. "When I first came here, I hadn't the strength to utter a word.

I had scarcely a hair on my head. I couldn't walk across the room, and I had to be lifted from my bed."

Then he explained that he had been born there.

Nearly every stage actor suffered from nerves or even stage fright at one point or another in their careers. Not Coward. He advised nervous colleagues on opening night to remember that "there's nobody in the audience clever enough to be up there in your place."

In October 1963, Coward and writer Harry Kurnitz were preparing the play *The Girl Who Came to Supper* and had a tryout in Boston. "An out-of-town tryout before Broadway," said Coward, "is like taking a girl home to meet your mother. You know she's not perfect, and you'll soon be told why."

The always urbane, elegant Coward once sat in a dentist's chair, and the doctor said: "Expectorate, please."

"What?" said Coward incredulously. "*me* spit? Never!"

Like every giant of the theater, Coward was asked for advice to give young actors. "Young people should go on the stage only when they feel that's the one thing they'd rather do above all else. The only advice I ever gave actors is to learn to speak clearly. Project your voice without shouting, and move about the stage gracefully, without bumping into people.

"After that," he concluded, "you have the playwright to fall back on, and that's always a good idea."

A British author named T.H. White owed a debt of gratitude to Coward. When he was an unknown writer, White brought the script for a new play to Coward and asked for advice. He took Coward's advice, turning his play into a novel, but kept the title, *The Once and Future King*. Years later, it was adapted into a musical by Lerner and Loewe called *Camelot*.

In addition to being a great playwright, actor, author, director, and raconteur, Coward could perform in French and was an accomplished painter. He once explained why he preferred landscapes to portraits: "A landscape can't talk back," he said.

His friend Sir David Lean, the great movie director, once sent someone to Coward for an audition for one of his plays. "What did you think of him?" Lean asked later.

"I fear the worst," Coward replied. "He has the eager look of the inefficient."

In November 1957, Coward's play *Conversation Piece* was revived in an off-Broadway production. The original had been performed twenty years earlier. "That's appropriate," he proclaimed. "Otherwise it would be cruel to the original principals. Ten years ago they still would have wanted to play the roles. But twenty years later, none of them minds when the role goes to another."

In 1955, Coward sent word that he wanted Lauren Bacall for the TV version of his play *Blithe Spirit*, in which she'd portray a ghost. "I wouldn't have to carry anything, would I?" asked Bacall. "I hate working with props. So what would I carry?"

"Only the play, my dear," replied Coward. "Only the play." Unfortunately, that production was never staged.

At the beginning of the wartime movie *In Which We Serve*, the *London Daily Express* headline from August 1939 is shown, reading: "NO WAR!" It was Coward's revenge on Lord Beaverbrook, who owned the newspaper and had opposed having Coward co-direct that movie with David Lean.

At a 1964 party in London, Coward noticed a young guest arriving and said to him: "Sit down, young man, and be satirical." It was Paul McCartney.

One night my father gave the young mayor of Minneapolis a tour of some of New York's nightspots. He brought the mayor, Hubert H. Humphrey, to a table full of friends who knew who he was and gave him advice on a wide range of subjects. Then my father noticed Humphrey was wearing white shoes and quietly suggested they were inappropriate attire for a New York nightclub.

Just then, Coward, the incarnation of sophistication itself, walked in, wearing white shoes himself.

A few years later, Coward made his TV debut. The reviews included letters from fans. They used words like "brilliant" and "amazing" about his acting. But he read one fan letter and tossed it away, saying: "He said I was only 'very good.'"

Coward appeared in his play *Nude With Violin*, and only the people in the first few rows were aware of some subtle touches he employed portraying the butler. In the first act, he wore a ruby ring. In the second act it was an emerald, and in the third act it was a diamond ring.

Early in the run of *Nude With Violin* on Broadway, Coward dined at the famed Algonquin Hotel before his performance. Two drama critics, who'd both been unkind to Coward's show, sat with their wives at a nearby table. Coward greeted them anyway.

"I shouldn't think you'd be speaking to us, after what my husband wrote," said one critic's wife.

Coward replied: "My plays aren't written for critics, but for audiences. And if you're worried about our business at the box office gentlemen, please don't be concerned. We're doing fine, compared to that play across the street."

Coward knew full well that both critics had praised the other show, but that it was doing poorly despite their raves.

One night Coward and Marlene Dietrich went to see Johnny Ray, the torch singer popular in the 'fifties. He was performing at the posh Empire Room in New York. A sudden rain and a slump in nightclub business caused the room to be less than full, and later Ray confessed his embarrassment to Coward.

"The test of an artist," Coward replied, "is how well he performs under adverse conditions." He then recalled being in a London theater emptied by an air-raid alert during the war, saying "Grace Miller, the star of the show, worked it as if it was a full house. The true artist gives of himself, no matter what. Tonight you did that, Johnny, you did that."

Coward was a frequent theatergoer whenever his performing schedule allowed. One night in May 1957, he saw Judy Holliday in *Bells Are Ringing* and backstage afterward told her: "What a treat it was for me to sit there and, after the first five minutes, know I wouldn't wince even once all evening."

Coward was one of many stars who had cameos in producer Mike Todd's *Around the World in 80 Days* but sent regrets about attending the huge premiere party Todd was staging at Madison Square Garden.

"I suspect the sincerity of any invitation to a party that comes complete with a general release for me to sign, waiving all rights in case they should happen to put me on TV," he said.

Opening night of *Nude With Violin*, Coward basked in the glory of being the star and the playwright of a hit. But it was tempered by his memory of the night his play *Cavalcade* opened in London. Everyone praised him except an actress friend. Finally he asked her about it, and she replied: "Everyone else can call your play tripe if they like to, but me? I liked it."

Eva Gabor liked *Nude With Violin*, and said: "Oh if I only had that talent. I'd write such big parts for myself and such little ones for everyone else."

In April 1955, Coward invited Ingrid Bergman to see him perform at the Café de Paris in London, with his compliments. She asked if it would be all right to come with another woman. "Sure," said Coward, "both of you come, with my compliments." Then she called, saying her friend couldn't come and she didn't want to come alone. That evening, two men, in white tie, called for her as her escorts, "with Mr. Coward's compliments."

When Eva Gabor made her stage debut in Coward's *Present Laughter* in February 1958, he stood in the wings and told her not to be nervous.

"You'll be fine," he said. "And if you do get nervous, remember there's a piano onstage. All you have to do is say to me: 'Darling, come out and play something,' and I will."

One day in 1960, Sir John Gielgud addressed a group of young actors and said they must never play to any one member of the audience. "That would diminish the quality of the performance," he said. He told them about his appearance in a production in London as an example.

"I noticed Noël Coward and a producer were in the sixth row. So I addressed my first six comic punch lines to where they were sitting." Then, when he came to the seventh punch line, he returned to that part of the stage to look back at where they'd been sitting, and noticed two empty chairs. They'd walked out.

When he returned to London after a trip to New York, Coward encountered a newspaper reporter. "Welcome back, Sir Noël," said the journalist. "Do you have anything to say to *The Star*?"

"Twinkle twinkle," said Coward.

On another occasion, he arrived in Sydney, and an Australian fan said: "Sir Noël, you're so famous for your wit. Say something witty."

"Kangaroo," came the reply.

North to Alaska was one of John Wayne's more popular movies. The shooting involved two months of continuous fight scenes in the mud. When it was over, Wayne asked wistfully: "I wonder why Noël

Coward doesn't write any more of those drawing-room comedies."

Coward attended the play *Advise and Consent* and noticed that one of the bit roles, a senator, was portrayed at that performance by Warren Caro, in real life a Theater Guild executive. Backstage he asked Caro how much he was paid.

"Four dollars a performance," said Caro.

"Hmm," replied Coward. "Grossly overpaid."

Coward was offered the starring role in a production of *The Entertainer,* the role portrayed by Laurence Olivier. "For me," he explained, rejecting the part, "a trained song and dance man, it would have been routine. But for Olivier, it was a tour-de-force."

Sir Michael Redgrave once voiced his high regard for Coward, but was quick to add that no man admires himself as much as Coward.

In response, Coward sent Redgrave a drawing of Noël Coward, by Noël Coward, admiring a statue of Noël Coward.

Coward epitomized class, no matter what the circumstances. When, for example, his play *Vortex* opened in London, he received a congratulatory letter from Lord Curzon, later viceroy to India, expressing pride that "a fellow Oxford man" had written the play.

Coward could've left it at that. Instead, however, he replied politely: "The only time I went to Oxford was to appear twice nightly in *Charley's Aunt.*" Despite his trademark sophistication and wit, Coward was largely self-educated.

Brendan Behan said: "Noël Coward is the most professional theater man in the world. If he were in East Joplin, Missouri, and he learned a show was playing in town, he'd go. Not only would he go, but he would stay to the end and applaud, with hands high, like royalty, for all to see."

Not everything Coward wrote was a hit. One of his shows, in which he also appeared, was a flop on the Paris stage in 1949.

Another of his plays wasn't doing well either. Coward's business manager described its box office as "mediocre."

"Close it immediately!" Coward ordered. When told it was making a little money, he replied: "I'm resolved to go through life either in First Class or in Third Class. But never Second Class."

In late May 1949, Coward went to see *South Pacific* the night understudy Dickinson Eastham was in the role made famous by Ezio Pinza. Coward later told the understudy he did well and deserved credit for gallantry. Then he told of the night he appeared in his *Private Lives* and had to announce to the audience that his costar, Gertrude Lawrence—then a huge stage star—was ill and that her role would be played by an understudy.

Coward heard the mass groan from the audience and saw some of them preparing to leave and get their refunds.

"I share your disappointment," he said from the stage, "but I should mention that the first time I saw Gertrude Lawrence was in *From A to Z* when she too was an understudy, for Bea Lillie. Who knows that tonight you may experience the same thrill that was mine, that memorable London evening."

There were no requests for refunds.

One night in New York Coward had to stay later than he'd wanted at the Little Club because the orchestra kept playing a medley of his hits. He said it reminded him of the time he was in Africa seated on a sun-drenched platform and had to pay attention to an all-women's orchestra playing his score from *Bitter Sweet*, off-key and off-beat. His grim smile remained fixed throughout the long recital, which seemed interminable, especially under the baking African sun.

When it was finally over, Coward politely applauded, which the conductor noticed. "You really liked it?" he asked.

Coward nodded, so they played it again; start to finish!

Somehow, Coward once found himself taking Joan Crawford's children to a screening of her movie *Possessed*, and then having to reassure them that their Mummy really wasn't doing all those naughty things and nothing really happened to her. She portrayed a woman in a psycho ward obsessed with a man.

In July 1949, Coward returned from New York to London aboard the *Queen Mary*. The only other passenger aboard ship he knew was Mrs. Robert E. Sherwood, wife of the playwright, who urged Coward to devise an unusual plan to assure they'd be protected from "dreary" companions for the ensuing weeklong voyage: "I shall line up all the passengers," he said, "and hold a monster audition."

Coward was once asked how he became sophisticated, since he hadn't come from lofty origins; his father had been a piano salesman.

"I remember the day it happened," he recalled. He and Gertrude Lawrence had just completed a vaudeville tour that paid them $40 a week. They decided to spend their savings on one big, fancy spree. They bought dress clothes and went to the swankiest café in London.

"And there I noticed," he continued, "that I was the only man in the room wearing white socks. I discovered that I no longer could trust my instincts, and I decided that I had to find out how sophisticated people think and what they do and how they dress."

In January 1962, Sir John Mills was starring on the London stage in *Ross*, as T.E. Lawrence, better known as "Lawrence of Arabia." Mills's first major role had been in Coward's *Cavalcade* back in the 'thirties. After one performance of that play, Coward introduced Mills to a theatergoer he called "Airman Shaw." Mills was struck by the

man's charisma and intensity. Later, Coward told him it was actually T.E. Lawrence, "Lawrence of Arabia" himself.

One night he dined with Katharine Cornell and Helen Hayes, two of the greatest stage stars of their time. They were talking about closing a long Broadway run and what they enjoyed most once a show had closed.

Helen Hayes said: "I love the thought that at last I can afford to catch a cold."

Coward's thought was: "Ah, I love that second cocktail before dinner which I can now enjoy."

At a party in New York, the discussion turned to an actress who'd had lots of plastic surgery: her face lifted, nose shortened, even legs straightened. Coward said of her: "She's had every part of her body broken, except her heart."

His friend, the actor Clifton Webb, lost his mother Maybelle at age ninety in August 1966. While Coward conveyed deep condolences, he later said of his friend, who was inconsolable, "I cannot be sorry for a seventy-year-old orphan."

One evening at a nightclub, Coward was introduced to Twiggy, the top model of the 'sixties. He took one look at her, then said to her manager: "My dear boy, promise me you won't do a thing to improve her."

In July 1968, Coward said he was not writing Broadway plays anymore because of the rudeness of theater parties. "They come in late, and miss the exposition. Then they talk, and leave too soon." Instead he was writing a once-a-week journal in longhand. He wrote: "I look upon the footlights as an invisible curtain, to keep us properly apart, the audience and me. And as for those who stand onstage too long, drunk with applause: dreadful!

"An actor who insists that his audience wouldn't let him leave," he wrote, "is like the politician who insists he was drafted to run for office; there is no such thing."

In April 1970, actress Arlene Dahl told

Coward she'd be spending the summer starring in stock productions of his plays *Private Lives* and *Blithe Spirit*.

"Darling," Coward replied, "you never can go wrong with the classics."

The next month, Coward sat through the five-hour revival of Ibsen's theatrical marathon, *Peer Gynt*, which has forty scenes. The eighty-year-old principals finally realize their lives have meaning at the final curtain.

Emerging from the theater, Coward wearily said: "Boy meets girl. At last!"

When Joan Crawford held a party at New York's "21" club honoring Coward, he later sent her a thank-you letter, which read: "It suddenly occurred to me I've loved you for thirty years."

Coward had a magnificent home in Jamaica where my parents visited him. It had two swimming pools—one with salt water, the other with freshwater. He also had a home in Switzerland and apartments in London and New York. He would occasionally get mail addressed simply as: "Noël Coward, The World."

"I just happen to be there when the mail arrived," he explained.

At the 1970 Tony Award ceremonies, Coward posed with fellow Brits Cary Grant and David Frost, then said: "Will somebody take this smile off my face?"

A director working on a Noël Coward play was lunching in Manhattan when Coward himself entered and approached his table.

"Oh, God," said the awestruck director.

"Quite right, dear boy," replied Coward. "Just don't tell anybody."

Myrna Loy asked Coward in early 1973 how he enjoyed *Oh Coward!*, the musical review of his songs.

"I adored it," replied Coward. "I even went home humming the tunes."

"I have never made a conscious attempt at being funny," he said. "That is for clowns, and I am not a clown. I'm a civilized human being with a God-given capacity for humor. Wit is like caviar. It should be savored in small, elegant proportions and not spread about like marmalade."

At his funeral, Sir John Gielgud quoted his favorite saying of Coward's: "The world has treated me very well, but then, I haven't treated it so badly either."

ALBERT EINSTEIN

Albert Einstein was my distant cousin. Albert Brooks, the comedian/director/actor can say the same thing. (His real name is Albert Einstein, too.) We're related through my grandfather on my mother's side, but he left the family some four decades before I was born. Still, I'm proud of the relationship, even though I was a terrible math student.

One of the earliest mentions of Einstein in the column came in April 1948, when it was believed that the Princeton professor would support Henry Wallace for President on a third-party line. "Not to worry," said a Democratic Party member. "Only about twelve people in the world can understand what Einstein's talking about, and none of them are registered voters."

A colleague visited Einstein and talked of his problems: inventories, sales force, bad debts, machinery, and equipment. "Do you have any such problems?"

"No," replied Einstein. "These are my only tools," he said, raising two leaky fountain pens.

Einstein's two tools of his profession were a pencil and his brain, so he could work anywhere—while walking, riding, dining—anywhere except while sleeping. He once had an appointment to meet a friend on a bridge. The man arrived an hour late and apologized. Einstein, who'd been staring down at the water said: "Oh, that's all right. I was busy working."

He once spent the night at the country home of a friend in New York. After he left, the maid complained to her employer that the guest had defaced the new wallpaper in the guest bathroom. There were figures scribbled all over the wall, figures like mathematical formulae. Only a few days before, Einstein had announced his newest concept of the Unified Field Theory, which was front-paged throughout the world.

His host then made two phone calls: The first to a Princeton mathematician for an explanation of the symbols, and the second to a framer to put a glass cover over and around Einstein's mathematical scribblings.

In the spring of 1944, a CBS producer once had an appointment with Einstein at Princeton, the day after daylight saving began. He arrived an hour late, because he'd forgotten to move his watch ahead. "What an embarrassment," he said to Einstein's secretary, "coming late to the man who changed the world's concept of time."

"Oh, that's all right," she replied, "Dr. Einstein never knows what time it is."

During his years at the Institute for Advanced Studies in Princeton, Einstein received all sorts of letters. One read: "Our committee, having heard you are the country's greatest thinker, would be greatly obliged if you would send us your six greatest thoughts." Einstein's reply: "God, country, wife, mathematics, mankind, peace."

Einstein visited a summer theater in 1952 near his Princeton home and was asked to come backstage to be photographed with the actors. "It's your duty as a person," said the theater manager. "It will help the show get publicity." "Publicity," said Einstein, refusing to pose, "is not my 'duty.'"

Still, Einstein was one of the most photographed men of his time. A visitor at Princeton in the fall of 1952 said to him "You're a scientist, mathematician, teacher, author. If you had to define your profession, which would you say?"

"My profession," replied Einstein, "is a photographer's model."

Many journalists wanted to interview Einstein, but few were granted permission. Gertrude Samuels, who wrote a magazine story about the Institute for Advanced Study, of which Einstein was a member, was one of the lucky ones. His secretary said: "You can only have five minutes with him." Samuels agreed. After the allotted time, Einstein said: "That's five minutes. Now it's my turn to interview *you!*" He then questioned her for an hour.

After the announcement was made that Einstein had finished the mathematical formulation of his Unified Field Theory, he was asked what reaction it had received from the American Academy of Advanced Science.

"I always have two kinds of audiences," he said, "the blind and the deaf. The blind ones never see, and the deaf ones are my colleagues who don't want to hear."

It was in 1933 that Einstein fled the Nazis and came to America. The first person he wanted to see was his old friend Professor Beno Gutenberg, the German-American seismologist, then at the California Institute of Technology. They walked across the campus in Pasadena, with their hands folded behind their backs, discussing the phenomena of the earth.

Meanwhile, a gust of wind bent the trees, the earth shook, and buildings trembled. They paid no heed to this, but continued their scientific talk, and then entered the college and glanced at the seismograph. Only then did they realize there'd been an earthquake, the famous 1933 Long Beach quake.

During the war, Einstein appeared in an Army film. He interrupted the shooting to speak to the cameraman: "You're photographing me and recording my voice simultaneously. But since light travels faster than sound, how can you explain the speed differential?" A resourceful officer looking on concocted an explanation: "Professor Einstein, when the movie is shown, the film projector is in the back of the theater and the sound projector is on the stage, so the light catches up with the sound."

Einstein told that to a friend in the film business, who gave him the real explanation: for the remainder of his tour. Although the picture and the sound are recorded simultaneously, the sound track on the film is spaced several frames behind the pictures.

In 1949, Einstein was approached by a publisher hoping to convince him to write a layman's explanation of the Theory of Relativity. Einstein agreed, but wrote a manuscript so complex that the publisher decided laymen couldn't understand it. But they paid him the advance anyway, since he'd written the manuscript in longhand, and they knew that someday it would be worth far more.

At a birthday celebration, he was presented a cake with one of his famous quotes written across it in icing: "The only incomprehensible thing about The Universe is that it is comprehensible."

Einstein considered Thorstein Veblen, the sociologist and economist, to be one of the greatest thinkers in America and wanted to own all of Veblen's works. A friend soon sent him the complete works, and offered to send him a biography called *The Definitive Life of Veblen.*

"No, thank you," said Einstein. "I'm not interested in Veblen's private life. His works speak for themselves."

Einstein's autobiography was only forty-seven pages long. He made no mention of his family or of his flight from Germany, but devoted his book to describing his philosophy, how he came upon the Theory of Relativity, and the future of his scientific field.

"I never read biographies," he said. "They consist mostly of lies. A biographer's main interest is the human interest stories, which are legends. A person should be judged entirely by his works, and his personal life and hobbies should be of no concern to anyone."

My favorite story about Einstein was told to me by Sid Caesar. On Friday afternoon, April 15, 1955, Caesar was deep into rehearsals for his weekly comedy TV program, *Your Show of Shows,* which in those days was done live. Late in the afternoon, he was told that Einstein's office was calling from Princeton and that the great scientist wanted to meet him the following Monday. Einstein especially admired Caesar's "Professor" character (which was an early version of Mel Brooks's *2000-year-old man* character, since Brooks was a member of Caesar's legendary team of writers). Caesar's phony German accent made the character hilarious.

At first, Caesar didn't believe the call was genuine, but when told the name of Einstein's secretary who was calling, he was convinced. He immediately cancelled the rest of the rehearsals, saying they could ad-lib the next show and somehow get by. This was a once-in-a-lifetime opportunity. He then asked his staff to get him every book in the library on the Theory of Relativity.

"I figured I could learn it in one, maybe two days tops," he recalled for me, in all seriousness. "After all, how complicated could it be?" So for the next two days, he immersed himself in trying to understand some of the most complex formulae and ideas ever conceived. He pored through everything in the library, and at the end of the weekend felt confident he could hold his own on the subject.

Monday morning, Einstein died.

J. EDGAR HOOVER

There never was a more curious figure in American history than J. Edgar Hoover, the longtime director of the FBI. Every holiday season, we received a Christmas card from him, usually in the same mail delivery as a card from Polly Adler, America's most notorious madam, or gangster Charles "Lucky" Luciano, America's "Public Enemy No. 1."

When I was six, we were in Washington and were given a private tour of the FBI headquarters. "Your tax dollars at work" provided our own personal Special Agent who took us around the old building. At the part where we were shown the FBI's counterespionage techniques—very low tech by today's standards—I turned to the agent and, impressed with the coded designs on the inside of envelopes and secret messages hidden under pencil erasers, said: "Boy! Lucky the FBI is on *our* side! Crime sure doesn't pay."

Fifty years later, a friend was doing a book, and under the Freedom of Information Act found the file Hoover kept on my father. (The director kept files on friends and foes alike.) There was an entry in the file saying something like: "Lyons's son said: 'Lucky the FBI is on our side!'" Again, your tax dollars at work.

My father would see Hoover on the director's trips to New York. Hoover was certainly not en route to Europe, since curiously he spent his entire life inside the borders of the United States.

In 1942, two German submarines landed off the U.S. coast; one off Long Island, the other off Florida. The spies were quickly caught by the FBI and would soon be tried, convicted, and, under wartime laws, executed.

Soon after they were captured, they signed full confessions, and made statements implicating friends and relatives. Two of the spies recognized Hoover when they met him, and one said: "You're Mr. Hoover. We know you from your pictures."

In the fall of 1940, Hoover was in San Francisco and visited Alcatraz, a few miles out in San Francisco Bay. He accompanied the warden on a tour of the nation's most secure prison. They walked past the rows of cells and then through a courtyard, where some of the prisoners were exercising. One of them hissed. Hoover turned and recognized him. He was an old acquaintance, George "Machine Gun" Kelly, who coined the phrase by which Hoover's men would forever be known: When he surrendered, he dropped his weapon and cried: "Don't shoot! Don't shoot, G-Men."

A few years later, Hoover visited another federal penitentiary, Leavenworth in Kansas, and met Robert Stroud, aka The Birdman of Alcatraz, later to be portrayed in the movie of the same name by Burt Lancaster. Stroud, a lifer, had become a world authority on ornithology and had bred 300 canar-

With J. Edgar Hoover in Washington, D.C., probably during my parents' honeymoon in November 1934. Fifty years later, I got a look at the file Hoover kept on my father.

ies in his cell. All were singing at the top of their tiny lungs.

Hoover bought one of Stroud's birds, took it home, and later told friends it never so much as tweeted one sound.

Revelations in recent years about Hoover's alleged "kinky" private life cast a different perspective on the controversial lawman, but in 1940, he was linked with Lela Rogers, mother of Ginger Rogers. Mrs. Rogers phoned Hoover to say that she had left town for the weekend. "Where are you?" he asked. "You're the G-Man," she replied. "So find out."

Hoover kept her talking while his agents traced the call.

When the rumors of the romance were at their height, Hoover lunched in New York and overheard Deems Taylor, the composer and music critic, talking about it with friends. "Why should Lela Rogers fall for a copper?" he wondered in a loud voice. Hoover got up from his table, walked over to Taylor, and said: "Just for that, if you're ever kidnapped, I won't raise a finger."

Hoover once met Shirley Temple, and, patting her curly locks, told the famous child star he'd get her whatever she wanted. Her request: "A machine gun."

The movie *The House on 92nd Street*, released in 1945, is one of the best docudramas ever made. It told the true story of a cell of prewar Nazi spies who used a house on Ninety-Second Street off Fifth Avenue and were done in by a double agent. Using a documentary style, the movie depicted the then-cutting edge technology of two-way mirrors to help trap the spies.

Hoover, who appeared in the film, was asked if the FBI had devised the mirrors.

"Not at all," he said. "They originated in the bordellos of Marseilles."

My family, incidentally, was on a list the FBI found in the house: a list of prominent New York Jews slated for execution if the Nazis had taken over.

Hoover said he once sent out a wanted poster to all police chiefs. It had the usual left profile, right profile, and full-face photos. A few days later he got a curious message from a small-town chief: "Your poster helped us capture all three."

Another time Hoover met the head of Scotland Yard, who was visiting Washington. He told the guest that FBI agents have to be lawyers or accountants and asked if Scotland Yard had similar requirements. "No, Mr. Hoover," replied the English lawman. "Those are the sorts of people we guard!"

Whenever he'd come to New York, Supreme Court Justice Tom Clark would frequent the Stork Club, New York's most famous nightspot. He'd always get the best table, dating back to his days as Attorney General. That is, except when Hoover was in town. It didn't matter that technically, as Attorney General, Clark was Hoover's boss.

Sherman Billingsley, the proprietor, who was meticulous about who got the best tables in his place, explained: "Attorneys General come and go. But Hoover goes on forever."

SINCLAIR LEWIS

The first American to win the Nobel Prize for Literature (1930), Lewis was best-known for the novels *Main Street, Babbitt, Arrowsmith, Cass Timberlane*, and *Elmer Gantry*.

A persistent autograph-seeker once asked him to inscribe a copy of his novel *Elmer Gantry*, about the hard-drinking con man turned amoral preacher.

Lewis complied and wrote: "To you, who are more like Elmer Gantry than anyone else I know—except that unlike Gantry, women won't fall for you."

On another occasion, he was appearing onstage in one of his plays called *It Can't Happen Here*. On his way to the theater on opening night on October 26, 1936, he was stopped by an autograph fan who was shocked when Lewis signed his name but under a message to the fan: "Why don't you find a hobby that isn't so annoying to other people?"

After the curtain came down, an envelope arrived backstage with the same message—signed by that autograph-seeker.

In April 1942, Lewis returned to his native Minnesota at the suggestion of his friends in New York. "They told me to find a quiet place to write, away from the distraction of Broadway. I've found just such a place to work on my novel. It's a cabin on the shores of a lake at the foot of a mountain—a great place to start a summer theater!"

In September 1944, he was at work on the novel *Cass Timberlane* and believed he'd have no problem meeting his deadline. "After all," he said, "*Main Street* took me almost fifteen years to write." He explained that he'd begun it while he was at college. He wrote 20,000 words, then stopped. A few years later he wrote 20,000 more words, and again he stopped. He finished that masterpiece in his third attempt.

Like every great writer, he was often asked for advice from young writers. "I know of no rules of the slightest value for learning to write. If there were any rules, there'd be a million successful writers in America today. I know of nothing to do beyond wanting to write, then writing."

Back in the 'thirties, Lewis was to sit for a portrait in France. When the artist arrived, Lewis was stretched out on a sofa asleep. The author was painted in that pose, and the painting wound up in a private home. Years later, when the Germans overran that country, they looted the home, but left the portrait hanging. After D-Day, the French reoccupied the house and stripped it of the remainder of its possessions, but again leaving the portrait alone. Thus the painting of the sleeping Sinclair Lewis has the distinction of surely being the only painting rejected by both the Nazis and the French army.

In 1945 Lewis was invited to join the Academy of Arts and Letters, although he once denounced it in a speech accepting his Nobel Prize in Stockholm in 1930. "Why did you join after you attacked it?" he was asked.

He shrugged: "Because they asked me to join. I couldn't resist joining a group which invited me to become a member after I'd attacked it."

Lewis was a native of Sauk Center, Minnesota. In 1915, he wrote *The Trail of the Hawk: A Comedy of the Seriousness of Life*. It was his third novel, but only had a printing of 3,000 copies. Still, it was one of the first novels about aviation, about a flier named Carl, who became known as "The Lone Wolf"and eventually married an Eastern heiress.

When the book was published, there was a boy living in nearby Little Falls, just thirty-eight miles away, who was to become a flier known as "The Lone Eagle," and who would marry an Eastern heiress, Ann Morrow-Lindbergh.

John Hersey, author of *A Bell for Adano*,

once applied to Lewis for a secretary's job. Lewis questioned the young man thoroughly and then was interrupted by a phone call.

"It's another applicant," Lewis told Hersey. "Let me see how you'd interview him." So applicant Hersey interviewed the rival, turned to Lewis, and said: "This man seems to be all right." "All right then," replied Lewis. "You're hired!"

While he was a great writer who won— and refused to accept—the Pulitzer Prize, and who was the first American to win the Nobel Prize for Literature, Lewis wasn't a wise investor in other people's plays. He put money into a show called *Good Neighbor* that opened and closed on Broadway on October 21, 1941. But he was undaunted.

"I'm like someone who's survived in a plane crash," he said. "I've got to go up again —immediately." But later he said: "Ahh for the good old days—before I ever heard of the American theater."

Lewis felt that his novels *Main Street* and *Babbitt* were more deserving of Pulitzer Prizes than the novels that won for other writers in those years. When his *Arrowsmith* was chosen by the Pulitzer committee, the author refused the prize and the $1,000. He said the prize was silly and the judges weren't bright.

He did, however, accept the $40,000 Nobel Prize, and went to Sweden to collect it, explaining: "The Swedes are remarkably bright."

Lewis once attended a tryout performance of a musical called *Very Warm for May*. At the party afterward, Lewis observed: "The music was wonderful but the direction was bad." The director left the table. Then Lewis's friend said: "The music was indeed wonderful but the production was bad."

The producer heard that and left the table. Finally Lewis said: "The music was wonderful but the show was terrible." Everyone then left the table except one man who said, "That's all right. I wrote the music. My name is Jerome Kern."

His friend Sir Cedric Hardwicke, the elegant British character actor, sent him a note in March 1949: "You are the bravest man I know, for deliberately endangering your life by continuing your career onstage as an actor."

Another former secretary for Lewis was Barnaby Conrad, the noted writer/sculptor/artist, and former U.S. Consul in Seville. He recalled the only time he ever saw someone reading one of Lewis's books. It was during an ocean voyage, and he noticed a passenger reading *Elmer Gantry*. Suddenly, however, the man slammed the book shut, walked to the rail slowly, and deliberately and tossed it overboard.

GROUCHO MARX & HIS BROTHERS

Late in his life, I interviewed Groucho Marx for my radio show on CBS. It wasn't a pleasant experience, because by then, 1976, he was rather frail and even more short-tempered and cantankerous than ever. Thinking back, I realize that there was a reason for his nickname.

But I'm certain Groucho wasn't that way with my father, who knew him for forty years. In a column in 1937, an item appeared about Groucho and his brothers, who were screening a rough copy of *A Day at the Races*. My father reported that they decided to add the first three notes of Rachmaninoff's *Prelude in C# Minor*. So Groucho

With Groucho Marx circa 1950.

cabled Rachmaninoff and asked how much he would charge them. The amazed composer cabled back: "One thousand dollars." The Marx Brothers sent him the check, the first money Rachmaninoff had ever received for that work, because, unknown to the Marx Brothers, it was never copyrighted and could've been used anytime without his permission.

Like many others in Hollywood of that era, Groucho had no love for Columbia studio head Harry Cohn, known for his iron-fisted rule. In February 1939, they had a disagreement, and Groucho stormed off the lot. He headed to a movie theater to cool off, sat through the newsreel, and waited for the feature to begin. Once the Columbia Pictures logo flashed on the screen, he said in a loud voice: "This movie drags, don't you think?"

In 1950, Groucho had his own TV quiz show, *You Bet Your Life*, which had begun on the radio. He made an observation any famous comedian will vouch for: that people would laugh at anything he said, even if it wasn't funny. Before Groucho and his brothers were stars, they performed the musical *Cocoanuts* onstage. Groucho had a line he thought was funny, which came after brother Chico tried to sell Groucho some ice cubes for fifty cents.

"For fifty cents, I can buy my own Eskimo and make my own ice," Groucho replied. Nobody ever laughed at that line. But in his later years, Groucho used a similar line in all situations. When a salesman told him a hat he wanted cost $20, Groucho said: "For $20, I can buy my own Eskimo and make my own hats." He'd say it about groceries or a car, always with the Eskimo reference. By then, although the line really makes no sense, people always laughed at it, just because it was Groucho, the famous comic, who said it.

That same year, Groucho received a lucrative endorsement offer that would've put his picture in every subway and train station across the country. "No thanks," Groucho replied. "I already *have* a moustache."

In his later years, he'd spend most evenings at home, listening to Frank Loesser's music from *Guys and Dolls*. Then every night, just before retiring, he'd take great delight in phoning Loesser in New York to tell him what a genius the composer was. Asked if a nightly call from Los Angeles to New York didn't inflate his phone bill, Groucho said: "Oh no, I tell Frank he's a genius, he quickly agrees, and I hang up."

Goodman Ace was a famous radio raconteur with a huge following in his day. He was a frequent guest at Groucho's California home. But eventually Groucho grew tired of Ace's prolonged visits. So Groucho began to drop subtle hints. He'd place Ace's luggage, fully packed, in his front hallway, and unscrew the lightbulbs, saying, "I figured you've stayed so long, you know your way around here in the dark."

The Ritz Brothers, a poor man's imitation of Groucho and his brothers, were the rowdiest act of their day. Their low comedy bits included the removal of their shoes and socks, pie throwing, mugging, and even nose wiping on each other's coats. Pretty tame stuff today, but pretty vulgar back then. One of the brothers asked Groucho for advice. "Try not to be so subtle," Groucho deadpanned.

The Marx Brothers' father was a tailor who had a phobia fatal to the trade: an aversion to touching people. His measuring therefore was sheer estimate, with his tape measure held at a distance from the customer. But he had to retire from being a tailor when his legs gave out and he could no longer flee angry customers after they'd tried on the ill-fitting suits he'd stitched.

A friend described his new baby as "short, fat, and bald." Groucho asked: "Did your wife give birth to my agent? Or, for that matter, *any* agent?"

In April 1946, the Pittsburgh Chamber of Commerce filed an official protest concerning a line in the Marx Brothers' movie *A Night in Casablanca*. In one scene, Groucho and a woman blew thick smoke rings at each other, after which Groucho said: "This is like living in Pittsburgh, if you call that 'living.'"

Groucho once dined at New York's "21" where he scanned the pricey menu. In protest, he ordered one lima bean. The waiter, unperturbed, dutifully brought it to him on a large plate. Groucho sent it back, however, because the bean wasn't peeled.

Groucho once played pool with Sir Cedric Hardwicke, who missed an easy shot. Later Groucho wondered: "How do you tell a British nobleman that he stinks?"

Groucho was the guest of honor at a séance, and thus, once the Ouija board was in place, the shades were pulled, and hands and arms linked, the others made the mistake of honoring Groucho with the privilege of asking the spirit one question, supposedly about the meaning of life. "OK, Spirit," Groucho began. "If you're so smart, what's the capital of South Dakota?"

One sunny afternoon in the spring, Groucho was walking down New York's swanky Fifth Avenue and spotted a woman wearing a huge brimmed hat. She took one look at him, lowered her eyes, and walked quickly away. This odd behavior intrigued Groucho, so he quickened his pace and finally, a block later, overtook her.

"Why are you avoiding me?" Groucho asked. "Who do you think you are, Greta Garbo?"

"Yes, I am," she replied, taking off her glasses. "I'm Garbo."

HARPO

Groucho wasn't the only member of the Marx family my father knew. Harpo, the one who never spoke onstage, was in real life a charming man who loved children, though he never had any of his own. I remember our family dining with him and his wife at Luchow's, the legendary old German restaurant. Every Sunday, it was *the* place to be.

In August 1942, Dalí painted a portrait of Harpo, but it was partially damaged by a storm. After he'd posed, Harpo glanced at it to see what progress Dalí had been making. He was surprised to see the painting was not surrealistic as he'd expected, but was an excellent likeness, showing him doing—what else?—playing a harp. "Thanks so much," he said to Dalí. "It's not finished," the painter replied. "It needs some final touches." Then he painted a lobster atop Harpo's head.

In July 1944, Harpo's brother Chico was in town and recalled how their unique act began. The brothers were appearing in a short play they'd done in vaudeville for many years. But when they performed the skits in New York, their uncle, a veteran vaudevillian named Al Sheehan, told them their act was outmoded.

So they wrote a new act. But just before going onstage Harpo realized they'd forgotten to write any dialogue for him. But Uncle Al reassured them: "Just go on and don't say anything." Thus was born Harpo's silence, the trademark of one of the most famous characters in show business history.

The night Rudolf Hess, Hitler's deputy, made his bizarre flight to England and crash-landed in Scotland on May 10, 1941, Prime Minister Churchill didn't get the urgent news until an hour after it had arrived, for he'd left strict instructions not to be disturbed. He was watching Harpo and his brothers in their finest film, *A Night at the Opera*.

On a trip to Israel in 1963 (which my father arranged), Harpo carried his famous wig in his pocket in case he had the urge to make his fans laugh. When he went into a café in Haifa, he learned one patron was celebrating a birthday. So he donned his curly blonde wig, inserted matches under his fingernails, lit them, and whistled "Happy Birthday."

In his hotel, Harpo somehow found a harp and began playing. "You play like King David, only not as well," said the manager.

"And you speak like King Solomon, but not as wisely," replied Harpo.

He and his wife were once houseguests of Ben Hecht, who wrote *Kiss of Death* and *Notorious*, among others. He marveled at all the mail Hecht received every day. During

With Harpo Marx, center, and Brendan Behan, all in Harpo wigs on July 10, 1961.

their stay, Harpo got only one letter—from President Franklin D. Roosevelt.

On a visit to George Bernard Shaw's home, Harpo kept staring at the great writer's beard. Finally he leaned forward, parted Shaw's beard and said: "Ah *ha*! Just as I thought. You're not wearing a collar!"

During the height of the Cold War, Harpo was invited to perform his comedy routines and his virtuoso harp playing in the USSR. But at the Soviet border, he was called in by a Customs official. "Mr. Marx is an artist," the interpreter assured the official, hopeful that somehow he'd seen one of Harpo's movies. Nevertheless the official demanded Harpo open his bags.

The bags contained the props of this unique artist: 400 knives, two starter pistols, bottles marked "poison," red wigs, and other suspicious items. The official then had Harpo open his harp case and ordered him to play the instrument. So there, in 25-below weather at the small border station, Harpo Marx, one of the great performers of all time, played his trademark instrument without even removing his gloves.

"Yes," the Russian official finally conceded. "You *are* an artist."

Harpo's routines were so famous they were frequently imitated, and not only by show business people. During his tour of the USSR, he extended his hand to greet an admirer. But as he did so, the man yanked his own hand back, dropping a dozen knives out from the sleeve of his coat, aping one of Harpo's best-known comedy bits. The man doing the Harpo impression was Maxim Litvinov, Foreign Minister of the Soviet Union.

After he tore the house down at the Moscow Art Theater with his famous routines, Harpo strode off the stage to thunderous applause. His interpreter then rushed backstage and told him the audience demanded he come out and speak. He refused. Again came the request. Finally, Harpo relented, even though no one in the audience spoke English. So Harpo cleared his throat, then recited the only speech he had ever memorized—his bar mitzvah speech of more than thirty years earlier: "As I stand among you, my dear friends and relatives, I realize that today I am a man." The audience went wild. "Go on! Go on!" yelled the interpreter.

"That's all there was to the speech," Harpo related. "After that, they gave me a watch, which Chico then swiped."

In their days at MGM, dubbing dialogue was still costly. So studio head Irving Thalberg ordered his screenwriters to "put a lot of stuff for Harpo to do in the script. It helps our foreign grosses."

In 1924, Harpo lost $12,000 gambling at a casino, at a time he could ill afford such a loss. Joseph P. Kennedy, who'd seen him lose the money, berated him for his foolishness and said he'd help Harpo by giving him two stock tips. He advised Harpo to buy a couple of little-known stocks. One was selling at 20, the other at 60. Harpo bought 200 shares of the cheaper stock and made a profit.

Years later, Harpo looked back at that incident and calculated that if he'd heeded Kennedy's advice about the higher-priced stock, his $12,000 investment—in something called *Coca-Cola*—would be worth $10,000,000.

At a stockholders' meeting of a company in which Harpo and his brothers had invested, they warned each other not to clown around, lest they not be taken seriously. But Harpo couldn't resist. When the general manager announced he was resigning to go into the ice cream business, Harpo raised his hand and asked: "What flavor?"

On a visit to New York, Harpo went into Tiffany's wearing a wig, beard, and overcoat disguise. On his way out, he tripped across the doorway intentionally, and dozens of diamond rings fell from his sleeves

and pockets. The guards detained him until the rings were proven to be fakes.

Several years later, he returned to Tiffany's, this time without his disguise. As soon as he entered, three humorless guards spotted him and, obviously warned about the previous incident, followed him all through the store, until one guard couldn't resist. He tapped Harpo on the shoulder and said: "No tricks this time, Mr. Marx."

Harpo tried his hand at painting, but with a bizarre result. He rented a studio, bought the proper equipment, and even ordered a model from an agency. She arrived, said nothing, disrobed, and posed for half an hour. Then she looked at Harpo's canvas, shrugged scornfully, put on her robe, and took the brush from Harpo.

Soon *he* was the model, she the artist. The painting turned out to be a broad, arid landscape of the Texas plains.

Harpo was a chronic deviser of shortcuts. In his Beverly Hills home he built special stairways and corridors to make quick passages to other rooms, and a compartment in his car was filled with maps with highway shortcuts specially marked.

One warm day in 1949, Harpo drove George Burns from Beverly Hills to Palm Springs. "There is no shortcut to Palm Springs," Burns cautioned him, aware of his penchant for trying quicker ways to drive. But Harpo wouldn't listen. Four hours later, however, he admitted they were lost.

"How do you know we're lost?" asked Burns.

"Just look outside," replied Harpo. "It's snowing."

In 1953, Harpo was hospitalized briefly but couldn't sleep at night because another patient nearby was moaning continually. Finally Harpo rang for the nurse and demanded a quarter. "Now," he said, about to flip the coin. "Heads I get a tranquilizer. But if it's tails, he gets it."

Harpo once noticed an old friend was

celebrating his birthday the next day. He wired him: "Twenty-five years ago, I dined with you on your birthday, and I bet you $10 that twenty-five years from then I'd remember the date." The friend gratefully wired him the money.

Harpo then began consulting *Who's Who* to find other friends with imminent birthdays. "Makes for good extra spending money," he said.

Harpo Marx, who brought so much laughter to children all over the world, had four adopted children of his own. It started when one of his friends was unable to accept a child offered for adoption and recommended the Marxes as foster parents. The infant quickly brightened their lives. When Harpo was asked how many more children he planned to adopt, he said: "As many as the number of windows in the front of my house. Then, when I leave each morning, I want a child at every window waving goodbye."

Soon after Harpo's autobiography, *Harpo Speaks!* was published in 1961, Harpo met Brendan Behan, the great Irish poet and playwright. Harpo began telling Behan a story about Hollywood in the old days. "Once, we were making a movie called *A Night at the Opera*," he began.

Behan cut him off with: "That's like Leonardo da Vinci saying: 'Once I was painting a picture called *The Last Supper*.'"

The following year, Harpo visited the Supreme Court. "Hello, Harpo," said Chief Justice Earl Warren, who continued walking into the court. Harpo lunched with Justice Felix Frankfurter, who reminded him of a telegram Harpo had sent in 1939 after Frankfurter had been nominated to the Supreme Court but not yet confirmed by the Senate. It read: "Tentative congratulations."

Harpo was once asked to donate his house in Beverly Hills for a one-man show by an unknown artist. He thought about it, then obliged, and a few of the pictures were sold. The grateful artist then offered Harpo six paintings as a gesture of appreciation. But Harpo declined. Big, *big* mistake. Years later, those paintings, by Paul Klee, were worth millions.

On a flight to New York, one of the flight attendants insisted on meeting Harpo to see if she could get him to talk. He responded to her questions with articulate whistles. "See?" he told her. "I can't talk."

On the same flight, a child insisted on meeting Harpo, but then thought he was Groucho. Harpo obliged by doing a Groucho imitation and routines for her.

The Marx Brothers' movies were always the most difficult to dub for foreign distribution. The job of handling Groucho's unique, rapid-fire idioms was next to impossible for a translator. That's why the first ten minutes of all the Marx Brothers' movies have faithful translations. But then comes the madness, as if the translator, in whatever language, had thrown up his or her hands and said: "The hell with it."

One night at a dinner party with Kitty Carlisle Hart, the actress, opera singer, and widow of playwright Moss Hart, Harpo was seated next to Walt Rostow, LBJ's foreign policy advisor. He paid little attention to Mrs. Hart until she mentioned that she'd starred with the Marx Brothers in their funniest film, *A Night at the Opera*. Rostow, a Marx Brothers buff, then turned to her, sighed, and as the dessert arrived said: "So at last we meet!"

After a live performance of *Cocoanuts* early in their career, the Marx Brothers' father overheard an audience member say: "Oh, they're not really brothers. Two of them are cousins." Papa Marx tapped the man on the shoulder and offered to bet him he was wrong. Not recognizing him, the man said: "For how much?"

"What odds will you give me?" replied Marx.

Gummo was often called "the other Marx brother," since he didn't participate in the

Harpo Marx pointing to the barbed wire harp sent by Salvador Dalí, 1946.

act. When his son Bob was a schoolboy, his teacher asked his father's name. "Groucho," said the boy. "Groucho Marx." When his father asked him why he used his uncle's name, the boy replied: "Because, Dad, whoever heard of Gummo Marx?"

CHICO

Chico was the Marx Brother who played the piano in a unique way and affected a horrible Italian accent. So nicknamed because he chased "chicks," he fancied himself one of the ablest cardplayers in America. It began when he took long train rides, spending hours in hotels and dressing rooms. He even had a prized deck of cards that he constantly shuffled. On the first night of a $7,000-a-week engagement in Las Vegas, Chico went to the casino and lost $27,000.

The owners realized he'd have little inspiration to work if he owed them so much money, so a settlement was arranged: Chico would work for four weeks without salary and then was barred from the casino. So the next night, Chico went across the street to another casino and promptly lost $13,000 at the poker table.

The next day he typed a letter to the American Playing Card Company: "Gentlemen," it read, "are you still manufacturing Aces and Kings? I haven't seen any in a long time."

He once was asked how much he'd lost in a lifetime of betting in poker games, on horses, prizefights, at pool, and ball games. "I've lost exactly $1,832,047.62," he replied, explaining that's the exact amount his brother Harpo hadn't lost gambling.

When asked how he joined his brothers in the act, Chico said it was simple: "My father happened to be living in the same home as my mother."

W. SOMERSET MAUGHAM

W. Somerset Maugham, also known as "Willie" to his friends, or "The Old Party," wrote enduring classics such as *The Razor's Edge, Of Human Bondage, Rain*, and *The Letter*. Like many great men of letters, he was often asked for advice to give young, aspiring writers. He once advised the mother of one such boy: "Madam, give your son $500 and let him go to hell—literally. Five hundred dollars will allow him to travel around a bit, and finally he'll become poor.

"He'll meet all kinds of people, and then, if he's got any writer in him, he'll show it."

Maugham once told my father how he became, quite by chance, one of the wealthiest writers of the twentieth century. It started with his sale of the movie rights to *Of Human Bondage*, which would star Bette Davis in one of her early hits and costarred Leslie Howard. Maugham's fee was $15,000, hardly a princely sum, even for those times.

He spent part of the money on a South Pacific cruise where aboard ship he met Bert Alanson, a shrewd San Francisco broker to whom Maugham entrusted the rest of that money.

In one year, that investment soared to $100,000, and ultimately to millions.

In September 1940, there was a proposal introduced in the House of Commons concerning a union between the U.S. and the British Empire, no doubt to make Lend Lease easier. Maugham announced his opposition, saying he preferred the British way of life, speech, and customs. For example, he ran into an old friend who'd just returned to London after a long stay in America. They began to speak, in the middle of the street, as cars whizzed by. Suddenly he interrupted her and said: "I know you've been living in America. But mind your British accent!"

The following year, Maugham was in New York and was helping in the casting of one of his plays. He and the producer were seeking an American actor who could be convincing as an Englishman. One actor began his audition, coughed and stammered, stressed the broad "As," swallowed half his words, and kept inserting "old boy" and "right you are" into every sentence.

"I don't think he'll do," said the producer to Maugham. "He's too English for this country."

"He's too English for *any* country," agreed Maugham.

Soon after that, Maugham met Harpo Marx, who couldn't get over his name. "'Somerset Maugham,'" Harpo kept repeating. "To me, that sounds like the name of a place—like 'Bowling Green' or 'Epsom Downs.'"

A San Francisco fan asked Maugham to autograph one of his books in May 1941, and the author obliged. In return, the fan sent Maugham a box of cigars. Back in New York the following week, Maugham received a phone call in his hotel room from a man eager to meet him. "Remember that guy who sent you those cigars in San Francisco? Well, I'm his brother."

"Sorry," said Maugham, refusing the offer. "That's not close enough."

Maugham recalled the last time he met Maurice Ravel, the French composer best known for *Bolero*. He told Maugham he admired Lincoln; he'd read as much as he could about him, his speeches, his achievements, his life. "I intend to write a tone poem about The Gettysburg Address," said Ravel.

"By the way," he asked Maugham, "how does the first line go again?"

For fifteen summers, he and my father had a reunion luncheon at Maugham's Villa Mauresque on the French Riviera. At one of those luncheons, he told his aide, Alan Searle, "Never marry a woman for her money. You wouldn't enjoy it because I know you dislike work."

Only once did he give my father advice. Every year, my father would bring one of my brothers and me to the reunion, and one year he said to one of us: "It's important that you and your brothers find out at an early age what you want to be and then start studying and working for it."

My father replied: "That's strange talk coming from you, who started out studying medicine, to me, who started out practicing law."

On another visit, he told my father that he was writing his autobiography, which he planned to have published posthumously, because in it he comes out so badly.

Near the end of his life, Maugham and Searle went to Switzerland and decided to become Swiss citizens. After eleven days, however, they renounced their new citizenship and returned home. "The Swiss are meticulous." he said. "They sent us a bill for eleven days of income taxes."

Paramount bought the rights to Maugham's *The Hour Before the Dawn*, which would star Franchot Tone and Veronica Lake. Maugham filmed an introduction and was seen sitting behind a desk. Richard Meland, Paramount's story editor, told the prop man to pile a large assortment of papers and reference books on the desk, appropriate, he believed, for a world-famous author. "The desk ought to look exactly the way yours does when you write."

Maugham arrived at the set for the shoot, pushed the litter off the desk, and left only a pencil and plain ruled paper.

"This," he explained, "is how I write."

In February 1944, Maugham sent copies of his new book, *The Razor's Edge*, to various Hollywood directors, including George Cukor. The author hoped Cukor would direct the movie adaptation. Cukor read it and liked it, but found one disturbing paragraph: a passage about a desire to learn Latin

Welcoming W. Somerset Maugham to New York in 1956.

and Greek and read Homer in the original. It seemed familiar to him, and then he remembered having heard Orson Welles say it, word-for-word. Cukor wrote Maugham and mentioned having heard Welles speak those very words.

Maugham replied, and naturally expressed resentment at being accused of plagiarizing Welles. Cukor then phoned Welles and recited the lines.

"Didn't you once say the same thing to me?" he asked.

"I did," replied Welles. "I'd read it in a script I received from Somerset Maugham—*The Razor's Edge.*"

A few weeks later, he discussed divorce with an American lady friend portrayed in *The Razor's Edge.* "I've got no reason for divorcing my husband," said the lady. "That hasn't prevented many of your countrywomen from divorcing their husbands when they have a mind to," said Maugham. "They get divorces because they expect to find in their husbands a perfection that English women only expect to find in their butlers."

In June 1946, Maugham visited the South Carolina plantation of Nelson Doubleday, the publisher (and father of the future co-owner of the N.Y. Mets). He stayed in the guesthouse, where a collection of his books had been shipped for his visit. Before they were returned to Maugham's villa on the Riviera, some visitors inspected them. They included rare first editions and autographed volumes. On one shelf, they found a first edition of *Of Human Bondage*. On the flyleaf, they found the inscription: "To W. Somerset Maugham, with deep gratitude."

It was signed: "W.S.M."

In July 1946, Maugham was about to return to France from New York and dined with fellow playwright Moss Hart, coauthor of *Once in a Lifetime, You Can't Take It with You,* and *Lady in the Dark.* Maugham conveyed some distressing information to Hart: "I never need more than one week to write the first act of any of my plays," he said.

"You mean that's all you needed to write the first act of, say, *The Circle?*" asked Hart, who always toiled for months over an act.

"Sir," he added, "You have ruined tonight for me, and many other nights to come!"

In October of 1946, Maugham returned to London, and an interviewer asked him about the changes he noticed since he'd left before the war. Maugham said the thing he missed the most was having bread with his meals. As a result of that interview, the Dorchester Hotel, where he was living, received at least twenty loaves of bread every week from readers for Maugham.

Ten months later, Maugham announced he was working on another book, and of the eighty-odd stories and novels he'd written his favorite was his first, *Liza of Lambeth.* He'd written it in 1897 while working as a doctor at a hospital in the London neighborhood of Lambeth.

The only literary critic he recalled as having liked it was Sir Edmund Gosse, himself an author and poet. Whenever Gosse met Maugham, he'd praise the work. But at their last meeting, Maugham's pleasure at hearing the critic's praise was muted by Gosse's following remark: "How clever of you, Maugham, not to have written anything else."

Rouben Mamoulian, who directed *Becky Sharpe, Blood and Sand,* and *Golden Boy,* among others, had an unusual collection of letters from Maugham. The first contained Maugham's report: "I did exactly as you said, but it didn't work. I'll try again." In the second letter, Maugham wrote: "I started it again, but it's still disappointing. I'm not discouraged, however, for I know I'll succeed."

The third letter read: "Tried again and this time I think I see the light." The final letter from Maugham announced: "Success at last! I've got it. After five vain attempts with your recipe for Russian soup, I've made *Shchi.*" (A Russian sauerkraut soup with ribs of beef, garlic, and cabbage.)

In late 1948, Maugham advised Garson Kanin and his wife Ruth Gordon, authors of *Born Yesterday, Adam's Rib, Pat and Mike,* and many others, on how to write when ideas were slow in coming. "Whenever I'm stumped," he said, "I just write my name over and over: 'W.S.M., W.S.M., W.S.M.'"

The Kanins tried it: they faced writers' block, and kept writing: "W.S.M," "W.S.M.," and, somehow, the ideas flowed!

In early February of 1949, Maugham was given a lifetime membership in the Overseas Press Club in New York. "This is a strange honor to go to a fiction writer," he said in accepting the membership. "Still, when I read the stuff of foreign correspondents, sometimes I recognize a bit of fiction there."

On a visit to Russia, Maugham met a man who asked if he was a writer. "I rather bashfully admitted that I was," said Maugham later. The man asked if Maugham would write a letter for him. "It's time I got married," he said. "Please write me a proposal."

Maugham wrote a flowery, endearing, lyrical, and passionate letter. But the man was displeased.

"This won't do," he said. "Couldn't you write something to this effect: 'How much money is your mother willing to give me as a dowry?'"

When he received an honorary degree from Oxford, he was asked to make a speech dedicating a new building. "How does one open a building with a speech?" he wondered. "Other than to say: 'I hereby declare this building open.'"

On the wall of his bedroom, Maugham had a portrait of himself painted by Marie Laurencin. The noted artist nearly always painted women, never men, so for this one she asked Maugham to wear a robe because she never learned how to paint a collar and tie. When the painting was finished, she asked for his dressing gown in payment.

Maugham was honored by the Queen, making him a Companion of Honor. The medal was presented at Buckingham Palace in a private ceremony. Maugham wore the formal morning clothes he'd worn at his daughter's wedding, but added: "I once owned a top hat, but it was destroyed in the Blitz. And as it seems unlikely that my daughter will have another marriage, I did not want to buy another top hat, so I rented one."

The investiture lasted just fifteen minutes, as the Queen, Elizabeth, was then "frail and beautiful. It's a difficult job, being a queen," he observed.

When Noël Coward made one of his frequent visits to Maugham's villa, he said: "Willie today asked my advice on two questions of grammar. Imagine: W. Somerset Maugham asked *me* about grammar. It's a case of the blind leading the blind."

On another occasion when Coward was Maugham's houseguest, he began extolling the beauties of his home in Jamaica.

"Jamaica?" scoffed Maugham. "That's a place for people who haven't been invited anywhere else."

One of Maugham's bridge companions

was the Queen of Spain (before the Spanish Civil War), and the first time they played, no mention was made of stakes. At the end of the hand, she did some calculations and said: "You owe me 75 cents."

He noticed she always wore a pear-shaped diamond pendant that looked familiar. "You saw it in Velázquez's portrait of King Philip II," she said.

Maugham was married in 1917 and remained so for a decade, and years later remembered his only encounter with New Jersey. There a justice of the peace performed the ceremony with the wedding couple sandwiched on line in front of the bench, behind and in front of drunks awaiting jail time.

In 1956, he announced he would leave his considerable estate to his daughter Liza, wife of Lord John Hope. However, his lawyer suggested that the inheritance taxes would consume most of his estate, so a better way would be for Maugham to give her everything now, and live off a weekly stipend she would provide.

"My dear Sir," Maugham replied to the solicitor, "I have your letter. I have also read *King Lear*."

When a musical version of Maugham's *Of Human Bondage* was proposed, Maugham wrote the songwriter his permission, adding: "If you can retain the integrity and spirit of the story, fine, but remember first to entertain."

In explaining why she agreed to star in a Broadway review for the first time in April 1956, Tallulah Bankhead quoted Maugham: "'A play should have a beginning, a middle, and an end.' A review doesn't. A review is absolutely the queen of non sequiturs— which is what I am, anyway."

Later that year Maugham came to New York thinking his days were numbered. So he wrote what he believed to be his last script, called *A Writer's Notebook*. It contained plots for stories he never got around to writing, and he bequeathed them to all writers.

Then he learned that the diagnosis had been wrong and he wasn't going to die soon after all. He then ordered just one change to his manuscript—eliminating that line about bequeathing story ideas to others.

When he returned home from a visit to Greece late in 1956, he said: "Awfully awkward, not knowing the language and all. But I did manage to meet one Greek who spoke English perfectly—the King."

Sinclair Lewis once came by for a visit and had cocktails with Maugham. Later Lewis wrote that English writers are lousy and their cocktails warm.

"Ever since," said Maugham, "I've made certain the cocktails I serve are always ice cold."

During one of my family's visits, Maugham seated my two older brothers around him at the lunch table. He was seated in front of a new acquisition, a Picasso from the artist's famous Blue Period.

"Because of that new painting," he said, pointing over his shoulder, "you're all going to get a somewhat skimpy lunch."

In his library was a large dictionary, and my brother George noticed that it was the same oversized Oxford dictionary we had in our home. My father said he somehow gets different words out of it than Maugham. "The same words," said my brother, "only Mr. Maugham uses them better."

When my younger brother Douglas and I got our turn to visit him, he said: "No writer has more than a certain number of books in him. I hope to write two novels I have in mind, and after that, I shall shut up and stop quite definitely, and spend the rest of my life in wine, women, and song."

He then bowed to my brother and me and repeated: "Wine, women, and song. I won't, because of the children, name the order."

When the Germans invaded France in 1940, Maugham was trapped on the Riviera with almost no money. He managed to escape, but not without great difficulty. After that, whenever he traveled, he did so with lots of cash, just in case.

In December 1959, Maugham was paid a visit by his business manager, and Maugham said of their relationship: "A business relationship which develops between friends is almost always sure to lead to disaster, but a friendship which develops between business associates is almost always sure to last."

When he turned eighty-six in 1960, Maugham told the press: "I don't believe in an afterlife. I don't have to face the prospect of eternal boredom in Paradise." A few years before, in Hollywood, he was asked if he believed in God.

"That's something I've wondered about and searched for in many places," he said. "I don't profess to know the answer, but I shouldn't think so."

Yousuf Karsh, the greatest portrait photographer of the twentieth century, had a photo session with Maugham and later said of his subject: "He's always interested in people, but never liked them."

PABLO PICASSO

The most famous painting by the most renowned, influential artist of the twentieth century was *Guernica*. Picasso's masterpiece, an homage to the Basque village obliterated by German and Italian aircraft in 1937, had been displayed in various cities in Europe and America.

Then in May 1939, it was scheduled to be displayed at a show under the auspices of the American Art Congress. At almost 400 square feet, it was the largest single piece of modern art extant.

On May 4, my father reported that the artist had a change of heart and cancelled the travel arrangements and permission to show the work.

The next week Picasso changed his mind again, finally agreeing. Had it not been for that one temperamental outburst, however, *Guernica* would've been lost forever.

That's because the French ship on which it originally had been scheduled for shipment sank in the harbor at Le Havre.

Soon after that, Marc Chagall said to his friend Picasso: "Such terrible things are happening in your country. All those wonderful El Greco paintings may be destroyed."

"So what?" replied Picasso. "I'll make others."

Two months later in Paris, Nazi Ambassador to France Otto Abetz came to Picasso's studio and admired *Guernica*, which had been returned there.

"This is wonderful," said the German. "Did you do this?"

"No," replied Picasso. "You did."

In September 1944, a month after the liberation of Paris, my father printed a story about Picasso and how he survived the German occupation. Although Hitler had called Modern Art decadent, Nazi officers would come by Picasso's studio and admire his works. They knew their value. Some came away from the studio with examples, never knowing they were fakes, imitations painted by the master's students.

Late in 1945, a GI was sketching on the Quai d'Orsay, on the Left Bank of the Seine, when a man approached him and admired his work.

"Oh, I can do better," said the young soldier. "These crayons aren't much good."

The other man scribbled his name and address on a scrap piece of paper and gave it to the soldier, who quickly put it in his pocket.

"You can come to my studio, where I have better supplies," said the man.

"Oh, do you draw too?" asked the GI.

"Yes, a little," came the reply.

Only later did the GI unfold the scrap of paper and see the name above the address: "Pablo Picasso."

In April 1946, the Museum of Modern Art wanted to have a one-man show of Picasso's works. They sent him an invitation, saying a visit to America by the most acclaimed living artist would be a historic event. But Picasso declined.

"For an artist to travel to America is no longer original," he replied.

Soon after that, the French industrialist Pierre Wertheimer, who had a vast art collection before the war, began efforts to restore it. The Nazis had seized his paintings and sold them off. Somehow he managed to get back forty masterpieces, from old masters to modern French works. One of the most difficult to reclaim was a painting by Picasso, which the artist had purchased after it had been sold and resold several times.

Picasso thus found himself in the odd position of having to surrender a painting that he had not only paid for but also painted.

That same month, June 1946, Picasso visited Henri Matisse's studio and was invited to take any painting. He chose the smallest and least attractive. Matisse urged him to take a better, larger one, but Picasso stuck with his choice, explaining: "Now, when people come to my studio and ask about this painting, I can say: 'Oh, that's a Matisse.'"

In Paris in August 1946, he attended an exhibition of Chagall paintings and asked Chagall about his four-year stay in America during the war. He listened and was startled.

Picasso, who'd come to believe America was a country concerned only with trade and profit, said: "You mean to say an artist really can work in America?"

For all his worldliness and international acclaim, he would never visit the United States.

Picasso might have come to America in 1947 at the behest of the Association of American Artists, but at the American Embassy in Paris some high official was warned that Picasso was an avowed Communist, and they would be responsible for his keeping out of anything to do with politics. The official declined, saying: "How can anyone ever dare guarantee the behavior of an artist?"

In October 1947, Picasso was visited by a French Communist Party member who complained that Picasso's paintings weren't Marxist enough.

"The visit of that official started me thinking," Picasso told a friend. "If those people ever come to power, I'll be arrested. But perhaps I'll still have my pencils and be able to continue drawing my pictures. Then it occurred to me that they might take away my pencils while I'm in jail. What then? And then I decided that as long as my tongue is wet and there is dust on the floor, I can make my pictures.

"And so I've come to the conclusion that I'm more an artist than a politician."

When Churchill lost reelection as prime minister to Clement Atlee, the message of condolence that touched him most came from Picasso: "If you had not been a politician, you could've made a living as a painter."

Before the war, Chagall and Picasso frequented the Café de Flore on the Boulevard Saint-Germain in Paris, a gathering place for artists, famous and unknown. They would while away the time making sketches on matchbooks. The other artists would wait, hopefully, for the two giants to leave these sketches or toss them aside, but they were always disappointed. Both Chagall and Picasso knew their worth, and at the end of the night they'd approach each other with outstretched hands and count off an even exchange.

Picasso had a friend who lived in Los Angeles and was asked about the state of the artist's love life. "If it's any indication," came the reply, "he recently offered to swap three of his recent paintings for three mink coats. Assorted sizes."

In November 1948, Picasso received the Legion of Merit, France's highest civilian honor, over the objections of several anti-Communist members. He received the formal delegation of officials at his home in Antibes on the Riviera, bare-chested, in shorts, his feet encased in sandals, holding in his arms the naked boy who was his acknowledged son.

A year and a half later, Picasso painted a portrait of a man who'd sat for him for many days. The portrait turned out to be an impressionist picture of the man with one eye in the middle of his forehead and the other over his heart.

In distress, the man asked: "But why didn't you paint me the way God made me?"

"Because," Picasso replied, "I do not agree with God."

In January 1951, a feud broke out between Picasso and Salvador Dalí, involving politics and art form. Picasso said of Dalí: "He is the most pretentious man the world has ever known—after The Eternal Father."

Then, discussing his own work, Picasso showed some friends his early cubist pictures, then examples of his Blue Period, and finally his ceramics.

"Have you ever produced any normal things that will become classics?" he was asked.

Picasso replied: "The only classical, normal work I've produced is my children."

Later that month, Monroe Wheeler, a member of the board of the Museum of Modern Art in New York, spent time with Picasso, and they talked of Picasso's pictures. Wheeler mentioned an unusual one he'd seen in a German museum. Picasso asked what he thought of it. "Frankly, I don't like it," said Wheeler. He then asked Picasso: "And what do you think of it?"

"If it's good," replied Picasso, "then fifty years from now they'll say it's mine. If it's bad, it will be attributed to my school or to one of my followers."

In May 1956, a movie about the artist called *Le mystère Picasso* was shown at the Cannes Film Festival. At the time Picasso was ill, and his doctor had instructed him to be in bed each night by 8:30. But the movie showing was for 9. So Picasso obeyed his physician. He got into bed promptly at 8:30, then climbed out, donned a dinner jacket, and went to the movie.

GEORGE BERNARD SHAW

My parents had a framed photo on the wall in our hallway of two men wearing long, white beards. One was my father, who was forty years old in 1946, and his beard was sketched on. The other man, whose beard was genuine, was George Bernard Shaw, and the photo was snapped by my mother at Shaw's home in Ayot St. Lawrence on his ninetieth birthday.

Less than two months after my father began writing "The Lyons Den" in 1934, he ran his first story about "G.B.S.," as the great writer identified himself. He reported Shaw's visit to New York, during which a young playwright invited Shaw to attend a rehearsal of that struggling writer's new show. Amazingly, the usually unapproachable Shaw agreed. During the performance, the young man complained about the lack of cooperation he was getting from the cast: "Just look at that ham," he said. "All he has to do in that scene is yawn, and we can't even get him to do that."

"Why not read him the rest of your play," suggested Shaw. "He'll yawn for a month."

In March 1938, toward the end of the Depression, Shaw agreed to have his plays produced in America at the WPA Federal Theater, saying he'd charge only $50 a week in royalties. "But let it accumulate and pay me at the end of the year. Provided," he continued, "America is still solvent."

Just after the outbreak of World War II, Clare Boothe Luce, the writer and future ambassador, met Shaw at his home in London, where the old man was at his desk writing. "Mr. Shaw," she said, "You're the first person I've met here. Who else shall I try to meet?"

"My dear Miss Boothe," Shaw assured her, "you've already met everybody."

Shaw was invited to the seventieth birthday party of fellow author H.G. Wells and gave the last testimonial. He arose slowly and simply said: "H.G., you're a nice fellow, but you can't write."

Before America entered the war in 1941, Roosevelt armed England through the Lend Lease program. Shaw made a short film about this for distribution in American movie theaters. He looked into the camera and said: "This film you're about to see is a remake of an old, stale play of mine. Recently you may have seen the movie *Pygmalion*, which was a remake of another old, stale play of mine. Shortly before that, you witnessed a production of *Heartbreak House*, yet another old, stale play of mine. I'm sending America all my old, stale plays. But that's a fair exchange, because America is sending us all her old, stale destroyers."

When *Pygmalion* won Shaw the Academy Award for best screenplay, he was unimpressed, saying: "They might as well have given George a medal for being King." But when he heard the Oscar was made of gold, he said: "Gold! In that case, send it over." However, when it arrived, Shaw discovered it wasn't made of gold after all. Indignant, he sent it to his producer in America, Gabriel Pascal, who returned it to Shaw with a note saying: "I don't want any junk either. This really belongs to you." For years the forlorn, much-traveled statuette lay covered with dirt and grime in Shaw's study in his home, now a museum. Finally it was restored to its luster and is on display to this day.

During the relentless German bombings of 1941, Londoners had a novel way of learning what sort of a day lay ahead of them. They simply watched out for Shaw's car. Each morning, Shaw would ask his chauffeur: "Do you think we'll have a bombing today?" If the chauffeur, who seemed to know about such matters, said no, Shaw would ride into London in his convertible, with the top down.

But if the chauffeur said, "Yes, we expect a bombing today," Shaw would use his hard-topped sedan, and his fellow Londoners would suspect they'd be in for it that day.

Later that year, a stripper named Margie Hart wrote Shaw. She was writing one of the masters of the English language to ask if he could suggest a nicer-sounding word than "strip-teaser." Shaw replied: "As long as more people will pay admission to a theater to see a naked woman than a naked brain, the Drama will languish."

Soon after that, Shaw met a man who'd written his biography years before. "It's been a long time," said the writer to Shaw. "The last time I saw you, your face was white, your beard red. Now your beard's white and your face red."

Shaw was continually getting requests for permission to produce his plays because they were surefire moneymakers. One came from the Bucks County Playhouse in Pennsylvania, planning to produce a revival of *Mrs. Warren's Profession* with Mae West in the lead role. Shaw's reply to the producer: "Unable to authorize any revivals," the telegram read, "until taxes here return to normal. If I can wait, and Mrs. Warren can wait, so can Miss West. G.B.S."

When another request came, from the Theater Guild in New York, he replied: "Because of the taxes, what you don't take in over there, I don't get over here."

Like Hemingway and most other great writers, Shaw edited his own work carefully. He tried to cut each sentence, phrase, or word he considered unnecessary. In August 1942, Shaw wrote a long letter to the Theater Guild and included an apology: "Pardon the extreme length of this letter, but I haven't got the time to write a short one."

Monty Woolley, the famed character actor of that era, is best remembered today for portraying the cantankerous radio personality in *The Man Who Came to Dinner*. Woolley had been considered for the role of Shaw in a planned movie biography. They'd met in 1927, a year before the crusty actor grew his own trademark white beard.

Shaw heard of the projected biography of himself and demanded a screening of *The Pied Piper*, in which Woolley starred. But after two reels were shown, Shaw ordered the screening stopped. He arose and said; "He's not to the type to portray me. He's much too scholarly and pleasant."

In February 1943, a list of "People-We'd-Like-To-Meet" was published, culled from visitors to England, which included Shaw. This despite the fact that there was a war going on, and that Shaw had famously refused to meet with a man known as a bore. "The trouble with him," said Shaw, "is that he lacks the power of conversation, but not the power of speech."

Nevertheless, several people in the survey persisted and tried to meet him. He sent them a postcard that read: "The Bernard Shaw you want to see no longer exists. There is nothing of him except an old man with his eighty-three years, living in an inaccessible village where he has no means of entertaining such distinguished visitors."

The day after D-Day, Shaw's *Heartbreak House* was performed in Oxford with Shaw in attendance. Three immortals of the theater starred: John Gielgud, Raymond Massey, and Flora Robson. The audience, aware of Shaw's presence among them, reacted to nearly every line with great laughter. When the curtain descended, Shaw addressed the hushed audience: "When I wrote *Heartbreak House*, it was a serious play, not a comedy. After tonight's performance, however, all I can do is give the producer, the cast, the director, and especially you, the audience, my most heartfelt curse."

During a trip to Hollywood, Shaw posed for a studio photographer. Surprisingly, he liked the results. So he paid for the prints of the photo by signing twenty checks, each for 10 pounds Sterling. "There are enough fools in the world," he explained, "who think my autograph is worth something. I understand that the prevailing price of my autograph is 25 pounds. So by sending you twenty checks, both of us profit. You can sell the 10 pound checks for 25 pounds and the buyers will want to keep my autographs so they won't cash the checks!"

A fan approached Shaw once and asked him to sign a photo of himself. He obliged, but signed on the back. "I'm not afraid my autograph would spoil my picture," he explained, "but that my picture might spoil my autograph."

In July 1945, Vivien Leigh met Shaw while shooting his *Caesar and Cleopatra*. Shaw recalled seeing her play the role of Jennifer Dubedat in his play *The Doctor's Dilemma* three years earlier. "You looked too respectable and ladylike in that role," he recalled. "Do you really think so?" the actress beamed. "Not any longer," replied Shaw. "Now that you've met me, you're neither respectable nor ladylike, so you'll certainly make a great Cleopatra."

His play *Pygmalion*, on which *My Fair Lady* would be based, was itself a big hit, frequently produced in revivals and by stock companies. The producers of one proposed revival were keenly aware of Shaw's crabby nature, so they sent him a carefully worded telegram: "I'm sure you will be pleased to learn that Gertrude Lawrence, with whom you are so friendly, will be starring. We know you'll take a friendly view, because we plan other Shaw revivals. Sir Cedric Hardwicke will direct *Pygmalion*, and we know how friendly you are with him."

Shaw replied in a typical manner: "Am 'friendly.' Wire with whom I can talk business! G.B.S."

Hardwicke, one of the great character actors of that era, lunched with Shaw, and the writer told Hardwicke he was his fourth favorite actor. "Who's ahead of me?" asked Hardwicke, not knowing what to expect.

"The Marx Brothers," replied Shaw.

At the 1946 premiere of a revival of his film *Caesar and Cleopatra*, Shaw was asked if the young Egyptian queen could really have done all the things attributed to her in the movie. "After all," Shaw was reminded, "she was only sixteen when Caesar visited Egypt."

Shaw explained: "The difference between wisdom and folly has nothing to do with age. Some people are younger at sixty than others at sixteen."

A passenger on an ocean liner noticed Shaw was a fellow passenger. He knew well enough to keep his distance, as Shaw sat alone, reading a book, lying on a deck chair. Since Shaw's reputation as being cantankerous preceded him, the man left Shaw alone. But he began to notice that every few minutes, Shaw would look up from the book and laugh, then he'd go back to reading and do it again. Finally Shaw put down the book and went inside. The other passenger had to know what book could make the great George Bernard Shaw laugh so often, so he quickly snuck over and looked at the cover: *The Collected Works of George Bernard Shaw*.

His first play to be staged was *Widowers' Houses* in 1892. At a revival in 1946, Shaw told the cast: "Courtesy is a waste of time, and at ninety I have no time to spare." During rehearsals, he watched from the rear of the theater, then handed out notes to everyone in the cast, except for the star. The actor beamed, assuming his portrayal was so good he didn't need any help, even from Shaw himself. Then he made the mistake of asking Shaw why he didn't get any instructions.

"Because," said Shaw, "no actor could possibly fail in the role you're playing."

Among his many honors, Orson Welles held the distinction of being the only person Shaw allowed to edit a Shavian play.

He'd telephoned Shaw in London for permission to edit *Heartbreak House*. "I never allowed The Theater Guild to cut, so why should I allow you?" asked Shaw. "Because," replied Welles, "they don't know how to edit. I do. I cut Shakespeare's *Julius Caesar* last season, and it was a hit."

"Shakespeare yes, Shaw no," came the reply. Undaunted, Welles called again the next week and said: "You were right, Mr. Shaw. I don't think your play can be cut, because each line is so brilliant."

"In that case," said Shaw, "you may cut."

In July 1946, to mark his ninetieth birthday, Penguin Books published *Pygmalion, Major Barbara*, and *St. Joan*. The publisher had requested permission to print a scene from *St. Joan* in a school textbook. Shaw refused: "I lay my eternal curse on whomsoever shall now or at any time hereafter make schoolbooks out of my works, and make me as hated as Shakespeare. My plays were not designed as instruments of torture."

A New York producer wrote Shaw regarding a record album of his recordings to be called "The Best of G.B. Shaw." The cast included such revered actors as Raymond Massey, Katharine Cornell, Maurice Evans, Gertrude Lawrence, and Burgess Meredith. Shaw expressed interest, but imposed one condition: "Schoolchildren must not be compelled to listen to it."

About that time, Shaw took ill and his doctor prescribed meat to give him energy. But the vegetarian Shaw refused. "Death is better than cannibalism," he proclaimed. "My will contains directions for my funeral, which will be followed not by mourning coaches. Instead there will be herds of oxen, sheep, swine, flocks of poultry, and a small traveling aquarium of live fish, all wearing white scarves in honor of the man who perished rather than eat his fellow creatures." He planned to leave most of his money to the Institute for the Formation of a New Alphabet.

In August 1946, H.G. Wells, Shaw's contemporary, died. One of the news services released an obituary written by Shaw. It was a frank appraisal of Wells and his work, but it would not be the final word in their exchange. A few years before that, the news service had asked Wells to write an advance obituary of Shaw, who by then was past eighty.

Wells wrote the piece stating exactly what he thought of the Irish playwright. Both obituaries, in which both authors appraised the other without ever suspecting that their opinions were being exchanged, were stored away by the news service. Since Shaw outlived Wells by four years, Wells got the last word.

When *Caesar and Cleopatra* opened in New York, the program gave credit for the lighting to one "G.B. Shaw." Back in London, Shaw was livid. "My stage name," he explained, "is Bernard Shaw. And I want people to respect it."

Shaw once met a young man who told him he was a playwright. "They also tell me you're a song writer," said Shaw. "That too, Mr. Shaw," said the young man. "Don't be a duck," Shaw advised. "A duck can swim but not very well. He can walk too, but quite awkwardly. He also flies, but poorly. So don't be a duck, young man." The aspiring "duck" was a young Noël Coward, who became a swan.

Another young man, an American GI with writing aspirations, once managed to meet Shaw, who told him that for twelve years he tried to get published before he found success. "So those years were wasted, I guess," said the young soldier. "Not at all," replied Shaw. "After eight years of trying, editors knew I wouldn't give up and that they would have to give in."

On July 26, 1946, my parents spent the day with Shaw on Shaw's ninetieth birthday, and my father took home movies with a 16mm color camera that had been used in the wing of a plane on D-Day. The London

papers got wind of it and said the footage was Shaw's farewell in front of a camera. But later he met my parents again and asked what my father was carrying in his bag. "A movie camera," replied my father. Then they went outside, and my father began to film Shaw again. But Shaw walked away. His neighbor later told my father that Shaw was walking away because he didn't want to be filmed.

"Nonsense," said Shaw, when he heard that. "I was walking away to provide action. The trouble with amateur movies is that the subject poses as if for a still camera. I provided the action." This from a man who disliked movies and hadn't been to a film in years.

In May 1947, Shaw received a visitor who asked to see his Nobel Prize. Shaw went upstairs, ransacked his rooms, but came down shrugging: "I can't find it." Then he explained that when he received the check that accompanied the Nobel Prize, he was plagued by hundreds of letter-writers who recited their needs, and asked him to send them money. He therefore announced he'd be returning the check to the Nobel committee. "But that only made it worse," he said, "and it brought twice as many letters from poor people. They wrote that since I could afford to return such a large check, I certainly could afford to send them money."

Shaw once was visited by J. Arthur Rank, the wealthy film producer. He was unaware of Shaw's cantankerous disposition. "You're a very rich man, Mr. Rank," Shaw began. "Who did you swindle to get so much money?" "I didn't swindle anybody," the shocked Rank replied. "I inherited it from my father."

"Then who did he swindle?" asked Shaw. "No one can amass a fortune without having swindled somebody."

My father had printed a report saying that Shaw was nearly broke, having given away large sums of money over the years.

Shaw heard about this and wrote: "I am not destitute. But war taxation leaves me nothing to spare. (Begging letter-writers please note.) Serious authorship does not produce best-sellers. No great play can compete with *Oklahoma!* during the author's lifetime, though over the centuries, *Hamlet* leaves the most popular potboiler nowhere. I could not afford to marry until I was past forty. Since then, I have made enough.

"And enough is as good as a feast. G.B.S."

Shaw met Sigmund Freud, whose analysis of the playwright was: "All intellect and no heart." When Shaw was asked about that quote, he replied: "Nonsense. I've been to the movies and felt an irritable desire to kiss Mae West."

In 1948, Lilli Palmer, the actress, bought a portrait of Shaw as a gift for Rex Harrison, her husband at the time. She sent it to Shaw for his inscription. He studied the artist's impression of him and wrote: "George Bernard Shaw. The original who is only ninety, looks twenty years younger and is much tidier."

Shaw usually replied to letter-writers with postcards that often read: "Mr. Bernard Shaw, having now no time for any except the most urgent private correspondence, must refer you to the founder of the Shaw Society. He is better informed on many points than Mr. Shaw himself."

Shaw was a fierce debater, especially when dueling with a contemporary. In 1948, for example, Shaw, then ninety-two, crossed verbal swords with Maurice Maeterlinck, a fellow Nobel Prize winner. The Belgian playwright, poet, and essayist was then a mere eighty-five.

"Shaw is an old chateau no longer even haunted by a spirit," he began.

Shaw shot back: "Maeterlinck has never been hissed or hooted at by an audience. After all, how can you hoot and hiss while you're yawning?"

To Ingrid Bergman he said: "A girl with your talents should only appear in plays by Bernard Shaw."

In December 1948, Shaw was visited by former heavyweight champion Gene Tunney, who was surprised when Shaw recalled their previous meeting twenty years earlier while Tunney held the title. A photographer had been following the champ for days, hoping for a picture. He snapped the two men, then submitted a caption to his newspaper: "Gene Tunney and friend."

Back in 1924, Shaw had bet on Tunney's challenger, Georges Carpentier, who was knocked out by the champion. Shaw was kidded for his bet but wired the kidder from London: "You and I are far too intelligent to accept such mundane things as a referee's count or a judge's decision in a prize fight. We both know Carpentier won the only victory that really counts—the moral victory."

The aforementioned Sir Cedric Hardwicke was a close friend of Shaw's and appeared in the original cast of *Heartbreak House*. Shaw showed up at the dress rehearsal and complained that an offstage explosion wasn't loud enough. Hardwicke assured his friend that all would be well come opening night, explaining that the producers had hired an explosives expert.

Well, opening night came all right, and as Hardwicke and the other actors flinched onstage when the time came for the explosion, nothing happened. They waited. Still nothing. Finally they had to press on and pretended there had been an explosion. The show ended, and while the audience was on its way out, the blast finally came! In fact it rocketed through the theater and tore loose a chandelier and injured a patron.

Shaw heard about a theatrical festival that included marionettes of himself and Shakespeare, so he wrote a playlet for the production.

"In this play, I fight a duel with Hamlet and chop off his head," said Shaw. "I did it just to find out if the clever puppeteer could manufacture a marionette whose head could be chopped off." Shaw was then ninety-three. At his birthday celebration, his friend Sir Cedric Hardwicke introduced Shaw to his sixteen-year-old son Edward. "In years to come," said Shaw, shaking the boy's hand, "you'll be proud to say you once shook hands with Bernard Shaw. And people will say to you: 'Who the hell is Bernard Shaw?'"

In November 1949, *The March of Time*, then a popular documentary/newsreel series, wanted to interview Shaw, one of many prominent people prognosticating on the coming half-century. They should've anticipated his response: "It is a common mistake of editors to fill their magazines or newsreels with interviews of prominent people. Instead, they should use the money to hire young, original writers."

When someone persisted and asked him about the coming half-century anyway, he replied: "When anyone asks me a question requiring an answer of over twenty words, they should accompany it with an offer of at least three figures."

The Devil's Disciple has always been my favorite Shavian work, ever since I saw the 1960 movie version giving Kirk Douglas and Burt Lancaster, two of my favorite actors, the chance to work together with Lord Laurence Olivier. But over the years, this masterpiece has been performed countless times onstage as well.

Back in 1950, one of the stage productions was in jeopardy. The frantic producers cabled Shaw saying they had yet to receive a signed contract from him. They'd begun hiring actors, assuming he would agree to the production. Finally a postcard arrived from Shaw: "You are very foolish to engage actors on such an assumption. I am an old man who might die before getting to sign the contract. Proceed, however, at your own risk."

Hardwicke was asked if Shaw had ever directed one of his own plays. Indeed he had, the actor recalled: a production of *Caesar and Cleopatra*. "But he had to quit after four days, because he found himself laughing too hard at his own lines."

When invited to join London's Centenarian Club in his ninety-third year, he predictably refused: "I never wanted to be a centenarian," he explained. "I dread it. And as for wanting to live my life over again—no. It would be a confession that I've wasted it. I'm still too busy to bother about happiness. I am nearly dead, but still earning and growing. Life is worth my while, and if it were not, I should end it."

Soon after that, Shaw received a visit from violinist Jascha Heifetz before a recital in London's Albert Hall. Shaw gave him some unusual advice: "Play one wrong note," he said. "Because nothing must be perfect in this world, or the gods become jealous and destroy it."

A producer kept hounding Shaw about getting permission to film several of his plays, but kept getting turned down. Four times came the request, followed by four denials. Finally came yet another request. The then-ninety-four-year-old Shaw wrote: "All movie rights to my plays belong to Gabriel Pascal while he lives. But take heart; Mr. Pascal leads a strange, strenuous life."

Shaw's friendship with Pascal went back to the 1920s when he met the then-penniless producer and gave him exclusive rights to produce movie versions of his plays, a right that made Pascal rich. They'd met in Biarritz where Pascal had seen a bearded man in shorts emerging from the water. He giggled, and Shaw asked why.

"You look funny," Pascal said. Shaw's reaction was to invite him to lunch, where the lifelong friendship was forged.

A young actor portrayed General Burgoyne in a summer stock production of *The Devil's Disciple*. One night an adoring fan came backstage to congratulate him. Soon after that, they were married. Then the actor tried for a part in another Shaw play in New York, but couldn't get in to see the producer. Frustrated, he wrote Shaw for help, and enclosed a photo of his wife, explaining how they'd met.

Another postcard from Shaw was the reply: "I no longer interfere with casting. Furthermore, at the age of ninety-four and after spending sixty-eight years in the theater, a photo of a girl, though very beautiful, no longer cuts any ice with me."

It was Shaw who first wrote the line now common in sports about "those who can, do. Those who cannot, teach." But he put it this way: "Someone who is doing all the time does not really have time to teach, nor is he necessarily competent to teach. For example, I couldn't teach you to write plays."

As Shaw neared the end of his life, all sorts of people contacted him, including a collector of autographed dollar bills. The man's collection included bills signed by prominent people all over the world. Naturally, Shaw refused and sent a postcard: "I will neither export a silver certificate nor deface a dollar. The law is the law."

The Hearst publishing company offered Shaw a fabulous fee to write, "How to Grow Old Gracefully." Shaw replied: "Write it yourself and save the money."

Shaw once gave a description of himself, in reply to an inquiry from the Shaw Society of America: "I have fifteen different reputations," he replied. "They include: a critic of art, a critic of music, a critic of literature, a Shelleyan atheist, a Fabian Socialist, a vegetarian, a preacher, and a philosopher. In all my plays, my economic studies have played as important a part as a knowledge of anatomy does in the works of Michelangelo."

A writer in Hollywood once foolishly tried rewriting Shaw's On the Rock, by Americanizing some of the characters. Naturally he got a terse message from Shaw:

"You probably have quite enough talent to provide your own characters. So stop wasting your time tomfooling with mine."

To a woman who'd corresponded with him for years, then wanted to sell the letters, he said: "I refuse to play the horse for your Lady Godiva."

Shaw left an unproduced play written many years before his death. He considered it most timely when he wrote it, but a producer decided against staging it. But ten years later, the producer changed his mind and asked Shaw to agree to present it in London.

Shaw's reply was terse: "No. Better never than late."

My mother once asked Shaw what he thought of television, then in its infancy. The reply was characteristically caustic and terse: "I cannot bear to look."

George Bernard Shaw died from complications suffered in a fall on November 2, 1950. One of the last penny postcard communications from Shaw was received by a Greenwich Village writer, advising him how to prepare for playwriting: "Sit in a chair for fifteen years. After that, work in a coal mine. Then perhaps, you'll be ready."

When I look at that photo of my father and Shaw, the link to the past two centuries comes to mind, when I remember that Shaw knew Charles Dickens, who was born in 1812! In fact, my father heard Shaw refer to Dickens as "a snob."

The veteran character actor Wilfred Hyde-White appeared in the movie The Browning Version, based on a Shaw play. In the spring of 1951, reminiscing about him, the actor recalled one of his first roles in London, a minor part in a Shaw revival. The actor asked Shaw during rehearsals how to read his one line.

"My dear boy," Shaw advised, "I want that one line spoken in the same way I want every line of my plays spoken: so that everyone in the audience will nudge his neighbor and say: 'Only Bernard Shaw could have written that line.'"

Hyde-White would later costar in *My Fair Lady* onscreen as Col. Pickering, based on Shaw's *Pygmalion*.

A few years after Shaw died, a report was issued that the distinguished classical actor Eric Portman would participate in "The Players' Pipe Night Saluting GBS." But Portman said he'd be the only speaker who wouldn't praise Shaw. "I knew Shaw," he said. "Worked for him. And thoroughly disliked him."

At one point before he died my mother wrote Shaw, saying she would be coming to London with my oldest brother George and would like the boy to meet Shaw. Again a postcard reply:

"He never heard of me and I certainly never heard of him. Take him to the zoo instead." So she did.

Knowing my late brother George Lyons, however, Shaw missed out.

THE DUKE & DUCHESS OF WINDSOR

I remember meeting the Duke and Duchess of Windsor, with my father, of course, on his nightly rounds. It was at "21" in the late 'sixties, and I found myself talking to him in Spanish! My father had told me the Duke was bilingual, so there we were, me a law school student, talking about who knows what in Spanish with the un-crowned King Edward VIII! He spoke Spanish quite well, actually, with a British accent.

The friendship between my father and the Duke, whose backgrounds couldn't have been more disparate, was genuine and long-standing. When the Duke died in 1972, my father's tribute column began: "One of the saddest events in life is the loss of a friend."

He first wrote about the Duke soon after the abdication, an international news sensation in December 1936. On the night before he abdicated, then-King Edward VIII called the woman for whom he was giving up the throne. Wallis Warfield Simpson, the twice-divorced American, was in Cannes. They knew their wires were tapped by government officials—perhaps for history's sake.

"Well, I've abdicated," he said.

"You fool," she replied.

The next day he arrived on French soil and said: "Here I am. I now have no place to go."

At a dinner party in 1938, the Duke was accorded the seat of honor next to his hostess. He looked around the large table and saw that his wife was seated faraway at the other end, with some minor members of royalty. "Are you looking for your wife?" the hostess asked.

"No," replied the Duke, barely concealing his annoyance. "I'm looking for Her Royal Highness."

In New York in April 1948, the Duke attended a board of directors' meeting of the Chesapeake & Ohio Railroad. Before he arrived, the head of the company briefed the board members on the strict rules of protocol: the slight bow of the head, remembering to address him as "Sir," or "Your Royal Highness," etc. But one board member, arriving just as the Duke entered and noticing the stranger in the room—whom he obviously didn't recognize—stuck out his hand and said: "Hi. My name is Bob. What's yours?"

Early in 1949, the Duke ordered some custom silk shirts with monograms, and then learned that the monograms would be expensive because of the crowns atop the initials. "I think I'll have the crowns removed," he told the Duchess.

"That wouldn't be the first time," she replied.

The Duke was an avid golfer, and soon after he teed off for a round in August 1949, he spotted two young caddies arguing. He intervened and settled the dispute, then asked them to walk the course with him.

"Aren't you the King of England?" asked the younger one. "No, my brother is," replied the Duke.

At the third hole the young American said: "You ought to be the King—or something."

Then the Duke asked him where he was from.

"Oklahoma," replied the youth.

"Oh, I saw the show," the Duke replied.

Late in 1946, the Windsors attended the opera and outside saw a policeman they'd met on several previous visits to New York. "Good evening, Officer Kenny," said the Duke. "How are you, Sir?" came the reply. When the Duke asked the policeman how he was, the answer was: "Fine, except for one thing: Please, just free the Irish, will you? Just free the Irish."

At a Washington luncheon the following year, the Duke, then living in the South of France, was asked when he'd planned to return to London.

"That's difficult to say," he began, "because the Archbishop of Canterbury objects because I married a divorced woman. The Archbishop forgets that his office was created by a predecessor of mine for the purpose of marrying a divorced woman."

Back in New York a few months later, the Duke was headed to a country club on Long Island when his car was stopped for speeding. The chauffeur said to the policeman: "If you tear up that piece of paper with your name on it, I'll give you a piece of paper with his name on it," pointing to his passenger. The policeman looked at the backseat, recognized the Duke, and got his autograph instead of giving him the ticket.

Late in 1950, Ethel Merman was starring on Broadway in *Call Me Madam*. Like most stars, she dressed casually going to the theater: slacks, loafers, and a sweater. Just before the curtain rose, she was handed a note: "The Boy and I are out front," it read.

She knew that "The Boy" was the way the Duchess of Windsor referred to her husband. The note continued: "Come dine with us after the show at the Stork Club."

Thus, for perhaps the first time in Broadway history, a star left the theater before the patrons, for once the curtain calls were over, Merman raced past the patrons, jumped in a cab, dashed home, donned a formal gown and her finest jewels, and was at the Windsors' table at the Stork Club before midnight.

On another evening at the Stork Club, the Duke was talking about television, in its infancy in February 1951. He marveled at the ability of speakers on the grainy tube to talk clearly while standing up, with few if any notes. He was reminded of the great speech he'd given on the radio in 1936, announcing his abdication.

"Yes," he said. "But I had the luxury of sitting down."

One evening the royal couple attended a party and Yul Brynner, starring in *The King and I*, was there. He danced with the Duchess, and someone observed: "She's probably the only woman to dance with two kings, but only one of them is working at it."

Back at the Stork Club, the Duke was seated at a table adjacent to my father. The Duke was speaking in Spanish to his guest, and my father spoke up, also in Spanish: he didn't want the Duke to think he was eavesdropping on him. So the Duke asked my father how he, a New York columnist, happened to speak Spanish.

My father told the Duke that when he was a young lawyer, his firm was training him to go to San Juan, Puerto Rico, for two years, to open a branch office, and had him take Spanish lessons. But then, my father explained, he met Sylvia, the woman who would become his wife, and a two-year separation was out of the question. So he started submitting stories to the established Broadway columnists of the day, and eventually became a columnist himself.

The Duke, who had been listening with rapt attention, finally said: "So you had a career and a life all planned out for you, then you met a woman, and all your plans changed? How fascinating! Do tell me more!"

Danny Kaye, one of the great performers of all time, was at a party where the Windsors were guests. He said: "I'll entertain you. And, in your honor, first I will perform an old English madrigal."

"Make it the last," replied the Duke.

Back in Paris in November 1951, the Duke was with some friends, and the conversation turned to the royal "We." The example of Queen Victoria's famous statement: "We are not amused," was given. The Duke explained that "We" is only used in official documents, never in conversation.

"So she probably never said that," he said. Then he added: "What's more, I doubt she was ever amused about anything."

Gardner Cowles, the founder and publisher of *Look* magazine, a rival to *Life* in its day, was a close friend of the Duke's. One evening the Duke marveled at Winston Churchill's incredible memory for events that occurred years before and his ability to turn a phrase, like "blood, sweat, and tears." Cowles, in turn, admired the Duke's memory. The Duke politely disagreed, but then said: "Churchill used that 'Blood, sweat, and tears' phrase once before, you know. It appears in *The Unknown War, Volume VI* of his series, *The World Crisis*."

The Windsors attended a performance of a play called *The Happy Time,* set in Ontario. The cast knew they'd be there, and kept sneaking peeks at the couple to gauge their reaction. One scene had a photo of King George V on the wall, and when the curtain went up the cast could hear the Duke tell those around him: "That's my father."

They chatted throughout the show, and once, when one of the stars, Leonora Dana, went offstage, Eva Gabor, awaiting her cue to go on, whispered: "What are they doing?"

"They're talking," she replied. "In fact, I once stopped and tried to listen to them."

By 1954, the Duke had finished his autobiography and said there wouldn't be a sequel. "It would be stretching too much of a good thing," he explained.

The Duchess was writing her autobiography as well, but the woman for whom the King of England gave up his throne told him: "It seems to me that mine has been the dullest life in the world."

The Duke's autobiography was previewed with excerpts in *McCall's* magazine in 1956, and he was asked if he helped with the story. "I helped with the photos," he replied, "mainly by posing for them."

While living at the Waldorf Towers in

1956, the Duke would often walk the Windsor dogs at night. One night he descended in the elevator, and it stopped at a lower floor. A butler got on, walking his employer's dog. The dogs became friendly, so the two strangers decided to walk together. They chatted, and when they returned, the butler suggested they go to a nearby bar for a drink. They did, and walked their dogs back to the Waldorf. When they entered the elevator, the butler said to the former King of England: "Oh, by the way, who do you work for?"

When Whitey Ford, the Yankees' Hall of Fame pitcher, beat the Milwaukee Braves in the opening game of the 1957 World Series, he celebrated at a café near his home in Glen Cove, Long Island. A neighbor was there and invited the Fords over for a nightcap, promising a surprise. When they arrived, their host went upstairs and returned, leading his sleepy, tousle-haired guest, who probably never heard of Whitey Ford: the Duke of Windsor.

Jack LeVien, who produced the acclaimed TV documentary about Sir Winston Churchill, made a film version of the Duke's autobiography, *A King's Story*. He'd screened the Churchill film for the Duke in his studio, and when the part came on screen where the Germans annexed the Rhineland in March 1936, the Duke said:

"Oh, I know all about that. I was King then, don't forget."

At the first showing of the film, the Duke was seen dabbing his eyes with his handkerchief when the scenes of his boyhood were flashed on the screen. During the newsreel scene of his grandfather Edward VII's funeral, the Duke began naming for his wife those in the procession:

"That's Franz Josef. And old Ferdinand," he said, identifying the Austrian Emperor and the Archduke, whose assassination in 1914 touched off World War I. He named them just before the narrator, Orson Welles, did.

When the screen showed his father leading him to his investiture as Prince of Wales, the Duke began humming along with the sound track, the song the Welsh choir had sung at those ceremonies so many years before.

He confided that Churchill had helped him with his abdication speech: particularly the portion in which he reminded his subjects that his brother George VI was blessed with a happy home and a family—blessings possessed by so many of his subjects, but not by him.

When the screening was over the former King of England asked my mother what she thought of the movie.

"Good casting," replied my mother.

My parents with Orson Welles at the Stork Club.

'40s

The Lyons Den

By Leonard Lyons

This decade saw our family grow; my brother Warren arrived on Irving Berlin's fifty-second birthday, May 11, 1940. I followed four years later, and my brother Douglas came along in 1947. By then we were living in an apartment on Central Park West, which my mother would call home for fifty-two years, as one by one, the men of the family left.

DiMaggio was a fixture at Toots Shor's every night, and New York was the baseball capital of the world with three popular teams. The Dodgers were usually second division teams, but did win pennants in 1941, 1947, and 1949, only to lose to the Yankees in the World Series every year. But the arrival of Jackie Robinson was one of the most significant events in American history. The Giants were never in the World Series in that decade, but their slugger Mel Ott would wind up his Hall of Fame career in 1947.

By then my father's picture appeared in the paper every day, and the *Post* changed from a full-sized paper to a tabloid. It was an "afternoon" paper, hitting the streets in time for the evening rush hour. Such a thing is inconceivable today, when New York has only four major papers (including Long Island–based *Newsday*), but back then the *Post* competed with Hearst's *Journal-American* for the rush-hour readers.

Wartime restrictions led restaurants to impose some rationing, with meatless Tuesdays and Thursdays, but the nightclubs still thrived. My father's routine was set, covering lunch places, writing the first draft of the column, then going out at night to make the rounds of the nightspots for later stories.

At the time, "The Lyons Den" was syndicated by the Hearst-owned King Features. (In those days before photocopiers, emails, and computers, the syndicate took tear sheets of the column, and mailed them to the 100 or so papers around the world that carried "The Lyons Den." A few days after the column had run in the *New York Post*, it would appear in the Los Angeles *Racing Form*, or the *Rome Daily American*, and elsewhere.

But after my father praised the Orson Welles film *Citizen Kane* in 1941, King Features dropped him, since the picture mocked William Randolph Hearst. The column was quickly picked up by the rival Hall Syndicate, which continued to distribute "The Lyons Den" for the next thirty years.

Broadway faced stiff competition from movies, but audiences still flocked to see musicals like *Pal Joey, Lady in the Dark, By Jupiter,* and, of course, *Oklahoma!* (which, because of its structure and choreography, would revolutionize the American musical theater and run an incredible 2,212 performances). The night it opened at the St. James Theater on March 31, 1943, Darryl F. Zanuck, head of 20th Century-Fox, whispered to his wife: "This show will run longer than World War II." Other musicals of note in the decade included *Carmen Jones, On the Town, Show Boat, Annie Get Your Gun,* and *High Button Shoes.*

It was the decade of Tennessee Williams, Ethel Merman, Brando's stage debut in *I Remember Mama,* and his starring role in *A Streetcar Named Desire,* with Jessica Tandy and Karl Malden. Laurette Taylor, Arthur Miller, Mary Martin, and Helen Hayes were flourishing. Ossie Davis debuted in *Jeb,* José Ferrer triumphed in *Cyrano de Bergerac,* which would win him the 1950 Best Actor Oscar on film. And I saw my first Broadway shows, the aforementioned *Oklahoma!* and, in 1949, *South Pacific* with Mary Martin and Ezio Pinza. A top ticket cost $7.50.

My father went to Germany in May 1945 with the First Army Press Corps and visited Berchtesgarten, Hitler's "Eagle's Nest."

And "The Lyons Den" ultimately reached a circulation of more than one hundred newspapers in syndication.

TALLULAH BANKHEAD

She was the tempestuous Alabama-born Broadway star, daughter of the Speaker of the House, niece of a Senator, and a woman who always hated the fact that Bette Davis was a bigger star. But she was one of the most colorful people of her time.

She only had two hit plays on Broadway: *The Little Foxes* and *Skin of Our Teeth,* but became a big star nonetheless with constant work in twenty-one other plays, including works by Shakespeare, Tennessee Williams, Thornton Wilder, Lillian Hellman, and Noël Coward. She had her own radio show, occasional films, and later, television appearances. She was constantly quoted in "The Lyons Den," because she always made news.

Representative William Bankhead said he never sought the job of Speaker of the House, but took it "because I was tired of just being known as Tallulah Bankhead's father." His daughter had hopes he'd become vice president in a Roosevelt administration.

"It's an easier job than Speaker," she explained. "As Speaker, you wield a gavel presiding over 496 people. But as Vice President it's only 96."

In July 1940, she went into rehearsal for a summer stock production of a play called *The Second Mrs. Tanqueray,* a melodrama about a woman with a past. Before rehearsals, she met with the director.

"How shall we begin?" he asked.

"Look here," she replied, "I have a certain amount of beauty. I have a certain amount of talent. And I have a certain amount of friends who'll come to see me. The rest is up to you."

She sat near David O. Selznick at a restaurant in Hollywood, aware that at the time he was casting *Gone with the Wind.* Hoping to get his attention, she wore a Confederate flag bandanna in her hair and said in a loud voice, in her deepest Alabama drawl: "What damn Yankee says I can't portray Scarlett O'Hara?"

Then, when the movie opened the next year, she attended the New York premiere and hissed whenever the Union Army was on the screen.

While rehearsing Clifford Odets's play *Clash by Night* in October 1941, Bankhead met the three-year-old daughter of the director Lee Strasberg.

"Do you know who I am?" she asked the little girl. She got no reply.

"Why, I'm Tallulah Bankhead," the great actress continued.

"Why?" asked the little girl and future actress Susan Strasberg. She would, years later, star in *Picnic* and, appropriately, *Stagestruck*.

In 1942, during the run of *Clash by Night,* the sound track of the movie *The Philadelphia Story* was piped in from offstage. One night, Philip Barry, who wrote that play, was in the audience and later threatened to sue. At the next performance, the sound was turned much lower.

After *Clash by Night,* she starred in Thornton Wilder's *The Skin of Our Teeth.* Before it went out of town for tryouts, the producer, Michael Meyerberg, had a run-through with an audience of potential investors. Magazine photographers were there, too, but when their constant popping flashbulbs annoyed her, Bankhead stepped out of character and asked them to stop.

Then she said: "I hate this play. It's a silly play." The backers, thinking she was still out of character, left, unaware that those lines, uttered as asides to the audience, were part of the script.

During the run of that play, Bankhead was visited backstage by Paula Strasberg, wife of the great acting coach (and little Susan's mother). She told Bankhead she was headed to an art gallery and said: "Can I pick up anything for you while I'm out?"

"Yes," replied Bankhead. "I'd like a hair brush, some foundation makeup, and one Renoir."

In April 1947, the *Saturday Evening Post* ran a feature article on Bankhead, and a copy was sent to her. She glanced at it, and told a friend: "How dare they say I put bourbon in my cup before my coffee? I have bourbon *in* my coffee."

In January 1949, she dined at the Stork Club and asked for a glass of milk served in a bourbon bottle. "I don't want people to think I'm ill," she explained.

After she saw Bankhead play Regina Giddens, the part she was to do in the movie version of *The Little Foxes,* Bette Davis went backstage and said: "You scared me to death. I'm a little afraid to play it now."

During a New York newspaper strike in January 1963, she read the Sunday comics to children on the radio, just as Mayor La Guardia had done a generation before. She did all the voices *except* Donald Duck. "For that one," she said, "I used my voice exactly the way I do at ordinary cocktail parties."

Early in her career, she appeared on the London stage and invited T.E. Lawrence— "Lawrence of Arabia"—to a party and said: "I adore brave men and he's the bravest." Asked about the possibility he'd refuse her invitation, she replied: "Refuse *me?* He's not *that* brave!"

There was a Broadway producer who often announced plays that never got put on. Once he announced he'd interview actors for "a Tallulah Bankhead play." A hopeful woman came to his office, but refused to be kept waiting. She was told she'd have to wait if she wanted a job in the Bankhead play. "I don't want a job in 'the Bankhead play,'" she said. "I *am* Bankhead!"

Howard Dietz, the great lyricist who wrote the words for *That's Entertainment,* one of the unofficial anthems of show business, said of Tallulah Bankhead's volatile way of life: "A day away from Tallulah is like a weekend in the country."

At a party in 1960, she met Dr. Karl Menninger and asked: "Do you think I should be psychoanalyzed?" The distinguished psychiatrist said: "That would be a wonderful experience—for the therapist."

Bankhead had a friend named Eddie George, who'd risen to feature billing on Broadway before deciding to become a stage manager. She asked him why he'd given up acting, and he replied: "In every play, there's a hero and a heel."

"And you always played the heel?" she asked.

"No," he replied. "I always played the heel's friend."

She once posed for a portrait by her friend Augustus John. She acceded to requests from museums all over the country to exhibit the portrait, saying, "That's why I moved back to New York from the country. I bought my country home just to provide a place for the portrait. And when my picture isn't hanging there, I don't care to be there either."

When she opened in *The Skin of Our Teeth* to rave reviews on Broadway, another actress said: "Tallulah's always skating on thin ice, and people want to be there when it breaks."

Backstage after a performance of the show, a distant relative visited her, and told her she had one more year of college. "Darling," said Tallulah, "how silly. I never finished the fourth grade. And look at me now."

She was the daughter of the forty-seventh Speaker of the House, Representative William B. Bankhead, and her uncle was Alabama Senator John Bankhead. When Congress threatened to cut funding for the Federal Theater, she tried to convince her uncle to filibuster against the bill by reading, on the Senate floor, "*The Life of General Robert E. Lee*—in two volumes!"

It didn't help. The Federal Theater lost its funding on June 30, 1939.

A movie studio planned to make a film from a play in which Bankhead was winning great reviews on Broadway. They sent their actress to New York to see the performance and copy it on screen. But Bankhead knew the actress was in the audience that night, and for once gave in to every actor's cheap tricks and exaggerations. Thus when the movie came out, critics made the inevitable comparison to the stage performance, and Bankhead was the clear winner.

In June 1939, Tallulah's father met King George VI and Queen Elizabeth in London. Later, a prominent London columnist who often wrote about royalty said: "I thought your Daddy behaved quite well before the King and Queen."

"Really?" Bankhead snapped at the haughty Englishman. "Funny, Daddy said the King and Queen 'behaved quite well' in front of *him*!"

That same month, she lunched in Sardi's in New York and saw Elia Kazan, the Group Theater director, who was of Greek-Turkish descent. She asked her husband if Turkey was an ally of the United States. "I think so," he assured her. "Good," replied Bankhead, beckoning to Kazan to invite him for a drink.

In early October 1939, she met Joe DiMaggio and confessed that even though she was first and foremost a N.Y. Giants fan, she was rooting for Cincinnati, the National League pennant winners, over DiMaggio and his Yankees in the World Series.

"After all," she explained in her Alabama drawl, "my grandpappy was a Colonel in the Civil War, and he'd turn over in his grave if he knew I was rooting for a team called 'The Yankees.'"

She appeared in only a dozen movies, most notably Alfred Hitchcock's *Lifeboat* in 1944. A movie executive once explained to my father why she appeared so infrequently on the screen: "Women who go to movies like to identify themselves with the stars. They pretend that they too are Greer Garson or Joan Crawford. But not Tallulah. Everyone knows there is only one Tallulah, and there never can be another."

She loved New York nightlife and often stayed out until dawn. One morning in February 1940, she returned to her apartment and asked the doorman if there were any messages.

"No, Miss Bankhead, no messages," he said.

"Come to think of it," she replied, "why should there be any messages? I've been out all night with everyone I know."

She would often seethe when roles she created on Broadway were turned into movie parts for other actresses. When, for example, she went into rehearsal for *Clash by Night* in 1941, without any apparent reason, she began to weep, then her sobs quickly turned into gales of laughter. The director asked her if anything was wrong.

"No," said Bankhead. "It's just that I decided to show all of you that I can act, that I can turn on tears and laughter at will."

The movie version of her role arrived a decade later—starring Barbara Stanwyck.

In May 1945, she visited Pittsburgh where a man sent her flowers and an invitation to go dancing. She agreed. Some months later in New York, he again sent flowers and an invitation go to dancing. She declined, saying: "Dahling, you don't understand. It wasn't you. It was Pittsburgh."

Her only marriage was from 1937 to 1941, to actor John Emery. They rarely retired before dawn, and Bankhead once said of him, "Poor dear. He's so tired—he's been up all day." Before her marriage, she assured her father, Speaker Bankhead, that she would not give up her name—yet he was the only one who, during her marriage, wrote to her as: "Mrs. John Emery."

She told her husband: "Darling, I want people to say: 'Mr. Emery, may I have your wife's autograph?' not 'Miss Bankhead, may I have your husband's autograph?'"

She toured in 1945 in a production of the play *Foolish Notion* with Emery, and agreed that her by then ex-husband was talented and handsome.

"But we were never meant for each other," she said.

"So why'd you marry him?" she was asked.

"Oh that," she replied. "That was just a slip of the tongue."

It was a lead item in the column on September 30, 1952, which put Tallulah Bankhead in perspective: "Her book was published this week, marking another career for the remarkable woman who never has needed more than one shot at it to attain eminence in any field. One radio program made her the most celebrated performer in the profession. One political broadcast with President Truman made her a White House favorite.

"She's only had one hit play so far, *The Little Foxes*, and yet is accepted among the foremost ladies of the Broadway theater. And one movie, *Lifeboat*, made her a Hollywood star."

A friend of hers was in town and went to see her on Broadway. But a woman in front of her refused to remove her hat despite repeated requests. So the friend, who'd seen the show before, finally got revenge. He leaned forward and whispered: "She dies of T.B. at the end."

Like any great actress, Bankhead would occasionally deviate from a script in a part she'd played over and over. It happened in 1950 when she was on tour in Noël Coward's *Private Lives*. When she returned to her native Alabama, she was performing in Montgomery and took her first curtain call waving a Confederate flag. And during her roughhouse battles onstage with her leading man, Donald Cook, she hurled a curse word at him the British-born playwright Coward never conceived: "Yankee!"

After the 1949 season, Joe DiMaggio closed up his hotel apartment in New York before moving back to San Francisco for the winter. He shipped all his belongings west, except his pet canary. He didn't know what to do with the bird.

Across the hotel hall lived Tallulah Bankhead, however, and she too had a pet bird. One of DiMaggio's friends was reported to be waiting for the proper moment, when she exercised her bird and put a sign on her door: "Keep Door Closed. Bird Out of Cage." He was then expected to open the door quickly, deposit DiMaggio's bird inside her room, and add what my father said would be "another puzzle to Tallulah's baffling life."

When her beloved N.Y. Giants won the World Series in 1954, she celebrated in a way she only did on closing nights of her shows. She served real drinks to friends; the drinks always contained the same ingredients referred to in the script of her last show. One was a mixture of port wine, vodka, and bourbon.

That year she supported W. Averill Harriman for governor of New York. Harriman was one of the richest men in America. "If I had his fortune," she mused, "I'd buy the N.Y. Giants and keep drinking forever—instead of interesting myself in public welfare."

A few nights after she said that, she was alone in her hotel room watching the election returns—Harriman won—and reached for a telephone. It fell off its shelf and hit her in the eye.

The next day, sporting a shiner, she said to reporters: "If you're going to print that I have a black eye, please say I got it from a divine man who gave it to me for saying 'No' to him."

At a 1949 performance of the Broadway play *Light Up the Sky,* she sat in front of two theatergoers who whispered that the character portrayed by Virginia Field wasn't really based on Gertrude Lawrence. "She's supposed to be Tallulah Bankhead," whispered one.

At that, Bankhead turned around and said: "Dammit no. You're wrong."

In December 1966, she received a lucrative offer for a TV talk show, five days a week. She refused, saying she'd be on opposite her favorite soap opera and couldn't bear to miss it.

In January 1960, she went backstage after watching Patricia Neal's Broadway debut in *Another Part of the Forest,* portraying the same character at an earlier stage than that portrayed by Bankhead in her famous performance in *The Little Foxes.*

"Darling," she drawled, "You're as good as I was. And darling, if I thought you only *half* as good as I was, that would've been a hell of a compliment."

Even though she moved to New York to pursue an acting career at fifteen, you could never take the Alabama out of her. For example, she was asked in 1965 by the noted agent of that time, Milton Goldman, if she grew any vegetables at her country home in Bedford Village, a tony town in upstate New York.

"Of course I grew vegetables," she replied. "I grew chives for my vichyssoise and mint for my mint juleps."

DAVID BEN-GURION

When my father made a visit to Tel Aviv, David Ben-Gurion, the first prime minister of Israel, told him that to be a good Jew you have to live in Israel. Looking around at the hospitals and other buildings financed by and named for prominent American Jews, my father replied: "Oh, you can be a good Jew and live in America, too."

Just before the state of Israel came into existence, a foreign diplomat urged Ben-Gurion to sign a treaty that would, he said, facilitate recognition of the new nation. But Ben-Gurion refused, saying Israel could never live up to its terms.

"Sign it anyway," the diplomat said. "This will only be a face-saving device: a formality. You don't have to live up to its terms."

"I can't do that," said Ben-Gurion. "Israel isn't yet powerful enough *not* to live up to our agreements."

Just four months after the birth of Israel, "The Lyons Den" reported that the American delegation arrived to present their credentials wearing informal attire. But the Soviets announced that they would present credentials to the Prime Minister in full formal attire.

When he heard that, Ben-Gurion quickly donned striped pants and tails, but couldn't find a top hat. Because of his famous wild, bushy white hair, it wouldn't be easy to find a hat to fit him anyhow. The Prime Minister therefore borrowed a top hat from an aide and kept it in his hand throughout the ceremonies, because it was two sizes too small for him.

Ben-Gurion assigned guards to protect the home of American Ambassador James G. McDonald and told them not to argue with the Americans at the embassy. "If they tell you their climate is best, don't argue. If they tell you their athletes are best, don't challenge them. Don't dispute them even if they should tell you America is bigger than Israel."

When a journalist came to interview the Prime Minister, he was prohibited from using a tape recorder. "It's useless to get him to change his mind," he was told. "Maybe I can convince him he's wrong," responded the determined journalist.

"Listen" said his aide, "a man who, without enough arms or munitions, declares war on and defeats seven Arab nations surrounding him, he's not easily convinced he's wrong about anything."

In May 1950, Ben-Gurion announced the migration of 70,000 Yemeni Jews, the tribe whose exodus from Israel was made 2,000 years ago, before the Roman conquest. They were untouched by modern Western civilization, but were brought back to Israel in airplanes. They refused to enter the aircraft until the Israeli pilot showed them the prophecy in the Bible that the dispersed Jews shall return to Israel "on the wings of eagles."

When the planes landed, Ben-Gurion later reported, the Yemenis were taken by car to temporary encampments. The cars began to move, and the Yemenis, surprised and confused, asked: "Why doesn't *this* thing fly too?"

In June 1952, Ben-Gurion addressed the Knesset, Israel's legislative body, and took off his jacket and necktie. Then he opened his collar. The other ministers protested this lack of formality, and Ben-Gurion replied that Winston Churchill had given him permission to do this.

"When I visited Mr. Churchill in London," he explained, "I tried to take off my jacket and tie and open my shirt collar. Mr. Churchill stopped me and said: 'Mr. Prime Minister, it's OK to do that in Jerusalem. Not here.'"

Ben-Gurion was a voracious reader, who

got most of his books sent from New York. In October 1952, the Prime Minister sent a request for seven items.

"Only seven items," his New York contact thought. "This month is easy." Then he went to a bookstore where he bought the first six items on the list.

The seventh was: *A Collection of Castilian Literature*, in 134 volumes.

By September 1953, Ben-Gurion, who'd already mastered Mandarin, was studying Spanish to read a book about Spinoza in the original version. He told that to some friends during dinner at his home. Then from the kitchen, his wife called: "Ben-Gurion? It's your turn." He ignored her. Soon she called again: "Your turn."

He then excused himself from the table, went into the kitchen, and took his turn washing the dishes.

Ben-Gurion announced his retirement many times. After he'd done it for the seventh time, an Israeli was asked by an American if that meant he was retiring at long last. "Not at all," came the reply. "He's like one of those stores in the Garment Center on Seventh Avenue in New York, which display signs saying: 'Going Out of Business.' It gives the proprietor a chance to unload some stock they don't want, hire new people, and make a different contract with the union."

A political opponent of Ben-Gurion's was skeptical about one of his retirement announcements. "The difference between the Messiah and Ben-Gurion is that the Messiah refuses to come and Ben-Gurion refuses to go."

In the fall of 1961, Ben-Gurion insisted to my father that he'd been misquoted about urging all American Jews to come settle in Israel. But then my father heard a man introduce himself as "Joe Cohen from Denver."

"So?" replied Ben-Gurion, shaking the man's hand. "When are you going to say you're 'Joe Cohen from Israel'?"

Another American said to the Prime Minister: "I've gone to Israel nine times."

"Why not come just once?" Ben-Gurion replied. "And stay."

On a visit to New York, the Prime Minister scanned the menu in a delicatessen and said: "We're still a young country. Israel could also have a dozen kinds of herring like I see on this menu. But first, we need an atomic reactor. *Then* comes the herring."

In June 1962, Mrs. Ben-Gurion introduced Broadway producer-director Hal Prince to the Prime Minister. "This is the producer of *West Side Story*," she explained. Ben-Gurion stared ahead blankly. "You know, *West Side Story*, Lennie Bernstein's musical."

"Lennie I know," he replied. "*West Side Story* I don't know."

Shortly after that, a German official said to Ben-Gurion: "It's gratifying to see that you've named your new music auditorium after the great German author Thomas Mann."

"No," Ben-Gurion corrected him. "It was named after Frederic Mann, the philanthropist, of Philadelphia."

"What did he write?" asked the German.

"The check," replied Ben-Gurion.

One night in 1962, Mrs. Ben-Gurion was awake and woke up her husband. "Ben-Gurion, tell me," said his American-born wife, "did you ever, *ever*, in your wildest dreams, imagine that someday you'd be sharing a bed with a Prime Minister's wife?"

Asked about his opinion of the recently formed United Arab Republic, a political merger of Syria and Egypt, Ben-Gurion said: "It's not 'united,' it's not 'Arab,' and it's definitely not a 'Republic.'"

Ben-Gurion appeared on Edward R. Murrow's *See it Now*, filmed at the Prime Minister's home deep in the Negev Desert. When the filming was over, Murrow told Ben-Gurion it was a good interview.

"It would've been a better story if you'd been here 3,000 years ago," said

Ben-Gurion, pointing down to a distant point on the horizon. "Down there, not many miles away," he explained, "is Mount Sinai, where Moses received the Ten Commandments. What a TV show *that* would've made!"

THOMAS HART BENTON

In 1912, the writer and critic George Jean Nathan teamed with columnist H.L. Mencken and another writer, Willard Huntington (later to create the popular detective "Philo Vance"), on a book called *Europe After 8:15*. The tome took two years to complete, and on the first day of publication many copies were sold. But on the second day, World War I began, killing sales forever.

In succeeding years, however, copies of that book became very valuable, because the illustrations were done by a young, then-unknown artist who would become America's most famous painter, Thomas Hart Benton.

He was one of America's greatest painters, and when he died at eighty-five in 1973, Thomas Hart Benton left a legacy of realist, stylized paintings and murals that captured a more innocent, yet sometimes turbulent time in America. A member of a prominent Missouri family, he traveled the country painting farmers, soldiers, sharecroppers, backwoods people, laborers, transients, and anything and anyone that captured the America of his time.

Benton's favorite subjects afforded him the chance to make political statements and depict a cross section of America. But getting inspired for such momentous works wasn't always easy. In August 1943, for example, he said: "At the moment, I'm painting little girls and goats with white fur and horns and white roses and hay fields, sunsets and other things of a peaceful sort. Meanwhile, I'm girding myself for another crack at the active concerns of the day."

Somehow, no doubt on a visit to New York, he and my father crossed paths, thus cementing a friendship between a Jewish journalist from the city's Lower East Side and a painter from the American heartland.

It was solidified when Benton spent two decades in New York.

Besides his talent at an easel, Benton was a skilled harmonica player, appropriate for a chronicler of that time. Early in April 1942, he and his son were in New York for the release of an album of recordings they'd made together: the father on the harmonica, his son playing the flute. Decca Records hired a large orchestra to furnish the accompaniment and, thinking the session would be a short one, paid top dollar for the best musicians available.

What they *didn't* know was that neither Benton nor his son read music. The Bentons played by ear. So for ten days, at top union scale, the large orchestra had to rehearse with the duo. Benton waived his performance fee.

In April 1944, Benton announced that his earlier plans to move East were changed, and, for the time being, he would remain in Missouri.

"This is *my* country," he explained, "and it furnishes the material and the tone of my work. I've made up my mind, to keep my feet in the dirt even if I do it in loneliness. Coming back across the state, with the green of the winter wheat and the pink of the peach blossoms, I found a dozen pictures. Missouri's outline, from cotton in the South to wheat in the Northwest prairies, touches about everything I'll ever have to say as an artist.

"When I visit New York now, other artists won't say: 'There goes that sonofagun Benton.' Instead, they'll say: 'Benton's in town.' And they'll come have a drink and laugh. That by itself is worth a little artistic loneliness."

In June of that year, Benton was in New York and ran into a musician friend, anxious to buy one of Benton's new paintings. He said he was willing to pay top dollar, but Benton replied: "One artist shouldn't buy from another artist. Let the public do the buying. If an artist pays for another artist's work, that isn't progress for the artist."

Unlike most painters, Benton occasionally lectured on his craft. "I speak in places where the women would look better if they removed their glasses—and the men would look better if they put them on!"

Three years later, the great muralist was at work on a complicated piece of his own devising, painting the Greek legend of Achelous, a river god, and Hercules, but in a Missouri setting! His patron on the huge project was the owner of a local ladies-wear store in Kansas City.

When the contract was signed, Benton told his patron: "The symbolism, the gathering of the fruits of the earth through the conquering of Achelous, who has changed into a bull for the battle, is appropriate for the locale."

"Look, Tom," replied his patron, "paint whatever you want. Just try to keep me in business."

In February 1953, my parents were in Missouri visiting the Trumans and stopped off at Benton's home for dinner. He and his wife Rita took my parents to the converted carriage house that became his studio, and then to his basement where his latest pictures were stored. There were Benton paintings on all the walls, except in the bedroom, where the sole decoration was an Orozco print.

Benton attributed his success to luck: luck and a bottle of bourbon that released his inhibitions and made him say the quotable things that stirred the world of art. For instance, he told my parents: "Few pictures painted today will last a hundred years, because commercial paint will disappear." That's why he only used his own homemade paints.

"We're all personalities who make ourselves out of fiction," he said. "I've been successful at fiction for almost forty years." Then, reaffirming his belief that artists should never sell their works to one another, he said: "We wait until some stockbroker makes a killing, then wants something to decorate his or her home. *That's* when we sell."

Benton created three murals for the Truman Library in Kansas City, but he destroyed his three efforts to paint a portrait of the former President.

"Truman has a great face he puts on for the public," he explained. "I was trying to get at the man underneath. I had him take off his magnifying eyeglasses, so that I could get the shape of his eyes.

"But Truman's secretary, Rose Conway, walked in and ruined it by saying: 'It's awful.' I tried it twice more. And she said the same thing again. The trouble is, I tried to make Harry Truman look like Caesar; she wanted me to make him look like Clark Gable."

In 1965, he learned that his home on Martha's Vineyard had been burglarized during the winter. "Probably by kids looking for liquor," he sighed. "Innocent kids, surely, or they would've known I always drink up all the strong stuff before closing the house."

Then he spoke of pop art, just coming into its own back then. "I'm all for it," he said, "because it's bringing art back to a human concern. It's marvelous. Each art movement has its genius. Jackson Pollock was never vulgar. He did only what he could do."

Pollock, in fact, had been one of Benton's pupils at the Art Students League in New York. "He had great taste in color," said Benton of his student whose canvases sold for fortunes. "He was well-trained under me. He had no pretense."

Benton had experimented in the new art forms as early as 1908, when he painted a few abstracts. "I burned them when I came back from the War," he said. "Because I thought they were derivative. But they were *me.* The Cleveland Museum owns two abstracts of mine; they're me!"

The Corcoran Gallery in Washington had no Benton work and was eager to acquire one. A judge from Washington phoned the artist on behalf of the Friends of the Corcoran to buy a painting. Benton said he had a suitable one called *Lord, Heal the Child.* He'd sell it for $20,000. The patron, he was told, would get in touch with him.

The next day, the patron phoned and offered to buy it for himself—for $15,000—keep it for two years, then donate it to the museum. Benton refused.

"How about $17,500?" the patron countered. Again Benton refused, adding that another man was interested in it.

"Oh, I know that tactic," said the patron, thinking this was just a bargaining ploy. In truth, Mrs. Benton had phoned a wealthy Texas cotton broker who'd always wanted that painting and said he could have it for $20,000. And so it was sold.

When the other patron phoned the next day, expecting more negotiations, Benton delighted in telling him: "You're too late."

Billy Rose, the largest stockholder in AT&T, was also a producer-showman who put on the fabled "Aquacade" at the 1939 New York World's Fair. He owned a large Benton oil painting, and had never bargained over the purchase price. It was on the wall of his home in Mount Kisco, New York, alongside works by Renoir, Chagall, Velázquez, Dalí, and Utrillo.

Then one day a fire engulfed the mansion, burning it to the ground. Firemen responding to the alarm were told about the priceless artwork inside, so they rushed in and realized they'd have time to save only one painting. Not being art devotees, they reasoned that the larger the painting the more valuable. So they lugged out the huge Benton oil, and the other paintings, some worth ten times as much, burned.

Included in the conflagration was a series of priceless paintings by Dalí called *The Seven Lively Arts.* They'd been commissioned by Rose in 1944.

When he heard about the fire, the lost masterpieces, and his own work being saved, Benton said of the firemen: "They're not only brave, but damn fine art critics, too!"

Benton owed an unusual debt to Robert Moses, the municipal-planning genius who conceived so many of New York's bridges, tunnels, highways, and parks with his vision of the future. He'd commissioned Benton to paint the mural for the St. Lawrence Seaway. But in Canada, the only authentic books for Benton's research for the project were in French.

"I'd lived in France four years," he said, "but that was fifty years ago. So I just stared at the page until it all began to come back to me. Now I can read Sartre's plays and the books of my youth in French."

So he owed Moses for his reacquired ability to read French.

In the fall of 1965, Benton was back in New York and told my father he'd just sold a painting for a record sum, but he wasn't pleased.

"An artist shouldn't want a record high sale," he explained, "because then his widow and kids pay for it. One half of an artist's output is never sold. The paintings become part of his taxable estate. It may be his best stuff, but nobody wants it. The inheritance taxes are based on his record high. Burn the picture, I say."

He mentioned some tax-saving devices, starting with foreign domiciles. "A Swiss bank account is OK for Picasso. He's a Spaniard living in France. But I'm a regional artist from Missouri. I've been written off four or five times, but I've come back each time. The Louvre says it takes thirty years to decide if a man's an artist."

Benton then spoke of Truman, calling him the greatest politician of his time, even greater than William Jennings Bryan. My brother Douglas, then seventeen, a political buff, was there and asked him why he so admired the only three-time major party Presidential candidate.

"Because everything Bryan advocated is in the statute books today," Benton explained.

But my brother, today a criminal defense attorney, cited Bryan's prosecution in the Scopes Monkey Trial. Benton shrugged: "It was in his old age, when he believed in Fundamentalism. It's easy for any lawyer to question the universal statement: 'God created the Universe.'"

But then the seventy-six-year-old painter and my brother found agreement on the penchant of Bryan's opposing counsel Clarence Darrow for quoting bad poetry. "It's always 'Omar Khayyam' in his summations," said Benton.

That had been a historic day, in 1964, for at the New York World's Fair earlier that morning, Benton had been at the Missouri pavilion and met several men who, though born in Pennsylvania and Illinois, respectively, found fame in Benton's home state: Stan Musial and his St. Louis Cardinal teammate, Red Schoendienst, are enshrined in the Baseball Hall of Fame.

INGRID BERGMAN

No movie star of her era—not Bette Davis, Joan Crawford, nor Barbara Stanwyck—has enjoyed the lasting popularity of Ingrid Bergman, a natural beauty who stood Hollywood on its ear from her first American film, a remake of her Swedish movie *Intermezzo* in 1939. She was a good friend to my father, for he was to be the one American journalist who defended her in her time of need.

The great Hungarian playwright Ferenc Molnár, whose *Liliom* starred Bergman onstage and was the basis for the smash-hit Rodgers and Hammerstein musical *Carousel*, had an idea for a surefire one-act Broadway hit: "It will be called simply: *The Reading of the Manhattan Telephone Directory by Ingrid Bergman.*"

In November 1946, Bergman, then at the height of her fame after films like *For Whom the Bell Tolls, Casablanca, Gaslight*, and *Spellbound*, took an unusual step for a movie star: she came back to Broadway to star in *Joan of Lorraine*. When asked the inevitable question about which performing medium she preferred, she said: "I don't see why there has to be a conflict. I love doing both. To me, it's all acting. If someone loves music and can play two instruments, it doesn't matter which one she plays."

During the run of that play, her costar Sam Wanamaker said: "I have the ideal job for an actor. Eight times a week, I get to hold Ingrid Bergman in my arms."

One night in March 1947, she arrived at a dinner dance and headed to the powder room. At least twenty other women were seated in front of the mirrors, including my mother, who later reported to my father what happened next. Slowly and deliberately, the women rouged their lips, applied mascara, combed their hair, and put on perfume. Then Bergman walked in, stood in front of a washstand, wet a washcloth, ran it over her face once, and then, wearing no makeup, and enduring the jealous glances of the other women, walked out smiling, and beautiful.

In November of 1947, she was filming *Notorious* for Alfred Hitchcock. After a day on the set, she donned the costume of a witch. Then she drove out to the Bel Air home of the Hitchcocks and rapped on the living-room window. When the startled couple appeared, she shouted: "Boo!"

The next year, Bergman was nominated for an Oscar for *Joan of Arc* but tore up her own ballot. She explained: "It would be immodest of me to vote for myself. But on the other hand, it would be too modest of me to vote for somebody else." That turned out to be Jane Wyman, who won for *Johnny Belinda*.

In March of that year, she lunched with my father and recalled her first screen role. It was 1931 in Stockholm, where one of her friends, working as an extra in a movie called *Landskamp*, promised her a job. During the Christmas holidays, when there was no school, the fifteen-year-old girl was taken to the studio, submitted to makeup, and at 11 a.m. walked through a crowd scene. She thus made one of the most inauspicious debuts for the legendary career that awaited her.

When the scene was over, she toured the studio, still in costume. Finally when she left, the guard at the gate asked: "Where've you been? The cashier's been waiting for you all day with your check."

"You mean I'm to be paid for this?" she asked.

When she went to Italy to make a movie with director Roberto Rossellini, a trip that would change her life, he told her there'd be no script; they'd create the dialogue before each scene. She then asked him about retakes, and he said he never heard of retakes and didn't intend to shoot any.

When, in 1950, she left her husband, Dr.

Peter Lindström, to marry Roberto Rossellini, she was excoriated in this country by self-described guardians of morality, so she moved to Italy. On February 6, 1950, my father wrote that a message saying "We Love You" was sent to her. It bore the signatures of a dozen of her friends from New York.

"They resented the fact that the first stones thrown came from those whose own morals could stand little scrutiny, and in some cases from those whose own children were conceived only to breed a wartime exemption under the Selective Service Act."

At the height of the controversy, Bergman received many letters from fans who told her they'd written letters of support to newspapers and magazines, but the editors were afraid to print them.

When she gave birth to twin daughters—one of whom would become the actress Isabella Rossellini—she said: "And I thought the only thing I would make when I came to Italy was movies." It was about that time that the self-righteous criticism of her personal life coming from America began to wane.

"Americans are a peculiar race," she said of this. "Their kindness exceeds their cruelty."

In *The Bells of St. Mary's*, she portrayed a nun, and in one scene she gave boxing lessons to youngsters. To prepare, she went to a bookstore to buy a book on "The Sweet Science." The salesman offered her one written by turn-of-the-century heavyweight champ Jim Corbett.

"He won the title by knocking out the great John L. Sullivan," he told her. "In fact, Corbett never lost a fight until he met Bob Fitzsimmons."

My father with Ingrid Bergman. My father was one of her few defenders in the press during her controversial divorce.

Ingrid Bergman replied: "So? Don't you have a book about Fitzsimmons?"

The day after she won the Oscar for *Anastasia*, she wrote my father: "'Hit 'em with your talent,' you told me, and it worked! So now the question is how to keep hitting. I'm getting somewhat feeble and middle-aged, but there's a lot of Viking blood left in the old gal yet!'"

In May 1957, starring on the Paris stage in Robert Anderson's production of *Tea and Sympathy*, she knitted onstage. After she'd knitted two sweaters and one scarf, she began to think about ending her run. She decided it would come when she finished knitting another sweater.

The next month, my father visited the Rossellinis in Paris, and she told him that French Customs officials viewed her Oscar statuette simply as a gold import and demanded duty, but 20th Century-Fox refused to pay. So did she. It took twenty-three weeks of the statuette's being quarantined for the Customs officials to relent and let her take it home.

She was asked to display her Oscar in the lobby for *Tea and Sympathy*. She refused, saying: "It has nothing to do with this play."

She didn't accept her Oscar in person. That night she was in the bathtub in Paris, where the ceremonies were broadcast on Armed Forces Radio. Her son Robertino Rossellini, who spoke no English at the time, shouted that he'd just heard her name mentioned. He carefully brought the radio next to the bathtub in time for her to hear her friend Cary Grant accept the prize for her: "Ingrid, darling, wherever you are...."

She shouted back: "I'm in the bathtub, Cary. The bathtub!"

Looking back on her life one time, Bergman observed: "I can't remember how I felt at twenty. At thirty, I felt so old. When I reached forty, I didn't feel as old as I did at thirty."

In January 1958, my father noted that an American visiting London for the first time got up early on his first morning in town to study the laborers of Britain on their way to work. The first "worker" emerged from the posh Connaught hotel and stepped into a Rolls-Royce. It was Ingrid Bergman. Then another "laborer" emerged and got into another Rolls-Royce. It was Cary Grant. Finally a third "worker" appeared and got into a Chrysler station wagon, only because his Bentley had been shipped home. It was William Holden.

By May 1958, Bergman's marriage to Rossellini was over. "Poor Roberto," she sighed. "How difficult it was for him, a Latin married to a Swede. How I prayed we should have had a hit movie together. Just one. But it didn't happen. Then I went and did *Tea and Sympathy* and *Anastasia*. That was so difficult for Roberto. The strange thing is that not one person so far has said to me: 'I told you so.'"

While filming *Inn of the Sixth Happiness,* she had a sobbing farewell scene with co-star Robert Donat. Only two takes were needed. Then she posed for a still photo of that scene and sobbed real tears again.

In August 1958, an issue of *Look* magazine quoted Ingrid Bergman: "Only one columnist, Leonard Lyons, was kind to me during my troubles." But so was John Steinbeck, who'd sent her a supportive cable. Other support came from Ernest Hemingway, who volunteered to fly back with her from Paris to be at her side for her return to New York.

In December 1959, Lauren Bacall visited Bergman in Paris, prior to Bacall's starting rehearsals for the play *Goodbye, Charlie*. When her guest turned to leave, the Swedish star booted Bacall in her seat, explaining: "Oh, in the Swedish theater that means 'Good luck.'"

In 1959, President Eisenhower returned to Paris for a parade down the Champs Élysées. Bergman and her children watched from the penthouse of the Pulicite Building near the Arc de Triomphe. As Eisenhower's motorcade reached the building, he suddenly raised his arms toward the penthouse where the actress and her three children were watching.

"He knows you! He knows you, Mother," the children yelled, proud that the President had apparently recognized their mother, even from afar.

She didn't have the heart to tell them that Eisenhower hadn't recognized her. He'd gestured only to that building where he'd maintained his headquarters after the liberation of Paris; the rooftop office had become the only Eisenhower Museum in France.

I met Bergman in London in 1964, lunching with my father on the set of *The Yellow Rolls-Royce*. She spoke of her daughter Pia Lindström who'd been given a one-day role in a De Sica movie. She had only one word about this: "Why?" (Ironically, I succeeded Pia as Film and Theater critic at WNBC in 1996.)

She spoke of old friends. "One grows fonder and fonder of old friends as one grows older. They know you, and you're at ease with each other. It's easier than learning about new people. And new standards." When she first went to Italy, she took with her a copy of the Production Code, the movie industry's censorship guidelines, which were abandoned in 1968. "We couldn't use the word 'whore.' They substituted 'strumpet.' I had no idea what the word meant at that time."

"Maybe I'm moving backwards. I guess I'm just old-fashioned after all."

MILTON BERLE

On May 19, 1934, a nervous young journalist walked up to Milton Berle, already a big star, and introduced himself. Thus began a friendship between my father and Berle that would last forty-two years. Even back then, Berle was accused of stealing other comics' routines. Indeed, he was somewhat affectionately called "The Thief of Bad Gags."

But he basked in that description. He'd been in show business all his life. His mother was a floor detective in a department store with dreams for her son. When he was six, his mother took him to Fort Lee, New Jersey, for a role in Pearl White's *Perils of Pauline*. His pay for one day's work on that 1914 film was $1.75. He would eventually become one of the richest performers of his time, having worked in vaudeville, radio, on Broadway, in nightclubs, movies, and become television's first superstar.

He needed no urging to perform. In May 1962, for instance, Berle was introduced to the members of the Friars Club and did an impromptu routine which lasted ninety minutes! It wasn't the first time he'd done that. Two years before, he'd been on a flight that ran into engine trouble and began circling and even dumping fuel—never a good sign. To keep the passengers from panicking, Berle jumped up and stood in the aisle, entertaining the worried fliers with his surefire routines until the plane landed safely.

Years before, he was in a Chicago movie theater watching a film when the film broke, and the announcement was made that a long delay would ensue. Sure enough, he jumped onstage, said: "I thought you'd never ask me," and did eighty minutes until the print for the movie was repaired and reloaded.

One night in June 1942, Berle was at a New York restaurant and spotted Tommy Manville, the asbestos tycoon who was married

My father with "Mr. Television." Milton Berle, "Uncle Miltie," changed the face of television. Berle was the first person he interviewed on May 19, 1934. They remained friends the rest of their lives.

an astonishing thirteen times to eleven women. At that time, Manville was on his fifth wife, and Berle noticed he was eating a bowl of rice. "Nice to see you, Tommy," said Berle, "and what a change to see you eating rice, instead of having it thrown at you."

Berle was once asked to come back to Broadway in a musical but refused. He cited his last run, a huge flop called *Springtime in Brazil*, a show that closed out of town without ever reaching Broadway. After the final curtain mercifully came down, the audience derisively shouted: "Author! Author!" In response a man in a gorilla suit was brought onstage. Berle then fired a blank gun at the man, and the gorilla keeled over. Then Berle announced: "That's all folks. Scenery for sale."

Berle said that he did 366 TV shows for NBC, and that added up to 28,280 hours spent in rehearsal.

When Berle and his wife moved to Hollywood, swapping their New York apartment with Oscar-winning actress Gloria Grahame and her husband playwright Cy Howard, Mrs. Berle first had to make certain their new bedroom was soundproof, since her husband was one of the lightest sleepers in show business. He once was kept up all night when a pigeon alighted on their windowsill.

Early on the morning after their first night in their new home, a large construction crew arrived at the next plot and began work on the foundation for a huge new home.

One night Berle introduced former heavyweight champion Gene Tunney to Mrs. Jack

Dempsey. "Your husband knows him," he told her.

In August 1947, Berle bet on a hundred-to-one horse, and it lost. A few days later he was hospitalized for a few days, and his doctor ordered that all newspapers be kept from him, to keep him calm and speed his recovery.

It was a wise decision; the next day that horse raced again and came home a winner.

Like any ex-vaudevillian, Berle had many talents, including card tricks. One day in 1960, he used Peter Lawford as a foil. He first wrote out the expected answer on a piece of paper, then said to Lawford: "Think of a card. Any card. Got it? Ok, now double it. Next add your weight. You following me? Double it again, and add your height. Ok, divide the number in half. What's your card?"

Lawford's reply: "The 217 of Clubs."

When veteran character actor Warren Berlinger (one of those actors whose face is far more familiar than his name) was starting out, he got his second role on Broadway in *Anniversary Waltz*. Before the curtain rose, his mother approached Berle, whose real name was also Berlinger, and asked if they were related.

"I want to wait and see the show first," he replied.

After the first act, he said to her: "Not bad. Could be he's my second cousin." At the end of Act II, Berle said: "Yes, I'm sure he's my cousin." And as the final curtain descended, Berle stood up and cheered: "How about a hand for my favorite nephew!"

One night during the Broadway run of *Take Me Along*, Jackie Gleason, the star, arrived in his dressing room to find Berle in his makeup, including a mustache:

"I thought you weren't coming," said Berle.

Later, when Berle returned after the show to congratulate Gleason, all he found was a note: "I knew I was great tonight. I saw you. Biting your lips."

Berle walked into the Little Club one night in June 1960, and a patron said: "Say, aren't you Milton Berle?"

"If I'm not, I've sure been having a lot of fun with his wife," Berle replied.

In September 1951, Berle was at the height of his fame, starring in a live network show every week: a program that would change

My father with Tony Perkins (far left), the great writer Paddy Chayefsky, and Milton Berle at El Morocco, circa 1962.

the face of television's "Golden Era." He was in El Morocco one night discussing the inexorable pace at which TV consumes comedy material. One of his writers explained: "When the program is over, as soon as the curtains close and we go off the air, Berle starts removing his costume, then begins: 'Now for the opening shot in next week's show, I think we should. . . .'"

An autograph seeker approached Berle and asked him for his signature. "Make it to 'Joyce,' please," said the fan. "How do you spell that?" replied Berle, who'd just gotten a divorce from Joyce Matthews.

Matthews, who appeared opposite Robert Alda in the movie *Mr. Universe*, had a role in which she merely posed and hardly spoke a word. She was asked how she rehearsed for this nearly silent role.

"It was easy," she explained. "Don't forget, I was married to Milton Berle for six years."

In all his theater, nightclub, and television routines, Berle made jokes about his brother Frank, who was his manager. Finally, after years of this his brother flared up in resentment, and they quarreled. That night, when Berle met with his gag writers preparing the script of his next show, he instructed them: "Wherever you see Frank's name in the script, take it out. Take out every mention of him. Never use his name again. Instead, use 'my brother Phil.'"

On his TV show in May 1951, Berle appeared with a monkey on his back and called it "Henny Youngman" seven times. Youngman didn't care: "Just keep saying my name. It makes no difference if you make a monkey out of me."

Berle and Youngman were friendly rivals. They were always at odds over their claims to gag material. One Christmas, Berle sent Youngman a large wallet with a note: "Hope this will hold all the money you've been making."

Youngman acknowledged it by sending Berle the largest trunk he could find with a note: "Likewise."

Bert Lahr, best known as the Cowardly Lion in *The Wizard of Oz,* saw Berle on TV mugging and leering at the camera. Later, he sent Berle a telegram: "I was never better." Then he wailed: "Milton's stolen my whole routine, except he can't do this," and quivered one cheek. When Berle heard about that, he replied: "Does Lahr mean this?" and quivered one cheek.

One of Berle's favorite stories involved a touring circus he saw in Europe, which advertised an eighty-three-year-old man who would dive ninety feet into six inches of water. The place was jammed. Then the bent, bearded, and wizened man walked out onto the platform.

"I'm eighty-three years old," he announced, in a thin, wailing voice. "And at eighty-three, to make a living, I have to dive ninety feet into that tub. Imagine your own fathers or grandfathers having to do this at eighty-three. A young person could get killed doing such a thing, and I'm eighty-three. So I ask you," he wept, "shall I dive?"

"No!" the touched audience shouted in chorus.

"Then," said the old man, "please clear the tent and make room for the next audience!"

Berle was a tireless performer. In 1946, for example, he was paid $10,000 a week to perform at the Carnival nightclub. He sang with the chorus, danced, and even did turns with the acrobats, working onstage longer than any other nightclub or theater performer. Nicky Blair, the proprietor of the nightclub said: "When you figure out how long Berle is on stage for each show, it works out to about 40 cents an hour."

George Jessel had a live stand-up comedy engagement at Loew's State Theater and explained: "This is my fourteenth engagement here. Milton Berle has worked here six times. That means, ladies and gentlemen, you've heard my jokes twenty times."

Fred Allen said of Milton Berle: "If ego were acid, Berle would've consumed himself long ago."

Berle was performing one night at a New York nightclub and recognized a friend in the audience, busy eating a steak. Berle chided him for eating while a star was performing.

"I can't take you on an empty stomach," came the reply.

One day in April 1962, Berle played golf with TV game show host and actor Hal March. Berle missed his first tee shot completely. Then Berle's second drive went out of bounds twenty yards away. His third shot was another dud: it dribbled a few feet up the fairway, and Berle started walking toward the ball.

"Hey, Milton," said March, "don't forget your lucky tee."

A few days later, at the Friars Club in New York, he was asked to stand up and take a bow. Instead, he did ninety minutes of jokes.

In January 1966, Berle attended a dinner in Sardi's and afterward spotted a friend at a nearby table. He quickly jotted a note to his wife, got an envelope from the restaurant, addressed it, and dropped it on the plate of his friend, saying: "I have no stamp. Please mail this."

Without hesitation the friend, Postmaster General Larry O'Brien, wrote on the envelope: "Postage due," and returned it to Berle.

Like my father, Berle loved introducing people from two different worlds: Whereas my father introduced Giants' quarterback Y.A. Tittle to Joan Miró, the Spanish surrealist, Berle introduced the Duke of Bedford to Max Asnas, owner of the Stage Deli, New York's most famous delicatessen.

"The Duke of Bedford," said Berle, "meet the King of Salami."

During the filming of *Moulin Rouge*, Berle suddenly appeared on the set in Paris, instead of José Ferrer, walking with shoes on his knees, portraying Toulouse-Lautrec. Berle was arrested for "trespassing."

His wife once said of him: "When Milton's with one person, he complains. When he's with twenty people, he performs!"

A Broadway comic once was depressed, and friends advised him: "Look up. Keep your head up." He replied: "What's the use? Every time I look up, I see Milton Berle's name in lights."

Before Berle went to Hollywood, he got his nose shortened. Seeing his new look, Groucho Marx asked: "Who messed with your face, Gutzon Borglum, that Mt. Rushmore guy?"

Jule Styne, later to write the songs for *Gypsy*, *Bells Are Ringing*, and *Funny Girl*, wanted Berle to star in a show Styne was producing called *Master of Ceremonies*. Berle had pen in hand, ready to sign on the dotted line, when he learned the show's author insisted he'd allow nobody to do any rewriting. Berle dropped the pen, then told his agent to "make the other deal."

That "other deal" was with Texaco, a TV venture that helped pioneer the new industry and made him the best-known performer in the land. "Uncle Miltie" became a household name and an American pop culture icon. In Europe, he signed hotel registers "Uncle Miltie, TV, U.S.A."

Berle was the world's greatest emergency act. When he worked the Chez Paree nightclub in Chicago, for example, he was awakened by a call to rush to the club because a troupe of performers was delayed by a snowstorm. Berle showed up in his pajamas and worked two and a half hours until the troupe arrived.

During a USO hospital tour, a nightclub gave a night in his honor. He did routines from midnight until 7:50 a.m.

Later, Berle attended the White House Correspondents' Dinner and was cornered by the respected college president and educator Dr. Milton Eisenhower, brother of the President. He had one question for Berle: "How do I get my colleagues to stop calling me 'Uncle Miltie?'"

In 1948, Berle signed a twenty-year contract with NBC. The next day, he met CBS head William S. Paley, who said: "The day your contract runs out in 1968, come see me."

The contract did run out in 1968, and his new contract with NBC was a lifetime deal.

When he appeared on Edward R. Murrow's *Person to Person* from his home in Beverly Hills, he confessed he wasn't much of a gardener but liked trimming hedges.

"So would you, Ed," he said, "if you lived next door to Joan Collins."

Actually it wasn't Berle's home. He'd swapped his New York apartment for several months with Cy Howard, who wrote the popular *My Friend Irma* show. When he watched Berle on the program, live from his own home, he sent Berle a telegram: "You promised no guests."

When Berle and his fiancée decided to become engaged, he took her to a jeweler to buy a diamond ring. She refused, saying instead she preferred a season box seat at the Polo Grounds to watch the New York Giants.

Like George Burns and Ernie Kovacs, Berle's trademark was a cigar. His wife Ruth would carry around a day's supply of cigars in her handbag for him. Then in October 1953, they were stopped at the airport in Rome and told one person couldn't bring in so many cigars to Italy. Berle told the Customs official half of them belonged to his wife.

Ruth Cosgrove Berle, to prove her husband correct, then casually lit up, blew a smoke ring, and didn't cough. They were allowed in.

Berle was a graduate of New York's Professional Children's School. "Kids from that school are different," he recalled. "When most kids meet me, they ask for an autograph. When I meet kids from my old school, however, all they want is a job."

In June 1959, Berle had three teeth pulled. The dentist used sodium pentothal: truth serum. Before the medicine wore off, he went to Lindy's for lunch with friends and said: "Ask me anything, except where my jokes come from."

Early in his career, Berle asked Hollywood columnist Sidney Skolsky to write a "tintype," a column about him.

"When you get big enough, I'll do it," said Skolsky.

Berle warned him: "By that time, I might be too busy."

Years later, after Berle had changed the face of television, Skolsky called him: "The time has come," he said. "Sorry, Sidney," replied Berle. "I'm too busy."

He and Gleason were friends, even though Berle once greeted the rotund Gleason: "You're three of my favorite comedians."

Gleason shot back: "I wish you were one of mine."

HUMPHREY BOGART

Contrary to his tough-guy image, Humphrey Bogart came from a well-to-do family, and as a young Broadway actor reportedly was the first to utter the now famous words: "Tennis anyone?" Today he remains one of the true icons of American cinema and pop culture, whose screen persona endures.

During the filming of *Passage to Marseilles* in 1943, Bogart toured the Los Angeles nightclubs but got lost en route home. He found himself adrift in a strange part of town at 3:30 in the morning. He then saw a lighted window and put his face against it. The lady inside, making coffee, saw him, but recognized him even with a five-day growth of beard. "Oh, it's Humphrey Bogart," she said, casually. "Come in." Then she woke her family to meet the star and showed him to the guest room where he spent the night.

The next day, he invited the family to the Warner Brothers lot for lunch.

In March of 1944, Bogart toured the war front, and one stop was Tunisia. At their hotel, another guest recognized Bogart and insulted him. A fight broke out, during which German planes flew overhead and bombed the hotel. After the attack, the manager glanced at the shattered roof and crumbled walls, then carefully wrote out a bill for Bogart for the furniture and tableware destroyed by the fistfight.

When Bogart was married to his third wife, Mayo Methot, she went to a preview-showing of *To Have and Have Not*. One look at the love scene between Bogart and young, beautiful Lauren Bacall, and she knew that reports of the "good work" between the two stars looked like the real thing. The next day she called her lawyer and instituted a legal separation.

One day in December 1945, Bogey was golfing at the Lakeside Club in Los Angeles with former welterweight champion Jimmy McLarnin. At the 17th tee, McLarnin was asked about a fight he once had with an opponent named Young Jack Thompson. "I fought him at the Oakland Arena," said McLarnin, "and I knocked him out with a stomach punch."

"That's impossible," said Bogey. "Nobody can knock a man out with a blow to the stomach." Then he bet the retired champ $500, braced himself, and McLarnin punched him in the stomach. Bogie's knees buckled and he collapsed, and lost the bet.

Knock on Any Door was a movie Bogey produced. One scene called for a robbery at a change booth at an elevated New York train station. "Writers are inconsiderate," said Bogart the producer. "If the author had made 'em stick up a bus instead of an El station, the production would've saved ten grand."

When the movie opened in March 1949, Bogey and Bacall were in the Stork Club when Harry Cohn, the ironfisted head of Columbia Pictures, walked in. He whispered a few words to Bogart. The actor then turned to his wife and beamed: "The picture's a hit."

"What makes you so sure?" she asked.

"Because," replied Bogey, "he referred to the picture as 'Our movie.' If he'd said 'Your movie,' it'd mean the picture was a flop." He later described the twin tasks of producing and starring as "comparable to taking instructions in schizophrenia."

CHARLES BOYER

Contrary to popular belief, Charles Boyer, one of the most suave and sophisticated of the matinee idols in movie history did not say the line always attributed to him from 1948's *Algiers*: "Come with me to ze Casbah." That was said in a "Looney Tunes" parody of the French star, by a character named "Pepe LePu," the skunk based on Boyer's Pepe Le Moko from the movie. Still, it did accurately characterize his famous matinee-idol screen persona, which he nurtured in some eighty films.

He was the first actor to be top-ranked in two languages. During the war Boyer did shortwave broadcasts to Europe and told a government official that he spoke French, English, and Italian.

"Only three languages?" the man asked.

"Yes, just three," he replied. "My father didn't want me to become a headwaiter."

Two weeks after they met in 1935, Boyer and British actress Pat Patterson were married in Yuma, Arizona. The minister asked: "Do you take this woman to be your lawful wedded wife?"

"I certainly would love to," responded Boyer, whose English back then was a work in progress.

"That's not enough," the minister said: "Repeat after me. You must say: 'I do.'"

The marriage lasted forty-four years.

Boyer was in Paris at the outbreak of World War II in 1939 and immediately joined the French army as a private. On the first day of basic training, he stood at attention with the other recruits. The captain who inspected them remembered Boyer's current screen role: "Yesterday on the screen I saw you in *Conquest.* You were Napoleon—today you are a private. Nature does not follow real life."

In July 1941, Boyer met Billy Rose, the wealthy AT&T tycoon/impresario/lyricist/showman.

Rose had been married to the comedienne Fanny Brice but then married Olympic swimmer Eleanor Holm, who was infatuated with Boyer. Rose introduced her to Boyer one night and said: "See? He looks like an ordinary suspender salesman with a toupee."

"I don't care," swooned his wife. "It's the man up there on the screen I'm nuts about."

In his movie *Tales of Manhattan,* Boyer wore a tailcoat in the opening scene. Later in the story, it wound up hanging on a scarecrow in a Mississippi cornfield. The studio prop department at 20th Century-Fox needed a worn dress suit for that last sequence.

They finally found one in a secondhand clothing store in Los Angeles. On the inside pocket was stitched the name of the previous owner: Wendell Willkie, the 1940 Republican candidate for president.

Boyer was asked which month he preferred in California, and responded: "Any month except October. By then, if I haven't acted in a movie, and with the end of the year in sight, I'd begin accepting roles I'd previously rejected."

In August 1948, Boyer returned to Champollion College, the French school he'd attended as a youth. The mayor of the village nearby welcomed him in a speech and wondered what would've become of Boyer if he hadn't gone off to Paris to act.

"I'd have become a great man," the screen star replied. "I'd have stayed here and become a teacher."

Boyer first became a romantic lead in Paris, where he appeared in a series of plays written by Henri Bernstein. After performing the first of these plays, there were 200 fans waiting for him outside the stagedoor after a matinee. "What a remarkable attraction you have in this new star," a friend told Bernstein about young Boyer.

"Yes, 200 fans are outside the stagedoor," he replied, "but unfortunately, only sixty-five were in the seats."

When Boyer starred in *Conquest,* Greta Garbo portrayed his mistress, Maria Walewska. On the days when they were to shoot scenes of Napoleon mistreating his paramour, Garbo would arrive and greet Boyer tersely and coldly. And on the days when there were to be love scenes, Garbo would greet Boyer warmly.

In July 1949, Boyer returned to New York after several months in Europe. As soon as he cleared Customs and sent his baggage to his hotel, he took a walk down Fifth Avenue and observed: "The thing about this city is that two hours after you're back here, somehow you forget you've ever been away."

Once on the French stage, years before he married, Boyer had to cry eight times a week, and he told his costar that every time he played that scene, he thought of a lost love. At one performance, however, try as he might, he couldn't muster up the tears.

His costar whispered: "What happened? Did you have a reconciliation?"

In November 1963, Boyer told a fellow he had just met he was tired after playing Sunday matinees. "I know how you feel about Sunday matinees," replied his new friend: Y.A. Tittle, the New York Giants' quarterback.

In 1971, Boyer made a return trip to his birthplace, Figeac, in France, and noticed something familiar about the men of the town. Most were wearing Boyer's old suits, sent there over the years by his mother.

Actor John Dall, who was featured in *Spartacus,* was asked what character he portrayed did the most to enhance the image of the American man.

"Easy," said the stage and screen actor. "It was in a play called *Red Gloves,*" he said. "I got to shoot Charles Boyer—eight times a week!"

WINSTON CHURCHILL

To my knowledge, Britain's greatest prime minister, and one of the towering figures of the twentieth century, never made a movie, starred on Broadway, nor hit a home run in Yankee Stadium. Even though "Jerome Avenue," right behind "The House that Ruth Built," is named after his American mother, Jenny Jerome. Sir Winston Churchill was the veritable face of the British Bulldog, who for far too long, single-handedly led the fight against the darkness and evil of Nazi Germany.

In the summer of 1966, a year after his death, my father and I visited Churchill's son Randolph, whose life, unfortunately for him, was overshadowed by the overwhelming persona of his father. Randolph's home was outside London, in East Bergholt in Suffolk. On his back lawn was a prefab hut, nearly 100 yards long. He took us inside, and as far as the eye could see were his father's papers, source material for the son's massive biography about him. I couldn't imagine such an overwhelming task.

Churchill met with Eleanor Roosevelt early in 1942 when the war was going badly. "You must feel an immense responsibility, being the leader of so many people and several nations," said the First Lady.

"I'm not their leader," said Churchill, who also commanded Canadian, Australian, and Indian troops in both theaters of war. "I merely express their will."

A few months later, Churchill was shown a photo of his grandson from *Life* magazine and was told how amazing the resemblance between them was. "Not so amazing," he replied. "All babies look like me at some stage." That baby would, twenty-eight years later, begin serving thirteen years in the House of Parliament.

In April 1943, Churchill met with a young

Royal Air Force flier who'd downed thirty-one German planes. "I can see you're awe-struck at being in my presence," said the PM. "But imagine how I must feel, being in *yours!*"

Later, some American visitors attributed the RAF's turnaround in attaining air superiority to engines better than those of the Luftwaffe. "It has nothing to do with the engines," replied Churchill. "It's the men who fly them. The RAF is the broad ladder by which the spirit of England ascends into the skies."

On long flights during the war, Churchill had a ritual. He'd awaken early, don an old robe, light a cigar, and move to the cockpit. He'd sit in the copilot's seat, where his valet would bring him his medicine. The valet would leave, Churchill would toss the pills away, make a nasty face, as if he'd swallowed the bitter medicine, puff his cigar, and take the plane's controls until breakfast was ready.

At one point during the war, an American pilot who'd flown the PM to Washington had been given a two-week leave afterward. So the pilot and his crew flew to San Francisco, his hometown. But as soon as they were settled in at a restaurant on Fisherman's Wharf, they received an urgent message: "The PM wants you in London Tuesday at noon." This was on a Sunday. They rushed to the airport, flew cross-country, then across the Atlantic back to London. Finally at noon Tuesday the weary pilot showed up at 10 Downing Street.

Churchill said: "Now let's have lunch." Only then did he realize he'd forgotten about the pilot's two-week leave, thinking he was in London all along.

Churchill was honored at a luncheon in Washington in October 1943. His large audience was mainly newspapermen and women. But the microphone began to ring when he started speaking. He banged it, then the podium, but it only got worse. So he pushed it aside and said in a loud voice to his large audience: "I have spoken in the great halls of England and America without these devices," he said. "What a feeble generation we've become."

He later gave the most unusual definition of America in responding to a question about a paper shortage due to the war: "America is the place where the newspapers are too damn thick and the tissue papers too damn thin."

When told that his predecessors, David Lloyd George and Neville Chamberlain, exercised regularly, Churchill replied: "We Churchills always die young. So why bore myself to death?" He would die in 1965 at ninety-one.

During the Yalta conference three months before the end of the war in Europe, a proposal was raised that the forthcoming United Nations should have a limit on the number of colonels in members' armies. Churchill objected. "I will not have the fumbling fingers of fifty-two nations meddling in the heritage of Britain."

In March 1945, Hollywood mogul Sam Goldwyn met with Churchill. Later, Goldwyn's only comment was: "Now *there's* a movie star!"

Soon after V-E Day, May 8, 1945, Churchill began to think about life after 10 Downing Street. He'd remembered David Lloyd George, Britain's PM during World War I, once musing on the same subject: "On that day when you stand at the right of the King on the balcony of Buckingham Palace, and hear two million people assembled there cheering, you say to yourself: 'There must be more I can do for these good people.'"

In September of that year, Churchill was voted out of office, succeeded by Clement Atlee. Then he was named a member of the Royal Order of the Garter, but he refused the honor. "How can I accept the Garter from the King when I've just gotten the boot from the people?"

He was back in Washington in March 1946, about to give his famous "Sinews of Peace" speech at Westminster College in Fulton, Missouri, where he would coin the phrase "Iron Curtain." At a dinner before the speech, he was asked about the Soviet Union's intentions, and gave an evasive answer. "Tell them what you really think, Winston," said his wife Clementine. He whispered back to her: "World domination, my dear. World domination."

He surely based that opinion on a four-and-a-half hour meeting he'd had with Stalin at Tehran. Stalin told Churchill about the political setup in the USSR and Soviet suspicions about America and Britain. "Do you think we're trying to gang up on you?" Churchill asked Stalin. The Russian nodded. Then Churchill asked: "What makes you think so?"

"Because," replied Stalin through his interpreter, "that's what I'd do, if I were you." Then Stalin added: "If you'd have been born in Russia, you'd have been one of the top men there by now."

In April 1947, Churchill was asked to write the inscription for a war memorial. He wrote: "In War, Resolution. In Defeat, Defiance. In Victory, Magnanimity. In Peace, Good Will." The memorial committee unanimously rejected it.

When he was a young man, he'd been the beau of the actress Ethel Barrymore. Churchill wanted her to decide if she'd like a life linked to English politics. So he gave a dinner party to which the only other invited guests were Neville Chamberlain, a future Prime Minister, and former Prime Minister David Lloyd George.

After an evening of long discussions among the political leaders of Britain, engagement rumors between the rising star of British politics and the young American actress ended.

Years later, a mutual friend visited Churchill, by then a former PM, and men-tioned Miss Barrymore. Churchill spoke of her with great affection and at great length.

Then the friend returned to New York and saw her at a discussion of a new play. He interrupted and said: "I bring regards from an old beau, Winston Churchill," he said.

"Oh, that's nice," replied the actress. "Now in the first act of this play. . . ."

Churchill once told a friend: "That which illustrates the fact that when a romance is ended the man never forgets, but the lady sometimes has a remarkable ability to drive it out of her heart and mind forever."

It was my father who'd first quoted Churchill's most famous comment on English grammar. He'd been about to broadcast a speech and sent a copy of his manuscript to the Foreign Office for official approval. It was returned with a small correction in his grammar. He'd ended a sentence with a preposition.

Churchill said of this: "This is the type of errant pedantry up with which I shall not put."

In 1948, he was returned to office as prime minister and went to a private room at the House of Commons. He asked the waiter for a whiskey and soda, but was warned that there might still be some lingering shortages and that such a drink would probably be unavailable. Nevertheless, the waiter returned drink in hand.

Churchill held it up proudly and said: "Recompense for having saved the British Empire."

In October 1949, Churchill was on a train across Britain and busied himself with his newspaper. The seat opposite him was occupied by a man about Churchill's age. Finally the man said: "Excuse me, sir, but is your name 'Churchill?'" "Yes," replied Churchill, glaring at the man before the next question came: "And would your first name happen to be 'Winston?'"

"It is," said Churchill, returning to his

newspaper. The man fingered his old school tie, continued to stare at perhaps the most famous man of the twentieth century, and smiled before asking his final question: "You didn't, by any chance, happen to attend Harrow, did you?" He had.

In 1949, Anthony Beauchamp, a prominent London photographer, was engaged to marry Churchill's actress daughter Sarah. But first he had had to ask her father for her hand. Few more daunting tasks ever awaited any groom-to-be.

They met in New York, and Beauchamp quickly came to the point. Churchill replied with a grunt. Then they spoke of other matters, and Beauchamp left for London. Mid-flight, over the North Atlantic, he sat up with a start, realizing he didn't know whether Churchill's grunt had meant "yes" or "no." (He'd said "yes." They were married.)

In August of 1950, Churchill described the United Nations as "a veritable cock pit where all kinds of men come to curse and growl." Then, when asked about people who heckled his speeches, he said: "I never mind heckling or having to answer anyone. So long as I and I alone have the microphone."

Churchill loved sitting in the front row at the theater. One night Laurence Olivier starred in *Henry V* at the Old Vic. He said it was one of his most difficult performances. "Mr. Churchill knew the play by heart," said Olivier, "and he kept muttering the lines, but a word or so ahead of me." Richard Burton once told me the same thing, and that he was always warned of Churchill's presence in the audience beforehand, so he could try to endure the distraction.

At a meeting with FDR, Churchill was accused by the President of showing off. "You with your fancy education, just because you studied hard at school and I didn't." Churchill replied to Harvard's most famous alumnus: "'Studied hard?' My

dear Mr. President, at school I was last in my class."

A magazine article about my father in 1953 said his friends included Harpo Marx, Joe DiMaggio, and Winston Churchill. My father corrected the author, saying that that was stretching a point. "I've had tea with the PM at 10 Downing Street," he said, "but that was where his son Randolph, who is indeed a friend, explained that his father feels he's already met everybody in the world he cares to know."

It was in July 1952, when my parents were at 10 Downing Street and met Churchill. Randolph had prepared my parents beforehand, telling them to be brief when the meeting came. "He just wants to know who will win the American elections in the fall."

Actually my father had met Churchill years before in New York, but thought he'd made no impression at that time. Still, when he was presented to Churchill, the PM said: "My son Randolph tells me you know everything there is to know about America. Tell me, Mr. Lyons, who's going to be your next President?"

My father replied: "Governor Adlai Stevenson of Illinois."

"But what about General Eisenhower?" Churchill asked. My father, remembering Randolph's admonition to be brief, blurted out that Senator Robert Taft of Ohio would be the Republican nominee. Then my father remembered that Churchill was familiar with American politics. He had an American mother, after all, and in 1928 he'd suggested a campaign slogan for the Democratic nominee, New York Governor Al Smith: "All for Al and Al for All."

Then Churchill asked about Stevenson's divorce. My father explained that Stevenson had never remarried, and it had been Mrs. Stevenson who'd sued him for divorce, but that wouldn't matter to the voters anyway.

The Prime Minister seemed unconvinced. "Mr. Churchill," my mother chimed in, "this only means that *Mrs.* Stevenson can't ever be president." Churchill smiled, and for the rest of their visit, never again addressed my father, but spoke only to my mother.

Years later, my father retold that story to one of Stevenson's sons, who said: "The irony is that Mother always wanted to be President, much more so than my father ever did."

In June 1956, Churchill was vacationing on the Riviera, and a neighbor adopted a stray puppy she'd found nearby. Churchill was walking past her house, and suddenly the previously cuddly puppy began to bark at him. That's why the neighbor, Brigitte Bardot, named her new best friend "Atlee."

He once had to decline an invitation to attend the Kentucky Derby on doctor's orders. "A pity," he said. "I'd have loved to have seen the headlines: 'CHURCHILL'S UP AT CHURCHILL DOWNS.'"

Art gallery exhibitors found it difficult to tell which of his paintings on display belonged to him and which to members of his family. For Churchill had a habit of giving his paintings to his children and grandchildren, but then, when visiting their homes, he'd look at his paintings and say: "I think that tree needs more leaves." Or: "I'm not quite satisfied with that landscape." Then he would take the paintings home and keep them.

Churchill described the English landscape, his favorite subject to paint, as "a place which would be a paradise, with only fifteen more degrees of sun."

Churchill was also one of the century's greatest historians; his history of the Battle of Hastings in 1066, for example, and his history of World War II are among the finest, most detailed accounts of those conflicts ever written. His literary agent, Emery Reeves, was at a party in New York and uttered a minor grammatical error. "Suppose your most famous client, Win-

ston Churchill, wrote that in a book?" he was asked. "I'd be thrilled," Reeves replied. "Because those books would quickly become collectors' items."

Jack LeVien was the documentary filmmaker who produced a memorable TV film series on Churchill's life. He once sent Churchill a pop song then on the charts called "The Battle of New Orleans," sung by Johnny Horton. It depicts a pivotal battle in 1815 in which the British were defeated. LeVien included a note that said: "Let this be a lesson to you."

Churchill replied; "Which side of this record had the lesson?" The flip side, the so-called "B" side of the record, was a song called "Never Leave Your Baby."

LeVien told my father that on a visit with Churchill, the former PM told him an astonishing story. During the Battle of Britain, on September 21, 1940, in a huge dogfight, the RAF fighters had only ten minutes of fuel left in their tanks. Then the Luftwaffe fighter aircraft, unaware of this, suddenly broke away from combat and headed back to their bases in France. Those ten minutes saved the war.

In April 1960, Winston Churchill was made an honorary member of the Metropolitan Club in New York, but an officer of the club told the press they wanted no publicity. He wanted it described only as "a club on New York's East 60th Street."

But he quickly changed his mind when it was pointed out that another club was on the same street: the Copacabana nightclub.

In 1945, an enterprising young newspaperman, fresh out of the U.S. Navy, decided to get a handle on the upcoming election for prime minister by doing man-on-the-street interviews. He thus correctly predicted that Churchill, despite being one of the principal architects of the Allied victory during the war, would be defeated for re-election. But just as he was about to file his story, he met Lord Beaverbrook, the powerful

British-Canadian press baron, who told him his conclusions were absurd, and that he'd be making a grievous error filing a prediction of a Churchill defeat.

So the young reporter never filed his prediction of an upset. Churchill lost, and the fledgling American reporter, John F. Kennedy, chose another career path.

In 1944, when FDR was undecided about running for a fourth term, Churchill advised his friend: "You are a soldier in battle, and you must keep going until the bullets of the enemy lay you low."

In July 1962, Churchill was hospitalized. When news of his improving condition was announced, he received a box of cigars from the group of reporters camped out several floors below his room. With the box came a note: "With good wishes from the reporters and photographers downstairs, to whom news of your progress has been of more than purely professional concern."

JOE DIMAGGIO

In March 1991, there was a baseball-card show in the large basement of the Armenian Church on Manhattan's Second Avenue. The star attraction was Joe DiMaggio, signing items for a long line of autograph seekers. My son Ben, then ten, accompanied me, and we sent word to DiMaggio that we wanted to stop by and say hello.

As soon as he saw us, the most iconic American sports star of modern times stopped the line and called us up on the stage. He put his arm around Ben, gently pushed me aside out of earshot, and began talking to him. Ten minutes later they were done, and I wondered what they had discussed.

"Dad," said Ben, "he told me what you were like at my age."

Ever since he retired in 1951, DiMaggio never seemed to know what to do with the rest of his life. "Mr. Coffee" and Bowery

With Joe DiMaggio at Toots Shor's circa 1970.

Savings Bank ads kept him in the public eye, and he coached for a time for the Oakland A's, wearing their garish green-and-white uniform. But he never seemed happy. Still, his reputation for being aloof wasn't the full picture. I knew him as warm and friendly.

No other figure in contemporary America enjoyed so much adulation. In 1969 he was voted the Greatest Living Player. While Willie Mays's fans might have had a case for their hero, it solidified DiMaggio's larger-than-life image.

My earliest memory of him was at a party my parents gave for the great actress Ethel Barrymore in 1950, where DiMaggio stood shyly in a corner of our living room among other giants like Fred Astaire, Adlai Stevenson, Ernest Hemingway, and Marlene Dietrich.

Twenty-five years later, at an Old Timers' game at Shea Stadium, he asked me if I'd still call him the best guest there, as I did as a child. I told him, of course.

My father first met DiMaggio in 1936, when Joe came to New York from San Francisco, where he'd been a big star in the Pacific Coast League playing with his older brother Vince for the old San Francisco Seals. They remained friends for forty years, and Joe's name appeared often in "The Lyons Den."

One early item concerned Joe and Groucho Marx. When Joe was tearing up the PCL with the Seals, Groucho had a party. Back then, the Hollywood Stars were the minor leagues' most popular team, as good as several major league teams back East. Groucho told his guests: "I've just arranged a trade with the Seals. I swapped two of our outfielders for a life-size photo of Joe DiMaggio."

During a road trip in the 1948 season, DiMaggio called his good friend Jackie Gleason. "Where are you?" asked Gleason.

"I have no idea," replied DiMaggio. "Let me check the towels in the bathroom."

As instructed, room service back in the hotel where he lived in New York knocked on his door with breakfast early one morning. DiMaggio looked out the window, saw a downpour, and instructed the waiter: "Never wake a ballplayer on a rainy morning."

On July 22, 1948, DiMaggio got an accidental hit on a checked swing. Lou Boudreau, the Indians' shortstop and manager, spotted Toots Shor, the restaurateur in Shor's box seat in the stands, aware that his place was DiMaggio's nightly hangout.

"Hey, Toots," he yelled, "what do you feed that guy?"

"Come by tonight," replied Shor, "and I'll show you." Sure enough, that night Boudreau turned up and said: "OK, show me."

Three years before he hit baseball's most famous home run, the so-called "Shot Heard 'Round the World," New York Giants' outfielder Bobby Thomson was told his stance was the same as DiMaggio's, with his feet set wide apart, bat held high. Then a friend noticed Thomson had changed his stance and showed him a photo of DiMaggio at bat.

Thomson studied the photo and said: "Oh well, in this picture, Joe had a 3-1 count on him."

"How'd you know that?" asked the friend.

"Because," replied Thomson, "he doesn't look worried."

After the 1948 season, DiMaggio was at his usual table in Toots Shor's and heard the owner disparaging two ballplayers, referring to them as "has-beens."

"Don't ever say that about a player," said Joe. "The only sure thing about ballplayers is that they eventually must be through. We're all bound to be 'has-beens' someday."

The following February before reporting for spring training, he vacationed in Acapulco, Mexico, and was invited to visit the local minor-league ballpark. The crowd cheered, and he was asked to take a few swings in batting practice. Joe obliged, but instead of the usual fastballs down the middle, the pitcher tossed a curveball, hoping to strike out the great DiMaggio and thus win glory. So Joe dug in, worked the count to 3 and 2, and singled sharply to left. Then he returned to his vacation, his reputation intact.

When he injured his right heel the following April, the baseball world talked about nothing else. "They tell me," said Joe, "that I've made this guy Achilles famous."

In June 1949, he began dating a showgirl who worked at the Latin Quarter nightclub. Either because of or despite that, his heel began to improve, prompting my father to write: "as long as DiMaggio keeps hitting, the lady's place in his heart is secure."

In August of that year, the Yankees had a rare day off, so DiMaggio stayed out on the town until the wee hours of the morning, something he hadn't done since the war. In the next game he hit three triples and later said: "Triples are harder to hit than homers, because a home run doesn't require exertion. But triples do."

His younger brother Dominic was the center fielder for the rival Boston Red Sox, and he was a very good player, too. In fact in Boston at that time, there was a song with the refrain:

"He's better than his brother Joe,
He's Dominic DiMaggio."

Dominic reached the majors in 1940. When he and the Red Sox came into town for their first series against the Yankees, Joe showed Dom all the tricky nooks and crannies in the deep recesses of center field at Yankee Stadium. He taught the rookie how to play the caroms and work the shadows of late afternoon, how to work the warning track, and position himself for certain hitters.

Then they headed to their respective locker rooms, but not before Joe invited Dom to his apartment after the game, where Joe would cook dinner. That day Joe

hit a sure triple to deep center, but Dom, instinctively remembering what brother Joe had taught him before the game, made a sensational catch against the wall.

As they passed each other in the middle of the inning, Joe said: "Nice catch, rookie, but dinner is off."

In December of that year, Robert E. Sherwood, one of America's greatest playwrights, who wrote *Abe Lincoln in Illinois, Idiot's Delight, The Best Years of Our Lives*, and *The Petrified Forest*, came into the Playwrights Producing Company's annual meeting. He'd just come from Toots Shor's restaurant and was holding his right hand high above his head. Sherwood, surely the tallest Pulitzer Prize winner, stood 6 feet 8, so that hand was *really* off the ground. He explained that he didn't want anyone to touch it, saying he'd just shaken hands with Joe DiMaggio.

When Babe Ruth died in 1948, DiMaggio was asked to be a pallbearer. Toots Shor met him at his hotel, and they took a cab to the funeral at New York's St. Patrick's Cathedral. As they approached, DiMaggio said he had to rush back to his hotel. "I forgot to bring the telegram inviting me to the funeral. They might not let me in without it," he explained.

James MacArthur is the actor best known as "Detective Danny Williams" on *Hawaii 5-0*. As a boy, however, he was affectionately called "Jamie" by his godmother Lillian Gish. One day in 1950, she took him to visit her sister Dorothy. When the visit was over, Lillian told her sister she had a surprise for little Jamie and showed her two tickets for the matinee of *South Pacific*. "I promised Jamie the biggest thrill of his life," she said.

They entered the elevator of the hotel, and it stopped two floors below to pick up another passenger. In walked DiMaggio, who introduced himself to the boy. Jamie gasped: "Thanks, Aunt Lillian. You sure kept your promise!"

Few people know that in his next-to-last

season, 1950, DiMaggio didn't use his own model glove. He preferred a Mort Cooper glove. Cooper was a National League pitcher, mostly for the Cardinals. DiMaggio liked putting his index finger and middle finger in the same compartment, which was easily done with that model glove.

DiMaggio missed three seasons in his prime when he was in military service. Thus it wasn't until 1950 that he got his 2,000th hit, in a game against the Cleveland Indians. That day DiMaggio gave the Indians' rookie and future M V P Al Rosen his biggest thrill outside the locker room. Rosen congratulated DiMaggio, who replied: "Thanks."

During his final season, 1951, the Yankees were in a pennant race with the Indians, and DiMaggio had a hitting streak going while he'd begun dating a woman. He got two hits the day after their first date, a double and a single. The next game, he hit a double—and a single, double, and triple in succeeding games. In all, six hits. The final game of the week, a Yankee win, brought them into first place to stay. His date that week, who he was certain had brought him luck, was an actress all right, but not who you think. No, he didn't meet Marilyn Monroe until the following year. This one was Marlene Dietrich.

After the 1951 season, DiMaggio retired, and he talked with a friend over dinner about how an athlete ages. "You start chasing a ball the way you've always done," he said, "and your brain immediately sends out commands to your body: 'Run, bend, scoop up the ball, and peg it to the cutoff man.' Then," he sighed, "your body says: 'Who, *me?*'"

In 1954, early in DiMaggio's marriage to Marilyn Monroe, brother Dominic drove up to their house. She was in short pants sweeping in front of the garage. Joe noticed Dominic looking at the most glamorous woman in the world and said: "And she can cook, too!"

In December of that year, the DiMaggios were in California during the holidays, and some of his New York friends expected they'd fly back for a visit. But one knew better. "Can you name anything better in life than Marilyn Monroe and warm weather for Christmas?"

By 1954, the Yankees still had not officially released him. Since they were in danger of losing the pennant to the Cleveland Indians (which they eventually did), DiMaggio was asked, since he was still technically Yankee property, if he'd thought of a comeback. By this time his friend and rival Ted Williams had surpassed DiMaggio's 361 career home runs.

"No comeback for me," DiMaggio laughed. "If I did try that, it'd only make Ted play longer." Williams would play six more years and homer in his last at bat, his 521st.

DiMaggio had a good friend named George Solitaire whose specialty was getting impossible tickets to Broadway's hottest shows at the last minute. He frequently accompanied Joe and Marilyn on the town in New York. "Every few minutes I'm with them," he said, "I shut my eyes for a few minutes. Just to give them some time alone." He compared sitting at a table with Monroe to being a bank teller: "I can look at the stack of $1,000 bills, and they look fantastic. But they don't belong to me."

Monroe revealed that one of the things that impressed her about Joe was that she "never saw a man so neat. If I wake up at 8:30," she said, "he's always dressed in a clean, pressed white shirt and tie. Usually with a jacket, too." Joe explained it as coming from his years living in New York. It seems amazing their marriage, though brief, lasted as long as it did. But they had an enduring love.

After he retired, DiMaggio attended the World Series, which in those years was usually played at Yankee Stadium. Just before the start of the 1955 Fall Classic against the

Brooklyn Dodgers, DiMaggio remembered he'd promised to take the son of a friend. So Joe picked up the boy, who was accompanied by a friend. Not just any friend: Earl Warren, the Chief Justice of the United States Supreme Court.

During the week of the 1954 Series, DiMaggio dined at Toots Shor's with Horace Stoneham, owner of the New York Giants. He'd once given DiMaggio a tie clasp inscribed: "To *the* Center Fielder." Now, four years into the career of Willie Mays, Stoneham asked: "Do you think you were better than my guy?"

"No," said DiMaggio. "I'd say Mays is better. I've seen him play. But then again, I've never seen *me* play."

DiMaggio had the excellent eyesight required of a slugger who hit for a high average. Nevertheless he had faint, bloodshot streaks in his eyes. He blamed that on the knothole in the outfield fence in San Francisco through which, as a boy, he'd peep to see his older brother Vince play for the Seals.

"The wind came sweeping through that old knot hole," he recalled. "My eyes still show the marks."

Spike Hennessey, a Seals teammate of Vince's (who would have a short, undistinguished major league career), caught young Joe peeping into the park and invited him to meet the other players. He also gave him a fistful of passes for future games. Young Joe wound up playing shortstop in the final three games of the season.

He had no contract and wasn't paid at first, and even had to pay his own way to the ballpark. Four months after being called up to the Yankees, he realized he'd forgotten to cash his last check from the Seals.

"All I wanted to do was play ball," he recalled.

Initially known as "Deadpan" for his quiet, stoic demeanor, he became an outfielder by accident. After pinch-hitting for the right fielder, he headed to the dugout. After all, he was a shortstop and had never played the outfield.

"Go out there! Go!" said his brother Vince. Joe did, remained there for the rest of his brief career with the Seals, was purchased by the Yankees, and became an icon of American sports as the greatest center fielder of his time.

A few years into his time as a Seal, Joe would eclipse his brother's records. His feats included a 61-game hitting streak.

In the fifty-sixth game of that streak, he hit a ball to an infielder, but the first baseman dropped the throw. It was a tough play, however, so the official scorer called it a hit, keeping the streak alive. Years later, DiMaggio gave a visitor a tour of New York. It was Steve George, the San Francisco sportswriter and official scorer on that long-ago afternoon.

"I owed him," said Joe.

Late in the 1955 season, Stoneham made DiMaggio a sensational offer for that time: $40,000 for just one time at bat for the Giants in a game against the pennant-bound Brooklyn Dodgers. But DiMaggio declined, correctly stating that he was still Yankee property.

By 1956, Joe and Marilyn had divorced. Then came word in June that she would marry playwright Arthur Miller. Mobster Frank Costello, then in the Federal House of Detention, received a visitor that day and had only one question about the outside world: "How's Joe doin'?"

In August of that year, a man from Brockton, Massachusetts, lunched at Shor's and asked him to get DiMaggio to come to his hometown for a public appearance. "If I could arrange that, I'd be a big man in Brockton," said the man, Heavyweight Champion Rocky Marciano.

In Rome that summer, the most famous Italian-American sports hero of them all was asked to demonstrate his skills. Wearing street clothes and batting one-handed to spare his aching back muscles, he blasted three pitches out of a local soccer stadium.

When DiMaggio attended the Sugar Ray Robinson–Carmen Basilio title fight in 1957, a fan asked DiMaggio for his autograph. While Joe was signing, the fan studied the bearded man with DiMaggio. "Hey, aren't you somebody too?" asked the fan. "Yes, I'm Joe's doctor," came the reply. The man walked away. The "doctor" was Ernest Hemingway.

On a trip to Rome and Paris, DiMaggio was recognized everywhere. "Oh, I'm known there, but not as a ballplayer," he commented. "They know me as the man whose name appears in Hemingway's *The Old Man and the Sea.*"

Then he flew to London and got a tour of the city from Sir Cedric Hardwicke, the elegant actor. He offered to take DiMaggio to a cricket match, "but only if you have about six months to spare."

In July 1958, he toured Macon, Georgia; Charlotte, North Carolina; and other cities in the Sally (South Atlantic) minor league. He'd played only a few seasons for the Triple A San Francisco Seals before being called up to the Yankees, and thus had no knowledge of life in the low minors, where all-night bus trips are common to this day.

DiMaggio went South at his own expense, visiting the ballparks and the young players, nearly all of whom would never make the big leagues. His appearance helped the gates of those small ballparks, especially when it was announced weeks in advance that the great DiMaggio would be there taking batting practice.

"I did all right, too," he said when he returned to New York. "With a 333-foot fence, I hit five of twelve out of the park."

He toured Army bases in the Pacific in 1960 and appeared at Little League games where the kid pitchers would try in vain to strike him out. After hitting a one-handed

home run, he gave that up. But just before the 1961 spring training season began, he announced he'd be in the Yankee camp in Fort Lauderdale and would take his turn in the batting cage. "Every kid dreams of swinging a bat," he explained. "That still applies to me."

In mid-June of that year, my oldest brother, George, who knew more about baseball than any fan I ever came across, got married. DiMaggio attended.

"George, I gave up a doubleheader at the Stadium to be here," he told my brother.

"So did I, Joe, so did I," replied George.

The 1961 World Series featured the Yankees and the Cincinnati Reds. Joe threw out the first ball at Yankee Stadium and was asked if he thought he could make the newly formed New York Mets, then busily stocking their roster with several aging stars.

"No way," he said. "After I threw out that pitch, I needed a rubdown."

In April 1962, my father arranged a luncheon at the United Nations with DiMaggio and Undersecretary General Ralph Bunche, winner of the Nobel Peace Prize. My father and Joe approached every checkpoint, but the security guards ignored my father's Working Press pass, saying only: "Oh, Hi, Joe. Come on in."

After this happened three times, DiMaggio said to my father: "Maybe I should've played just one more season."

In 1964, George "Twinkletoes" Selkirk, DiMaggio's former teammate, said of him: "That guy DiMaggio had real class. He changed into fresh underwear every day."

At a lunch with former Philippines President and UN General Assembly President Carlos Romulo, who'd played baseball as a boy, DiMaggio was asked if "there is anything prettier than a double play."

"Yes," replied DiMaggio. "A triple and a slide into third. Nearly everybody's moving. A beautiful thing."

Just before the start of the 1966 season,

DiMaggio noticed Yankee hitters weren't taking enough batting practice. "We used to spend half an hour in the cage before a game," he recalled. "Our pitchers on that 1936 team could hit better than the Yankees of today."

The end of the season proved him right. The Yankees finished last in the league for the only time in their history, 26½ games behind the Baltimore Orioles, and with a team batting average of just .235.

Joe once was introduced to an adoring seven-year-old boy, born more than a decade after he had retired. Expecting the same type of meeting he'd had with children countless times, DiMaggio was shocked when the boy asked him something no fan, journalist, not even a baseball historian, had ever asked:

"How many outs did you make?"

He stopped, thought a moment, and replied: "Oh, about 6,000."

Jack Valenti, the motion picture industry's well-known lobbyist, had previously served as an aide to President Johnson. Word came one day that Joe DiMaggio would be visiting the White House. Valenti got himself on the list of invitees, and said to the President: "Joe's always been my hero."

"Mine too," replied LBJ.

The September 4, 1948, issue of *The New Yorker* had a profile about me and DiMaggio's influence on my batting stance. The article reported that my family had bought an RCA television in 1944, the year of my birth. It was one of the first in New York, and I was thus the first of my brothers to be born into a television home.

Influenced by TV, I held a bat for the first time at four, took Joe's wide-legged stance, and told my father to smoke one in. He blinked and lobbed a gentle pitch toward me, which (so I've been told) I hit more than a hundred feet to the outfield.

A passerby in Central Park saw this and said: "I'll be darned if he doesn't swing exactly like Joe DiMaggio."

The next day, my father closely watched "The Yankee Clipper" on television and noticed I not only batted like him, but even slid into second base the way he did. I'd either pop up quickly after the slide or fade away, and brush off my trousers just above the knees, a reflex action, even if there wasn't any dirt.

The night after that, Joe was at his usual table at Shor's, and my father showed him what I was doing in the park. "I don't do that, do I?" Joe asked.

The following afternoon he doubled and told my father that evening: "By golly, I *do* do that."

The last paragraph of the article reported that "association with amateurs, namely his older brothers, who started playing baseball before television came into the household, has corrupted him. 'He's beginning to play like a kid again,'" said my father.

JOHN GARFIELD

Born Jacob Julius Garfinkle on Manhattan's Lower East Side, he was one of Hollywood's grittiest tough-guy actors, an enormous star with films like *Gentlemen's Agreement*, *The Postman Always Rings Twice*, *Body and Soul*, and *Pride of the Marines*. Victimized by blacklisting during the McCarthy era, he was just thirty-nine when he died of a heart attack. But his thirty-two films still resonate with an acting style presaging today's antiheroes.

In 1931, a young actor, then working as an apprentice at Eva Le Gallienne's Civic Repertory Theater, wrote playwright Albert Bein, asking for a job in Bein's new play, *Heavenly Express*. "I can play the part of Julio well," he pleaded. "And even though it's a walk-on, I can make something of it."

In 1940, the play was produced on Broadway with Garfield, by then a Hollywood star, signed to play the leading role. But Bein first demanded he read that letter aloud to the rest of the cast.

Early on Garfield was often cast in prison pictures for Warner Brothers. Sitting in the office at the studio, wearing a pinstriped suit, he once negotiated for an escape from the genre by saying: "It's taken me years to get from horizontal stripes to vertical ones."

In March 1942, Garfield had just completed some tough-guy scenes opposite Spencer Tracy for the movie *Tortilla Flat*. He phoned his friend Chico Marx at the Hillcrest Country Club, and Marx put a friend on the line, saying: "I have someone who can fight you."

"Wanna fight me?" said Garfield, playfully, still in his tough-guy role, to the voice on the other end of the line. "I licked the Dead End Kids in one picture and flattened Jimmy Cagney in another. I'm pretty tough."

"I fight pretty good too," said the voice.

Julius Garfinkle, aka John Garfield, and Dana Andrews flanking my father at the Stork Club on the set of Daisy Kenyon *in 1947. My father had a cameo, later described as "unconvincing."*

"OK," replied Garfield. "I'll be over soon. By the way, what's your name, buddy?"

"Joe Louis, Mr. Garfield," the gentle voice replied.

After a pause, the actor replied: "Oh, call me 'John'—Mr. Louis."

Also in March 1942, Garfield was on a flight to Tucson and met Mary Pickford. They discovered they were both scheduled to make political speeches, supporting opposing candidates. Garfield said their respective audiences were probably convinced how they would vote, and suggested they switch audiences to make it more interesting. She agreed, but her sponsors refused to allow it.

In December 1942, Garfield was under suspension from Warner Brothers for refusing to play a role in a movie that called for him to portray a murderer who attacks a blind girl and then beats a dog.

"I don't mind playing a murderer," he explained. "And movie fans might forgive an actor for playing a role in which he attacks a blind girl. But for my beating a dog? For *that* they'd boycott my movies."

In 1943, he was longing to portray George Gershwin. He lobbied Warner Brothers. He learned how to sit at a piano and make it appear as if he played it expertly. But the role went to a younger, debuting actor, Robert Alda (father of Alan), for the movie appropriately titled *Rhapsody in Blue*.

"This is no reflection on you," director Irving Rapper told Garfield. "You probably could've played Gershwin well, but it just wouldn't be convincing if John Garfield appeared wearing a top hat entering Carnegie Hall."

My father and Garfield had something in common. They'd go to the same New York dentist and try to have all necessary work done in one sitting. In Garfield's case, his time in the chair sometimes lasted ten to fourteen hours. Garfield would transact all his New York business from the

chair, since his time in the city was so limited.

During one session, Maxwell Anderson, the playwright who wrote *What Price Glory*, *Winterset*, and *Key Largo* came to the dentist's office and began reading a script to the patient. Suddenly, Garfield winced.

"The play?" inquired Anderson.

"No," said the actor, "the drilling."

An hour or later, Garfield called out in pain again.

"The drilling, right?" asked Anderson.

"No," mumbled Garfield, his mouth filled with cotton, "This time the script! Ouch!"

One night in November 1944, Garfield was at the Stork Club telling of visiting Anzio, Italy, as well as Yugoslavia, South America, and other distant places during his two USO tours. Another actor listened and asked: "What's the first thing I must do about going?"

"The first thing," replied Garfield, "is to look in the mirror when you wake up and ask: 'What am I doing? What am I doing here with a war on?' Then you say to yourself: 'Nothing else matters but the war. Contracts, pictures, costars, they don't matter. I've gotta go.' Then, you go."

That same day, my father wrote of Garfield's Italian front visit, from which he brought back a German Luger pistol, sold to him by an American sergeant for $100. It came with the assurances of the soldier that such an item was difficult to obtain. Later, almost every GI Garfield met wanted to present him with a Luger for nothing.

Months later, back on the studio lot, Garfield saw that sergeant who'd sold him the Luger again. "I tried to duck meeting you here," confessed the soldier, Congressional Medal of Honor winner Charles "Commando" Kelly.

In late January 1948, a snowstorm hit New York while Garfield was in town. He was there for the golden wedding anniversary of his aunt and uncle, who lived in

Brooklyn. So Garfield, unable to find a taxi, went with his wife on the subway. All the passengers recognized the movie star and kept staring. All except one elderly couple. Finally the woman approached and said; "Say, aren't you Julius Garfinkle from Livonia Avenue in the Bronx?"

"Yes," Garfield replied to his long-ago neighbor.

"Hmm, we thought so. Haven't seen you in years. So what's new, Julie?"

The end of December 1948 saw Garfield back in New York, and he saw Henry Fonda at Sardi's one night. Fonda had heard Garfield was in rehearsals for Clifford Odets's play *The Big Knife* and asked him how things were going.

"Going into rehearsals in a new play is like having an affair with a new girl . . ." Garfield began. Then he stopped and stammered, pointing to the woman on his arm: "By the way, Hank, I'd like you to meet my wife."

Garfield's son David was a year ahead of me in high school at the Fieldston School. We were teammates on the baseball team. A sometime actor, he too would die before his time, and like his father, from a heart attack. When he was a boy in 1951, David's father made his debut on TV in *Showtime USA*.

"I'm doing this to impress my son," said Garfield. "His schoolmates didn't believe him when he told them his father is a great actor. But they didn't believe him because they haven't seen me on television."

SAM GOLDWYN

I remember going with my father to the home of one of Hollywood's founders, Sam Goldwyn, in Beverly Hills in January 1965. Our host was a tall, charismatic man, then eighty-six, with a high-pitched voice that somehow belied his iconic place in the history of the movies.

Born Samuel Gelbfisz in Warsaw in 1879, Goldwyn frequently got his name in the papers for mixing up English words and phrases. (However, many of his "Goldwynisms" were made up by a publicist.) Among the most famous quotes attributed to Goldwyn is: "An oral contract isn't worth the paper it's written on." And he also said, a famous sculptor "once did a bust of my wife's head."

He never directed a movie, but produced some 138 films, from 1917's *Polly of the Circus* and the original, silent version of *Ben-Hur*, to *Dead End, The Westerner, The Little Foxes,* and *The Pride of the Yankees*. He often appeared in "The Lyons Den."

In 1925, the young Sam Goldwyn attended a party given by publishing magnate Condé Nast. There he saw a young woman named Frances Howard surrounded by a group of admiring men, gushing about her beauty. The film producer cleared a path through the starry-eyed, smitten men and simply said to her: "You're wearing your hair wrong. It spoils your looks."

The next day he called her for a date. "I said the only thing I knew to impress you," he confessed.

They were married two weeks later!

After the success of his first two movies in the silent era, Adolph Zukor, one of the founders of Paramount Pictures, invited Goldwyn and his brother-in-law and partner Jesse Lasky to discuss a movie deal. The conference began, and Zukor offered both men a cigar, but they said they didn't smoke. Later, the two partners decided that if they were to put up the same kind of op-ulent front Zukor did, they had to learn to smoke cigars. So they stopped to buy some, went home, and gave it a try. Both inhaled and became ill. Although a cigar is part of the image of an old-time Hollywood mogul, Goldwyn never smoked one again.

One of the associate producers in Gold-wyn's studios was preparing the produc-tion of a movie about Custer's Last Stand. (It eventually went to Warner Brothers as *They Died with Their Boots On.*) He wanted to be certain his boss, Sam Goldwyn, knew the story of the famous Battle of the Little Big Horn of 1876.

"Of course I do," said the Polish-born Goldwyn. "I know all I need to know: Custer lost."

Veteran screenwriter Jo Swerling was re-cruited by Goldwyn to write *Hans Christian Andersen* with Danny Kaye in the title role. "I can't work for you for a while," said the writer. "I'm under contract to Paramount, and you can't get me."

Goldwyn laughed and said: "You never knew I got you away from 20th Century-Fox to write *The Pride of the Yankees*, did you?" Goldwyn then explained that he'd been playing gin rummy with Fox studio head Darryl F. Zanuck and won a climac-tic double-or-nothing hand. But instead of money, he got the right to hire Swerling to write that classic film, which starred Gary Cooper as Lou Gehrig.

One night in late June 1950, Goldwyn and his wife were in London and dined at the home of Sir Alexander Korda, perhaps England's Goldwyn counterpart. Korda produced such classics as *The Private Life of Henry VIII*, *The Four Feathers*, and *The Thief of Bagdad*.

At one point during the meal, Mrs. Gold-wyn blurted: "Wait a minute! Aren't you two suing each other?" Indeed they were, in a dispute concerning the movie *The Scar-let Pimpernel*. Both producers had forgotten about the lawsuit, and they proceeded to settle it over glasses of brandy.

Goldwyn was known as a publicity hound. "When you write nice things about me, I feel fine," he told my father. "And when things about me which aren't so nice are printed, I feel awful. But worst of all is when you write nothing about me."

In 1954, Goldwyn was discussing the ad-vantages he enjoyed as an independent film producer. When he learned that the movie rights to the smash-hit Broadway musical *Guys and Dolls* would be sold under a sealed bid, he immediately called a meeting of his board of directors. "You like it?" asked one board member. "Then buy it."

The board of directors of Goldwyn Stu-dios was comprised of Mrs. Goldwyn and their son Sam Goldwyn Jr., one of today's independent movie moguls.

A publisher asked Goldwyn for his list of the ten greatest actors and actresses in Hol-lywood. Goldwyn agreed to give him some-thing but submitted only nine names. "Just in case someone calls, wondering why they weren't on the list," he explained, "I can say I forgot to put them on as the tenth."

At a story conference one afternoon, where the participants usually debate the merits of each scene, everything went uncharacteristi-cally smoothly: not an argument, not a sug-gestion, everyone in agreement. "That can only mean one thing," said Goldwyn, when he heard about it later: "A lot of trouble."

One night at their home in Hollywood, the Goldwyns had dinner and a movie for their children and grandchildren. They screened *Hans Christian Andersen*, during which the youngest grandchild began to squirm.

"Don't worry," said their grandfather, "it's just like TV."

In the spring of 1961, Goldwyn was dis-cussing the dangers of stardom and some of the odd things he'd seen happen over his decades in Hollywood. He and his wife once attended a dinner given by a silent movie star, for example, who had amassed a fortune. Many tables were spread around the lavish pool area, and everyone had a gold plate. There was an orchestra and a huge serving staff.

The day after the dinner, however, the sheriff arrived and foreclosed on the house and all its contents.

When Charles Lindbergh went to Hollywood to sell Goldwyn the rights to *The Spirit of St. Louis*, Goldwyn entertained him, addressing him as "General." "He's a colonel," whispered an aide.

Once Lindbergh said he was asking for $1,000,000, Goldwyn spent the rest of the meeting addressing him as "Lindbergh." Warner Brothers would eventually make the movie, a classic, with James Stewart as the aviator.

"Genius is 10 percent inspiration and 90 percent exhaustion," he said. "When geniuses work for me, I supply the exhaustion." As for complimenting his staff, he only did that "after the public has spoken. An 'artistic success' is only a success," he continued, "if it sells tickets."

He had the right to assume such an attitude, since Goldwyn was the only Hollywood producer of his time to invest solely his own money.

On a train ride to Philadelphia to see a play in pre-Broadway tryouts, Mrs. Goldwyn noticed an incredibly beautiful young woman. She introduced herself and set up an appointment with her husband. He liked the young woman and offered her a $500-a-week contract to be a "Goldwyn Girl," promoting the company. She would've followed other young hopefuls like Lucille Ball, Paulette Goddard, Betty Grable, Jane Wyman, and Virginia Mayo, who got their starts that way.

Nevertheless, the young woman refused. "I'm working as a model," she explained, "only while I'm learning to become an actress, Mr. Goldwyn. I'll then go to Hollywood, but only after I've learned to play a role."

The young woman heading from New York to her home in Philadelphia that fateful day was Grace Kelly.

Goldwyn's *Best Years of Our Lives*, the greatest postwar film about soldiers adjusting to civilian life, won nine Oscars. The idea came when his wife showed him a wartime photo of wounded GIs coming home.

"Frances," he said. "That's my next movie."

His perfect movie, in his eyes, was *Wuthering Heights*—the original version. He'd signed a London stage actor named Laurence Olivier, thinking he was ideal for the script. But the early "rushes" (the print of the previous day's scenes) were unsatisfactory because Olivier was screaming his lines. Director William Wyler couldn't tone the actor down.

"I sent for Larry," said Goldwyn, "and showed him the rushes. I told him a movie set isn't a stage where the actor must raise his voice to be heard. The microphone is a delicate instrument. Larry understood; he went back, and there was never any trouble again."

Bette Davis was starring in *The Little Foxes* for Goldwyn and refused to reshoot some scenes after a disagreement with director Wyler. She walked off the set, changed into her street clothes, and prepared to leave the lot. Goldwyn arrived and suggested she phone her lawyer, warning her that he would sue her for all damages incurred.

He knew she had money; he'd just agreed to pay her an exorbitant fee for the lead role of *Regina Giddens*. Davis did indeed consult her attorney and her accountant and told them of a possible lawsuit by Goldwyn. A few minutes later, she quickly changed back into her costume and reshot the scenes.

CARY GRANT

Sometime in 1980, my wife Judy and I ran into Cary Grant. I can't recall the circumstances, but I do remember what he said to her: "You know everyone imitates me saying 'Judy, Judy, Judy,' but I never said that in any of my movies."

My wife, who is fazed by absolutely nothing, was speechless. She simply looked up at Grant in adoration.

Every man wanted Cary Grant to portray him in the movies; the epitome of style and elegance, he was loved by everyone who knew him.

It seemed as if every man of his time tried to carry himself like Grant. He had his clothes tailored in Hong Kong. In fact, his Chinese tailor displayed on the street in front of his shop a life-size cardboard photo of Grant wearing one of the tailor's suits, with his hand extended, pointing to the entrance.

On June 14, 1939, Grant saw the play *The Philadelphia Story* and went backstage to congratulate his friend Van Heflin, whose performance had drawn raves from the critics.

"You're very good in the role," said Grant, "but you won't play the part in the movie version."

"Why not?" Heflin asked.

"Because I will," said Grant, correctly predicting that Clark Gable, producer/star Katharine Hepburn's first choice for the big-screen version, would not wind up in the role.

Grant began as a stilt walker under his real name, Archie Leach, and worked for the Shuberts, owners of a string of New York theaters. Whenever he'd return to New York, years later, he'd leave a note for J. J. Shubert saying: "A. Leach would like to see Mr. J. J." Shubert would always reply: "We're not using any stilt walkers this season."

Grant attended a party in 1943 where the hostess brought her daughter to meet him.

With Cary Grant on the set of The Pride and the Passion *near Madrid in July 1956. I took this photo.*

The film star shook the girl's hand, and she beckoned to him to bend over so she could whisper something in his ear. "Mr. Grant, I've been in love with you all my life," imparted the ten-year-old.

Grant was asked why his marriage to Barbara Hutton, the richest woman in the world, didn't last. "Tell you why," Grant explained. "I was making $14,000 a week and still felt like a kept man." Another reason might have been the fact that Hutton had a longtime chauffeur whose name was Archie Leach!

I first met Grant on the set of *The Pride and the Passion* in Spain in July 1956. Grant had arrived in Madrid several months before, and on his first day in town was anxious to visit the Prado, one of the world's greatest art museums. Speaking no Spanish, Grant gestured to the cab driver, saying: "Goya. Velázquez." The driver gave a slightly puzzled look, smiled, and nodded. He then took Grant on a half-hour drive to the outskirts of the city, leaving him in an empty lot at the corner of Goya and Velázquez streets.

Frank Sinatra costarred, along with a young Sophia Loren, in *The Pride and the Passion*, and Grant said of the crooner: "Frank's a fine actor. Most actors think only of how they look while filming a scene. Not Frank. He has the right thoughts, pace, adjustments; no false motions. The same as in life." (Ironically, Sinatra had won an Oscar for supporting actor three years before for *From Here to Eternity*, but Grant, who appeared in seventy-two features, never won one.)

Then he spoke again of his ex-wife Hutton, and mentioned some of her problems as the richest woman in the world—the target of schemers, drunks, the envious, and the arrogant. Once he'd heard a man ask her bluntly: "How does it feel to have a lot of money?" Hutton replied: "Very nice, thank you."

Grant's third wife was actress Betsy Drake, who was a passenger aboard the plush Italian ocean liner *Andrea Doria* when it sank in the Atlantic, after colliding with the *Stockholm* on July 25, 1956, while Grant was in Spain and was unaware of the accident. Friends from all over the world quickly sent him hundreds of cables inquiring about his wife. When he returned to his hotel, he found the batch of sealed cablegrams and picked one at random.

It was from his wife, by that time aboard the liner *Ile de France:* "All's well. Not a scratch." The *Ile de France* dateline on the cable puzzled him, since he knew she'd been booked on the *Andrea Doria*. Not until he began reading the rest of the cablegrams did he realize that the Italian liner had sunk.

Finally he was able to phone his wife, and he began to cry. "Relax," she said. "I'm fine. Now go take Sophia Loren to dinner."

In *The Pride and the Passion,* Grant had to carry both Sinatra and Sophia Loren away from danger. Asked the difference, he said "Sophia is so beautifully counterbalanced."

Grant enjoyed making movies abroad. It was his desire to see the world that first drove him to acting. He was twelve, too young to join the British Navy, but he knew that actors traveled, so he left home to join a road show, thus starting a show-business career lasting half a century.

My father told the story of how one morning, Howard Hughes suddenly appeared at Grant's Palm Springs home, walked into the kitchen, and prepared cereal for himself. The eccentric billionaire glanced at a young blonde woman wearing glasses, sitting in the corner where she embroidered. A few minutes later, without saying anything, she got up and left. The next day Hughes phoned Grant and suggested they meet for dinner. "And bring your wife's secretary," Hughes said.

"Oh, that's no secretary," said Grant. "She's my costar, Grace Kelly."

HOWARD HUGHES

I recently heard Howard Hughes described as "the Bill Gates of the twentieth century." Absurd. Gates is open, does public appearances, donates hundreds of millions to charities, and seems outgoing and engaging. Hughes was a maniac for privacy and was the personification of eccentric. And while one of the richest men in the America of his time, he was probably a tenth as rich as Gates.

Hughes dated Katharine Hepburn in the 1940s and suggested she include television rights to any movie contract she signed. She replied, "What's television?"

An actress who'd expected Hughes to marry her ordered expensive silverware and table linen bearing their intertwined monograms. When Hughes married someone else, the rejected woman had Johnny Meyer, Hughes's former aide, intercede with him about the cost of the monogrammed silverware and linen. Hughes replied: "Tell her to marry Huntington Hartford."

Joe Frisco, a Broadway vaudevillian, was on a winning streak at the dice table in Las Vegas and turned to a man in sneakers, who stood next to him, quietly watching the run. "Hang around, kid, and I'll buy you a pair of shoes," he said. That "kid" was Howard Hughes.

Hughes's methods of operation were always unconventional, to put it mildly. The ceromonies designating him "aeronautical adviser to the New York World's Fair" in 1935 were delayed half an hour while he'd sent out for a clean shirt.

The first time my father met Hughes was at New York's Colony restaurant. My father had been invited to dine with Alfred Hitchcock. As Hughes approached the table, Hitchcock, aware of Hughes's aversion to the press, assured him that he could speak frankly and in confidence in my father's presence.

Hughes simply nodded, then turned to Hitchcock and said: "So tell me: How do I buy MGM?"

He had Jane Russell under contract for eighteen years, but saw her only once every four years. He phoned his top aides at all hours of the night, making sure they'd first been alerted and were standing by to receive his call. One such call, made at 3 a.m., roused his aide's wife who said: "I've no doubt it is important, but my husband has had no rest for days and needs the sleep."

Hughes called her back to say there was a suite in her husband's name at the Waldorf. "Have him check in now. And when he's had his sleep, have him call me."

He preferred phone calls to face-to-face conversations because of his deafness, incurred in his California plane crash on July 7, 1946. After he recovered consciousness, he sent for his secretary and dictated instructions to the heads of all his companies about how to keep his enterprises going.

When New York Mayor William O'Dwyer banned *The Outlaw*, Hughes said: "I'll just wait until he's out of office, and no, the movie won't be outdated. Jane Russell and a Western can never be outdated." When neighbors objected to the marquee's blinking lights, saying it cost them sleep, he sent the plaintiffs in a suit against them a reply and a dark eyeshade.

In January 1965, my father took me to Las Vegas en route home from California. We hadn't told Hughes we'd be in town, and yet, after we'd arrived, we were contacted by Hughes's people and a guide sent to our hotel for a private tour. This was when he was holed up in the Desert Inn, presumably watching *Ice Station Zebra* over and over, walking on Kleenex boxes, unshaven and with little contact with the outside world.

Not surprisingly, our guide, who told us he was a retired general, wondered how we rated such preferential treatment. "How well do you know Mr. Hughes?" he asked my father.

"Oh, I've known Howard since his time in New York."

"Really?" replied our guide, sounding surprised. "When was the last time you saw him?"

"I think it must've been around 1947," replied my father with a straight face.

And yet, somehow, Hughes knew we'd arrived in town.

He once had a heated argument with screenwriter Arthur Caesar about a film. Finally, Hughes said: "Do you have six million in cash right now? I do." Caesar said, "No, I don't. But I do have six friends."

In July 1938, a guest stopped to talk to the manager of the St. Regis Hotel in New York. "Checking out, Sir?" asked the manager.

"Oh no," replied Hughes. "Keep that suite for me. I've got my clothes up there. I'll be back in a few days."

He didn't tell the manager, but by "a few days," Hughes was referring to the length of time he'd need to fly around the world, which he was about to do.

Soon after that, Hughes was photographed at the Stork Club with Ginger Rogers. The photo was never published, and Hughes sent for the photographer in his hotel. "Please give me the negative," he pleaded. "Ginger and I are just friends. If that picture is published, it'll get me in trouble with my real girl." The photographer agreed and gave Hughes the negative. Then he coughed suggestively and said: "Forget something, Mr. Hughes?"

"I did," replied the multimillionaire aviator. "I'm flying back to Hollywood tonight, and my feet are cold. Would you mind giving me your woolen socks?" He got the socks.

In February 1946, Hughes was at the controls of one of his TWA Super Constellations, flying some friends from Los Angeles to New York. During the flight, he called the steward up to the cockpit and said loudly: "What do you have to drink?" Several times he asked for a drink, and finally, the steward said: "Will vodka do?"

The passengers, naturally, were horrified, since their lives depended on Hughes remaining sober.

But the steward ignored them and brought a bottle of vodka to the cockpit; whereupon Hughes poured it onto a rag and used it to clean the fogged-up windshield.

His maniacal distrust of strangers became an obsession. When in July 1946, for example, he was a patient at Good Samaritan Hospital in California, he wouldn't permit a nurse to change the bedsheets. Instead the job was done by the highly paid treasurer of the Hughes Tool Company.

His doctor said if he didn't follow orders and stay in his room to recuperate they'd have to take drastic measures. Then the doctor got the city to assign a deputy sheriff to stand guard, under orders to keep everybody away from the patient, including Lana Turner whom he was dating at the time.

The actor Dick Powell inadvertently demonstrated how thoroughly Hughes operated. In September 1946, Powell purchased a plywood boat from the Hughes subsidiary corporation that manufactured them. But the boat leaked, and Powell mentioned it to Hughes.

"Return it to my board of directors," said Hughes, "and we'll give you a new one."

Powell then called for a new boat, and the board of directors came out to examine it with him. But by that time, it was a completely new board of directors. Hughes had fired their predecessors.

In 1947, Hughes's company built the Hercules Flying Boat for the Navy, which insisted, therefore, that a Navy pilot make the maiden test flight. Hughes refused saying: "I have six million dollars invested in that plane, and if anyone's neck is going to be broken, it'll be mine."

The plane was described in the newspapers as the "Hercules." When Hughes saw that, he phoned his office and told them to refer to the boat as the "H-4," indicating it was the fourth model his company had built.

"The 'H' is for 'Hughes'—me, not 'Hercules.' I worked on it, and it should be identified with me instead of with a Greek who's been dead 4,000 years."

During a night drive through the California desert in November 1948, he stopped at a diner and gas station. It was 100 degrees, and he noticed a kitten, panting in the heat. He tried opening the door of the restaurant. "Sorry, sorry, we're closed," said the owner.

Hughes replied: "I'll give you $5 for a glass of milk," after paying for his gas. The man opened the diner, brought out a glass of milk, and accepted the money.

Hughes then poured the milk into a plate, put it on the dusty ground, and called: "Here, Kitty, Kitty," and drove off into the steamy night as the cat lapped up the cool drink.

When Hughes crashed his plane and nearly lost his life, his aide Johnny Meyer tried to see him in the hospital, but Hughes, near death at that time, was under doctors' orders to have no visitors. Meyer then remembered that on the beach near Balboa, California, Hughes owned a small cabin to which no one had ever been invited.

Suspecting there might be things inside Hughes wanted no one to see, he flew to Balboa, found the cabin, and noticed the sign on the door: "No One Permitted to Enter Under Any Circumstances." Determined to deal with any sensitive information or materials inside that he knew his boss would want destroyed or at least put in a safer place, he broke down the door. Inside the dark room he saw the windows covered with heavy Army blankets. The room was in disarray; trousers over a chair, socks under the bed, and blueprints strewn in the corners. He studied the blueprints but could find nothing confidential about them. There was nothing behind the blankets, either.

So Meyer flew back to the hospital, and when the doctors finally permitted him to see Hughes for a few minutes, he said: "Don't talk, Howard. Just nod or shake your head." He told Hughes he'd flown to the Balboa cabin to search for anything Hughes might have wanted destroyed.

"I found nothing," said Meyer. "Would you want me to go back for anything I missed and remove it?" Hughes shook his head. Meyer then asked: "Then why the heavy blankets over the windows?"

Hughes opened his eyes and spoke one word: "Mosquitoes."

After he'd bought RKO Studios and had taken a famous late-night secret tour of the grounds, he said simply "Paint it." In 1950 Hughes got a visit there from a producer. As the lunch hour approached, the producer, who had a dining room, kitchen, and staff at his studio, suggested: "Why don't you come over to my place, and have lunch with me?"

"No," replied Hughes, aware that such an invitation would involve encountering strangers and appearing in public. "You have lunch with me." Hughes then opened a brown paper bag that contained a bottle of milk and two sandwiches. The second sandwich was an emergency one, for any last-minute "luncheon" guest.

Hughes was a man of whims. There was the time, for instance, when he wanted to fly a TWA Constellation, then still a new plane, to Berlin. His TWA associate refused to permit this, because the plane hadn't been in service very long, and he feared an accident on such a long flight might impair travel on the other planes the company had bought.

So the next day, Hughes's lawyer phoned the associate and said: "My client wants to know how much you want for your interest in TWA."

The man named his figure, and by nightfall Hughes had bought out the associate's stock.

Producers Jerry Wald and Norman Krasna signed a lucrative deal to make movies for Hughes in 1952. "We're our own bosses," they told Groucho Marx at the Screenwriters' Guild dinner. "We have artistic integrity, and independence, and complete autonomy. All that Mr. Hughes has over us is the right of approval or disapproval."

In 1952 he was dating Mitzi Gaynor, who one night told him she wanted to go dancing. Hughes promised he'd take her the next night. True to his word, he took her to the nightclub she mentioned. They were, however, the only ones in the room that evening, for he'd bought out the place for the night.

In June 1954, Hughes's company was filming *Underwater!* with his favorite star, Jane Russell. The shooting was done near Kona, on the island of Hawaii. Hughes instructed his crew to stay there and film only on cloudless days. One afternoon the sky was cloudy, and one of the technicians took his rowboat and fishing rod out into the bay offshore. After an hour without a bite, he suddenly felt a fierce tug on the line. He reeled it in, sure he'd caught a monster fish.

But it was a sign attached to his hook by a playful swimmer with a diving mask. The sign read: "GET OFF YOUR SEAT AND GO BACK TO WORK. HOWARD HUGHES."

In late July 1968, my father sat with veteran actor Ben Lyon and his wife, Bebe Daniels. Lyon recalled starring in Hughes's memorable *Hell's Angels* in 1928. Soon after it was completed, silent films became obsolete, so Hughes decided to remake it in sound, all except the aerial shots. His search for a new leading lady ended when Lyon spotted a blonde in a satin costume testing for another movie. Her name was Jean Harlow.

Lyon brought her to Hughes for a screen test at noon. By nightfall, she'd been tested and signed. Lyon was delighted—except when Hughes decided to bill the new star above Lyon's name. Hughes agreed, after a lawyer was called in, to top-bill Lyon, but in watercolors, saying: "At the first rainfall, your billing will be washed away."

Lyon took flying lessons for the role and Hughes sent an unusual Christmas gift: a parachute with a note: "Here's one Christmas package I hope you'll never open."

For a time, Hughes lived in New York and—naturally—was registered under an assumed name: "J. Alexander." A reporter spotted Hughes lunching in the hotel dining room and, uninvited, sat down and asked: "Is it true that the Hughes Tool Company is a monopoly?"

"Not at all," replied Hughes. "People who want to drill for oil and not use the Hughes Bit can always use a pick and shovel."

In March 1967, Hughes was living in isolation at the Desert Inn in Las Vegas. He'd been occupying an entire floor since the previous October and suddenly was asked by the management to leave. "But I'm paying well for it," he protested.

Management countered by saying they would make more if that floor were occupied by high rollers, people there to gamble in their casino. Hughes then offered to buy the hotel for $13 million. And did!

Once he took over, new rules were instituted. None of the maids was ever allowed to see him. When it came time to clean his rooms, they were required to call first so he could move into the adjoining penthouse.

When Marilyn Monroe was seeking a separation from Joe DiMaggio while filming *The Seven Year Itch,* she needed a hideout from the press. So she sought help from her personal photographer Sam Shaw. (Ironically, Shaw's photo of her on the subway grating, which DiMaggio witnessed, helped precipitate their separation. Shaw also took the photo of Marilyn "flirting" with my father with my mother looking angry, which is on the cover of this book.)

Shaw arranged with her studio, 20th Century-Fox, for her to stay in Betty Grable's vacant bungalow on the studio lot, with a direct line to studio boss Darryl F. Zanuck. Monroe lived there for several weeks until the separation story died down.

Hughes knew that Zanuck worked late and phoned him there at all hours. He never knew that the "secretary" answering Zanuck's phone was no secretary at all, but Marilyn Monroe.

In 1969, Hughes wanted his old friend Dave Chasen, owner of one of Hollywood's most famous restaurants, to dine with him in Las Vegas. By that time Chasen was ill, and his wife said he couldn't go anywhere without being near his doctor.

So Hughes sent his own plane to Los Angeles and flew the Chasens to Las Vegas. With their doctor.

GEORGE S. KAUFMAN

He was one of the wittiest writers of his day, the author or coauthor of the Marx Brothers' best film, *A Night at the Opera* (for my money the funniest film ever made), along with screenplays for the Brothers' *Cocoanuts*, adapted from his play, *Animal Crackers*, and others, not to mention *The Man Who Came to Dinner*.

In 1937, Kaufman went to see a Broadway play that was so bad that, during the second act, he tapped the woman seated directly in front of him and asked: "Madame, would you mind putting your hat *on?*"

In March 1938, Kaufman was a guest at a formal dinner. After the meal he surveyed the large dining room, turned to his hostess, and said: "You have a good layout here with good food, excellent service, and if you get enough people to talk about this place, you'll do some business."

"Yes," replied his hostess: First Lady Eleanor Roosevelt. "And besides," she added, "it's got a great location."

Kaufman was playing bridge in April 1938, teamed with Herman Mankiewicz, coauthor of *Citizen Kane*, who was playing badly, making blunder after blunder.

"Listen, Mank," said Kaufman, "when did you learn how to play bridge? And don't tell me it was 'this afternoon.' I want to know what *time* it was this afternoon!"

In February 1944, Kaufman announced that he'd just changed his will, and it provided that he be cremated, with his ashes to be tossed into the face of a producer he disliked.

In 1946, Kaufman attended a party where the hostess decided to have her guests play a parlor game. She distributed pencils and sheets of paper to each guest. When she gave them to Kaufman, he said: "I can't write. I mean it, I can't write. And I have the opening-night reviews to prove it."

In May 1947, Kaufman signed a contract

to direct the movie *The Senator Was Indiscreet* with William Powell. He left his New York apartment at 410 Park Avenue, took a train to Hollywood, 3,000 miles away, and was given the script. Scene one was set at 410 Park Avenue, New York.

Kaufman hated to travel, especially by plane. In fact, he claimed membership in the "Newton Was Right" society. "I don't want to go anywhere where I can't be at 58th Street and 6th Avenue in New York at midnight if I want to," he explained. He said that when forced to travel to Europe, he preferred "the largest ship possible. The ideal way of traveling to Europe would be if they could launch Central Park."

In the early days of television, Kaufman appeared as a panelist on a show called *This Is Show Business*. On one show, a young actress and future best-selling author named Jacqueline Susann appeared, saying that alien spaceships were real. "Don't you believe me?" she asked.

Kaufman replied: "In 1929, I took advice on the stock market from the Marx Brothers, so there's no reason why I shouldn't believe you about flying saucers."

Kaufman was proud of the fact that he had no technological knowledge at all. Neither did his friend Jack Benny, who said: "I have no idea how an airplane stays up, nor what makes a car go." Kaufman matched that by saying: "I'm still trying to understand why a hammer works."

Soon after that, Kaufman's play *The Phantom Ship* had an out-of-town tryout near a theater where another Broadway-bound play, *The Good Fellow*, was also in previews. He went backstage to visit the star of the second play, Ruth Gordon. Kaufman complained that his comedy wasn't getting any laughs. She complained, too, saying her drama was getting unwanted laughter.

Kaufman suggested they swap audiences.

DANNY KAYE

Long before there was Jonathan Winters, Robin Williams, or Martin Short, there was Danny Kaye, who could sing, dance, tell jokes, conduct a symphony orchestra, ad-lib, and do accent humor better than anyone. He performed in vaudeville, starred on Broadway, in live appearances, and TV and movies. His *Hans Christian Andersen* was a masterful, if somewhat controversial movie in which Kaye played the great Danish children's storyteller.

It was deemed "controversial" because some Danes objected to an American portraying the most famous Dane of them all. So after the film was released, Kaye went on a goodwill tour of Denmark to soothe the locals.

His comedies like *The Secret Life of Walter Mitty, Knock on Wood,* and *The Court Jester* are as funny today as they were in his time. And his fame was enhanced by his work as an international ambassador for UNICEF, which allowed millions of children from developing nations to be delighted by his endless talents.

As for accent humor, just look up "Tchaikovsky Danny Kaye" on YouTube and you'll be amazed. He recites the names of several dozen Russian composers at breakneck speed in a scene from *Lady in the Dark*.

Or if, like me, you live for baseball, his tribute to the Los Angeles Dodgers on YouTube is a must-see. (Kaye, by the way, was a part owner of the Seattle Mariners when they first entered the American League.) When you've done that, try "The Pellet With the Poison" sequence from *The Court Jester*, and you will laugh until your sides ache. There was no one like him.

In June 1942, Kaye attended a party in New York for the exiled King George of Greece. This was during his country's occupation by the Germans. Spyros Skouras, the Greek-born president of 20th Century-Fox

A rare photo of my father and his archrival, Walter Winchell, with Danny Kaye, taken on a back lot at Goldwyn Studios in 1950. "Damon" in Kaye's inscription refers their efforts as cochairs of the Damon Runyon Cancer Fund.

was there, and he used a phrase in Greek in speaking to the King.

Kaye interrupted, saying the pronunciation was incorrect, and recited the phrase. Incredibly, the King agreed. "Where'd you learn that?" asked the amazed Skouras.

"I learned it from the guy behind the counter in the drugstore in Brooklyn where I grew up," replied Kaye. Then he entertained everyone by attempting to break his record of forty seconds in reciting the "Tchaikowsky" number from his movie.

"Time it, Your Majesty," said Kaye. The King did, and Kaye finished it in thirty-two seconds.

In a column from July 31, 1942, my father reported that he and my mother entertained a young British bombardier spending his leave in New York, and took him to see

Kaye and the jazz singer and pianist Hazel Scott. The flier was so impressed he promised to drop two bombs on the Germans in their honor, and sure enough, word came that he'd written their names on the first two bombs he loosed somewhere over occupied Europe.

The day after he was rejected for military service and classified 4-F, Kaye announced that he would do a USO tour entertaining the troops, and added that he would perform at bases where no other entertainers had been able or willing to visit.

In October 1945, he flew to Pearl Harbor on tour. It was in a military transport, and he was later asked about the flight.

"It was comfortable," he said, "except for the last eleven hours."

On November 20, 1945, Frank Sinatra was taken ill just before opening an engagement at New York's Waldorf-Astoria Hotel. Kaye and his wife were there at a front table, and Sinatra, learning this, sent word to Kaye asking if he could go on instead.

Kaye agreed, and did a complete performance, with his wife Sylvia Fine playing the piano in accompaniment. When it was over, he returned to his table and asked the waiter for the check.

He did indeed receive a check, but the waiter added: "For you, Mr. Kaye, no cover charge."

In June 1946, actor Sam Jaffe of *Lost Horizon* fame was talking with a writer about the enormous talents of a young comic named Danny Kaye. Playwright Ferenc Molnár, who wrote *Liliom* (on which *Carousel* was based), overheard them and agreed.

"He's hilarious," said Molnár.

"Did you see him on screen or on stage or in a nightclub?" Jaffe asked.

"Oh, none of those places," replied Molnár. "I just shared an elevator with him at the Plaza Hotel. Hilarious!"

On May 20, 1948, Kaye was in the Stork Club, having just returned from London. He told of his fabulous reception in England and the night King George VI and Queen Elizabeth came to see him at a Command Performance. When they visited him in a private room afterward, the royal couple stayed for half an hour. Then the King said that it was time for them to leave. Kaye leaped up, wild-eyed, shook his head in mock rage, while he jumped up and down and roared: "No! No!"

The Queen waited for his pretended tantrum to subside and said: "Very well, then. We won't leave," and they stayed for half an hour more.

The proprietor of the London Palladium, where Kaye played the Command Performance for the King, recalled that he'd refused to hire Kaye a decade earlier for $150 a week. Kaye's salary by this time was $15,000 a week.

A newspaperman who wanted Kaye to meet George Bernard Shaw, reported that Shaw said: "Kaye? Who's he?" Then he was told that Danny Kaye was an unusually talented comedian. Shaw replied: "Bosh. That's not true. There hasn't been a talented new comedian since Charlie Chaplin."

In January 1965, my father took me to Las Vegas and to Kaye's one-man show. It was an evening of sustained genius.

If there was a secret to Kaye's greatness, it was endless curiosity. Aviation, baseball, tongue twisters, and medicine all fascinated him. He was a perfectionist. To learn golf, he took lessons from top pros and shot in the 70s. Flying intrigued him, so he studied intensely and qualified for a transport pilot's license. Absorbed by surgery, he was permitted to watch countless operations.

In 1962, Kaye suffered from a mysterious pain in his side, so he flew his own plane to the Mayo Clinic in Minnesota. Dr. Charles Mayo himself told Kaye it was an inflamed appendix and needed surgery.

"Have you done this operation before?" Kaye asked the world-renowned surgeon.

"Yes," replied the doctor. "Twice."

In September 1960, a year after Kaye qualified as a pilot, his father, always reluctant to fly, finally gave in and agreed to climb aboard his son's plane, explaining: "Danny, I've lived three score and ten, and any experience after my allotted span is sheer gravy."

In 1958, Kaye conducted a symphony orchestra at Carnegie Hall. But he didn't walk in blindly like other non-conductor guest leaders. To prepare, he spent six hours at WQXR, the classical music radio station of the *New York Times*, studying recordings of orchestras conducted by Arturo Toscanini, Eugene Ormandy, and others performing the same pieces he was to conduct.

Dimitri Metropolis, the great conductor, was the only one in the auditorium that night who didn't laugh at Kaye's routines, because he was fascinated by Kaye's talent and obvious preparation.

In July of that year, Kaye made his return to nightclubs in Las Vegas after a gap of twenty years and was told by the management that he hadn't lost anything. "You were so good, in fact," said the manager of the hotel, "even the losers were laughing."

Even after years as a movie star, Kaye wouldn't let a single year pass without appearing on a stage somewhere in the world. "If you think you'll tire me out before I tire you out," he told an audience in San Francisco, "I'll let you in on a little secret: No one in the world enjoys hearing me entertain—more than me!"

In December 1955, Kaye was at the posh Empire Theater in Paris, where he saw Maurice Chevalier perform. Chevalier introduced Kaye from the stage, and later Kaye said he hoped to introduce Chevalier from an American stage.

And so he did a few months later. Chevalier had never seen Kaye work, except in films, so he went out of his way to see him live. And sure enough, Kaye reciprocated the honor of being introduced from the stage in Paris, by doing it for Chevalier to his audience—in Dayton, Ohio.

Israel's most celebrated general, Moshe Dayan, visited Los Angeles in 1960 and phoned Kaye, who'd promised to show him around the vast city. Kaye whisked the general to the airport, and they boarded Kaye's private plane for an aerial view. Then he flew him to Palm Springs for lunch and an inspection of the orange groves.

"I'll show you more on your next visit," Kaye promised General Dayan. "By then I'll have my pilot's license."

When Kaye was studying to get that pilot's license in 1960, he ran into trouble on the navigation exam. So he rushed home to California and asked his thirteen-year-old daughter Dina: "Do you remember how to do long division?"

"Yes," the child replied. Kaye, whose brief schooling didn't include much arithmetic, asked his daughter; "Can you teach me?" She did. He passed the exam and got his license.

Dana Wynter costarred with Kaye in *On the Double* and was asked if it was difficult working with a comic.

"Only in the love scenes," she said, "trying to kiss my leading man—without laughing!"

One evening in 1951, Kaye and his wife had guests for dinner, including a studio executive known for his taste and inability to be impressed. Kaye decided to challenge that. After dinner, he invited the executive to his bedroom and took out a silk robe that bore the initials: "F.D.R." The Roosevelt family had bequeathed it to Kaye.

The executive studied the robe, felt the material, then said: "A fine robe. Now all you have to do is change those initials."

It was in a Midtown Manhattan nightspot called The Martinique, where on a night in 1940 he performed to a nearly empty house. But one of those in the audience was Billy Rose, the impresario, who was impressed.

"But you didn't laugh," Kaye said later.

"Guys like me don't laugh," replied Rose. "We nod."

Kaye's father was the guest of honor at a party at his son's Beverly Hills home. The other guests included Tyrone Power, Claudette Colbert, Douglas Fairbanks Jr., and Jack Benny. His father sat next to Benny and watched his son do crazy but brilliant routines, entertaining the guests.

"Mr. Benny," said Kaye's father, "I used to be just as crazy as my boy Danny—but I didn't get paid for it."

In May 1950, Kaye spent a week in Paris and mastered a French accent. Frenchmen complimented him on his perfect accent, acquired by his sensitive ear and talent for mimicry.

"Yes, I have an accent," he said, "but no vocabulary."

But Kaye did know some French words—two, in fact: he could say "Surgeon dentist" in French, which he'd utter with twitching lips, rolling the "R" and using the nasal "N." A producer then offered him a role in a French film at a sensational fee.

"I'll take the part," said Kaye, "if the role is that of a man with a constant toothache."

In June 1966, Los Angeles Mayor Sam Yorty took a short flight in a new Lear jet, part of a promotion. Once the plane reached its cruising altitude, he thought the back of the head of the pilot looked familiar, and mentioned it to the aviator. The pilot turned around, and it was indeed Danny Kaye, who among other talents, occasionally flew test flights for Lear.

In December of that year, Garson Kanin was directing a production of *Die Fledermaus* for the Metropolitan Opera. Mary Costa was starring and had difficulty doing some comic mannerisms for the role.

"Here," said director Kanin, finally, "let my assistant show you what I mean."

Out leaped Kaye and demonstrated.

In September 1971, Kaye told Alfred Hitchcock he'd always wanted to star in one of Hitchcock's movies. "The only problem with that, Danny," replied Hitchcock, "is that you'd have to play your role in a straightjacket."

HELEN KELLER

Helen Keller was one of the most courageous, brilliant, and accomplished women of the twentieth century, and frequently appeared in my father's column. There was the time, for example, in February 1943, when Harpo Marx serenaded her. Not on the instrument that made him famous but on his brother Chico's favorite, the piano. Keller kept one hand on the piano to feel the vibrations and kept swinging the other hand to and fro, in accompaniment.

Soon after that, she lunched with her companion-translator Polly Thompson and critic George J. Nathan. "Oh, Mr. Nathan, I remember you," she said. "Because twenty years ago, in reviewing a musical show, you wrote that the chorus girls' costumes 'looked like they'd been picked by Helen Keller.'"

She first voted in the 1944 presidential elections, but had to take a literacy test. This despite the fact that she spoke English, French, German, and Italian, and was a graduate of Radcliffe College. She passed.

At lunch a few days later, she met Robert Montgomery, one of the big movie stars of that era. They shook hands, and he returned to his table. Before he left the restaurant, he came over again to say goodbye. Such was the remarkably sensitive touch of Keller that when he placed his hand in hers, she recognized him and said: "Oh yes, Mr. Montgomery. Nice meeting you."

In September 1944, before storms were identified with people's names, "The Great Atlantic Hurricane" hit the East Coast and knocked out the lights of Keller's home. Her companion Thompson was frightened at being in a dark house while the storm raged outside. She went upstairs to Keller's room where the great lady was lying in bed calmly reading her book in Braille. "There's a hurricane outside," said Miss Polly.

"That's nothing to be frightened of,"

replied Keller. It wasn't a surprising statement, since she'd once entered a lion cage because she wanted to touch one of the beasts.

"I think you ought to know what a hurricane's like," said Miss Polly. Keller agreed, opened a window, stuck her head out into the wild storm and repeated: "It's nothing to be frightened of."

In 1944, Keller and Miss Polly visited the studio of sculptor Jo Davidson. She placed her sensitive hands on one of the busts in the studio and said: "This is President Roosevelt, isn't it?"

"Yes, it is," replied the sculptor.

Keller continued to touch the bust, then said: "This was made while he was younger than when I visited him recently."

"Why, yes," replied the amazed Davidson. "It was made in 1937."

"So that accounts for the difference," said Keller.

The Miracle Worker, about her life, opened on Broadway in 1959 to rave reviews. Anne Bancroft and Patty Duke would later recreate their stage roles as Annie Sullivan, Keller's first teacher, and the young blind-and-deaf Helen in the movie version and win Oscars. Both learned the hand sign language that Keller used, so as to make their performances more authentic, and they would communicate that way during rehearsals.

"Look at them," said another member of the cast. "They're talking about us behind our backs, right in front of us!"

During the run of the play, Duke visited Keller's home in Connecticut. They walked in the garden and talked through the fingers-in-the-hand language, the way Keller communicated. Three weeks later, Keller met Bancroft, and when they too communicated that way, Keller said: "She talks just like Teacher."

One night at the famed Copacabana nightclub, Keller and Miss Polly came for a performance by Sophie Tucker, the brash singer known for performing risqué songs. Her accompanist, Ted Shapiro, noticed the two communicating with their fingers in each other's hands, and slowed his tempo whenever the song seemed complicated.

Later, Tucker asked Keller: "Are my songs too naughty for you?"

"How could they be?" replied Keller. "They seem to bring joy to everyone."

CHARLES LAUGHTON

When I think of Charles Laughton, of course Captain Bligh in *Mutiny on the Bounty* comes to mind, as well as memorable roles in *The Hunchback of Notre Dame, The Private Life of Henry VIII, Advise and Consent,* and *Spartacus.* Oh, and the delightful *Island of Lost Souls,* the ancient, now-campy horror classic. He had a screen career that spanned five decades and was one of the most respected actors of his time.

As part of his preparation for the role of Captain Bligh in 1935's *Mutiny on the Bounty,* Laughton went to Gieves & Hawkes, the old Savile Row tailor shop founded in 1771, which for several centuries had dressed British naval officers. He asked the clerk what the Royal Navy uniform of the real Captain Bligh might've looked like.

"What year?" asked the salesman.

"1784," replied the actor.

"Just a minute, sir," said the clerk. He then went to the bowels of the store, pulled out a dusty scrapbook, and presented Laughton with Bligh's original order form, plus the measurements and sketches of Bligh's uniform.

Laughton's name first appeared in "The Lyons Den" on June 15, 1937, in an item in which my father reported that Laughton said that despite his film successes, he confessed that he'd saved no money. He had only one tangible piece of evidence to mark his screen triumphs: a painting that hung in his living room of four nudes studying a collection of fruit. The artist was one Pierre-Auguste Renoir.

In September 1938, the master print of his movie *St. Martin's Lane,* later to be renamed *Sidewalks of London,* was quietly shipped back to London for "dialogue revision." The Cockney dialogue proved unintelligible to American preview audiences.

During the filming of *The Hunchback of Notre Dame,* Sir Cedric Hardwicke and his fellow cast member Thomas Mitchell were watching Laughton acting. Hardwicke turned to Mitchell and whispered: "Do you want to know what I think of Laughton? He's a *screen* actor."

When it came time for Hardwicke to do a scene, Laughton and Mitchell watched, and Laughton whispered to Mitchell: "Do you want to know what I think of Cedric? He's a *stage* actor."

"The trouble with both of them," Mitchell said later, "is that neither is Irish."

A year later, Laughton confided that taxes consumed 82 percent of his income and that his role of Quasimodo in *The Hunchback of Notre Dame* "is one luxury I'm permitting myself."

A few weeks later, in October 1939, Alfred Hitchcock, who'd recently come to Hollywood, was asked what he found most difficult to photograph. He replied: "Children, dogs, trains—and Laughton."

At the first showing of *The Hunchback of Notre Dame,* Laughton was in the audience. He seemed unmoved during the screening, but then became excited as soon as the film was over.

"I didn't come here to see this movie," he confessed. "I came to see the next thing— the Donald Duck short."

When Garson Kanin was set to direct *They Knew What They Wanted* with Laughton in 1940, he was warned by friends in Hollywood that Laughton was very demanding and difficult to work with.

"Nonsense," said Laughton when told of this. "I'm impossible only when I work with those half-wits. They think I'm unreasonable because they don't understand me."

Then Kanin and Laughton met with the producer to discuss casting a leading lady. Laughton began insisting that "there is only one woman for the part. She was born for it, and I can't see anyone else in it."

When asked to name the actress, Laughton replied: "Jean Harlow," who by then had been dead for three years. Carole Lombard got the part.

In May 1942, Laughton appeared on a radio program written by Norman Corwin, the great radio writer. Laughton studied the script at his hotel, was satisfied with his recital of the lines, and went to the studio. There, however, he was unable to interpret the lines to his satisfaction.

"When I sat in my easy chair at the hotel," he told Corwin, "I was able to read my lines perfectly, but now I can't."

Corwin solved the problem: he had the hotel easy chair brought to the studio. Laughton sat down, the microphone was brought over, and he read his lines perfectly.

In *Arch of Triumph*, Laughton portrayed a sadistic SS man, and an interviewer asked him about all the psychopathic roles he'd played: Captain Bligh and others.

"Did these roles ever disturb you?" he was asked.

"About three years ago," Laughton replied, "I had a press agent who announced that I no longer would play heavies—that I'd accept nothing but sympathetic roles. The story received wide publicity, and as a result, I didn't get an offer of a job for a whole year.

"That's the only time I nearly went crazy."

In March 1949, Laughton, Burgess Meredith, and Franchot Tone were in Paris shooting *The Man on the Eiffel Tower*. A published report said that the three stars were arguing among themselves. Their press agent learned that a Hollywood columnist was in Paris and arranged for the stars to go with the journalist to a club in Montmartre and revel in camaraderie. At midnight, Laughton whispered to the other two actors: "Now may I go to my hotel? I'm due on the set at 8 a.m."

Tone and Meredith dissuaded him. Then at 2 a.m., Laughton finally left, despite their protests. The columnist notified the press that it was true—the movie stars were indeed fighting among themselves.

Henny Youngman, the king of the one-liner jokes, once posed for a photo with Laughton and mugged for the camera. Laughton noticed this and said: "My dear fellow, even a Hollywood actor never would try to steal a *still*."

When he checked into the famed Hotel Algonquin in New York in September 1950, he stayed in his room a while, then began to crave the company of other actors. So he went downstairs and asked the manager: "Any other hams in the house?"

In September 1952, a friend called Laughton to settle a bet. Knowing he'd portrayed King Henry VIII, he wondered how many wives the King had. "I say eight," said the friend.

Laughton replied: "You're mistaken. Only six."

Then he recited the famous mantra about Henry's many trips down the aisle: "Divorced, Beheaded, Died; Divorced, Beheaded, Survived."

In March 1953, Laughton directed a stage production of *John Brown's Body*. It starred Tyrone Power, Judith Anderson, and Raymond Massey. In its pre-Broadway tour they played San Diego, where Massey suddenly became too ill to continue and Laughton was forced to replace him.

He began the performance at the footlights, explaining the situation to the audience and saying; "Ladies and gentlemen. I know I look about as much like Abraham Lincoln as a pink elephant."

In 1954, Laughton, between screen roles, found a new calling. When his wife, actress Elsa Lanchester, called him a "loafer" for staying around the house, he called his agent to get some work doing readings: Shakespeare, The Bible, The Gettysburg Address. At first he volunteered his readings at a Veterans' Hospital, then went out on tour.

In one city, his agent arranged for him to appear on a morning disc jockey's program. Laughton refused. But his agent convinced him that the show was highly rated, and it would sell tickets to his readings.

Laughton endured the predictable series of inane questions, and then the DJ said: "Mr. Laughton, I've been enjoying your movies for years. I feel I know you. Do you mind of I call you 'Charlie?'"

"Call me 'Chucky' if you like, you imbecile," the regal British actor replied.

Laughton portrayed Captain Kidd in *Abbott and Costello Meet Captain Kidd*. Fran Warren, who appeared in the film, wondered why the distinguished actor agreed to such a role.

"I now enjoy an adult audience. This way, I can reach the children too," Laughton explained.

By 1955, he'd established himself as a director as well, with stage work including *Don Juan in Hell*, *The Caine Mutiny Court-Martial*, and on screen with *The Night of the Hunter*.

He described his evolution to directing as "feeling like one of the girls who's become the Madam."

In October 1956, Laughton opened on Broadway directing and starring in a revival of Shaw's *Major Barbara*. Ruth Gordon had a reunion with him and reminded him of her London debut in *The Country Wife*. She'd complained to Laughton that her director had hired a sixteen-year-old boy to portray a ninety-year-old man. Furthermore, her leading man was another unknown.

Laughton spoke to the director who hired the boy: Alec Guinness. Then Laughton offered to play the leading man's role for free. But the director wisely decided to keep that unknown in that role. His name was Michael Redgrave.

A few months later Laughton was preparing to appear on the Ray Bolger–Elaine Stritch TV show, and one of the writers for the series gave him his script. He started rehearsing the lines, beginning with: "Every time I walk into a theater, no matter what its size, to me, it's a temple, a shrine, a place of worship." Laughton tossed the script aside, saying, "Sorry, I just can't say that."

"But Mr. Laughton," replied the writer, "I got those words out of your own book!"

During the run of *Major Barbara* in 1957, Laughton heard a lady say about him: "Gracious, does he have to wear his hair that long?" He wheeled around and told her: "Madam, I get $5,000 a week for wearing my hair that long."

Another lady commented on Laughton's weight and told him it was dangerous, adding that her brother was a doctor.

"Madam," snapped Laughton, "my brother is a plastic surgeon—and you've got a double chin."

In the previews of *Major Barbara*, Laughton insisted on reciting his lines with his hands in his pockets, despite the protests of the show's producer. When it opened in Boston, however, for the first time he played the role with his hands free; the producer paid the wardrobe mistress an extra fee to sew up the pockets in Laughton's costume.

During the filming of *Witness for the Prosecution*, Laughton had a dispute with his wife and costar Elsa Lanchester.

"You don't scare me," she said. "Remember, I once played *The Bride of Frankenstein!*"

During the filming of *Spartacus*, Laughton was chatting with costar Peter Ustinov, when somehow a tourist found her way to the set and told Laughton she was a huge fan. She especially loved his magnificent performance in *Cat on a Hot Tin Roof*, obviously confusing him with another rotund actor, Burl Ives.

After she left, Ustinov warned Laughton

that such people often return to apologize once they realize their mistake.

Sure enough, she did return, and Laughton introduced her to Ustinov, saying: "Meet Edward G. Robinson."

"You can't fool me," said the woman, "You're Walter Hustinov."

Early in 1962, Oscar Levant and his wife checked into the Algonquin Hotel in New York, but were delayed in reaching their room because that famous hotel has only one passenger elevator. When Mrs. Levant told this to the bellhop, he replied: "Charles Laughton stayed here for twenty-eight years. He spent twenty of them waiting for this elevator."

GYPSY ROSE LEE

Gypsy Rose Lee—the most famous, talented stripper, performer, and raconteur of her day. The wonderful Broadway musical and subsequent movie *Gypsy* couldn't come close, really, to recreating her incredible charisma and *joie de vivre*. Her son Erik was one of my friends when I was growing up; we were born a month apart, and my parents were friends of Gypsy's.

Coincidentally, Erik also became a critic on TV, in San Francisco. Only after his mother's death did he and the world learn that his father was director/actor Otto Preminger, the result, I was told, of a one-night stand. I'd see Gypsy every Christmas at the home of a mutual friend, and even back then I marveled at how she could light up a room with her wit and laughter.

Born Rose Louise Hovick in Seattle, what made her famous wasn't her beauty; she was rather conventional looking at best. It was her brilliant way of spoofing the art of striptease, of using her wit to tease her male audience. When, for example, she was invited to a Hollywood costume party in May 1937, she replied: "But I haven't a thing to wear—and glad of it!"

One night in Hollywood, Gypsy dined with Roland Young, the character actor from movies like *The Philadelphia Story* and *Two-Faced Woman*. "We're going to do a play on Broadway together," she told friends at the table, turning to Young and adding: "Aren't we?"

"Yes," came the slightly bewildered reply, since no play had ever been discussed.

"Here's how it'll start," Gypsy continued. "I'll come out onstage and start acting. . . ."

"Yes, and if you try acting, I'll strip," he interrupted.

Soon afterward she announced she would indeed return to Broadway, and was asked to pose for a series of photos for a magazine. She obliged, but emerged from the photographer's studio depressed: "I kept telling 'em I'm legit now," she said. "But all the cameraman could yell was 'Drop it a little lower—lift it a little higher.'"

In 1940, she'd insured the jewelry she wore in her performances with Lloyd's of London, and listed her profession as "actress." She'd worn the jewelry in burlesque while living in a poor neighborhood. Then Lloyd's found out their new client was the famous striptease star, and they immediately doubled her rate.

So Gypsy decided to show 'em; She moved to the upscale Murray Hill part of Manhattan, almost next door to where tycoon J.P. Morgan had lived. Then her new home was burglarized.

Gypsy performed at the 1939–40 New York World's Fair, but before she opened, painters worked on a new sign announcing: "'The Streets of Paris,' Gypsy Rose Lee Starring." But when quitting time came on the Friday before the fair opened, the painters laid down their brushes and went home. The famed producer Mike Todd took one look at the incomplete sign and spent Friday night whitewashing it, for, as left by the workmen, it read: "'Streets of Paris,' Gyp."

She was a mystery writer, too, whose best-known work was *The G-String Murders*. In one of her books, she gave the first rule of burlesque: "Wear something long enough to keep the police away and yet short enough to lure in the customers."

After one of her books was published, she sat next to a literary critic at a luncheon, the same critic whose review had called her book "third rate."

"How did you dare call it 'third rate' when others said it was only second rate?" she demanded.

When the government's wastepaper conservation program asked Gypsy to contribute the manuscript of her book to their fund drive, they said Benny Goodman had donated his old orchestrations, and other writers had given their manuscripts. She agreed but said her manuscript had already been donated elsewhere.

When the publicist for the government drive tracked down the people who'd received her manuscript, they refused to give it up: "It's more valuable here," they said, "to allow posterity to be able to mark the present trend of American literature." And so the manuscript for *The G-String Murders* remains the proud possession of the archives of Princeton University!

During the war, the Stage Door Canteen was a gathering place for soldiers in town, and stars frequently appeared there to meet and mingle with them. When Gypsy arrived, the soldiers naturally insisted she entertain.

"But I'm not prepared," she protested, no doubt knowing what they had in mind. Finally, when they insisted that her "specialty" didn't require preparation, she agreed—and proceeded to deliver a long lecture about her book, *The G-String Murders*.

At her wedding ceremony to Alexander Kirkland in 1942, she looked at the guests and noticed they all were dressed in conservative clothing, except for one woman wearing a low-cut evening gown. It was the minister's wife.

Soon after her marriage, she arrived at a nightclub where the patrons playfully yelled: "Take it off! Take it off!" She then held up her ring finger and said, "Not with this on."

One day in early September 1947, George Cukor (often called "The Women's Director" because of his ability to entice great work out of his actresses) gave a luncheon. The guests were Katharine Hepburn, Ethel Barrymore, Fanny Brice, and Gypsy Rose Lee.

There was a thunderstorm during the lunch, and the lights went out.

"Suppose we suddenly were entombed here," said Gypsy, "and stayed this way, here at this table, dressed as we are, for thousands of years. I wonder what the archeologists of the future would think when they found us."

One guest decided that archeologists of the future, knowing only that the particular occupations of the guests were varied, would conclude that Hepburn was the stripper, Gypsy the lady of social background, Brice the distinguished actress, and Barrymore the comedienne.

In April 1953, she reflected on the fact that in the preceding year, she'd made more money than she had in her long career. She was asked if she ever felt any embarrassment as a stripper.

"Only at the beginning," she recalled, "but that didn't last long. Only the first hundred stares are the hardest."

Returning to New York from a long tour another time, she sighed: "I've worked so steadily that for the last eight months I haven't had a stitch of clothing on my back."

By 1960, she'd been divorced again and was visiting her friend Ethel Merman, who had created the role of Gypsy's domineering stage mother, "Mama Rose," in the stage version of *Gypsy*. Gypsy lamented to her friend: "Ethel, I live in a townhouse with twenty-six rooms, but right now, there is still no room for a man."

In January 1961, Gypsy was in San Juan to star in a production of *Auntie Mame*, and was accorded a royal welcome. At the theater on the night of her premiere, she heard singing in the street outside her dressing room. She was moved, hearing the crowd singing the "Star-Spangled Banner." So she went outside, and the crowd began to chant: "*Yanqui* go home! *Yanqui* go home!"

Long after she'd retired from stripping, Gypsy met a young woman who was just starting in the business. "Remember," she advised her, "men don't go to nightclubs to be educated or inspired. Bear that in mind when you walk onstage."

Gypsy was once asked if she'd used a ghost writer, and indignantly replied: "I write my own books, catch my own fish, and my son Erik is *not* adopted."

OSCAR LEVANT

There was never anyone like Oscar Levant—the actor, raconteur, concert pianist, author, and continually depressed pessimist. For some reason, he took a liking to me more than any of my brothers, and we visited him in his home in Beverly Hills. I loved the quips, the hypochondria, the brilliant observations, and sour-faced aura of the man. Levant was a world-class pianist, songwriter, and the quintessential sad sack best friend to the stars in movies like *An American in Paris* and *Rhapsody in Blue* (playing himself). His autobiography was titled *Memoirs of an Amnesiac*. And his other books, *A Smattering of Ignorance* and *The Unimportance of Being Oscar* bespoke his outlook on life.

A close friend of George Gershwin and Aaron Copland, he was also a witty panelist on radio and later television shows, demonstrating a rapier-like wit and deadpan expression.

"I'll tell you how long I've known Doris Day," I heard him say one time, referring to the squeaky-clean, All-American aura of the singer and movie star.

"I knew Doris Day *before* she became a virgin!"

In August 1937, my father reported that Levant, who'd lived in hotels most of his life, finally was "getting domestic," as my father put it. He had found an apartment in Hollywood. His first step was to try to arrange for milk deliveries. Back in those days, milk was delivered every morning to doorsteps across America. Levant naively placed an empty milk bottle outside his front door with a note inside requesting regular deliveries.

A few weeks later, Levant heard George Gershwin discussing the arts, music, and creative work.

Oscar Levant, with his usual expression, joins my parents at the Waldorf-Astoria Hotel in November 1939.

"George," he asked Gershwin, "Tell me —if you had to do it all over, would you fall in love with yourself again?"

In April 1938, Levant met a young woman in Hollywood and asked her to dinner. She agreed, but said her mother had to meet him and a relative as well before granting permission to go out with him. Levant then brought his "uncle" to meet the girl's mother.

The dinner date never took place, because the "uncle" chased the mother all over the house. It was Harpo Marx.

When he was thirty-two in 1939, Levant announced he would never again be seen in short pants. "I'm officially too old to be a child prodigy any longer," the piano virtuoso explained.

During the time he was wooing actress June Gale, he phoned her from New York. They'd had a tiff, and her sister answered, saying June refused to speak to him. "I don't blame her one bit," said Levant, "but I've paid for three minutes of long distance—so could *someone* talk to me?" They were married a few months later.

At the ceremony, Oscar kept asking his best man: "Seriously, do you think I'm making a mistake?"

Then he realized he'd forgotten the ring; so at the last minute he dashed out to a nearby costume jewelry store and bought one. At first it was listed at $15, but Levant told the dealer it wasn't worth that much, so he got a bargain—$14.

In February 1940, Levant assured his friends that he and his wife would never have children.

"I don't have enough room in my pockets for pictures," he said. "And anyway, some columnist would probably write: 'The Oscar Levants are expecting a bundle from hell.'"

Oscar and his wife June had three daughters.

Just before his wife delivered their first child, Levant was asked about the nursery. "We're doing it in barbed wire," he deadpanned.

"I'm glad I have three daughters," he said. "I couldn't control sons. But with my daughters, I'm just one of the girls."

In-between rehearsals for a concert in 1941, Levant was asked if he was going to portray himself in his next movie.

"Due to my limitations," Levant replied, "I'm forced to."

Levant often took his friend Alfred Gwynne Vanderbilt out on the town with him. When he took him to dinner at Lindy's in New York in April 1940, several waiters, recognizing Vanderbilt, waited on them, as did Leo Lindy, the proprietor.

Later, Lindy saw that Vanderbilt had left his plate nearly untouched.

"Oh him," said Levant. "He's just a shill I use to get better service."

On a visit to New York, Levant fell ill in his hotel room. The self-described "World's Foremost Hypochondriac" asked for a doctor, "but only one who knows music and who doesn't talk much."

Another time in New York, Levant complained that he didn't like most Broadway plays because "they take my mind off myself." In Sardi's, the theatrical restaurant, later that evening, Sir John Gielgud came by his table and said he was a great admirer of Levant's.

"Thanks," replied Levant, "but you ought to be more discriminating. Especially at your age."

Levant was urged to move to New York to do a TV show in 1960 but refused. "Hollywood has everything I need," he explained, "my home, my friends, my family, and my enemies. All live here." Eventually he did do a show, and when it got renewed Levant received a telegram from his producer: "Congratulations, Oscar, and remember to keep sick."

Levant must have spent half his life on

his psychiatrist's couch. After a periodic checkup, however, he was finally declared fit.

"All this means," he sighed, "is that I'm going back to my old self again—God forbid!"

In fact, he was in therapy for thirty-five years. He recalled his classmates in high school back in his native Pittsburgh, saying: "Some studied law. Others studied medicine. I'm the only one who studied to become a patient."

In July 1940, Moss Hart offered Levant a role in a summer stock production of *June Moon*. "I turned that role down in the original, ten years ago," Levant reminded him, and refused again.

"But it's an easy part," Hart said to the piano virtuoso. "All you have to do is play."

"I don't want to be typecast," said Levant.

In June of the next year, Levant dined at Lindy's with Garson Kanin and Danny Kaye. When the check came, all three grabbed for it. Kaye let go first, then Kanin, leaving Levant holding it.

"Garson," he said, "what happened to that strong grip of yours?"

When their second daughter was born a few weeks later, Oscar visited his wife June in the hospital. She awoke and asked, "What's our baby's name?"

"I don't know," replied Oscar. "I haven't asked her yet."

When Columbia Pictures renewed his contract in November 1943, Levant insisted in the negotiations that one word be inserted: "happy." Thus the contract read: "Columbia Pictures is *happy* to renew. . . ."

One afternoon in 1946 he was walking on West Fifty-Seventh Street in Manhattan with Vanderbilt, and they entered an art gallery. Vanderbilt was looking for an Utrillo to add to his collection. Levant spotted a painting and asked: "How much for that?"

"Two thousand dollars," the proprietor replied.

"I'll give you a thousand," replied Levant.

"Sorry, I can't do that," came the reply.

Levant said: "Good for you. Don't drop your price. With a Vanderbilt here, I just wanted to say I was the only one who made an offer."

One day, Levant and Harpo Marx were walking along Fifth Avenue and passed a wedding emerging from St. Thomas Episcopal Church. There were newspaper photographers, guests, the wedding party, the couple's getaway car, the lot. A crowd was gathered, and the police only asked two people to move on: Levant and Harpo—because they were shouting: "It can't last! It can't last!"

In the Stork Club one night, Levant was asked what book he was reading. "I've given up reading books," said Levant, "because it took my mind off myself." When the bill came, he asked his friends: "Do you think a 500 percent tip is enough for someone with an inferiority complex?"

On another visit to the Stork Club, Levant noticed several couples at various tables whom he knew were involved in surreptitious romantic affairs.

He commented, "I've discovered that the thing which takes up the least amount of time yet causes the most amount of trouble is love."

At dinner one night at the Stork Club, café society pianist Eddie Duchin asked Levant to make a baseball wager with him, but Levant refused, saying: "Betting would ruin my boredom."

Undaunted, Duchin later tried to wage a bet with Levant involving slugger Hank Greenberg and oft-wed Tommy Manville. The bet would be: Greenberg would hit thirty home runs before Manville would marry yet again. It was never sealed, however.

A few weeks later, Levant went to the Polo Grounds to see the Giants, and a fan recognized him, asking, "Are you who I think you are?"

"Madam," he replied, "I didn't come to the game to identify myself."

He gave one of his finest supporting performances in the movie *Humoresque* in 1946. Before he saw the film at the opening, a friend offered to show him the glowing reviews from the newspaper critics.

"Not until I see the film," said Levant. "I'm afraid it might prejudice me."

Although he was usually morose, Levant did laugh at a joke, occasionally. In fact, he once laughed so hard that six pills popped out of his mouth.

Levant went to parties every so often, but he was not the type of guest who knew when to leave. Hours after the last guest left a party at Ira Gershwin's house, for example, Levant remained. Finally the great lyricist gave Levant his hat and coat and said: "Oscar, it's time to go. I will forgive you for eating and not running."

At another party, Levant arrived and greeted his fellow guests, actually smiling! "That's to dispel the legend that I'm rude," he explained.

One day late in 1957, he was in a producer's office and was lamenting the fact that Hollywood showgirls weren't as beautiful as they had been back in the 1930s. "Look at this one, for example," he said, pointing to a glossy photo. The producer then explained that the photo he'd chosen was that of Jackie Maye, a noted female impersonator of the time.

But speaking of beautiful women, one night in Sardi's, Levant noticed the young Joan Collins at the next table, wearing a dress with a plunging neckline, leaning low over the table. He kept staring, naturally, and finally leaned over and said: "Joan, I think I've seen every part of your body in the last few minutes except your forehead." She obliged and parted her bangs. Years later when I interviewed Collins, she confirmed that story.

His long-suffering, patient wife June sued him for divorce several times. One time he suggested she hire a lawyer who was a mutual friend. He assured her the lawyer was capable and wouldn't charge her an unreasonable fee. She agreed. Then he called the lawyer and tried to convince him not to accept the case, but to no avail. Levant never spoke to the attorney again.

On a visit to New York, Levant ran into an old friend and said: "You look terrible; you look exhausted, you need a shave, and you look like you haven't slept in a month. No wonder people think we're brothers."

A friend of Levant's told him he had to go home and get a good night's sleep to be ready for an early appointment with his psychoanalyst. "It seems such a waste of time," said Levant, "to be stretching out in a bed to be up in time to stretch out on a couch."

A mother asked Levant if there were any shortcuts her piano-playing son could take, rather than face the daily drudgery of practicing.

"I've been searching for a shortcut for twenty years," he replied. "Meantime, I just practice."

One night my father went to a party with Levant where Levant met a young TV actress named Marjorie Winters. Fifteen minutes later, Levant said: "You're in love with that young fellow who just came in."

"Whatever gave you that idea?" she asked, seemingly bewildered.

"You didn't say hello to him, and before he came in, you were quiet. Now you've become effervescent. You suddenly started to smoke and put your cigarette out after just two puffs. And a minute ago you laughed loudly at something I said. It wasn't that funny. You laughed to make him think you were having a great time. You must have had a quarrel with him, but you're stuck on him."

Six months later, the actress and that young man were married.

After a concert in 1952, Levant, who described himself as "a well-adjusted neurotic," phoned his wife to say that even though the concert had been a great success, he felt, as usual, depressed. Later he phoned her again to say he felt better. "Now I'm just desolate," he said.

Composer Sammy Fain, who wrote "Love Is a Many-Splendored Thing," "Secret Love," and would win two Academy Awards, came to Hollywood from New York the same time Levant arrived from his hometown, Pittsburgh. Both went to the Beverly-Wilshire Hotel, and were assigned adjoining rooms where they devoted the nights to composing.

After a few days, Fain received a notice from the manager of the hotel, requesting him to move because his piano was too noisy at night. Fain asked Levant if he too had received such a note, but Levant said he hadn't. The day after Fain moved out, he checked with the manager about the person who'd complained about his piano playing. The manager gave him the name of the guest: Oscar Levant.

Music critic Virgil Thomson visited Levant in 1951 and noticed that on Levant's piano were two compositions, two newspapers, two half-empty cups of coffee, and the radio and TV were at full blast. Then Levant entered and said: "Why can't I concentrate?"

Levant's presence in any movie added the element of droll humor. He was one of the best character actors of his era and lent a wry perspective to the proceedings. But he was unable to appear in one projected musical, and the part was rewritten. The musical was none other than *Singin' in the Rain*, with Donald O'Connor in the rewritten role. This led to O'Connor's brilliant "Make 'Em Laugh" number, one of the greatest, most athletic, exhilarating in movie history.

One Day in February 1951, Levant lunched in New York with Jule Styne, the composer of *Gypsy*, *Funny Girl*, and *Bells Are Ringing*. Styne swallowed a pill, then realized, to his horror, he'd taken the wrong pill.

"I just took a Dramamine pill! Oscar, what'll I do?"

"Quick!" replied Levant. "Book a reservation on a train or plane and head to the terminal immediately!"

Levant was in New York to discuss television projects. Producers knew he was one of the world's greatest raconteurs and wits and thus hardly needed a script. Plus there were his talents as a concert pianist, which he could use on a talk show to fill in any gaps in discussions.

At a lunch meeting with a producer, Levant was humming a tune he was composing. The producer urged him to write it down. Levant replied: "Not for twenty-four hours. I figure if I can't remember the tune the next day, nobody will."

Those talks came to fruition when he landed a TV show and flew back to California. But before he left for Beverly Hills, Levant hired a maid to take care of the New York apartment while he was in California.

"Her main job, actually," said Levant, "is to answer the phone." Asked why he didn't simply hire a telephone answering service, he replied: "Because I don't want to call the service and hear them tell me that nobody's called. It's bad enough that nobody calls me, but I don't want the service people to know that, too."

Asked how he relaxes, Levant replied: "That's easy. I just grit my teeth. I'm relaxed."

After another return to New York, Levant was surrounded by friends who marveled at his many talents.

"Thanks," replied the perennially neurotic genius, "but my attitude is that adulation doesn't take the place of self-pity."

His TV show turned out to be short-lived, however. After only a few weeks, it was cancelled. But he was philosophical: "As it turned out," he explained about his negotiations with the network, "neither of us was too good for the other."

When he came to New York on business one time, he phoned his wife June in California and said: "I'm here alone. Now I have no one *not* to talk to."

He was giving many one-night concerts on a tour in 1950, and while it was successful, he said: "I don't like doing that. It interferes with my piano practice."

When Levant sat for an interview, he insisted it take place on a Friday, "so that I'll be able to visit my psychoanalyst over the weekend, to get over the interview."

One day Levant made a long-distance, person-to-person call to a music critic in New York.

"How are you, Oscar?" said the critic.

"At these rates," replied Levant, "I can't afford to tell you."

In 1949, Levant visited the office of an executive who had decorated his bookshelves with volumes selected only for size and color. He picked up one of the books—its pages still uncut—and saw it was *The History of Western Civilization.*

"Good!" said Levant. "As long as he's not going to know anything, he might as well not know anything about something highbrow."

Levant's most serious movie critic was Bosley Crowther of the *New York Times.* "I know he's honest and that's what I don't like about him," said Levant, "because when he says he doesn't like me, he really means it."

After a night at the Stork Club, Levant was wondering if he should leave a small but appropriate tip or a large one. "If I leave a small tip," he said, "the waiter will sneer at me. But if I leave a large tip, I'll be able to sneer at the waiter. That's all tipping really means."

One day Levant read a movie column item in a trade paper that referred to a star's "vitality" because the actor had submitted to 123 consecutive hours of close-ups without tiring.

"That's not vitality," said Levant. "The feeblest actor in Hollywood never shows signs of tiring when the camera is doing close-ups of him, and the most powerful actor weakens during long shots.

"In Hollywood, vitality is when you show no signs of getting tired during long shots of you—and some other actor is getting all the close-ups."

Levant told his friend Peter Lind Hayes, the actor and TV personality of the time, that he, Levant, "hates music."

"Then why on earth do you perform concerts all over the country?" asked Hayes.

"Because I like to mix with people. But at a distance."

Levant always thought there was something wrong with him. One day, for example, he coughed and patted his ribs and complained to his wife June: "Either I have a chest full of congealed emotions, or bronchitis."

Levant went to a screening of a movie he disliked and later was asked his opinion by the producer.

"If I were you," Levant said, "I'd advertise it as 'the movie nobody dared make.'"

In January 1962, while the press agent for the play *The Egg* was preparing his program notes, he heard Marcia Levant say her father is Oscar Levant. The press rep's escort, Marshall Breeden, said: "Oh yeah, right. Your father is Oscar Levant and my mother is Joan Crawford."

"But Oscar Levant *is* my father," Marcia Levant protested.

"Well," Breeden replied, "Joan Crawford once *was* my mother." Breeden's father was Phil Terry, who was Joan Crawford's third husband.

Her parents came to New York to attend her opening, and came by train, since Levant didn't like to fly. He told the maid at the Algonquin Hotel: "Please bring me more blankets; You see, I didn't get much affection when I was a child."

In the spring of 1966, Levant had an extensive hospital stay, interrupted by brief visits home. He told a friend: "My home is a nice place to visit, but I'd hate to live there."

GEORGE S. PATTON

I never met General Patton, of course, but I did meet George C. Scott, who, although the third choice for the title role in *Patton* (after Robert Mitchum and Rod Steiger turned it down), gave one of the greatest portrayals in movie history.

The first time my father mentioned "Old Blood and Guts" Patton was in August 1942, when the spit-and-polish general was teaching desert warfare. He wrote that Patton had one favorite way of ending the war, a line paraphrased in the movie: "Put Rommel in the Nazis' best tank, and put me in our best tank, and let's fight it out. This duel would settle it."

In November 1944, Patton was making his historic dash through France, at the head of his Third Army, and sent word to headquarters: "I want just three things," he said. "Gas. Ammunition. To be left alone."

John Hersey, author of the then-popular novel *A Bell for Adano,* had made some undisguised references to Patton. He only met the general once. "Oh, the correspondent from *Life* magazine is here," said one of Patton's aides on that occasion. Patton disliked *Life*'s calling the profile of him "Old Blood and Guts."

The general drew his ceremonial saber and held it at Hersey's middle. Then they both laughed, chatted briefly, and Hersey left. They never, never met again.

The movie *Patton* correctly depicted him as a stickler for the Army's dress code. His soldiers had to have shined shoes, buttons polished, and ties knotted. One day during training in the States, he noticed a man atop a telephone pole. Patton spotted the man's open collar and that he wasn't wearing a tie. He ordered him to come down immediately.

"What's your name and what company are you in, young man?" asked Patton, sternly.

"My name is Cook," replied the man, "and my company is 'Bell Telephone.'"

An officer assigned to Patton's headquarters encountered the general's bull terrier, who was suspicious of all strangers. "That's Willie," Patton explained. "He bites people." Patton told the officer to sit. He obeyed. Willie noticed this, and placed his head gently at the officer's feet.

"Okay," Patton reassured the officer. "And when Willie likes you, you're in!"

Patton and Eisenhower inspected the Buchenwald concentration camp together after it had been liberated. They saw the ravaged bodies, implements of torture, crematoria, piles of shoes, human hair, gold extracted from teeth, and other shocking sights. Eisenhower noticed that Patton lingered behind and said: "Come on, George."

Patton, the toughest general in all of the Army, stood there, horror-struck, and said: "No, I can't take it."

When Patton's men met up with the Third Ukrainian Army, he and the Soviet general held a celebration. After the speeches were made and the toasts gulped, the shrewd Russian general, who'd noticed Patton's sidearm, a custom-made gun, drew his own pistol, an old, standard-issue firearm, from his holster and presented it, beaming, to Patton.

Knowing exactly what the Russian was up to, Patton nevertheless reluctantly and resignedly drew his pistol from his own holster. It had a fine ebony handle and four diamonds in it, a flamboyant indication of his rank. Going strictly by the rules of protocol, he grimly presented it to the smiling Soviet general, in "exchange."

In August 1945, Patton was about to return to Europe, and attended a dinner at which George Jessel, the actor/"Toastmaster General of the United States," was, as usual, master of ceremonies. Jessel told a few stories. Then he introduced General Jimmy Doolittle, whose bombing raid on Tokyo early in 1942 boosted America's morale soon after Pearl Harbor. Then came Patton's turn to speak.

"There are two brave men here tonight, ladies and gentlemen," he began. "Truly brave. The first unquestionably is General Doolittle. And the second is George Jessel, who must be very brave, because tonight he told a joke I first heard at West Point—in 1909!"

When Nazi Field Marshal Kesselring was captured at the end of World War II, in his wallet was found a piece of paper on which was written: *"Der Angriff ist der besten Verteidigung,"* which translates as: "The attack is the best defense." Kesselring explained to his captors that he'd visited the American War College in 1931. The piece of paper was signed: "Patton."

Another Nazi, SS General Walter Krueger, agreed to surrender, but only directly to Patton. He refused to surrender his pistol unless it was to Patton. The arresting captain said: "Take your choice. Either I let you keep your pistol and march you through the city to Patton's headquarters, with your hands over your head, or I take your pistol and let you ride to see the general in my jeep." Krueger surrendered his pistol and entered the jeep.

Two months before his death in October 1945, Patton discussed great soldiers of the past: Napoleon, Hannibal, and Genghis Khan. "What about Julius Caesar," he was asked. "Caesar?" replied Patton, contemptuously. "That guy couldn't have made colonel on my staff."

Late in 1944, General John C. Lee, Eisenhower's chief of Services Forces, gave a dinner in France honoring General Patton and his staff. They spoke of the casualties, and death, and the way they'd prefer to die.

"When I go," Patton said to General Lee, "I'd like it to be in battle. That's the way to finish, fighting to the end."

"I disagree with you, George," said Maj.

General Maurice Rose. "I prefer to survive all battles, and to die in an ordinary way. Well, let's say in a traffic accident."

General Rose was killed in battle in Germany, and Patton died in a traffic accident.

EDWARD G. ROBINSON

The most amazing fact about Edward G. Robinson, born Emanuel Goldenberg in Romania, an icon of American cinema, is that he was never even nominated for an Academy Award! Robinson rose to fame in the early days of Warner Brothers and enjoyed a noble, respected career that spanned half a century. He is probably the greatest character lead actor of them all.

He made his Broadway debut in 1916, billed twelfth at the old Hudson Theater in *Under Fire,* and would appear twenty-nine more times on Broadway, even after becoming one of the movies' biggest stars.

My father and I visited him at his home in Beverly Hills in January 1965. Robinson proudly showed us his magnificent art collection, which included works by the great French Impressionists. But he cautioned me that "for every masterpiece you own, there may be ten terrible paintings in your basement. It's how you put the collection together that makes it great."

During World War II, Robinson broadcast messages over the BBC to occupied countries in seven languages: English, French, Romanian, Russian, German, Polish, and Finnish! When he was asked to give a voice level, he did it in a perfect Oxonian accent. The actor was one of only two people ever permitted by the BBC to smoke a cigar while broadcasting. The other, of course, was Sir Winston Churchill, England's wartime prime minister. After all, where else would they find a movie star fluent in seven languages.

In March 1943, a young man was about to invest all of his money in paintings and asked Robinson for advice.

"Don't do it," the great actor said. "Because it will change your life completely. First, you'll have to rearrange your house, because many people will want to see the paintings, and you'll be anxious to exhibit them. You'll soon be invited to judge art shows, and museums will ask you to join their boards of directors, hoping you'll bequeath the collection to them. And you will join the boards out of vanity. Finally, you'll have to change your will in case your son or daughter shouldn't like the paintings willed to them.

"So unless you really love the pictures, don't start a collection."

Nearly a year later, Robinson was in New York and visited the Museum of Modern Art. He walked through the galleries and stopped to admire a painting by Grant Wood. He studied it from various angles, walking to the left, then to the right, taking a few steps back, and then peering at it close up. He noticed one corner of the painting had been dirtied. Robinson drew his handkerchief and polished the spot by using the standard, low-tech method—first wetting the handkerchief on his tongue.

Of course a museum guard saw this, rushed up to the screen star, and shouted: "Stop it! You can't do that here!"

"Oh yes, I can," replied Robinson, pointing to the card under the painting. It read: "Loaned by Edward G. Robinson."

Like some others with a vast art collection, Robinson began painting, too, and soon afterward said: "I've been painting only one year, and already I can hit the canvas with my brush—nearly every time."

In August 1944, Robinson visited France just after the liberation. Probably because the soldiers had seen him in *Little Caesar* and *Bullets or Ballots*, or countless other such films, he was permitted to fire from an artillery battery in the direction of some distant German installations still in operation.

When he returned to New York, Robinson boasted that he had proof that he had struck a successful blow at Nazism, for an expert Army cameraman photographed the explosion caused by his firing of the gun. Robinson then proudly carried the treasured photograph, for all to see, with its official Army inscription: "Able Gunner Edward G. Robinson."

In January 1945, he was at a dinner in Washington and spotted a notable guest. "I'd love to get his autograph," said Robinson, who had always given but never requested autographs.

After the dinner, Robinson himself was surrounded by autograph seekers, but made his way through the crowd to the dais and meekly asked the guest of honor, General of the Armies George C. Marshall, the highest-ranking soldier of World War II, for an autograph.

By March 1948, Robinson's art collection had become legendary. A visitor to his home asked about how to start a good collection.

His response: "First, you must have the guts and passion to buy your first good picture. That picture will dictate your buying the second good one. And the two, in turn, will tell you what others to buy."

A few months later, Robinson was a guest at the town house mansion of Billy Rose, showman, producer, and largest stockholder in AT&T. He was anxious to get an assessment of his collection from the art connoisseur Robinson. The actor studied the collection, stopped in front of one painting, and puffed on his famous cigar before saying: "That's a Hals, isn't it?" referring to the seventeenth-century Dutch painter Frans Hals.

"Yes, it's a '*Hahls*'," replied Rose, triumphantly correcting Robinson's pronunciation.

"What did it stand ya?" asked Robinson.

"30 Gees," Rose replied, in the vernacular of a Robinson gangster movie.

Robinson smiled, indicating it had been offered to him for much less. Rose smiled back, indicating that he could now get twice as much for it.

When Robinson was appearing with the Theater Guild in their stage productions in New York, he told them he was leaving to begin his career in films. A talent director for a major studio then told him: "But, Mr. Robinson, I don't think you'll do. You're too short to be playing leading parts with a movie company. No one would believe you as a lead."

"Really?" replied Robinson, undaunted. "I suggest you tell that to the president of your studio. I'm three inches taller than he is."

Robinson and his first wife, Gladys Lloyd, divorced in 1956, after twenty-nine years of marriage. Their divorce, however, came as no surprise to my father. On a visit to the Robinson home shortly before their separation was announced, my father noticed that his wife, an amateur painter, had put her paintings on display in front of and covering a Picasso, a Manet, and a Degas.

"That marriage is in trouble," my father later told my mother. Once their divorce proceedings began, Robinson needed to raise money for legal fees. He was forced to sell his beloved collection to Greek shipping magnate Stavros Niarchos, who displayed most of the masterpieces on his huge yacht.

A visitor onboard to see the paintings studied the collection, then said to his host: "Somehow it seems strange, Stavros, to buy, in a moment, a collection that took another man a lifetime to acquire."

"Don't blame me," replied Niarchos. "Somebody had to buy it."

Later the magnificent collection, a reflection of Robinson's sophisticated and expert taste in art, toured museums around the world, billed as "The Stavros Niarchos Collection," which broke Robinson's heart.

By October 1960, Robinson had begun rebuilding his collection, explaining: "I have to make a picture to buy a picture." He even refurbished his house to accommodate his new paintings.

"Paintings are tyrants," he said. "They dictate the architecture of a house. I have no swimming pool. Instead, I have added a new gallery. And then I finished the house to please the paintings."

When *The Prize*, one of his later films, opened in 1963, it played Radio City, and Robinson was in the audience opening night. He played two roles in the film and said of this: "Seeing myself from the audience playing two characters is one of life's most enjoyable love triangles."

His costar in the film, Paul Newman, said: "Eddie's a Method Actor like me. But his 'method' is to act circles around his fellow actors."

CARL SANDBURG

I wish I'd been there when Carl Sandburg, the great poet, author, and foremost Lincoln biographer, said: "Imagine how much richer American history would have been, had there been a Leonard Lyons in Lincoln's time." It must've been one of my father's proudest moments.

In April 1941, my father wrote that Sandburg attended a formal dinner in New York. So, for the first time, he came in black tie. He'd bought a black bow tie. His shirt, however, was blue. "The blue shirt," he explained, "means 'no surrender.'" He then told his host: "It said 'black tie.' If you wanted me to wear more formal attire than that, you should've said so."

On April 14, 1941, the Illinois-born Sandburg made his first visit to a New York nightclub. First he went to the Stork Club, then Café Society. There a customer recognized him and said: "Today is the seventy-sixth anniversary of Lincoln's death. We should be weeping."

"I did all my weeping when I wrote *Lincoln*," Sandburg replied. A year earlier he had turned down a high-priced lecture fee to make an address at Lincoln's grave. "That was fitting," he explained, "for it was my final punctuation mark to *The War Years*."

The Hamilton University Forum invited Erskine Caldwell, author of the classic *Tobacco Road*, to deliver a lecture at one of its sessions. But they withdrew the invitation and invited Sandburg instead, explaining: "The price was the same, but Sandburg also plays the banjo at his lectures."

A writer from California sent Sandburg his newest manuscript and asked that Sandburg read and appraise it. Six months later, the writer sent another letter asking if Sandburg had read it. Six months after that came a third letter. Finally he wrote the postmaster at Flat Rock, North Carolina, where Sandburg lived, asking him to hand deliver his letter and wait while Sandburg read it.

"Well," said Sandburg, who took thirty years to write his prizewinning Lincoln biographies, "We'll just have to send this man's work back to him. He's in too much of a hurry."

Sandburg entered West Point in 1899, in the same class with Douglas MacArthur, but he was dropped two weeks later. He always believed it was for deficiency in arithmetic. But in 1952, he discovered the superintendent's letter, which gave an additional reason: Sandburg's grammar wasn't up to West Point standards.

"I didn't know the definition of a verb," the Pulitzer Prize winner recalled. "Who knows? If I had known back then, maybe *I* would've been running the war in the Pacific!"

That same year he was offered a high fee to write an endorsement for a brand of beer. He turned it down, then out of curiosity tried the beer, and grew to like it.

Soon after that, he received a letter from an Army officer stationed in Germany, saying that he and his wife had just finished reading Sandburg's novel *Remembrance Rock*. They'd read it aloud to each other every night, a process that took a year. Sandburg vowed then and there never again to write a book that couldn't at least be read in a few days.

When Ernest Hemingway won the Nobel Prize for Literature in 1954, he was quoted as saying he thought the prize really belonged to Carl Sandburg. When he heard that, Sandburg said: "Thirty years from now, some bright young person, sitting around, will ask: 'Say, did Carl Sandburg ever win the Nobel Prize?' And then some brighter young person will say: 'Yes, Ernest Hemingway gave it to him.'"

Sandburg revealed that he'd tried his hand at songwriting but didn't get very far.

My parents with Carl Sandburg on the seventy-sixth anniversary of Lincoln's assassination on April 14, 1941. Sandburg said if "The Lyons Den" had been around in Lincoln's time, history would have really known what New York was like.

He couldn't get past the first line: "There goes my date . . . my mate . . . my fate."

He also tried his hand at writing a play, but never got past the first scene. "That's the difference between a writer and a poet," he said. "A writer writes what he can, but a poet writes what he *must*."

In 1956 he published his *Complete Book of Poems*, which sold for $7.50 and contained 863 poems. "What a bargain." he proclaimed. "That's less than a penny a poem!"

In 1958, Sandburg was one of those who supported parole for Nathan Leopold, one of the two convicted murderers in the infamous "Crime of the Century" in the 'twenties. When Leopold was granted parole, he was headed to Puerto Rico to live and work. Changing planes in New York, he phoned Sandburg and told him where he'd be living. Sandburg later said: "It's strange, but my old regiment [in the Spanish-American War], the 6th Illinois Volunteers, slept one rainy night in that same spot in Puerto Rico, sixty years ago."

Early in 1961, Sandburg was in Hollywood to speak at a Friars' testimonial dinner honoring Gary Cooper. He asked George Jessel, aka "The Toastmaster General of the United States," what his speech should contain. "I needn't tell you, the great historian, what to say about a highly overpaid cowboy."

Sandburg's speech began: "Gary Cooper is America's most beloved illiterate."

In April 1961, Sandburg appeared on CBS on a show about the Civil War and was asked how he preferred to be introduced. "It really doesn't matter if you call me a poet, a historian, biographer, guitar player, folk singer, or minstrel," he replied. "I'd rather be known as a man who needs only four things in life: To be out of jail, to eat regularly, to get what I write printed, and then, a little love at home . . . and a little outside." He was eighty-four at the time.

Three years later, President Johnson was hosting a meeting between the presidents of the railroads and the railroad union leaders in the Cabinet Room of the White House. During the negotiations, L B J opened a door and brought in Sandburg and his brother-in-law, and contemporary, Edward Steichen, one of the greatest photographers of all time. The President said to the negotiators: "I just wanted you to see what two tough guys look like."

The only time Sandburg ever posed for a portrait was for a painter named Miriam Svet, who happened to be the wife of movie mogul Dore Schary. Sandburg never had the patience to sit still for a portrait, but agreed only because Schary was a Civil War buff and kept talking about historic battles and old generals while his wife kept painting. And that's the portrait hanging in the Smithsonian Institution's collection of prominent Americans.

In October 1965, my father brought the great historian to the Stork Club. Owner Sherman Billingsley, never known for having spent much time in libraries, asked my father: "What does he do?" "He's Carl Sandburg. He writes books," replied my father, in shock at the question.

Billingsley replied: "Tell him to mention the Stork Club sometime."

A soft drink company offered Sandburg a small fortune to endorse their product, but he declined just as he'd done with the offer to appear in an ad for beer. "Don't you ever do endorsements?" the soft drink company official asked.

"I believe I wrote the longest endorsement in history," said Sandburg, "endorsing Abraham Lincoln. A million-and-a-half words of endorsements."

In 1962, my father was in Los Angeles with my brother Douglas. They went to the 20th Century-Fox studios, where Sandburg was working on a film called *The Greatest Story Ever Told*. His screen credit was unique: "In creative consultation with Carl Sandburg." My father and Sandburg spent some time together, and as they were parting, my father asked: "Carl, is there anything I can do for you?"

Sandburg said, "Lennie, I'd like you to patch up your feud with Walter Winchell." My father had had a well-known feud with Winchell, the most powerful columnist of his day. Winchell, who carried a gun, had even threatened to kill my father, although that was probably said in a perverted sort of jest.

Thinking that Winchell was 3,000 miles away, back in New York, he said: "Sure, Carl, anything for you." Sandburg said: "Good! Now come with me, Lennie, he's right next door!"

My father was shocked when Sandburg led him to the adjacent bungalow, and walked in on Winchell—without knocking. As my father told the story years later, he literally caught Winchell with his pants down. Douglas took a photo of the three, Winchell, Sandburg, and our father, all shaking hands.

JOHN STEINBECK

I was lucky to have met some of the world's greatest authors, who were friends of my parents. There was Hemingway, of course, a close family friend; William Saroyan, W. Somerset Maugham, Richard Condon, Norman Mailer—and John Steinbeck. He was a tall, barrel-chested man, perhaps the only one of that elite group who could be mentioned in the same breath as Hemingway.

His first appearance in "The Lyons Den" came on May 13, 1937, when my father wrote that Steinbeck was working on the dramatization of his book *Of Mice and Men*. He originally envisioned that it would be performed with no intermission, explaining: "Intermissions destroy the mood." He was later convinced otherwise by a producer.

A friend gave Steinbeck two white mice, in honor of *Of Mice and Men*. A few weeks later, she wrote the Steinbecks asking how their new pets were doing.

"I know about men," the author wrote back, "but now I've learned about mice. From those two we now have 114!"

When the book became a best-seller, Mrs. Steinbeck said they would celebrate by making household purchases in keeping with their new station in life. Steinbeck agreed. His first purchase was a new typewriter.

Sam Harris produced *Of Mice and Men* on Broadway and was impressed by Steinbeck's huge build. The producer long ago had managed "Terrible" Terry McGovern, the turn-of-the-century bantamweight and featherweight champion, and told Steinbeck he'd like to promote a fight between the author and Joe Louis, then the heavyweight champion. A few weeks later, Steinbeck won the Critics Circle Prize and wired Harris: "Never mind this. What I'd like you to do is get me some fights!"

In April 1939, Steinbeck's next book, *The Grapes of Wrath*, had been bought by movie mogul Darryl F. Zanuck. But the author told my father he wasn't interested in the money. In fact, he said he budgeted himself to live frugally, on only $1,800 a year. Furthermore, he always traveled in secrecy, avoiding fans and publicity. Headed to New York to complete the sale of the book to the movies, he left California by train, since his wife wouldn't permit him to fly.

Just as the train pulled out of the station, however, he was paged to receive a telegram. Thus discovered by his fellow passengers, he was besieged by autograph-seekers and retreated to the bathroom for five hours. He got off in Salt Lake City and flew to New York.

Nunnally Johnson wrote the screenplay of *The Grapes of Wrath*, but not without extensive consultations with Steinbeck. After their first story conference in April 1939, an exhausted Steinbeck said: "If men from Mars ever come to Earth, I'll bet they all look like Nunnally Johnson."

Two weeks later they had another long, successful discussion about the screenplay, then celebrated over dinner. Lots of wine was consumed. The next day, however, neither could recall what ideas they'd decided upon.

When he was in Chicago in October of that year, reporters couldn't find Steinbeck. They checked all the swank hotels. But they overlooked the Cass Hotel, a $9-a-week establishment where Steinbeck was surely the most famous guest.

During that stay in Chicago, Steinbeck visited the Lying-In Hospital where the movie *The Fight for Life* was being filmed. Between takes he regaled the interns and nurses with tales from his home region in Northern California. Not recognizing the tall, husky author, one intern said: "Those are wonderful stories, Sir. You ought to write a book."

In 1940, Steinbeck won the Pulitzer Prize but didn't keep the $1,000 that came with it. In Monterey, California, he discovered a young, unpublished author who needed money to complete his first novel.

"When I started to write," said Steinbeck, as he gave the budding author the money, "my father loaned me $1,000. It supported me while I was writing *Tortilla Flat*. I was able to repay that loan only after *Of Mice and Men* was published, but by that time, my father had died.

"This," he said, "is the $1,000 I owed my father. Don't pay it back to me. But when you're a successful writer, give it to another young author who shows promise and who needs it, so that he too can pass it on."

In July 1940, Steinbeck was still collecting royalties for the movie version of *The Grapes of Wrath*, but didn't invest any of it in stocks or business enterprises. Instead, those royalties were deposited in a savings bank and spread out among his thirty accounts.

By this time he was world-famous, but he refused to pose for pictures, lest his face become so recognizable he wouldn't be able to go and be a part of the lives of the ordinary people who were the subjects of his novels. It was late in 1940, and war clouds were gathering. Steinbeck said he was taking as many sunbaths as possible, because he foresaw the approach of air raids and blackouts, and a deep suntan was "the last remaining luxury of a human being."

Before Lewis Milestone bought the movie rights to *Of Mice and Men*, Steinbeck conferred with Mervyn LeRoy, who was also interested in it. "I've been thinking a lot about it," said LeRoy, who would later direct *Mister Roberts*, *The FBI Story*, and *Gypsy*. "It's the scene where George kills Lennie. Well, that should be out of the movie version. He doesn't have to do it."

"Mr. LeRoy," replied Steinbeck, no doubt controlling his temper. "It took me almost 200 pages to show inevitability, and now you want to destroy that with one phrase."

"Yeah," replied LeRoy. "Wonderful, isn't it?"

Tortilla Flat opened in New York in May 1942. A few weeks before, "The Lyons Den" carried the following item about the movie: "*Tortilla Flat* provided a field day for scene-stealers. Spencer Tracy said John Garfield tried to steal a scene. Frank Morgan tried to steal it from Garfield, Akim Tamiroff tried to steal the scene from Morgan, and the trained dogs in the picture stole it from everyone." Tamiroff, however, did the best job of scene-stealing. He wore a torn sock, and when the camera was focused on the sleeping men, he attracted attention by wiggling his exposed toe.

In February 1944, Steinbeck was a war correspondent in Africa and Sicily. One of the Allied conquests he covered was the Isle of Capri, one of the most romantic places on earth. The officer commanding the small invading force proclaimed his admiration for writers and a sense of the appropriate. So he said: "I'm now giving Capri back to the writers. It's therefore fitting that you, Mr. Steinbeck, one of America's greatest writers, should do the honors." So it was that Steinbeck's words dictated the official terms by which Capri was liberated from Fascist rule.

Oddly, Steinbeck and Hemingway didn't meet until May 1944, in New York. An onlooker was fascinated by Hemingway's full beard and noticed Steinbeck had started to grow one, too. "Mr. Steinbeck," she asked "why the beard?"

"Obviously, an affectation," he replied.

"And you, Mr. Hemingway? Why the beard?"

"Obviously," replied Hemingway, "to cover a rash."

Still in New York the next month, Steinbeck met Oklahoma Senator Josh Lee, who told the writer he enjoyed *The Grapes*

My father with John Steinbeck in 1958. I have no idea why my father was wearing that silly hat.

of *Wrath*. "Except that California got the grapes," he sighed, "and Oklahoma got the wrath."

Later that summer, Steinbeck met Jimmy Durante, who reminded Steinbeck of the parody of *Of Mice and Men* Durante had included in his show *Keep Off the Grass*. "Sure, I remember," said Steinbeck. Durante then asked Steinbeck to return the favor. Steinbeck agreed, saying he was working on the next edition of *Sea of Cortez*, a nonfiction book about marine biology. Nevertheless, Durante insisted he be mentioned somehow.

Thus in the next edition of *Sea of Cortez*, the index listing the scientific names of all the fish referred to in the book included a listing for: "Durante, Jimmy, p. 599." The book was 598 pages long.

In October 1945, Steinbeck was at the Stork Club, New York's most famous nightclub, and he and a friend were discussing numbers. The friend began to jot down figures on the tablecloth, but Steinbeck stopped him and gave him a piece of paper. He always protected tablecloths from being defaced, because as a young man he'd worked in a laundry, cleaning them.

Shortly after the war, Steinbeck revealed he'd conceived a secret plan to distribute counterfeit money throughout the Reich. It would have cost the Germans a fortune, possibly wrecking their economy. FDR suggested that Steinbeck discuss it with Henry Morgenthau, Secretary of the Treasury. "No, we can't do that. I put people in jail for counterfeiting."

"We also put people in jail for murder," Steinbeck responded, "but that's what they're doing on the other side."

Morgenthau never authorized it.

Steinbeck stuck to his principles of living frugally and avoiding the spotlight. In March 1946, a prominent agent approached him and said: "I think I can get you a lot of money for writing a screenplay for MGM."

Steinbeck said: "But I don't want to write a screenplay for MGM."

The agent replied: "Now I *know* I can get you a lot of money for writing it!"

In September of that year, he finished his novel *The Wayward Bus*. At the Stork Club one night, my father asked him how he feels when a novel is finished.

"Lost," said Steinbeck. "I've been living with the people in this book for all these months, and now I'm through with them. It's like waving goodbye to people on a boat, people you like and know you'll never see again."

In April 1948, Steinbeck was boarding a night flight for California from New York. He met an old friend, and they planned to sit next to one another, but the passenger seated next to Steinbeck refused to exchange his seat.

"Absolutely not," replied the man. Two hours into the flight, the man was about to fall asleep, then he saw a strange animal in a box in Steinbeck's lap. That kept him awake all night. It was Steinbeck's pet gopher, "Willie," whom the writer was bringing to Hollywood as a gift for songwriter Frank Loesser.

One year later, 1949, the organizers of the Cultural and Scientific Conference on World Peace invited Steinbeck to join the list of sponsors, but he refused, saying, "I've known the horrors of war and the horrors of conferences. I can't decide which is worse."

At a Hollywood party one night in 1950, the drinks were flowing freely. Late in the evening, a screenwriter, who'd had a few too many, took offense at something Steinbeck said, and asked him to step outside. "And take off your glasses," he said. Steinbeck replied: "Fine by me, but let me remind you I'm not wearing glasses; *you* are!"

In October 1952, Steinbeck wished to change his official voting residence from California, and so he went to register from his new home in Manhattan. But as a first-time voter there, he was required to bring a diploma to prove his literacy. But he didn't have his diploma. So the clerk asked him to take a written literacy test.

Then he realized he'd left his glasses home. So the Pulitzer Prize winner and author of the recent best-seller *East of Eden* was permitted to vote only after signing an affidavit of literacy. His wife had to hold his hand to show him where the dotted line was.

In August 1954, Steinbeck was using a portable recording machine, and dictated the script for a forthcoming musical. He sent the recordings to the office of his New York producers to be transcribed. A secretary, new on the job, did the transcription, but the dialogue seemed odd. Obviously new to Steinbeck's writings, she'd changed "he don't" to "he doesn't" and "ain't" to "is not" to make it grammatically perfect.

Joan Blondell, a movie star of that era, bought a copy of Steinbeck's *The Red Pony*, and paid $14, then an exorbitant price for a book. She brought it to a party where Steinbeck was a guest.

"Fourteen bucks? You got clipped," said Steinbeck while inscribing the book, thus making it at least 100 times more valuable.

In 1955, the Rodgers and Hammerstein musical *Pipe Dream* was having its Boston tryouts. At one performance, a man in the orchestra section coughed and talked constantly during the first act. He even sighed and grunted loudly whenever the audience laughed at any of the jokes. At intermission, the man seated next to him said to him: "My name is John Steinbeck. I wrote the novel *Sweet Thursday* on which this show is based. Now if you don't come back for the second act, I'll give you a refund."

By October 1956, Steinbeck was once again wearing a beard but complained that "the man with the beard always gets stuck with the check." He explained that "waiters can't distinguish one diner from another. So if all of us reach for the check, the waiter gives it to the one he recognizes: the guy with the beard."

In February 1958, the Steinbecks vacationed in the Caribbean. They visited the Rockefellers' Caneel Bay Plantation on Saint John Island in the Virgin Islands. Many other guests where there, including New York Mayor Robert F. Wagner, who received the following note: "We should meet. As the only two Democrats here, we must stand together. John Steinbeck."

One night in 1958 at Sardi's, the famous New York theatrical restaurant, Steinbeck was discussing the politics of the day: "Nixon is the rich man's poor man, and Rockefeller is the poor man's rich man."

Steinbeck attended the opening night performance at New York's Village Gate of the famed classical harmonica player Larry Adler. After the performance, Adler told Steinbeck he was completing his autobiography, called *From Hand to Mouth*, but was having trouble finishing it.

"Just how *do* you finish a book?" he asked Steinbeck.

"Did you get an advance from the publisher?" asked Steinbeck. Adler said he had.

"Just think of having to return it. That'll make you finish the book."

It took his winning the 1962 Nobel Prize for Steinbeck to give the first speech of his life, in accepting the award. Arthur Miller told him not to be nervous, since the speaker always knows what he's about to say and the audience doesn't. Later, the King of Sweden mentioned that he used to be nervous about speech making, but had many years to practice while Crown Prince.

At the dinner afterward, the King sat next to Mrs. Steinbeck, and they discovered they both grew flowers as a hobby. They then arranged a swap: his tulips for her Long Island roses.

Never one for formality, Steinbeck had bought a white tie full-dress suit for the Nobel ceremony, then told his wife he wanted to be buried in it.

"I want to get at least two wearings out of it," he said, "one standing up, the other lying down." Actually he wore it at least one more time in between those two events: to a white tie dinner at the Kennedy White House in April 1963.

After he returned from Stockholm, Steinbeck, now a Nobel Laureate, was offered several other prizes. One was the Literary Father of the Year award. He declined. The same group called back ten minutes later and offered him another prize: The Father of the Year award. Again he declined. The next day, the Dog Writers of America offered him a prize for Best Dog Book of the Year, for his wonderful book *Travels with Charlie*, about his cross-country trip accompanied only by his French poodle Charlie. Again he declined.

He had no illusions about his lasting fame after winning the Nobel Prize. Soon after he returned to New York he said: "It'll soon be over. About five days. One good murder case in the press, and the Prize will be forgotten."

John O'Hara was delighted to see Steinbeck win the Nobel Prize, and wrote him: "Congratulations! I can think of only one other American writer who deserves it."

Steinbeck met Marc Chagall, who said: "We have it easier, because we can try different colors, other materials. But you are limited to words." Steinbeck said painting was more difficult, to which Chagall said: "But there is no Nobel Prize for art."

"And maybe that's a good thing," replied Steinbeck. "A Nobel Prize for art might have a disastrous effect on the artist's future work. The Peace Prize winners can't do much peace work after that, and the writers often have to stop writing. The prize money goes anyway."

Two years after he won the Nobel Prize, Steinbeck was invited to the USSR, which for years sold his books without ever paying him—or anyone else for that matter—the royalties to which writers are entitled. He was asked to make a radio address to the workers in the publishing industry throughout Russia. He took the mike and said he was glad to speak to his fellow toilers in the book publishing industry instead of to their bosses, who'd been cheating him and probably cheating them as well.

A young correspondent about to go to Russia in 1965 asked Steinbeck for advice. He advised him to prepare by reading Gorky, Tolstoy, and Dostoyevsky. "No man can hope to understand Russia unless he's read those authors. You can learn more truths about a nation from its novels than from its textbooks."

In 1967, after a visit to South Vietnam, where his son was serving, Steinbeck applied for visas to North Vietnam and China. His name was, of course, known to both legations. He answered every question on the applications, including a request for him to list every book he'd ever written. The visas were then denied him.

Later that year, he was asked to toast a couple at their wedding. "I can't wish you happiness; you have that now. Nor would I wish you sadness; that will come. But I *can* wish that you'll comfort each other."

His best-selling book *Travels with Charlie* first appeared in *Holiday* magazine. Then the editor, Ted Patrick, wrote *The Thinking Dog's Man* and asked Steinbeck to write an introduction to that book. Steinbeck agreed. He wrote about why he can't write introductions, and took 4,000 words to explain.

"Writers," he observed, "are entertainers. They're rated just above the seals and far below the clowns. If some, like Homer, turn out to be great, that's fine and all to the good. But primarily the writer is an entertainer. But before a writer can be deemed truly great, in addition to possessing rare talent, he must have been dead at least 200 years."

HARRY S. TRUMAN

I've been lucky to have met several U.S. presidents: most recently Bill Clinton, as well as Reagan and Nixon. I wish Adlai Stevenson, who hosted us at his home in Libertyville, Illinois, in 1954, had been on that list. Indeed, the following year, I ran for president of my fifth-grade class at P.S. 9, but came in second.

Governor Stevenson sent me a telegram the next day—I guess when the "returns" were in!—consoling me, saying it's not so bad to come in second for president.

But my experience with Harry S. Truman was unique. In 1952, he welcomed my family to the White House, where he gave us a tour of the private quarters. I was eight, and my younger brother Douglas was five. At one point, Mrs. Truman, aka "The Boss," took us aside and into another part of the living quarters to meet her mother, Madge Wallace, shortly before she died. Mrs. Wallace was born in Jackson County, Missouri, in 1862. That always amazes me, since I can say I met someone born during the Civil War and the Lincoln Administration.

I've been told that while the President was showing my parents the recently renovated South Portico, I had my feet up on his desk in the Oval Office. When they returned, my parents were, of course, mortified, but the President laughed and said: "Better he sit there now than when he's grown up."

By then, my father had known the Trumans for a decade; the first mention of HST in "The Lyons Den" came in November 1942, when then-Missouri Senator Truman described a conference as "a slightly organized waste of time."

In October 1944, my father reported that Senator Truman had a good friend in John Snyder, vice president of the First National Bank of St. Louis, whom Truman would later appoint as secretary of the Treasury.

When Truman's name began to be mentioned for the vice presidential nomination, Truman promised Snyder he'd never accept it.

But once the Democratic National Convention of 1944 got underway in Chicago, Truman's name was again high on the list. When he heard that, Truman called his banker friend and asked to be released from his promise. He was released, and Truman got the nomination.

A month after he'd become president, following Roosevelt's death on April 12, 1945, Truman had a visit from a friend and invited him to use the White House swimming pool with him. After they changed, they approached the pool, when suddenly six Secret Service agents appeared and accompanied them.

Nearing the pool, the president said: "You don't want this job."

Immediately after being sworn in, Truman entered the Cabinet Room. Bob Hennagan was there. He was a Missouri politician who as chairman of the Democratic National Committee was the man who'd convinced FDR to name Truman as his running mate. He was seated next to President Truman and asked the newly inaugurated Commander-in-Chief if there was anything he could do for him.

"Yes," replied Truman. "You can go to church and pray for me."

In late May 1945, Truman awarded the Congressional Medal of Honor to Infantryman Jake Lindsay at a joint session of Congress. All the members of the Cabinet were assembled. Before ascending the podium, Truman approached Attorney General Francis Biddle, tapped him on the shoulder, and said: "I want to see you a minute." Biddle nodded and stepped aside. Truman then uttered six words that marked the first change in the Cabinet from the Roosevelt Administration:

"Can I have your resignation today?"

Later he appointed Biddle to be a judge at the Nuremberg War Crimes Trials.

On a Sunday in 1945, Truman asked a White House employee to bring a hammer to his bedroom. The employee went to the carpentry shop and then to the machine shop, but both were closed. A Secret Service man found the carpenter's weekend address and went there. The carpenter immediately donned his overalls and rushed back to the White House, where he went to the President's room.

"All I wanted is a hammer," said the President. "I'm hanging some pictures in my room and like to do it myself."

A Scandinavian diplomat was in Washington in September 1945. Asked the difference in diplomacy between FDR and Truman, he replied: "Under Roosevelt, every day was Christmas. Under Truman, every day is Thursday."

One day in October 1945, Truman had band leader Kay Kyser over for lunch. Kyser told the President his eighty-four-year-old mother had stayed up until 3 a.m. the night before to watch her son entertain at the Naval Academy's Centennial celebration. Later, Kyser's mother arrived at the White House, and Truman said to her: "You shouldn't stay up so late, Mrs. Kyser. You should go to bed early."

Then Truman added: "I get that from my mother so often, it's a pleasure finally to tell it to someone else."

On December 5, 1945, the war had been over for more than three months, and Truman could afford to relax a bit. He entertained film producer Hal Wallis and gave him a package of matchbooks as a souvenir. Each matchbook read: "I stole this from Harry S. Truman."

Wallis thanked the President and pocketed the matches. "That was just an ordinary one," said the President, who then took out another package of matches and gave it to Wallis.

The new matchbooks had inscribed on their covers simply: "The President."

"Impressive," said Wallis. "Did you have these made?"

"Oh no," said the President. "They come from the President Hotel in Kansas City."

Seven years before my visit to the White House, the President had invited my parents and my two older brothers, George and Warren. George Lyons inquired about the President's mother, Martha Ellen, whom the President always called "Mama" and who was then ninety-two. Mr. Truman showed George her picture and assured the boys that their mother, too, would be proud of them if they studied and worked hard. My brother Warren mentioned me (I was thirteen months old) and asked the President if he had any sons. "No," replied Truman. "Just Margaret."

Then he gave my brothers his latest set of matches, with the same inscription on a matchbook he would later give to me. Theirs read: "Swiped from Harry S. Truman."

In February 1946, Truman lunched with several actors, including William Bendix, who asked HST what he planned to do when he left office.

Truman replied: "It's wrong for a former President to go into retirement. When we're in the White House, we accumulate a certain amount of knowledge and experience—perhaps, in some cases, not much—but enough to be useful to our government. This knowledge and experience should not be wasted. But under our present laws, there is no provision for utilizing the capabilities of a former President in any capacity.

"When I leave the White House, I hope to continue to serve this country. I'll go back to Congress, as John Quincy Adams did."

At the 1946 White House Photographers Dinner, Truman was asked to pose with two guests. They requested that he stand in the middle.

"I always stand in the middle," replied the President of the United States.

In August 1948, every election poll put Truman's Republican opponent, New York Governor Thomas E. Dewey, far ahead. Truman was even urged to drop out gracefully, that it wasn't too late to save face. He replied by telling the doubters that when he was running behind in the polls for re-election to the Senate in Missouri against Manvel H. Davis, FDR called him and suggested the same thing: that he drop out of that race. Roosevelt promised him a government post of almost equal importance.

"I promise you, Mr. President, I'll be elected," he told FDR. Then he told a visitor: "And I give you that same promise, although I may be the only one who thinks so. I will be elected."

Still far behind in the polls for the election of 1948, Truman and his vice presidential candidate, Alben Barkley, were asked by a photographer to pose for a photo. "Mr. President," said the photographer, "my paper doesn't have a large circulation, but you may get some votes out of this."

The two candidates posed for twenty-five photos, after which Truman slapped Barkley on the back, saying: "You know, Alben, I don't think Dewey would be doing any of this darn foolishness."

Four days after he was inaugurated in 1949, Truman said he never doubted he'd be nominated by his party. "Anybody who sits behind this desk and can't get his party's nomination is a hopeless man. Even Hoover did it."

At a White House dinner for correspondents, Truman discussed some of the privileges that come with the Presidency. "There are some, that's true," he said. "The President does have them all, except that the job gives him no time to take advantage of any of them."

The next day he told a group of White House visitors: "Everybody keeps asking for my autograph and forgets that maybe I'd like some autographs, too. So here," and he passed out slips of paper for them to sign.

In November 1949, President Truman received a letter from Saudi Arabia's King Ibn Saud. It came in a large fancy envelope covered with an impressive assortment of royal seals. Inside was a letter that began: "Magnificent One."

"Does he mean *me?*" asked Truman.

A few days later, Truman announced his support of a program to admit 100,000 displaced Jewish persons into Israel. Then a second letter came from King Ibn Saud to the President. This one began: "Dear Sir."

Early in 1950, a freshman Congressman took his family to the White House to meet the President, who showed the young legislator a map marked to indicate every whistle-stop Truman had made on his successful come-from-behind 1948 campaign.

"I know what you're thinking," he told the young lawmaker. "When I first came to Washington, I wondered how the hell I ever got here. Six months later, I was wondering how the hell *everyone else* got here!"

In July 1950, a visitor to the White House asked about Mrs. Truman's health; she'd been suffering from a cold. The President said she was better. Then he stared out the window and spoke of his need for her. To illustrate this, he drew from his desk drawer an old, faded photo of Bess Truman. He removed the pins that held the picture to the frame. Between the photo and the cardboard back was a card on which was written: "God bless you and bring you safely home to me, my love, Bess." Mrs. Truman had given it to the President during World War I, on the eve of his departure for France and the battlefront.

President Truman was an avid pianist, but only once were his talents broadcast to a national radio audience. It was on Election Night, from the Kansas City hotel suite where he was awaiting the returns. He sat alone in his room, playing the piano, and his daughter Margaret was asked if she would open the door to let the music be heard on national radio. She obliged—but only when the President got past a difficult portion of the piece to a part she knew he could play flawlessly. When that difficult part came around again, she closed the door.

Margaret Truman, an avid concert singer, appeared on a radio show with Ginger Rogers, also from Independence, Missouri. The script called for the actress to ask the First Daughter: "How's the Judge?" "Oh, Dad's not a judge any longer," Miss Truman was to reply, before ticking off all of her father's subsequent government posts.

"Can't hold a job, eh?" Rogers was to reply. But Margaret Truman refused to say the lines.

"Poke fun at me if you like, but I won't be used as a means to poke fun at members of my family," she told them.

In September 1951, Truman visited a Washington exhibition of a Viennese art collection. One of the items on display was a fifteenth-century hunting horn. The President stopped to admire it, picked it up, examined it, then asked his guide: "Does it still work?"

"Why, I don't know, Mr. President," the guide replied. "No one's ever tried it."

"May I?" responded the President.

"I don't see why not," said the guide.

And so, the thirty-third President of the United States blew into an Austrian hunting horn that probably hadn't been used in nearly six hundred years.

It worked.

During his Presidency, Truman had to move across the street to Blair House between December 1949 and March 1952, while the White House was undergoing a major renovation. He became uneasy about the number of guards assigned to accompany him, morning, afternoon, and evening, from his new home to his office. He suggested that a bridge be built between both places to avoid the need for the detail of bodyguards. He was overruled, however, and reminded that such a bridge would only be temporary, and also that a bridge can be blown up.

In October 1951, Truman announced the Soviet Union's second atomic bomb test, and recalled the first time he ever heard of an atomic bomb project. It was while he headed the Senate's War Investigating Committee. He'd learned of a mysterious secret project, costing more than $2 billion, about which no one had any information. So he called Secretary of War Henry L. Stimson and began to ask questions.

"Please don't inquire, Senator Truman," Stimson replied. Truman had faith in Stimson and asked no further.

The Trumans had good friends from Kansas City named Evans who sent the President homemade pies during his visits to that city. When he returned there in April 1952, Truman wondered why the pies had stopped coming. Mrs. Evans explained that she thought they were unwelcome since nobody had ever thanked her for them.

When she resumed sending pies to the Trumans, she received a letter on White House stationery. It was signed by President Truman and his dinner guest that night, Dwight D. Eisenhower.

In May 1952, a young friend of the Truman family dined with the First Family and John W. Snyder, by then secretary of the Treasury. The young man gave Secretary Snyder a dollar bill and asked him to sign it. Truman noticed this and warned that writing on any bill could make it invalid, and it was illegal. But Snyder wrote his name anyway.

"Let me sign it, too," said the President. He wrote above Secretary Snyder's signature: "This bill is invalid if offered for exchange. Harry S. Truman."

In September 1952, General Eisenhower,

the Republican nominee to succeed Truman, paid a visit to the White House. He told Truman he'd just returned from Europe and said that people "were spreading stories about my wife and even about my son."

Truman replied: "If you're going to get into politics, I suggest you go right over to Republican HQ and get one of their elephant hides for yourself." Then he spread his index finger and thumb into a long span, adding: "This thick!"

In October 1952, Truman was making a whistle-stop tour, campaigning for Adlai Stevenson. At one stop, in Kalispell, Montana, a cowboy rode up on a Palomino, and the President walked over to him and said: "I bet I can tell you how old that horse is." He then grabbed the reins, parted the horse's jaws, counted its teeth, and said: "Five years?"

"And four months," replied the amazed cowboy.

As his days in office began to dwindle, he reflected on the momentous decisions he'd had to make and whether his successor would ask for his advice.

"They generally don't," Truman reasoned. "Children seldom listen to their elders, and the same usually goes for presidents, too. Both prefer to make their own mistakes."

In December 1952, a group of government officials paid him a visit at the White House, and Truman revealed that, after taxes, his take-home pay for that year was a paltry $4,200.

The President invited my parents to dine with them on the Trumans' last night in the White House, January 19, 1953. When it came time for dinner, Truman had headed toward the formal State Dining Room, but then was reminded that this would be an intimate family dinner, in the smaller dining room adjacent. During the meal, he mentioned a telegram he'd received after his last fireside radio chat. It had come from Mrs. Bob Fitzsimmons, widow of the former heavyweight champion. "You're a champion too," she wrote.

At the start of the meal, the President, aware that my father had been licensed to practice law before the Supreme Court, appointed him a federal judge. My mother, perhaps because of her conversational skills and rudimentary knowledge of Spanish, was named ambassador to Mexico.

They resigned over dessert, having served "from soup to nuts" (as my father liked to tell the story).

During the meal, the President reminisced about the speeches he'd given. There was a time when words came to him with difficulty. He told my parents of his first campaign speech, in Jackson County, Missouri. "I got up, said nothing, and sat down," he laughed. "I had nothing to say. They liked that. People rarely come just to hear speeches anyway. I got elected."

Truman reflected on earlier campaigns and remembered that in none of them did he ever have the support of the press. "A dusty old car and a lot of traveling to meet the people won for me each time."

Official White House statistics show Truman signed his name about 167,000 times a year. His signature never changed over the years. Some old Jackson County bonds that he'd signed were found, and Truman compared his old signatures with those done as President. The same.

As the evening neared its end, Truman realized that for the first time in many years, he had no homework, no documents to study, none to sign. More important, he had no regrets about his decision to drop the two atomic bombs on Japan: a decision that affected millions; perhaps the most difficult decision any President has ever had to make.

The last thing he said to my parents at

the end of the evening was: "I've done the best I could, the best for the people. I hope it was enough."

In 1934, when Harry Truman had left Independence, Missouri, for Washington as the new senator, his neighbors presented him with luggage. Nineteen years later, President Truman's baggage when he left the White House included the battered remnants of those suitcases with which he'd arrived at the capital.

Once Eisenhower was sworn in, Margaret Truman, for the first time in her life, addressed her father as "Mr. Truman." She told him it was the first time she could address her father that way, the first time in her life he had no title, held no office. He'd been a Jackson County judge when she was born, then chief judge, U.S. senator, vice president, then the thirty-third President, and finally, again, a private citizen.

In the years after his presidency, he'd often visit New York, taking reporters on his morning "constitutional," during which many of them had trouble keeping up with him. On an earlier visit to New York, while still in office, my father had offered Truman tickets to the Broadway musical *Gentlemen Prefer Blondes*.

"Thanks, but no thanks," said Truman. Then looking toward Bess, he said: "Some gentlemen prefer gray."

On their post–White House visits to New York, the Trumans often attended Broadway shows. In 1961, they went to see the show *Do Re Mi*. Phil Silvers, TV's Sergeant Bilko, was the star of the show and was told the Trumans were in the house.

"Quick!" he said to costar Nancy Walker before his solo clarinet number. "Hum me 'The Missouri Waltz.'" She hummed a tune, which he played instead of the song in the script. The song he usually played was: "Beautiful Ohio."

On another occasion in New York, Truman corrected a friend who'd referred to him as the "ex-President."

"An 'ex-President,'" he said, "means you were turned out of office after one term. I wasn't." Truman preferred "former president."

Early in 1954, he was back in town and couldn't take his morning walk because of a snowstorm. Instead, he fulfilled a longtime desire to visit the Metropolitan Museum of Art, where the director, Francis Henry Taylor, gave him an 8 a.m. tour. Truman, who'd read every book in the Independence, Missouri, library by the time he turned sixteen, gave a running commentary on the times and the people and places depicted in the paintings.

Dr. Taylor then reminded Truman that he was one of the few recent heads of state who didn't paint. Churchill, Eisenhower, and even Hitler painted.

Truman, referring to his abilities on a keyboard, said: "Oh, I'm an amateur in another field." Dr. Taylor took the cue. He unlocked a sixteenth-century piano on display and invited Truman to play in the Metropolitan where it was still too early for the public to witness this historic moment. But the piano was so old, no sound came out.

"There's only one piano in worse shape than this," said Truman, "and that's the one in the White House."

Setting out to return to his hotel, Truman waved to workers shoveling snow in the cold outside the museum.

"That's the advantage of being a former President," he said. "If I were campaigning, I'd have to go out in the cold and shake hands."

A few weeks later, reminiscing about all of his campaigns, Truman said he had voted for himself only once. "That was in 1948 when I figured I needed every vote."

In December 1955, my father accompanied a troupe performing the Gershwin classic *Porgy and Bess* to Moscow. Truman, who'd been sent daily copies of "The Lyons Den" after he left office, wrote my father. He warned him "not to get into any trouble in Russia. Remember, I'm out of office and am in no position to bail you out."

Truman returned to New York in October 1956 on a train that was due in at 6 a.m. Several friends came to greet him, sure he would stay in his berth for at least an extra hour of sleep. So they arrived at 7:30, but he was long gone.

"I'd been up for at least an hour," he explained later. "I never could get used to your city hours. I keep farm hours: up at 6 a.m., and if I have cows, then it'd be up at 4 a.m."

In 1957, a proposal had been put forth to give the President's Cabinet the power to remove him from office if its members felt he was unable to carry out his duties. Truman lectured at NYU's School of Education that May and opposed it. "It would weaken the Presidency," he said. "Besides, if I were President and on my deathbed, and the Cabinet came to look me over, I'd fire them all."

Whenever he'd visit New York, Truman often signed autographs, especially dollar bills. "It's another way of fighting inflation," he said, "by taking these bills out of circulation. People save these bills; and by not cashing them in it becomes an interest-free loan to the government."

In March 1958, Truman was honored at a dinner in Philadelphia. He tried to cut short all of the lavish praise heaped upon him because, he explained, he might miss his plane to Kansas City, and his waiting wife Bess would be angry.

In July 1958, the Trumans sailed home from Europe aboard the S.S. *Independence*. During the voyage, Truman got a haircut from the ship's assistant barber. His boss lamented the fact that he'd been at lunch when Truman came by the ship's barbershop. "When will I ever get another chance to cut a President's hair?" he asked.

Truman heard about that, and on the last day of the voyage came in for a second haircut.

The next month, Truman revealed a little-known incident concerning Roosevelt's first vice president, John Nance "Cactus Jack" Garner. On Garner's last day in office, January 20, 1941, only three people came to say goodbye. One was the then-Senator Harry Truman.

Years later, when Truman was campaigning for election to a full term in the White House, his train was due to reach Uvalde, Texas, Garner's hometown, at 6 a.m. He wired Garner that a reporter thought the former vice president would never appear at the train station. Not because of the early hour, but because he'd been against FDR's New Deal.

Truman bet the reporter that Garner would be there. At six the next morning, the train pulled in. Only one person was at the station to greet Truman: the thirty-second Vice President of the United States, John Nance "Cactus Jack" Garner.

In 1959, Truman was reminiscing about his Presidency and his controversial decision to fire General Douglas MacArthur as commander in Korea. "I dreamed I gave him an order," said Truman, "and he obeyed."

One of the few things I hated about my childhood was being forced to take piano lessons. I had no talent, no interest, and today use that as the reason I didn't wind up in the Red Sox outfield, next to my idol Carl Yastrzemski. In December 1961, my parents took my brother Douglas and me for a reunion with the Trumans, who were in town, hoping that the best piano player ever to live in the White House would encourage us to keep taking lessons.

But Truman, to my everlasting gratitude, crossed up my parents by saying: "Boys, don't play unless you get fun out of it."

When Lyndon Johnson was campaigning

for vice president in 1960, he came to Truman for advice, since he'd been through it all in 1944. Truman advised Johnson that the first speech was the most important one. It was best, he advised, to appear at a place and occasion as distant as possible from Texas and the Texas image. Johnson therefore selected Boston for his first speech.

As soon as he arrived, his Democratic hosts had him ride a horse, and gave him a 10-gallon hat to wear, to look like the Texan he was.

ORSON WELLES

I recently found a recording of my father being interviewed on some radio show about fifty years ago. He described Orson Welles as "my best friend." I'm not surprised, given the time we spent with him, especially in Spain. His youngest daughter Beatrice has become one of our good friends, so the association continues.

If he'd never made a movie nor set foot on a Broadway stage nor uttered a word on radio or television, Orson Welles would've still been the most amazing person you'd ever meet. He filled a room in every sense of the word. Welles was huge by then, with a trademark gigantic cigar and a laugh that shook the walls. He was an expert in magic, politics, history, art, literature, culture, music, world affairs—and bullfighting. Besides Ernest Hemingway, who'd arranged for my first summer traveling across Spain with the great matador Antonio Ordoñez,

Joking with Orson Welles circa 1940.

Welles was the only other American all the great matadors wanted to impress. And he tutored me, honing my knowledge of *"La Fiesta Brava."* He was many people rolled into one. A genius.

His father had been somewhat of an inventor. In 1913, he had discarded all the inventions for the automobile he'd been working on because he was certain cars were just a passing fad. He turned to aviation, but decided that that was just a fad, too. He came to the same decision regarding the radio, the medium that ironically would make his son world famous twenty-five years later. Instead, he devoted all his time to inventing a collapsible kit for picnics, of all things. And from that he finally made his fortune, because when America entered World War I, the collapsible kit became standard army equipment.

On Sunday night, October 30, 1938, Halloween eve, Welles and his Mercury Theater cast shocked the country with their all-too-realistic performance of H.G. Wells's *War of the Worlds*, setting off a panic from thousands of listeners who thought a real invasion was taking place in New Jersey. The next week, my father reported in his column that Macy's requested 10,000 copies of the program and that several NBC radio engineers in New Jersey had called their office in Rockefeller Center during the broadcast, asking how long they should stand by their posts. The next day, they were called in for reprimands. Not because they believed that Martians had invaded, but because they were thus admitting they'd been listening to Welles's broadcast on rival CBS!

A few days later, Welles spotted a friend on a mid-Manhattan street, crept up behind him, then yelled: "Boo! I'm the man who scared a nation!" During the broadcast, Welles mentioned the General Motors building, so Pontiac presented him with a painting of Martians attacking a 1939 model of their car.

When I knew Orson Welles, he was married to actress Paola Mori, a titled Italian brunette of stunning beauty. My father had befriended Welles years earlier, when he was married to Rita Hayworth. They were at ease together.

But Welles had a strange way of doing some things. He didn't know how to handle money, a requisite skill for any producer-director. His movie *The Trial* had only one cast member uncredited: his wife Paola. A simple oversight. But he admired other filmmakers who could handle money, especially producer Dino De Laurentiis, who hired him to direct the Abraham-Isaac-Jacob portion of *The Bible*. "Dino became a success," said Welles, "because he started doing that which nobody else in Italy did. He paid his bills."

Perhaps his inability to be overly concerned with money dated back to his youth. When he was fifteen, he went with his guardian to open the vault left by his late father. It contained his bequest to Orson: a gold ring—from which the diamond had been removed and hocked! When asked once why he was directing a portion of someone else's movie, he explained: "An Angel came unto me and said: 'Orson, get thee down to De Laurentiis and sign—For $200,000.'"

One evening during the war, Welles was at the White House, and President Roosevelt said: "Orson and I are the two greatest actors. He stirs up the world while I pour oil on the troubled waters."

On another occasion, he was invited to attend the Gridiron Dinner, one of Washington's most prestigious events, and sit on the dais with the President. He arrived on time, but fled before entering the room. The banquet proceeded, and the Gridironers began presenting their skits. When a friend noticed Welles had mysteriously left, he phoned him at his hotel room. "You must take a bow," said the friend. "They're doing the Martian skit. Why'd you leave?" "I noticed everyone else was in white tie and tails," said Welles. "I was only wearing a tuxedo."

In August 1939, Welles moved his family to Hollywood. Their next-door neighbor came over to welcome them. He introduced her to his young daughter. "Does she want to be an actress?" asked the neighbor. "Not until she's at least two," replied Welles. "I want her to have a normal childhood."

"Very sensible," replied the neighbor: Shirley Temple.

He had unusual work habits. For example, he was set to produce, direct, write, and star in a movie called *Heart of Darkness* in 1939. But he had to postpone the production indefinitely. A visitor saw the first page of his screenplay and noticed that Welles had written only one line of direction: "*Heart of Darkness* by Orson Welles. Scene One, Opening Shot. I enter. (Close-up) Fadeout."

When he agreed to direct the film version of *The Trial*, the Franz Kafka surrealist drama, he never intended to costar as well. "I asked all the British knights—Olivier, Gielgud, Richardson, Redgrave, and Jackie Gleason, but couldn't get any to agree," he explained, thus providing probably history's only sentence that had both references to British acting knights and Jackie Gleason.

He had the mixed blessing of writing, directing, and playing the title role in what is generally considered the greatest movie of all time, *Citizen Kane*, when he was just twenty-six, and forever would try to top himself. At the closing credits of a private screening, Charlie Chaplin got up and shouted; "Welles is a genius."

"But Charlie, you're the only genius in Hollywood," said Mrs. Douglas Fairbanks Jr. "Well, now there's another in town," he replied.

René Clair, the great French director, saw *Citizen Kane* and proclaimed that it would influence moviemaking for generations. "Every director will henceforth use some of the Welles technique, either deliberately, or unconsciously," he correctly predicted. When someone questioned this, Clair told him: "There's already one director who's already taken four ideas from the Welles film: *me!*"

For a time Welles lived in New York. It was while process servers were seeking him, so he leased a hideaway apartment on West Eighty-First Street. Nobody in the neighborhood knew he lived there until one night when Welles came home late and had forgotten his key. He stepped through the large, heavy glass door, revealing his presence to the neighbors. Word spread quickly, and the next day the process servers found him.

Among his endless talents, he was a superb prognosticator. Early in 1944, he was entertaining soldiers at a base in Alaska and predicted the details of the most closely guarded secret of the war: the exact date of the D-Day invasion. He put it on a piece of paper, which was then sealed. The paper was unsealed after June 6, and handed to the commanding general of the base. He looked at the paper and said: "We're in a helluva state, when I, a general, am kept in the dark on a top secret, while a civilian, an actor with White House connections, is let in on it."

He once was invited to compete on a TV quiz program. Welles was assured he'd win between $150,000 and $200,000. "But what if they throw me a question about football?" asked Welles. "I don't know the first thing about football." He was assured he'd have a look at the questions before the show. "I was shocked," he told my father. "There are schoolteachers dreaming of a prize like that. And I'd be competing against people who honestly felt they could win." Thus Welles, who could write plays, novels, and

Orson Welles with my mother Sylvia, November 1938.

movies, do card tricks, act, make political speeches, who even "sawed" Marlene Dietrich in half, at last found something he could not do: Go on a rigged TV quiz show.

He and his wife Paola took daughter Beatrice everywhere with them, tutoring her years before homeschooling became popular among some parents. "Beatrice can read, write, add, paint, dance, and speaks three languages. Girls are born knowing things," said Welles.

In September 1944, Welles told my father some of the strange consequences of his *War of the Worlds* broadcast. He received many crank notes, including from one writer who sent him a series of threats, vowing to shoot him during a performance of *Julius Caesar*, the play that Welles produced shortly after the broadcast.

This production of *Julius Caesar* was done in modern dress. In one scene, Welles had to stand alone in front of the stage, with a series of spotlights on him. "I was afraid

that at any moment a shot would ring out," he confessed. "I made a wonderful target. It may have been the first time an actor shied from the spotlight. And it was the only time I was glad a play I produced had a short run."

In 1945, a roll call was conducted by the Independent Citizens Committee for the Arts, Sciences, and Professions. "Fredric March?" called the chairman. "Present," replied the great actor. Several other names were called, and the chairman then called out: "Orson Welles?" "Omnipresent," he replied in his famous deep voice.

The next year he produced, directed, and starred on Broadway in *Around the World*, adapted from Jules Verne's *Around the World in Eighty Days*. It had sixty-five speaking parts and thirty-four scenes. In fact, not one but two drama critics reviewing the show said Welles had "thrown in everything but the kitchen sink." So the second night, Welles took his curtain calls holding a kitchen sink. It didn't help. The show closed after just seventy-four performances.

For a year and a half, Welles's Mercury Theater employed a young, aspiring actress as its telephone operator. "Such is my ability to spot raw talent," Welles would joke years later. Her name was Judith Tuvim, and she shot to stardom and won the Oscar for best actress as Judy Holliday.

My older brother Warren was stagestruck at an early age. He would go on to win an Obie award for coproducing John Guare's early masterpiece *The House of Blue Leaves* in 1971. But it was Orson Welles's advice early on that helped mentoring him. "Don't encourage him, don't discourage him from a career in the theater," Welles told my father. "Just courage him."

He then wrote my brother a letter of advice: "Listening to your elders is sort of a tax levied on youth in the theater. I suggest that you pay this tax conscientiously, and when you get old yourself, for God's sake, try not to talk so much. I urge you to give us elder troupers the treatment we need, not what you think we deserve. Remember how much harder acting is for those of us who imagine we've begun to learn a little something about it. To say nothing of stage fright.

"An actor doesn't recover from stage fright; he acquires it through bitter years of experience. Someday it may fall to your lot to find yourself working with some elderly character lady who has no stage fright at all. There are about seven of these in the Western hemisphere and unless you are a child actor or a cunning little puppy dog, such an actress will wrap up your scene and carry it briskly away from you. All of the more venerable character men suffer from stage fright, if only because they have played some time in their careers with one of these terrible old ladies.

"Learn to applaud. It's hard work. By the last curtain call your arms should ache as though you'd been conducting a symphony. When you find yourself sitting in an audience, and find it in your heart to approve, set a good example to those around you.

"Just remember that in every generation, there are one or two actors adored by their critics and detested by their colleagues. They serve a purpose; when you're a hit, remember that these bad actors have had much better notices than you ever will. If God made you an actor, it would be ungrateful of you to make yourself a critic. There are enough critics in the world, and there is no such thing as a superfluous ovation.

"During rehearsals, never say to the director: 'I don't see the part like that' or 'That's not how I feel it.' There are a dozen correct ways of doing any part, one of which is bound to approximate what even the stupidest director thinks he has in mind. Your own preference or interpretation can always be quietly smuggled into your performance. Even when the director catches you red-handed with this contraband, he can't do much about it. Unless, of course, you give him an argument.

"In a rehearsal, remember a suggestion is the actor's best weapon. If the director likes your suggestion you've won the point; if he doesn't, you've put him on the defensive. Your objection puts you in his power but not, it's true, for very long. Like Hamlet, every director tries to persuade his cast to play the show as he rehearsed it. But once the curtain is up, the greatest director you'll ever work with is instantly traduced to a single—probably anguished—member of your audience. This is your unique and awful advantage as an actor. Don't abuse it.

"When you get yourself some fans, by all means fool and flatter them that you're modest. A modest actor is obviously a mythical animal. But like the unicorn or the griffin, the fact that he doesn't exist in no way interferes with his decorative and pleasing appearance.

"Humility, on the other hand, cannot be faked. Anchored, of course, to respect, humility in our profession is always founded on a passionate love of the theater and its institutions. I assume you have that—that your need to use your talent was irresistible. This is why people who aren't on-stage regard actors with a certain sidelong glance. Everybody would like to be on the stage. If this weren't true, there wouldn't be any theater because there wouldn't be any public.

"Caruso once told my mother that he always made the high notes seem harder than they really were for him because he never forgot that his audience was composed entirely of tenors. The urge to act is universal. What separates real actors from the rest of the population is that they have completely abandoned themselves to the urge. The rest congratulate themselves that they have outgrown the childish trait of showing off. The fact that some people actually are paid handsomely, forgiving themselves of this failing, gives rise to feelings of irritation and envy.

"Finally, never ask your director how to 'do' a part. Stand six feet away and do your damndest."

While Welles was a brilliant raconteur on almost any imaginable subject, oddly he was not adept at a task any grade-schooler could master: "I can't spell out loud." He said that one day in 1958 on a visit with my father. He then wrote out his title by marriage, "Count Welles-Girfalco." My father said: "I've known you as a producer, star of the WP-Federal Theater, director, playwright, would-be politician, novelist, lecturer, but never as a member of Rome's nobility."

They were in Toots Shor's famous New York restaurant, and Welles, who never feared any man and who commanded any room he entered, nevertheless spoke in hushed tones, just above the din any popular nightspot created. He didn't want the boisterous proprietor to make fun of his title. His father-in-law, he explained, was a count with two daughters and no male descendants. Therefore his daughter Beatrice was a countess, and that, under Italian law, automatically made Welles a count. He explained that the title could be temporary if his sister-in-law, then pregnant, gave birth to a son, who would then take over the title. "I just want to be a count long enough to trump Lord Laurence Olivier and by protocol be accorded a better seat at the table at dinner."

He admitted he'd been wrong about the success of television when it became widely available in Italy a few years earlier. "I'd thought no one would watch," he recalled, "because Italians love to talk. But I was wrong, only because they put the TV on in bars and restaurants and talk back to it."

At that time, one of the TV critics (not this reporter: I began twelve years later!) had been caught reviewing a program that had been switched and never aired. "I can't pretend to be indignant about that," said Welles. "When I was fifteen, I was a ghost music critic in Chicago. I gave a singer named Giovanni Martinelli a bad review in a French opera named *La Juive*. I hadn't seen it, of course, and never was told that the opera troupe had switched to *Aida* that night."

Then Peter Ustinov and his wife joined them. "I too have a title," the jovial actor and author said: "I'm a baron. From Wurtemberg. It's a permanent, though Ukrainian baron." Thus ended an evening that began with my father meeting two international acting stars, but ended with a conversation between Baron Ustinov and Count Welles-Girfalco.

Welles once made an intriguing suggestion to my father: "New York realtors ought to subsidize the Broadway theater. If you take away the theaters, then New York is just another Cincinnati."

With Ernest and Mary Hemingway at the Finca Vigía in
San Francisco de Paula, near Havana, Cuba in December 1952.
They genuinely enjoyed each other's company.

'50s

The Lyons Den

By Leonard Lyons

The 'fifties were a turbulent time in America; the Civil Rights movement was forming, there was a war—I'm sorry, a "police action" as President Truman called it—in Korea, then a new man in the White House, and the shameful blacklisting of actors—part of the Red Scare and the scourge that came to be known as "McCarthyism."

While my father didn't write any columns condemning the witch hunts—his was not that sort of column—he did make it a point to publish anything newsworthy that some of the victims did, actors who were forced to leave Hollywood and find work in theater, radio, or television in New York. Other columnists, by contrast, named names, and careers were damaged or ruined.

On Broadway, Rodgers and Hammerstein, Frank Loesser, Lerner and Loewe, and Comden and Green were in their heyday. Big hits included *Brigadoon, Call Me Madam, Carousel, Guys and Dolls,* and a newcomer, a former TV director named Yul Brynner, became a star in *The King and I.* So did Judy Holliday, who followed *Born Yesterday* the decade before with *Bells Are Ringing.*

Other musical hits included *Top Banana* and *The Boy Friend,* which brought a nineteen-year-old Julie Andrews to New York in 1954, and saw her star in an even bigger hit, *My Fair Lady,* two years later.

Kismet, The Pajama Game, Li'l Abner, Damn Yankees, The Music Man, The Sound of Music, and *Fiorello!* made this the greatest decade of the American musical theater.

It was also the decade of Arthur Miller, Tennessee Williams, and plays like *Look Back in Anger, Two for the Seesaw, The Diary of Anne Frank, Bus Stop,* and *The Chalk Garden,* to name a few.

In baseball, the New York Giants won the pennant on October 3, 1951, with Bobby Thomson's "Shot Heard 'Round the World," the most famous home run in history. It actually *was* heard around the world via Armed Forces Radio. Three years later, when the Giants won it all, Willie Mays joined Duke Snyder and Mickey Mantle as the three greatest center fielders of their era; in one city, all at once! And the following year, 1955, "The Boys of Summer," "Dem Bums," the Brooklyn Dodgers, won their only World Series, beating the favored Yankees.

The "other" New York Giants beat the Chicago Bears to win the 1956 NFL championship, and though they lost to the Baltimore Colts two years later in "The Greatest Game Ever Played," it was the game that made pro football a national phenomenon on network television.

TV, which was luring people away from movie theaters, was in its Golden Era, with Westerns, variety shows, and stars like Milton Berle, Sid Caesar, Ed Sullivan, Jackie Gleason, Phil Silvers, Lucille Ball and Desi Arnaz, Burns and Allen, and Ozzie and Harriet on the most popular shows.

Hollywood countered by devising Cinemascope, 3-D Cinerama, and VistaVision to lure fans back.

New York nightclubs were still thriving, with places like the Little Club, the Harwyn Club, and perennials like "21," Toots Shor's, the Copacabana, the Latin Quarter, and El Morocco very popular. Sardi's, the theatrical restaurant across from Shubert Alley in the heart of the theater district, remained an institution.

My father resisted an offer to host a variety show like his competitor Ed Sullivan, fearing his column would suffer. But my mother Sylvia was a panelist on a short-lived quiz show called *Who's the Boss*, in which panelists tried to guess the secretary-contestants' famous bosses. Leroy Anderson's "The Typewriter" was the theme song.

It was the decade of our family's visits to Hemingway in Cuba, Truman in the White House, and Adlai Stevenson in Libertyville, Illinois.

And if you consider the year 1960 part of this decade, Kirk Douglas broke the blacklist by giving screenwriter Dalton Trumbo his professional name back on movie credits, where it belonged, for *Spartacus*.

It was an amazing time.

LAUREN BACALL

In December 2006, I spent an hour interviewing Lauren Bacall at the Bay Street Theater in Sag Harbor, New York. Before we went onstage, I showed her color photos from the early 'forties—her modeling days. She looked at them matter-of-factly, which I thought was perfectly in tune with her demeanor as one of the coolest, most alluring movie stars of all time.

She insisted we'd met before. "I knew all the boys," she said, referring to my three brothers and me, but I assured her that somehow I was the only one who hadn't had the honor. (She'd attended my brother Douglas's bar mitzvah, but arrived late. By that time I'd left to play in my high school football game.)

It was an incredible hour. She reminisced, she joked, she didn't miss an incident. As if it were yesterday. *Now* she's met "all the boys."

When Anthony Brown was producing *Tobacco Road* on Broadway, he interviewed a student from New York's Julia Richmond High School for a job. He asked if she could dance the Charleston. The young woman, who was an infant during the heyday of that dance craze, nevertheless said she could do it She improvised. The producer laughed and called the rest of the cast over to watch the girl pretending to do the Charleston. The young student grinned, repeated her assertion that she knew the old-fashioned dance steps, and continued to improvise.

Brown turned to the assembled actors and said: "She has a lot of nerve. I'll give her the part." Thus, billed as "Betty Bacall," she was hired. The show ran just sixty-two performances in the spring of 1942.

In 1944, producer Max Gordon was about to enter Sardi's restaurant when a girl selling copies of *Actors' Cues* magazine, at a nickel apiece, asked him to buy one. Gordon said: "You're too beautiful to be doing this. You should be in a show. Come and see me."

Next day, she came to his office, and he hired the then Betty Perske as an understudy for a show called *Franklin Street*, which closed out of town.

She met and costarred with Humphrey Bogart in her first film, *To Have and Have Not*, in 1944. By February 1945, when she and Bogie had dinner with friends, their romance was obvious. They held hands during dinner, so Bogie had to crack and eat the lobster being served with only his left hand.

In September 1948, three and a half years after they'd married, Bacall and Bogie re-turned to their home in Los Angeles and found her jewelry was missing.

"What makes you think we've been robbed, Baby?" asked Bogart.

"Because my jewel box isn't here," she replied. Then, as Bogie stalked through the room in his best detective manner, searching for clues, she finally said: "Bogie! Enough of *The Maltese Falcon*. How about calling the police now?" He did.

Three years after Bogie's death in 1957, she was briefly wooed by Frank Sinatra. But that didn't last long. Then, a few weeks later, they came face-to-face at a crowded party. Sinatra smiled, reached for the roses

A kiss from Lauren Bacall circa 1968.

in a nearby vase, and extended some to her.

She spurned them and, walking off to take the arm of her new beau, said simply: "Too little, and too late."

In March 1966, she was at a dinner for Prince Philip hosted by 20th Century-Fox mogul Darryl F. Zanuck. She was asked if she'd curtsy to Philip.

"If he curtsies to me, I'll curtsy to him," she said. "In this world, you get what you give."

Prince Philip went to see her on Broadway in *Cactus Flower* and, backstage, said to her: "You were splendid!"

"Thanks," Bacall replied. "So how about taking me out?"

In October 1967, Bacall marked two years in *Cactus Flower* and told my father she always tried to make the performance seem as if it were her first time in the role, and quoted the advice Olivier had given her: "Remember, there are people out there seeing you for the first time."

That was, by the way, the same reason Joe DiMaggio played hard every day, remembering that there were people in the stands who'd never seen him play before.

In January 1968, she advised a young actress to make demands on a producer. "You don't ask, you don't get," she said. Then she thought a moment and added: "Except for David Merrick: You ask, and you don't get."

In September 1968, news spread around New York about a woman barred from the Plaza Hotel's famed Oak Room for wearing pants. When she heard about it, Bacall stood up at her table at the Russian Tea Room, turned to her tablemate Yves St.

Laurent, and said: "I'm wearing pants. Look at me. In pants. Every woman today wears pants. I'll be at the Oak Room tomorrow night in pants. Let's see if they dare stop me."

In November 1969, Bacall was attending Roddy McDowall's party when Danny Kaye arrived with Jackie and Aristotle Onassis. After the introductions were made, Bacall said to Onassis, whose ocean-going yacht— the world's largest—had a helicopter on it: "You still have that rowboat?"

Bacall was nominated for a Tony in April 1970, for her role in *Applause*. One of her competitors was Katharine Hepburn for *Coco*. Her agent, Peter Witt, told her not to agree to perform a number as the finale of the telecast; Hepburn was a formidable opponent, he reasoned, and if Hepburn won, Bacall's performance, no matter how good, would be anticlimactic and would also diminish the star.

Alexander H. Cohen, the producer of the show, wasn't convinced. He thought she had a good chance to win and bet Witt his client would take the prize. The bet was a dinner—anywhere in the world.

When Bacall won the Tony, Cohen said he'd be looking forward to dinner with Witt—in Cannes.

Hepburn, incidentally, gave her rival a photo as a gift. Showing no bitterness at not winning the Tony Award, she inscribed it: "Aunt Kate."

A few days later, Bacall ran into Danny Kaye and told him they'd worked together on Broadway. Sort of. It was the production of *Let's Face It*, the Cole Porter musical at the Imperial Theater.

She was an usher.

MARLON BRANDO

In his later years, Marlon Brando seemed to be a parody of himself, aping earlier performances, using his famous nasal delivery, and, sometimes, reportedly never bothering to memorize dialogue. Instead he'd have cue cards just off camera.

But by then he'd established himself as one of the great actors of his or any generation. Like his contemporary, the ill-fated James Dean, he was a star who transformed the way subsequent actors approached a role.

In 1946, early in his career, Brando was in rehearsal for the play *Truckline Café* at the Belasco Theater. His director was the great Harold Clurman. Ever the introvert at rehearsals, Brando's voice could hardly be heard. Many in the cast thought for sure he'd be fired.

But not Clurman. Aware of the rumors, he assembled the cast and told them: "I want you all as witnesses." He turned to the young Brando and said; "Someday you're going to be a big star, a great big star. And when I'm a broken-down director, promise me you'll support me."

Brando laughed nervously and made that promise.

The following year, Brando electrified the American theater as Stanley Kowalski in *A Streetcar Named Desire*, opening December 3, 1947. "The Lyons Den" reported how he got the role: Originally it had been planned to have John Garfield star, but negotiations broke down when Garfield insisted he could leave the show with four weeks' notice if he got a movie role.

Brando's name came up in discussions, but the producers couldn't find him, because back then he had no known address. (This was before he roomed with Wally Cox.) Finally they tracked him down, and Brando walked across Broadway with an agent, Bill Liebling, headed to meet the show's author, Tennessee Williams.

Liebling, a former singer, knew Brando liked to sing and that it put the actor at ease, so during their walk to see Williams, Liebling began to sing "Dear Old Girl" to himself. Then, as if on cue, Brando began harmonizing, and they sang all the way to Williams's office. There the actor was signed for the role that would change everything.

Before he achieved stardom, he worked as an elevator operator between roles. But producers had seen him onstage, and one offered a movie contract. Realizing he hadn't received the proper training, however, Brando turned it down, saying: "No thanks. I like my present job."

Then he got an offer for a stage role and watched the British producer read portions of the script, in a high voice with odd gesticulations. Brando watched, in fascination, never said a word, and walked out.

Then the Broadway star and director Alfred Lunt auditioned him and asked Brando to say a few words.

Brando did: "Hickory . . . Dickory . . . Dock." And he walked out.

Brando's work in *A Streetcar Named Desire* in 1948 was so well received, his director, Elia Kazan, gave him an unusual gift: a series of prepaid visits to a psychiatrist.

Stanley Kramer, who produced Brando's first movie, *The Men*, in 1950, told some friends that Brando's supposed idiosyncrasies were exaggerations by the press. Then he excused himself to call Brando. He dialed the number, then asked for "Frank McGregor." Then he explained that Brando only takes calls for "Frank McGregor."

In 1954, Brando had a brush with the law over unpaid parking tickets involving his motorcycle. He was brought into a stationhouse between the matinee and evening performances of *A Streetcar Named Desire*. No one recognized him because he was dressed casually. He admitted he'd overlooked the five summonses, but as he pulled his hat out from a pants pocket, six more summonses fell out.

Brando liked to relax in the office of Eddie Jaffe, a New York press agent in the mid-'fifties. He liked not being treated like a star and could relax there. One day, a visitor to the office phoned an actress and said: "Hey, there's a big movie star here." Then he covered the mouthpiece and whispered to Brando. "Quick! Talk like Kirk Douglas."

When he starred as Napoleon in *Desirée*, the designer of the $7,000 ermine coronation robe draped it over Brando just before the cameras rolled.

"Boy," said Brando, surveying the robe, "they musta killed a lot of weasels to make this one."

During the shooting of the courtroom scene for *On the Waterfront*, supporting player Ed Cramer, who portrayed a policeman, fidgeted with the metal number on the collar of his uniform. He asked Brando if the number was pinned on straight.

"Look, Ed," said the star, "if the only thing the audience looks at is the number on your uniform collar, then this picture can't be much good."

Brando directed the movie *One-Eyed Jacks* and had a scene in which his character was drunk. Carrying Method Acting to its logical extension (assuming all the characteristics of the person he was portraying), he drank half a pint of vodka before rolling the cameras and did the scene tipsy.

The next day he watched the rushes (the rough footage), liked what he saw, and kept that take in the final print.

In a scene in the movie filmed in Death Valley, Brando's character was chased by a posse. At the end of the gallop he called to his costar Karl Malden: "Let's play cowboys and Indians some more" and ordered the crew to shoot the scene again.

He also shot another scene again, even though he'd been told it was performed perfectly. "I know," he said of the scene,

in which Malden performed. "I just like to watch Karl work."

The casting director of *One-Eyed Jacks* said he hated having to choose some extras and deny employment to others. Brando showed him how to cast extras: "Don't hire those who meet your eye, perk up and smile, and try to exude personality," he said. "Those are the type who'll try to stick their faces into the camera."

Adolph Zukor, by then the elderly chairman emeritus of Paramount, the studio he founded, looked at the long shooting schedule for the movie and said, "In that same amount of time, the pioneers were able to settle eight Western states."

Before shooting, Brando had lectured the cast about the importance of being alert at all times. A few days later, however, he noticed one of the cowboy extras studying his script intently. Brando snuck up, snatched the man's prop pistol from his holster, and said: "See? You weren't alert."

Later, he tried it again, but this time the cowboy swung the rifle he was holding and hit Brando with it, sending the star to the hospital.

He had some intimate love scenes with Anna Magnani, but they were later toned down in the editing. When she saw the final print, the fiery Italian actress called out: "Cowards!"

In April 1960, Brando requested a copy of Ionesco's surrealistic play *Rhinoceros*, in which the actors turn into rhinoceroses. He explained: "This would make a good adult Western."

In August 1964, Brando visited the Paris set of *Lilith* and met its star, Jean Seberg. "I had a crush on you when I was a little girl," she gushed. "I even wrote you a letter asking you to come live with me."

Brando surveyed the beautiful Seberg and said: "Why don't you write another one?"

In 1968, Brando was the original choice to portray Butch Cassidy, with Paul Newman as Harry Longabaugh, aka "The Sundance Kid." But Brando, probably to his everlasting regret, turned down the role, moving Newman to his role, and upcoming star Robert Redford into portraying Sundance.

The movie's title was then changed from *The Sundance Kid and Butch Cassidy* to, of course, *Butch Cassidy and the Sundance Kid*.

Brando once assisted a detective on a night patrol in which a mugger was caught. The detective had Brando call it in to the precinct, and the star learned later the report read: "Assisted by a civilian, Marlon Brando."

"It's second billing, but I'll take it," he remarked.

My father and younger brother Douglas were visiting the set of *The Chase*, today a forgotten, underrated drama in which Brando starred with Robert Redford, Jane Fonda, Robert Duvall, E.G. Marshall, and Angie Dickenson. Brando portrayed the honest sheriff of a present-day Southern town who, in the scene being filmed that day, gets severely beaten by thugs.

Brando insisted on additional makeup to make his beating look even more realistic and shocking. Then he overheard the studio guide telling my father that he'd been attending drama classes in his spare time.

"Give it up," advised Brando. "Only five percent ever make it as actors. I have so many friends among the others. They're all neurotic. Give it up."

Actress Fran Heflin once recalled working with the young Brando on Broadway in his debut production, *I Remember Mama*, which arrived at the Music Box Theater in October 1944. She knew he was an actor with a remarkably wide range of interests. She'd spotted him offstage carrying two pieces of reading material: a comic book and a book on the life of Sigmund Freud.

YUL BRYNNER

In most cases, a movie star is defined by one role, if he or she is lucky. But Yul Brynner, a onetime director at CBS in the Golden Age of TV, is defined by three: His Oscar-winning portrayal of King Mongkut of Siam in *The King and I*; Chris, the black-clad lead gunfighter in *The Magnificent Seven*; and Pharaoh in *The Ten Commandments*. His exotic looks and mysterious origins added to the mystique, along with his clipped speech and unidentifiable accent.

Actually, Brynner didn't create the part of King Mongkut. Rex Harrison did in *Anna and the King of Siam*, the nonmusical version of the true story in 1946. On Brynner's opening night in 1951, he received a telegram from Harrison. It read: "The King Is Dead; Long Live the King."

When the show opened to rave reviews, Brynner's four-year-old son proudly told his classmates: "My father's in a big hit."

"What's a 'big hit?'" he was asked.

"It's like a home run—only in the theater," replied the younger Brynner.

Soon after the show opened, Brynner received two visitors backstage. They discussed with him the proper use of pronouns when conversing with royalty. The visitor offered an opinion, and Brynner replied: "Your Highness, one thing I won't dispute with you is The King's English."

The visitors were the Duke and Duchess of Windsor.

Brynner got his start by walking into a producer's office, sitting on the floor, and playing a guitar. Then he said: "I've been hungry too long. You're putting on a Chinese show. I'm Chinese. You must have a role for me."

"Yes, I do," said the producer, Michael Myerberg. "It's the leading role opposite Mary Martin. It's yours. It's called *Lute Song*." Brynner got the job even though he wasn't Chinese at all.

In *Lute Song* he had the line: "Ten thousand volumes have I read." As the run of the show wore on, to keep each other fresh, Brynner changed the line each night, according to the size of the house.

Thus, on a night when the house was about 70 percent filled, he'd say: "Seven thousand volumes have I read." So when he said one night: "I read a book once," the cast knew the house was nearly empty and the show's run was soon to end.

The day after *The King and I* opened, Brynner phoned his agent and ordered him to search for another leading part.

"But, Yul," said the agent, "this show will surely run for years."

"I know," his client agreed. "That's why I'm telling you to start looking for a part this good now. It may take you fifty years."

In September 1951, Brynner was under the weather one night. He was even given some oxygen to ease the pain. Then the call came from the theater, inquiring about the understudy going on.

"That won't happen," said Brynner. "I'll be there." Then he explained: "I'm conscious, right? And as long as an actor is conscious, he goes on."

Later that month, Brynner took his young son Rocky to dinner and said he could order anything he wanted. So he said, "I'll have a hot dog and a root beer." The waiter replied they didn't serve either. The boy turned to his father and asked: "What kind of a place is this?"

The restaurant was "21," New York's most famous posh eatery.

Brynner was a boxing fan and had a TV in his dressing room so he could watch the Friday night fights from Madison Square Garden. But unless the fight ended in a knockout, he couldn't watch the last two rounds to a finish because he had to go onstage. In the death scene at the end of *The King and I*, the Siamese Prime Minister places his head on Brynner's chest. Friday

Yul Brynner and Celeste Holm at Sardi's circa 1965.

nights, he'd whisper something to the dead king. "Not a farewell," he revealed, "but the name of the winner of the main event at the Garden."

When I interviewed Brynner in the 1980s, he'd returned to Broadway for yet another revival of the show that had made him world-famous. He told me he learns something from every performance, something other actors have disputed as being impossible in a long run. What they didn't realize is that Brynner constantly inserted subtle changes that only the other cast members would know about.

For example, in the scene with "Sir Edward Ramsay," the King tells the British representative how many children he has. "One hundred forty-two," he'd say. "Next month, I'm expecting seven more." The first figure is variable, so Brynner was free to change it and use any other number he chose, just to keep the cast fresh for each performance.

This nightly change in the number spawned a backstage betting pool among the musicians in the pit and the crew. The winner would be the person who picked the number closest to the one uttered by Brynner.

The follow-up line the Englishman says to the King is: "Well, there's certainly no problem about an heir to the throne."

One night when Brynner uttered the numbers, that line got a big laugh from two people sitting front row center: Queen Juliana and Prince Bernhard of The Netherlands, who had four daughters but no male heir.

The morning after the show opened to historic reviews, Brynner, who'd struggled all his life, knew it was time to splurge. So he had breakfast at "21." He ordered scrambled eggs and caviar.

Not ten minutes after he won the Best Actor Oscar for the movie version of *The King and I,* the theater across the street from where the ceremonies took place had changed its marquee to read: "ACADEMY AWARD–WINNER YUL BRYNNER IN THE KING AND I."

While filming *Anastasia,* Brynner arrived at the studio in a chauffer-driven Rolls-Royce. He'd bought the car via an ad announcing that Greek shipping tycoon Stavros Niarchos had ordered it for his wife, who decided, after one ride, that it didn't suit her personality. Brynner picked it up at half price.

At another point in the shooting of *Anastasia,* Brynner, in London, read that Eleanor Roosevelt had arrived in Paris. He telephoned her, and she invited him to lunch. Given a day off from filming, he eagerly accepted, and drove to the airport, flew to Paris, drove to the luxurious Hotel Crillon, lunched with the former First Lady, then drove back to Orly Field for the flight back to London.

She never knew he'd come to the luncheon from London. She thought he'd been staying in Paris.

In February 1962, Brynner was cast in the lead opposite Tony Curtis in *Taras Bulba,* an exotic action thriller set in the Ukraine in the late sixteenth century. "Of course I'm perfect for such a role," said Brynner. "After all, do I look like the boy next door?"

There was always a mystique about his birthplace. In mid-April 1962, Brynner obliquely addressed this by observing: "My wife was born in Yugoslavia of German parents, educated in Paris, and raised in Chile. I was born in Mongolia of Swiss parents, grew up in Paris, and became a star in America. Our baby will therefore apply for admission to the United Nations."

He was believed to have been born in everywhere from Outer Mongolia to Brooklyn. "I don't mind talking about my life as an actor, but before that will forever remain private," he noted.

When I interviewed him, I said: "You can tell me. You were really born in the Bronx, right?" He laughed, and said he was born on an island near Russia. He never did anything to settle the contradictory theories.

In December 1962 in a magazine article devoted to *Taras Bulba,* Brynner's age was listed as forty. He then wrote a letter to the editors thanking them, but correcting his age. "I'm forty-three," he wrote. "It's not merely a question of accuracy," he continued, "but I'd rather have the public say: 'My, he's a young-looking forty-three' rather than 'an old-looking forty.'"

Brynner's sister Vera was a singer and once performed with him on the Paris stage, without telling the director they were siblings.

"He found out," she recalled, "when in a passionate love scene, I simply patted him on the head."

In January 1963, Brynner flew to Acapulco on Frank Sinatra's private plane. He and the singer got into a serious gin rummy game during the flight. It was so serious, in fact, that Sinatra told the pilot to fly the long route—via Mexico City—so they could finish their game.

RALPH BUNCHE

Twenty-five years after he graduated from high school, Dr. Ralph Bunche became the first African-American to win the Nobel Peace Prize. He soon got a letter from an old high school teacher admitting that it was because of his race he'd been kept from the honor society, and apologizing for that.

Dr. Bunche and his wife Ruth were good friends of my parents and were regulars at our home each spring for our Passover seders. Only years later did I appreciate the contribution to world peace he had made through his efforts in the Middle East. I knew him back then as a wise, gentle man who adored the rituals of the Passover holiday.

When he returned from Oslo with the 1950 Nobel Peace Prize, he celebrated with friends from Howard University. One guest was an instructor working on his doctorate, who'd run into financial difficulties. He told Bunche he had been about to secure a bank loan when he played the numbers and won.

"I figured if the Lord was good enough to have one of us win such great honors, I felt He was thinking kindly towards all of us," he said. He then explained that ever since he'd seen the photostat of Bunche's Nobel Peace Prize check, which was for $31,728.61, he'd been playing the first three digits of the sum awarded to Dr. Bunche. He finally won after playing "317" over and over.

Dr. Bunche wore only one piece of jewelry, a gold ring decorated with the signs of the Zodiac. He'd bought it in Madagascar years before, from a native who'd spotted Bunche as soon as he stepped off the boat.

"Nice ring for an American gentleman. Just $15." he said. The man followed Bunche for the entire day until Bunche finally bought the ring, but for just $7. It was one of his early experiences in bargaining.

"What annoyed me was that I knew right away I'd buy the ring." He added: "And what annoyed me more was knowing all the time that he also knew I'd buy it."

In mid-October 1951, Dr. Bunche was visited by Norman Corwin, the famed writer and radio dramatist who was preparing a show for the UN. He and Dr. Bunche spoke for an hour or so, during which the diplomat explained the complex functions of the UN Trusteeship Council. Later, Corwin returned to Bunche's office with a tape recorder, asking him to repeat what they'd discussed earlier—but for only one minute. Unfazed, Bunche said merely: "There cannot be any sound foundation for peace in the world unless the 200 million colonial people may look forward to freedom."

Nearly a year later, he met with General Douglas MacArthur, who'd led UN forces in Korea and who spoke about the future of the UN as a peacekeeping force. The important discussion between the diplomat and the soldier did not, however, take place at the United Nations but at a Dodger-Giant doubleheader.

One night in 1953, Dr. and Mrs. Bunche came to our home for dinner. My two older brothers, George and Warren, wanted to watch a mystery show on TV. Brother Douglas and I wanted to watch a comedy. To settle this standoff, our parents asked Dr. Bunche, who'd settled major disputes between Israel and the Arab nations, to help. He said he wouldn't dare get involved in such an impossible-to-solve dispute, but finally resolved it. By flipping a coin!

In 1956, just after the Suez crisis, Dr. Bunche was given the task of organizing the UN peacekeeping force, consisting of 4,500 soldiers from eight nations.

"I'm a field marshal of sorts," he said, "but with a small 'f' and a small 'm.' That's because I'm the only person ever called upon to raise a non-fighting army."

The Bunches gave a party for Marian Anderson in December 1958, and the Nobel Laureate was asked by the great singer

With Dr. and Mrs. Ralph Bunche, the Nobel Prize winner, circa 1968.
The Bunches loved coming to our Passover seders.

where the framed proclamation about his prize was hanging. He explained that the scroll came in an elegant box and would've been dislodged if it was framed. However, there was a framed document concerning the prize. It was written by Ralph Bunche Junior, who was six at the time. On the hand-ruled lines the boy had written: "I am happy you got the Nobel Peace Prize. Love, Ralph."

In early March 1960, Dr. Bunche was crossing Times Square just as the lights were changing. The traffic cop called to him: "Hey, can't you read?" Dr. Bunche said he could read, as the cop pointed to the "Don't Walk" sign. "The light had changed while I was crossing," said Dr. Bunche. After that response the policeman asked to see his identity papers.

After inspecting the papers of a man who'd been awarded fifty-one honorary degrees and the Nobel Peace Prize, the policeman said: "I don't care if you're the President. No jaywalking."

"Sir," replied Dr. Bunche, "I can read."

A few weeks later, he'd seen the Broadway show *The Best Man,* and visited the stars, Melvyn Douglas and Frank Lovejoy, backstage. He then was asked to mediate an imminent actors' strike. "I'd rather try my hand at settling the Israeli-Arab differences than stepping into something as complex as a fight between actors and producers," he replied.

In the turbulent summer of 1963, Dr. Bunche was in Mississippi, as one of the leaders of Civil Rights marches. At all times he was surrounded by four white Mississippi motorcycle cops. "I didn't know if I was being honored, guarded, or watched," he said later.

In July 1966, Dr. Bunche umpired a celebrity softball game in Yankee Stadium in which my father played the outfield. By that time, the diplomat's eyesight wasn't what it used to be. So he told each pitcher about his poor vision and said: "We'll use the honor system. You tell me what it is, and I'll call 'em that way."

In 1951, Dr. Bunche addressed the student legal society at the University of Virginia. The president of that group had demanded Dr. Bunche be allowed to speak. That young law student was also a future United States attorney general, then senator from New York: Robert F. Kennedy.

MARC CHAGALL

Few of my parents' friends ever affected them as deeply as did Marc Chagall. One of the three foremost painters of the twentieth century (Picasso and Dalí being the others), he was in some ways a spiritual link for my parents to their ancestors' lives in Eastern Europe. He'd come to our home Friday nights during World War II when he was living in New York, for it was the only home in town where he could be certain the food was kosher.

I once saw him look at a painting in our home by Joan Miró, the great Spanish surrealist, and scoff: "Drek," which in Yiddish means "Shit." But he was a gentle man, always with a twinkle in his eye and a wonderful outlook on life, no matter how dark it was during a great deal of his lifetime.

Late in 1945, my father returned from a trip with the First Army Press Corps to Berchtesgaden, Hitler's lair. One of the things he brought back was a proclamation awarding a Nazi Iron Cross to a Colonel Otto Benzin for some accomplishment—if you can call anything ever done by anyone wearing that uniform such a thing. And it was signed by Hitler himself.

Chagall saw it at our home and asked to paint his answer on the blank portion of the parchment. He was careful to sign it on the same line as Hitler, and, referring to Hitler's failed career as an artist in Vienna as a young man, shrugged his shoulders and said: "Two painters."

Years later, he returned to our home, and said he had to finish it. He took the parchment to his studio in New York for a few days. Then he returned it. He'd painted himself making love to his wife, a flying violin player, the burning ghetto, and jubilation in the streets at the liberation of Paris, led by the artists. The painting stretched all over the Nazi side of the parchment. He told us he did that to show that though

Leonard Bernstein, Marc Chagall, and my father, July 1960.

threatened with castration by Hitler and Goebbels, he'd outlived Hitler. "In case somebody ever tries to separate the two halves of this," he explained.

In January 1946, a soldier returned from the war proudly holding two Chagall paintings that he said he'd bought in Berlin. "I'm proud to have brought them from Germany," he said. "The work of this great artist is too good to be owned by a Nazi."

Then he met Chagall's son-in-law who told him they were probably fakes. Chagall himself confirmed this after inspecting them.

Noting the disappointment and embarrassment of the soldier, Chagall, through an interpreter, said: "Maybe we can do something about this." He took the canvases, washed away the paint, added back in the same scenes, signed his name and said: "Here. Now they're genuine."

Chagall had agents assigned to buying back some of his early paintings created when he was so poor. Some were painted on tablecloths, bedsheets, and even on shirttails. He reacquired those he felt could be improved.

On two occasions, however, as he applied paint and brush to his repurchased pictures, he retouched them so much that he finally decided they weren't good enough—and destroyed them.

Before the war Chagall left Paris on a trip to Berlin. His friends and fellow painters Soutine and Modigliani lived in the same house, and Chagall left his studio unlocked, merely tying a piece of string around the doorknobs. He believed his friends would guard his possessions.

But when he returned, everything was gone. He did find a few of the stolen paintings and bought them back at low prices. He found his largest painting—worth millions today—being used in a henhouse as a fence separating the hens from the roosters.

In 1936, when civil war came to Spain, he said to Picasso: "Such terrible things are happening in your country. All those wonderful El Greco paintings may be destroyed."

"So what?" Picasso replied. "I'll paint others."

Unlike Picasso, who lived his entire life without visiting America, Chagall came here often. After he returned from New York to Paris in 1946, Chagall gave a one-man show that Picasso attended. He listened to Chagall talk about his four-year stay in New York and was astonished. "You mean," asked Picasso, who believed America to be concerned only with trade and profit, "an artist really *can* work in America?"

The very night of his return to Paris, my parents walked with him down the Champs Elysées and along its narrow, twisting side streets. He told them his feelings on returning to the city he'd fled just before the Nazis arrived.

"As my ship neared Europe, I began to understand Cézanne, Daumier, Corot, and the others. For here, everything is set for the artist. All he or she has to do is reproduce the setting. But America is dynamic, with a broad, grandiose background. By immersing yourself in it, by diving into it, you get style. You must contribute something to its strength," he said on the lamp-lit street near the Place de la Concorde.

When he first arrived back in Paris, Chagall was surrounded by reporters who fired questions on all subjects. "Painters shouldn't talk," replied the shy, gentle Chagall. "All the trouble that painters get into is caused by words. If you really want my opinion on anything, come to the studio, and I'll paint you a picture that will answer your questions."

In December 1955, my father and Truman Capote were named "group historians" for the touring company of *Porgy and Bess* for its tour of Russia. It was the height of the Cold War, and few Americans were allowed into Soviet Russia.

The night before he left, my father was with Chagall and told him he was traveling to Chagall's native land. "You must visit my hometown of Vitebsk," he said. "How will I know it?" asked my father, smiling, no doubt, and handing Chagall his small pocket notepad.

And so Chagall drew a sketch of his village and presented it back to my father, thus making our family possessors of The World's Smallest Chagall.

Among most of his contemporary artists, Chagall was the only one who was Jewish. Thus he alone was marked for execution by the Germans. Late in 1946, he received a bill for 5,000 francs from the *Argus de la Presse*, the French newspaper clipping service he had used in France before the war. The service had never discontinued clipping articles about him, however, and the bill was for all the clippings that appeared in the Nazi-controlled press during the Occupation. The articles denounced him and his work and damned them both forever.

There was a large exhibit of Chagall's works in Chicago, and it drew record crowds. Friends took him to a local nightclub where an artist roamed from table to table, sketching the customers. He sat at Chagall's table and began to sketch the painter, not recognizing him.

"No, no, this isn't how it should be done," said Chagall. "I'll show you." He then sketched a self-portrait. The nightclub sketcher glanced at it and said: "That's the way Marc Chagall would do it."

"You're right," said Chagall. The sketcher then asked for the portrait, and thus, not realizing what he'd been given, became the owner of a Chagall.

In February 1946, Chagall received a form letter of application to the Scenic Artists Union. He dutifully stood on line with a crowd of other applicants for membership. As instructed, he brought paints, brushes, and samples of his work. His "samples" were his paintings he'd borrowed from the Museum of Modern Art in New York. But he was hungry, so he left the paintings at the union offices to get some breakfast. When he returned to pick up those paintings—worth a fortune—the union officials decided to waive the admission test and welcomed him.

In December 1947, Chagall met a man who'd earlier paid a large sum for a Chagall painting, but when he met the artist, was unable to describe it. "Does it look like this?" said Chagall after sketching an outline. "I think so," replied the man, "but I'm still not sure." Chagall sketched some more. "Well, does it have this in it? And this? And this?" he asked, continuing to fill in the sketch, which had by that time become an exact reproduction of the painting the man had bought.

"Yes, that's the one," said the man, reaching for the now-precious paper.

"I thought that must be the one," said Chagall, beating him to the sketch and tearing it up.

"Don't try to paint for a living," he advised my older brothers on another visit to New York. Then he said if he hadn't become a painter he'd have been a poet or composer of symphonies.

My father visited Chagall in Paris, who offered to introduce him to any artist he'd like to meet. "How about Utrillo?" my father suggested. "He's mad," Chagall replied, a bit sadly.

"How about Rouault?"

Again Chagall sighed: "Also mad."

Finally my father said: "And Picasso?"

"Unfortunately," Chagall replied, "not mad."

He lived the last part of his life in St. Paul de Vence on the French Riviera, and some friends came for a visit one day. One noticed lots of chickens running around the backyard and said: "Looks like some good meals coming up."

Chagall, who often used chickens as a motif in his works, said: "Never. Chickens are never eaten in this house." Then he added: "But in restaurants, of course, one sometimes forgets."

In May 1960, a wealthy New York woman posed for a portrait by Chagall. He delivered the painting, which showed her holding a cow in her lap. "Why the cow?" she asked.

"That's how I see you," he explained.

Brandeis University invited Chagall to paint a mural, and he accepted. "If I sell a painting," he said, "it hangs in the room of a rich man's home, where he alone can see it. But a mural at a university will be seen constantly by generations of youngsters." His largest murals, incidentally, adorn New York's Lincoln Center.

On another visit to New York, he was stopped at Customs when his ship arrived and asked if he was the same Chagall who'd passed through New York a few years before. He said he was.

"In that case," replied the Immigration officer, "where's the sketch I was promised? Salvador Dalí delivered one of his."

Chagall stayed in a posh hotel on the Upper East Side. A friend waiting for him in the lobby noticed the paintings on the walls—a Romney, an Edzard, even a Laurencin, and over the bar a Miró. He asked the hotel manager: "Don't you have a Chagall?"

"The Chagalls are over there," the manager replied, pointing across the street—to the Metropolitan Museum of Art.

Early in 1961, back home in France, Chagall stopped by his local bakery. The baker said: "I understand you're a painter. If you paint a picture of me, I'll give you free bread for one month."

Chagall was intrigued that someone, especially living near his home, could be so oblivious to his presence in the town and to his world-acclaimed art. So he painted the portrait for the baker. The next day, however, the painting was returned, and the baker, holding a painting surely worth more than he'd make in a lifetime, said: "My wife doesn't think this picture becomes me. So I can't give you free bread for a month. All I can give you is croissants."

A restaurant in Paris announced it would soon be displaying a Chagall. The artist heard about this and tried to stop it, saying: "I don't want my paintings hanging in restaurants." He failed.

Mrs. Chagall, resigned to seeing her husband's painting hanging in the restaurant, went there and showed the owner how she hung her husband's works, with extra wire in the back, so they wouldn't fall from the wall. It turned out he needed her advice with the Chagall. The next month, thieves broke into the restaurant and stole nine other paintings. But they couldn't budge the Chagall.

On a visit to Chagall's home in August 1963, my father got to see a few of his early paintings, including *The Married Couple of the Eiffel Tower,* which France used on its new eight-franc stamp. Another of his early canvases—the largest one in their home—was presented by Chagall to a new museum in France. He deemed that huge red painting typical of his life and work. Most of those pre–World War I works had been left by Chagall, rolled up under his bed in Paris, when he went to Russia in 1918. Years later, he finally located them.

In their talk that day, my father said something positive about something, and Chagall said: "You believe that? My specialty is doubt. To be absolutely sure is not right, not right. But don't think I'm a pessimist. Never."

Chagall met the great Armenian-American author William Saroyan, who told Chagall he'd kept an easel, brushes, and drawing paper in his Paris apartment for twenty-five years. "But I'm not yet a painter who writes," he told them. "I'm still a writer who paints."

Then there was the time Chagall and his wife were in New York and met the great American artist Ben Shahn. Both of them looked the role of nonconformist artist that night: Chagall in his wide-brimmed brown hat and plaid shirt, and Shahn in his seersucker jacket, tan slacks, and white socks. Their wives were impeccably attired.

Seated at the next table were Richard Nixon and his wife. My father recalled the last time he'd seen Nixon, and that he'd introduced him to Greta Garbo. Nixon's wealthy friend Elmer Bobst, an art collector, said he was bidding for a Chagall at a New York art gallery. My father brought a message from Chagall to Nixon: "He's just made you a generous offer," said my father to Nixon. "Next time you want to buy one of his paintings, he'll sell it to you directly, with no dealer. You'll save a fortune."

Without hesitation, however, Nixon replied: "Next time I buy a painting it'll be by an American."

When it was announced that Chagall murals would adorn the Paris Opera, it was also announced that his works would be exhibited in Tokyo. He was invited to attend that exhibition and was asked if such a long trip would be too tiring. "It's not as far a journey as I've made from my village in Vitebsk in Russia to the ceiling of the Paris Opera," he said.

In March 1966, an American photographer was shooting the huge Chagall stained-glass windows in Jerusalem. He noticed a shaft of light coming through the open heavy door. He called the security guard to close the door. The guard obliged, then stepped outside. The photographer finished the job, came out, and thanked the guard for closing the door.

"You think you're the only person who came in here and told me to shut that door?" asked the guard. "Chagall asked me, too, last week."

When my father asked Chagall if he was satisfied with the way his enormous murals appeared in Lincoln Center, Chagall said: "I'm never satisfied." A friend sent him a photo of a Chagall he planned to buy. Chagall wrote him that it was a forgery. His wife studied the photo and said it was such a primitive fake that it must have been done by children in an art class.

Then Chagall told my father an intriguing story of his youth. He once was paid a lot of money during the Russian Revolution. He'd been designing sets for a local theater, and his fee was paid with a mass of paper bills issued by the short-lived Kerensky government. The money, however, wasn't worth the paper on which it was printed. That is, until Chagall used a roll of it in lieu of canvas and painted on it.

The theater director admired the young painter's work in that novel medium—money—and asked Chagall for it. The artist presented it to him. After all, it was only Kerensky money. Nobody knows what happened to it.

My father then told Chagall the line Hemingway had said to him in the Louvre: "If you look at a painting often enough, you own it." And Edward G. Robinson, a noted collector and art connoisseur, told my father and me: "The owner of a painting is only a temporary custodian. That goes for the artist, too."

Chagall agreed: "I never look at a painting and say: 'That's mine.' I never even say 'That's good.' I see a flower, I know when it's good. But a good Chagall? I wouldn't know. Talent is God's, and I don't know if He gave me any."

In 1965, LBJ invited Chagall to the White House, and Lady Bird gave him and his wife a tour, which included an introduction to her new granddaughter. Chagall was asked his opinion of the White House and said: "Marvelous, I saw three Cézannes there."

Time magazine asked for a self-portrait for a cover story on Chagall. He sat in front of a mirror and drew twenty sketches. None pleased him. Then his wife suggested he do one from memory, without looking in the mirror. He did, and that's the one *Time* used.

SALVADOR DALÍ

The friendship between my father and Salvador Dalí was one of the most unlikely imaginable. Here you have a poor Jewish boy, born in the slums of New York's crowded Lower East Side, who years later delighted in the company of Spain's most eccentric artist.

In 1956, on my first of what would be (to date) twenty-five trips to Spain, Dalí invited my parents and me to his home in Cadaqués, Port Lligat, in the northeast part of Spain: the Catalán country. I remember him gesturing to me to sit down and be comfortable. Without looking, I did. The "chair," however, was an elephant skull. He then gave me a hard candy, even though I hadn't asked for one. But he intentionally dropped it at my feet, and it exploded in a tiny puff of smoke. That was Dalí.

He frequently visited New York, a city he loved. It was also where America's most important art galleries were. So Dalí, who cut quite a figure walking with his pet ocelot down Fifth Avenue, let the city know he was in town. He spoke a strange sort of English, leaving out words whenever he felt the need, with an unconventional Spanish accent.

"No, myself like Picasso very much, but different positions," he said, leaving the listener to ponder the precise meaning of that statement.

He once sent Harpo Marx a harp as a gift, only the instrument was strung with barbed wire. A few days later, Harpo sent Dalí a photo of himself with a pained expression, seated next to the harp, with all ten fingers bandaged.

He once announced that, with thinning hair, he would soon be wearing a wig, and decided finally to shave his long trademark mustache. He explained that wearing a wig *and* his mustache would be too ostentatious. Following that announcement, he was swamped with requests for strands of his mustache hair.

One of Dalí's best-known portraits was of Sigmund Freud, painted in 1938. A mutual friend had introduced them, and Dalí gave the friend the painting. "Dr. Freud liked your painting very much," the friend later told him. Within a year, Freud had died. Dalí subsequently got hold of a book written by his friend, but published only in Europe, and it revealed that he'd never shown the portrait to Freud. He didn't have the courage, because he thought it was the portrait of a man soon to die.

Dalí criticized abstract art: "Those who buy such paintings will find that their money will become abstract." He quoted Jean Cocteau, who once said to Dalí: "The man who was the first to say: 'Her cheeks are like roses' was a true poet. The second man to say that was an idiot."

When worlds collide: Dalí once met Bill Veeck, then the owner of the Cleveland Indians. "I do not understand much about your work," said Dalí. "Well, Bub," Veeck replied, "that makes two of us."

On another occasion, he met former Indian player Lou Boudreau, then of the Boston Red Sox. "We have much in common," said Dalí, who'd never seen a baseball game but had a vague notion about it nonetheless. "After all, baseball is not unlike my paintings. There is surrealism in baseball: men wearing strange clothes, most of them crouching for objects frequently unattainable, and played in moonlight. Surreal, all right."

My father was once asked to paint something for a charity auction and kept putting it off. "I dislike doing anything poorly," he wrote, "even if labeled the work of an amateur." The day before the "painting" was due, he met Dalí, who showed him a painting he'd nearly completed and was planning to give to my father and mother. For a moment, my father had a strange impulse to sign his name to the Dalí painting and send it to the auction.

In the end, however, Dalí signed it. My father had feared that someone might bid low for the painting had it borne my father's signature instead of Dalí's.

"You should've stopped me from signing it and put your name on it," laughed Dalí. "People would've laughed. Not at me but at the fools who couldn't recognize a true Dalí work of art."

He once wrote a screenplay about a cauliflower. "I find that a cauliflower best represents the state of my mind," he explained.

Dalí had a friend who was a star of the Parisian stage, and he said he was planning a show around her. "When the curtain goes up," he said, "you will be sitting in a bathtub filled with bubbles. Then a motorcycle will be shown coming right out of the bathtub. Then another and another, and when the curtain comes down there'll be thirty motorcycles dashing about the stage." He paused, noticed the actress's astonished look, and beamed: "The French press will go wild, because they won't know how it's done. And as yet," he sighed, "neither do I."

When he was invited to appear on a TV show in New York, the hostess suggested he bring Gala, his wife, to the telecast. "Perhaps I may bring two Indian princesses," Dalí replied. "Perhaps I may bring one or two kings. Perhaps I may bring some animals. And perhaps I may not show up at all."

The daughter of a rich New York socialite was born with an odd growth on her throat, which a surgeon removed immediately, assuring the parents it would leave no mark. The traces of the operation faded over the years, and the surgery was forgotten. Then late in 1956, the father commissioned Dalí to paint the girl's portrait. When the painting arrived, it included a tiny mole scar, which no other naked eye ever noticed.

He once paid his wife's hospital bill in

With Salvador Dalí at the Stork Club circa 1954. The brilliant surrealist from northeast Spain and the columnist from New York's Lower East Side enjoyed each other's company over many years.

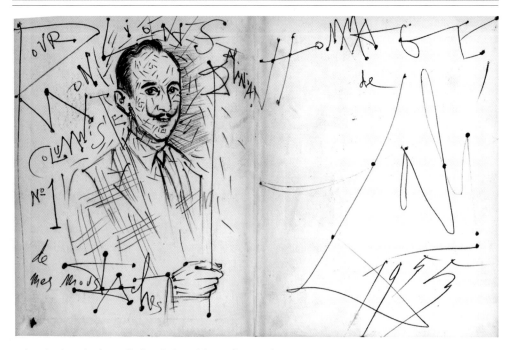

A drawing by Salvador Dalí of my father with a Dalí mustache.

person. The cashier noticed the lenses on his eyeglasses had been hollowed out, to make room for the live ants crawling there.

Dalí was in a New York nightclub and was presented to a young actress suffering from laryngitis. They tried communicating by writing on notepaper. But it didn't work. Her writings made sense. But his sketches were surrealistic and incomprehensible.

"The best way for people to forget all the woes of the world is to wear very tight shoes," he observed.

He once said to Jackie Gleason: "I'll do a portrait of your little boy." "I don't have a son. I have a daughter," replied "The Great One." "No matter," Dalí replied. "I'll paint him anyway."

Dalí was sitting with friends one time in New York, and Picasso's name came up. "People are always comparing me with Picasso," said Dalí. "I will tell you the difference. Picasso is a great artist. So am I. Picasso is a rich man. So am I. Picasso is a communist. I am *not*."

He had a feud with Picasso, who described Dalí as "the most pretentious man in the world, after the Eternal Father." Of Picasso he said: "He's provided a great service. Picasso has pushed ugliness to such extremes that all the rest must benefit by comparison."

Diego Rivera, the great Mexican artist, said of Dalí: "He's the finest arranger of shows in the magazines, windows, and in the sale of paintings. He is successful because his paintings look—at the same time—modern enough to be sold but ancient enough to get into the conspicuous collections."

When he heard what Rivera had said, Dalí responded: "I have profound respect for sincere political beliefs, with one exception. Any kind of propaganda in art is a tremendous mistake. As between Picasso and Rivera, my choice is definitely Dalí."

Dalí was once asked why Russia has never produced a great painter. "The air, the light, the sensualities all have something to do with it," he explained. "One place has it, another doesn't. The way truffles can be found in France but never in Connecticut."

After they'd known each other for fifteen years, Dalí insisted my father's English was improving. "I understand you better now," he explained.

In 1963, Dalí was hit by a New York taxicab. But he got up, uninjured, and tipped the driver. He explained: "I look around slowly, to see if I'm dead. I'm not. I feel so glad I'm not dead I tip the driver for not having killed me."

Two journalists in Paris were interviewing him, and he explained: "The two most important things in life are boiled noodles and the white meat of chicken." Then he shrugged: "It's obvious."

Dalí, who did a portrait of my father with a Dalí mustache as you can see here, never did cut his own in spite of his earlier announcement. He explained that his mustache acted as "my radar to the unknown."

KIRK DOUGLAS

I once was on a flight from LA to New York, and seated nearby was Kirk Douglas. He'd known my father from Douglas's earliest days on the New York stage, and remembered meeting me several times over the years. Since I had three brothers, he probably was confusing me with one of them, but I didn't tell him, of course. I would eventually interview him five times, with each being more enjoyable than the last.

He gave me a lift home from the airport, and en route said something profound: "An actor, if he's lucky, has one, maybe two roles for which he'll be remembered. I've been very lucky." Indeed he has, with movies like *Lust for Life*, *Seven Days in May*, *Gunfight at the O.K. Corral*, *The Vikings*, *Spartacus*, *The Devil's Disciple*, *20,000 Leagues Under the Sea*, *Lonely Are the Brave* (his favorite), and *Detective Story*, to name just a few classic roles. They have cemented his screen persona in the pantheon of American cinema, unmatched by all but a handful of leading men.

I told him that I met my future wife at a 1971 critics' screening of a Kirk Douglas movie. Oh, it wasn't one of those great roles. No, it was in a potboiler (as the *New York Times* describes such turgid films) called *The Light at the Edge of the World*. He put on a serious face, punctuated with that world-famous snarl: "If you ever mention that movie to me again, I'll punch you in the nose."

"My life is a 'B' movie," he once told my father. "No one would believe it." Indeed. He was born the son of an impoverished Russian Jewish immigrant in the mill town of Amsterdam in upstate New York. He literally lived on the wrong side of the tracks.

"I'd hear the trains go by and wanted to go wherever they were going." He arrived at St. Lawrence College penniless, relying on food donations from friends. Then the administrator discovered it and berated him in front of the entire class. But by the time he graduated, he was the president of his class, had his own suite, car, and private telephone, and was headed to New York to seek his fame and fortune.

Twenty years later, he returned, an international movie star, to receive an award from the school—presented by that same administrator who'd humiliated him.

He spent a year or so working at a settlement house and scrounging for work, unable to find acting jobs. He was living near the Bowery, the neighborhood synonymous with New York's downtrodden, and he went to the Salvation Army for a Thanksgiving dinner. After a long wait on line, he was very disappointed to learn that, just as his turn came, the kitchen had run out of dinners.

A year later, he was feasting in the Fifth Avenue apartment of Katharine Cornell, then the reigning queen of the Broadway stage, for he'd landed a small part in *The Three Sisters*. Actually, his debut was hardly a role at all. Talk about inauspicious! It was at the Ethel Barrymore Theater on December 21, 1942. "I wanted to play a soldier, but someone else got that role. All I got to do was play an orderly and carry a samovar behind Edmund Gwenn. But after the soldier called out '*Yo hooooo*,' I was his offstage echo. I did a better '*Yo hooooo*' than he did!"

"I like to think of acting as an art," he continued. "I like to do something creative with it." Unlike most actors, Douglas rarely used stuntmen. His most dangerous stunt came in *The Vikings*, when, as the prince of the invading horde, he used the handles of axes thrown across a castle moat to climb over the top and open the gates.

"When I had my helicopter crash in 1991," he recalled, "the doctor looked at the scars on my back and observed: 'I see you do your own stunts.'"

"I hate doing fight scenes," he said. "You can get hurt, and that holds up production." But *Champion*, one of his earliest hits, was full of fight scenes, of course, since he played a coldhearted boxer.

In one scene, Douglas's character, "Midge Kelly," was presented with a statuette of a boxer as his prize for being named outstanding athlete of the year. Director Stanley Kramer kept the statuette on his desk as a memento. Douglas decided to borrow it overnight, without Kramer's knowledge, and surprise him with an inscription engraved on its base. But he dropped it, and one of its hands broke off.

The next day, Douglas returned the statuette, which now bore the inscription: "For Stanley, who can lick this movie business with one hand. Kirk."

The premiere of his movie *Ace in the Hole* was held in Albuquerque, where the story was set. At the opening, Douglas was startled by some unexpected laughs. They came in a scene, where as a reporter yearning for escape from that city to a larger media market, he cites his complaints, which include the fact that there is no restaurant in New Mexico that serves chicken liver or garlic pickles. After the opening, Douglas learned why the line got a laugh. He was taken for dinner to a New York–style delicatessen next door to the theater, and was served chicken liver and garlic pickles.

During the McCarthy Red Scare era, Douglas made a speech recalling his immigrant parents, who settled in upstate New York. But he carefully avoided mentioning the country of their births. "I'll only say my mother still can make the best plate of borscht this side of Minsk."

When one of his sons, Joel, was attending a school in Manhattan, he was living with Douglas's first wife Diane, an actress. She was spotted in a TV drama by a classmate of Joel's, who asked him: "So your mother's an actress?" "Yes," replied the boy proudly.

"And what does your father do?"

"Oh, he's a traveling man," Joel replied.

Douglas had a magnificent art collection with works by Chagall, Rouault, Utrillo, and Vlaminck, but none by Van Gogh. That was ironic, because he nearly won the Oscar for portraying the troubled artist in *Lust for Life*, but lost to Yul Brynner for *The King and I*. "I couldn't afford a Van Gogh," he said. "Besides, if I'd bought one, I'd have felt I painted it myself!"

Douglas and his wife eventually sold much of their artwork to fund the restoration of several hundred inner-city playgrounds in Los Angeles, and they attended the ribbon-cutting ceremonies of every one.

Douglas began shooting *Spartacus* with Stanley Mann directing, but the early scenes displeased Douglas, who was also the film's producer. So he reluctantly fired Mann and hired a young director named Stanley Kubrick. Two years later, Kubrick used just fifty actors in directing *Lolita*, a far cry from the 50,000 extras in *Spartacus*.

"Kirk liked having a lot of people around," said Kubrick.

He was one of the first postwar actors to produce his own movies, under the aegis of "Bryna Productions," named for his mother. She lived to see his name—and hers—in lights.

"The fact is, my own company has to compete for my services as an actor," he added. "I'd have liked to have done a play every season on Broadway. I was in ten flops, and I never was a hit there." He did star in the Broadway production of *One Flew Over the Cuckoo's Nest* in 1963, running a mere eighty-two performances. When he was having trouble getting the movie produced, he turned over the rights to his son Michael, who cast an actor twenty-four years younger than his father named Jack Nicholson, who won the Oscar and solidified his own stardom.

"I see my movies twice," he said. "First to see how I did, then to see how everyone else performed." Douglas said that his proudest achievement wasn't one of his performances. No, it came with the movie *Spartacus*, in which blacklisted screenwriter Dalton Trumbo had his good name restored to the credits. "What could they do to me?" asked Douglas, who produced and starred in that sword and sandal classic. "The sky wasn't going to fall."

Several years ago, Douglas was in Pakistan doing a documentary on the Afghanistan refugees on the border. "We were eating strange foods, and I thought I'd be wise and explain Thanksgiving to them. After all, it's one of the most American of holidays. We sat with a tribal elder who said: 'To us, every day is Thanksgiving.' Some of the Mujahadeen seemed to know who I was. But they never showed it. They're so wrapped up in their own problems and lives. All they asked for was guns, not food."

In 1995, I wrote *101 Great Movies for Kids* and included *The Vikings,* one of Douglas's greatest, for older kids. It was perhaps Douglas's most demanding performance, one of the few films ever made about the fearsome Norsemen.

"That was a difficult shoot," he recalled. "I was very egotistical. I insisted we film on location at the Hadanga Fjords in Norway. It rained almost every day. I was an undefeated wrestler in college, so I insisted on doing all my stunts, including walking on the oars.

"At the beginning of the movie, Tony Curtis, who portrayed a slave, hurls his hunting hawk at my face, saying 'Kill!' The rest of the movie, I had to wear a white contact lens over my left eye to make it appear to have been torn out. I could only wear the lens for half an hour at a time, and one day it got stuck. I was young then, so I managed, but I'd never do something like that again."

Then he quizzed me: "Remember the

scene with the baby? That was little Jamie Lee Curtis, Tony Curtis and Janet Leigh's child," he said proudly. "Her screen debut." Actually there were two babies, the usual practice. The other was Douglas's infant son Peter. The daily call sheet giving the assignments had an added request for props: "Warm milk will be served on the set at 11 a.m. There will be pauses hourly for 'necessary changes.'"

My godfather, Sidney Kingsley, wrote *Detective Story*, probably the first play set entirely in a contemporary police station. It was the forerunner of *Dragnet*, *NYPD Blue*, and today's *Law and Order*. Ralph Bellamy starred in it on Broadway, and Douglas got the role on screen, as a short-tempered but dedicated detective with personal issues.

He prepared for the role by riding around midtown New York with real cops and even booked a suspect at the Forty-Seventh Street precinct. "I was fingerprinting the guy," Douglas recalled, "and he recognized me."

"'Aren't you Kirk Douglas?' he asked me. So, not wanting to blow my cover, I said, 'If I were that guy, with all his money, would I be in a place like this booking you?'"

The same thing happened during rehearsals for *One Flew Over the Cuckoo's Nest*. Dressed in tattered clothes in the now-famous story of inmates at a mental institution, Douglas stepped outside for some fresh air. A passerby glanced at him and asked: "Aren't you Kirk Douglas?" "Are you kidding?" he replied. "Dressed like *this*?"

Douglas once played a round of golf in a pick-up threesome. The other two players, portly businessman types, hit balls fairly close to the middle of the fairway. Then Douglas, in a shirt that showed off his rippling muscles, addressed the ball, and hit a slice to the right. "THAT'S *Spartacus?*" said one of the men.

After a dinner at Luchow's, then one of New York's most famous downtown res-

taurants, not far from where he spent his impoverished years in the Bowery, Douglas was recognized by a beggar. Douglas gave him some money. "I never missed a movie of yours," said the beggar. Douglas gave him some more but first said: "Don't let me catch you spending this on one of my movies."

His father sold rags from a one-horse cart. That is, until a group of local anti-Semites killed his horse for spite. When Douglas opened in *One Flew Over the Cuckoo's Nest* tryouts in New Haven, Connecticut, his wife Anne wired: "Don't worry. I wouldn't mind going back to a horse and wagon if need be. Love."

"I've always been drawn to portraying people with deformities," he once told me. "I look for the weakness in strong people I portray and the strength in weak people. That's because drama is chiaroscuro, light and shade, contrast. And what greater contrast is there than between strength and weakness?

"I used to argue with John Wayne about this. It was while I was shooting *Lust for Life*, and we had drinks together. He was furious with me. 'How can you play such a sniveling weakling?' 'Duke, I'm an actor,' I replied. To me, it's always been clear what's make-believe and what's reality."

The most dramatic scene in *Spartacus* was his crucifixion. He makes a poignant near-death farewell to his wife, Varinia, played by Jean Simmons. He looks down at her, too weak to respond as she holds up their infant son to say goodbye. The first take went well—until the audio man realized he'd picked up the radio broadcast of a Dodger game being played nearby.

"I create an illusion of being Spartacus and Van Gogh," he told me. "The audience is supposed to get lost in the role or the movie. I have the responsibility of knowing what I'm doing.

"I hope I don't see myself trying the same

old tricks. If I can see a second of transformation in my performance, then I know I did well. I'd love to play Picasso, but Anthony Hopkins has trod that path before in *Surviving Picasso*.

"Everyone imitates me, including my sons. One time we were watching [mimic Frank] Gorshin doing me, and I was going along, following him. My son Peter was watching, too, and said: 'Dad, Gorshin can do you better than *you!*'"

He never did a Kirk Douglas "imitation," so to speak, better than his incredible performance in *Gunfight at the O.K. Corral*, opposite his favorite frequent costar, Burt Lancaster. Douglas played the tuberculosis-afflicted Doc Holliday. "The trick," he explained to me, "was to keep track of when I coughed. I couldn't cough in every scene, and since movies aren't filmed in sequence, it was tricky to spread out the coughs and make it believable.

"When you mentioned that movie, I got to thinking. Back then we needed only a few shots to kill the bad guy. Today they need machine guns with hundreds of shots. All we needed was one or two."

In his 2007 book, *Let's Face It,* he wrote that people say the old days were better. "I'm beginning to think they were. The younger generation is inheriting a mess. Let's face it. The world is a mess. Even though I've written nine books, I'm an actor. But I love writing because it gives me the opportunity to play young men, old men, and there's no director around to criticize me. I'm the head of the studio."

Douglas starred in *The Indian Fighter*, filmed in rural Oregon, and liked the area so much he bought a nearby ranch. This was over the objections of his business manager. "What on earth do you know about ranching?" he was asked. "Plenty," replied Douglas. "After all, I've already made two Westerns."

Here's an example of how some Hollywood studio heads operate. One reached out to Douglas to star in the movie version of *Pal Joey*, after trying in vain to get Frank Sinatra for the role. Douglas, who'd sung a memorable song in *20,000 Leagues Under the Sea*, was nevertheless hesitant about starring in a full musical. "This isn't a musical," said the executive. "It's for a real actor. Like you. You can learn the singing and dancing."

Douglas agreed, but didn't sign a contract. First he devoted weeks to song-and-dance lessons. Then Sinatra became available and was quickly signed. The next day, the studio executive told his secretary he was leaving for a vacation. "And by the way," he added, heading out the door, "please phone Kirk Douglas and tell him thanks. We got Sinatra."

Perhaps the best collaboration between Douglas and Lancaster was *Seven Days in May*. It was a still-relevant movie, directed by John Frankenheimer, about an attempted military coup to take over the U.S. government. Douglas played Marine Colonel "Jiggs" Casey, aide to the treasonous chairman of the Joint Chiefs of Staff, Air Force General James Matoon Scott, played by Lancaster.

"We wanted to film in the Pentagon," Douglas recalled. "But once the Defense Department read the script, they refused. But first we stole a shot. I'm seen walking into the real Pentagon in the uniform of a Marine full colonel, my character, heading to the office of the Joint Chiefs. Two real Marines saluted me. I guess they noticed the silver eagles on my shoulders. We got the shot we needed. Then they built a mock-up of that huge building. To make the corridors look endless, we dressed little people in uniforms at the far end.

"While we were filming the movie, Vice President Johnson invited me to lunch at the White House. JFK spotted me and came over. 'I hear you're making *Seven Days in May*,' he said. 'Uh oh,' I thought. 'It's a great book,' said the President. What a shame he never lived to see the movie. But he did lend his friend John Frankenheimer, our director, the real Oval Office where Freddie March played the President."

In *The Big Sky*, one of his lesser films, Douglas's character lost a finger. In *Ace in the Hole,* he was stabbed in the stomach with a pair of scissors. He was crucified in *Spartacus* and shot to death by a suspect in *Detective Story.* There was the falcon claw to the eye in *The Vikings,* and his plane was shot down in *In Harm's Way.* "Let's face it," he laughed, when I read him that list. "I'm a poor insurance risk. But one of my early jobs was as a singing telegraph delivery boy. Nothing could be more difficult than *that!*"

In April of 1960, a delegation from Congress was given a tour of the American Embassy in London by Ambassador John Hay "Jock" Whitney. The walls were adorned with the Whitneys' vast personal art collection. One congressman, who apparently knew little about art, stopped to study the Van Gogh self-portrait, thought about it a moment, and remembering only *Lust for Life* blurted out: "Look! Kirk Douglas!"

A man once walked up to Robert Mitchum and gushed: "Oh wow! Kirk Douglas! I loved you in . . ." and then named twenty of Douglas's finest hits. Finally, exasperated, Mitchum said: "What do you want?" "Please sign this for my boss. He'll be so impressed," said the man. "Make it out to 'Bill.'"

Without hesitation, Mitchum pulled out a pen and wrote: "To Bill. Drop dead and go to hell. Sincerely, Kirk Douglas."

One night at a Broadway opening, I spotted Douglas before the curtain rose. We chatted briefly. The first act droned on and on, and to pass the time and try to stay awake, I began writing down the names of Douglas's movies. At intermission, I'd scribbled down a large number of movies and proudly showed them to him, saying sometimes critics use unconventional methods to endure bad theater. He smiled, then counted the titles.

"Fifty-five," he said. "Impressive. Only thirty-five to go. One movie for every year of my life."

JACKIE GLEASON

Every New Year's Eve in New York, WPIX, my old station, carries on a wonderful tradition: they run *The Honeymooners* from midnight for twelve hours. I can think of no better way to start off the New Year. And they run that wonderful show's best season, 1955–56, the one that has spawned a cult all over the country.

Ask anyone of a certain age about the episode in which Art Carney, as Ralph Kramden's best friend Ed Norton, sleepwalks, for example, and a perfect imitation is sure to follow. Or the episode in which Ralph throws his back out. Say "Hello, Ball," and members of the cult will explode in gales of laughter.

My two favorite episodes, for the record, were the one in which poor Ralph crams for a week, trying to learn every modern song ever written for a quiz show, only to . . . well, I won't give it away and "Chef of the Future." The key line to trigger laughter from that one is: "Can it core a apple?"

After Milton Berle became television's first and greatest star, along came Sid Caesar, then Jackie Gleason, whom my father saw virtually every night, holding court in Toots Shor's restaurant. But he knew why he was the center of attention at the best table, all right.

"When you're a hit," he said one night in 1954, "everybody listens. Success makes you an expert on anything."

Just a year before, after his star began to rise when he'd been the original lead in the TV show *The Life of Riley*, he was in Boston where a local newspaperman said Gleason couldn't be considered a real actor.

My mother with "The Great One," Jackie Gleason, probably at Toots Shor's, circa 1968.

"Could you, for example, recite the so-liloquy from *Hamlet?*" I can hear Gleason as Ralph Kramden, nervously wiping his face and saying: "Hammanah Hammanah . . ." to that one.

But a few weeks later, he returned to Boston, saw the same reporter in a local nightclub, mounted a table, and recited the soliloquy flawlessly (perhaps as his other famous character Reginald Van Gleason III) and flew back to New York.

In his early days, Gleason had worked at the Miami Club in Newark, New Jersey, where one night he studied a mobster who wore a big diamond ring. "I watched to see how he handled that ring on his finger, just in case I ever got rich enough to buy one," he said.

It was about that time, when he was still staying in cheap hotels, that a drummer he knew urged him to buy an iron. "You can press your suit and also fry eggs on it," said the drummer. Gleason took his advice and pressed his suit before a performance. Then he tried to fry two eggs on it, but they remained stuck on the iron. He phoned the drummer. "Oh, I forgot to tell you," said the musician. "Before you start frying eggs on the iron, call Harry, our trombone player. He'll give you some trombone oil."

Years later, he'd made millions and drove down Fifth Avenue window-shopping. "I looked and looked," he said, "and couldn't think of a single item I cared to buy."

Soon after that, seated at his favorite table in Shor's, he stared at the calm, be-spectacled man sitting across the table. They'd just met, but the comic hadn't caught the name. "Tell me," said Gleason, "do you hate me because of my millions?"

"Not at all," replied the man, "the more the merrier." It was James A. Michener, whose typewriter had earned him millions of his own for *Tales of the South Pacific, Sayonara, Hawaii*, and *The Bridges at Toko-Ri*, all of which became successful movies.

In early April 1955, Gleason was so popular he had control of three hours of programming on CBS Saturday nights. "The measure of your success depends on your indifference to it," he said. "If you seem indifferent, they pursue you. The only man who should ever press is a tailor." He was asked why comics always seemed sad offstage, in real life. "Because," he said, "when success comes, inhibitions set in. You're being watched. Inhibitions make you sad."

My father noticed that neither his new gold cigarette box nor his gold lighter was monogrammed. "I never do that," Gleason explained. "I'm a mercenary guy. Someday I might have to hock them." Gleason had just signed a new contract for $11 million.

Only once in his life did Gleason travel abroad. One of the reasons is that he could never get the hang of foreign currency. In his defense, back then, British money was very complicated, especially when it came time to figure out tips. Gleason had an ingenious method of dealing with this, however. When he'd leave a cab at his London hotel, he'd give the driver a handful of coins and walk away. If he didn't hear the car drive on immediately, he'd stop and walk back and give the driver more coins until the driver, satisfied with the amount, drove away.

His secret retreat was in Bermuda at the home of Alfred Steele, the industrialist who at the time was married to Joan Crawford. Gleason went there on vacation and took along 400 pounds of prime beef. Since the kitchen there wasn't big enough to store such a large amount of beef, Gleason sent it to a nearby hotel, and ordered portions served to him each day. But the kitchen staff at the hotel feasted on it, and instead sent him Bermuda beef, unbeknownst to him.

When Gleason was a young comic, he later told my father, he was doing stand-up one night and a heckler kept interrupting him. Gleason stopped the show and told the heckler to meet him outside. It turned out to be "Two Ton" Tony Galento, the former Newark bartender who floored Joe Louis in their heavyweight title fight. He easily flattened "The Great One."

In September 1955, his TV competition was the soft-voiced singer Perry Como. "I'm not worried," said Gleason. "Not a bit. When songs start taking the play away from laughter, that'll be the end of TV."

On vacation in Phoenix in April 1956, Gleason was invited to make a presentation at the local racetrack. He stood on one side, the equally rotund racetrack official stood on the other, and in between stood the tiny winning jockey of the featured race. Gleason looked at the two men and said: "We look like a sandwich at a cheap restaurant."

Gleason's first sponsor for his TV show was a coffee company, so at Christmas he sent coffee to all the columnists, including my father. The next year he switched sponsors to a breakfast food company. So everyone received breakfast-food products at Christmas. The following year his sponsors were a pen company and electric razors, which dutifully were sent out to the usual recipients that Christmas. Finally Buick became his principal sponsor, and that Christmas we received a beautiful 1956 Christmas card.

Gleason had a manager named "Bullets" Durgom, who, after a dispute in early 1957, refused to return his client's repeated phone calls. So Gleason rented a large monkey in a cage and sent it to his manager's home with a note: "*Now* will you answer my calls?" Durgom retaliated by having Gleason's bathtub filled with Jell-O. Gleason countered with a series of fifty-pound packages of foul-smelling agricultural products, one package to be delivered every half-hour. Finally the manager answered the phone.

One night at Shor's, Gleason sat with Dame Sybil Thorndike, the great British actress who confessed she'd never heard of him. He invited the grande dame of English theater to join him on an episode of *The Honeymooners*. She asked him what he would do, and he said; "Oh, I'll just shuffle around." He continued to advise the British actress: "Audiences determine the sensitivity. Always sandpaper your sensitivity so that it's always raw. I never rehearse, so whatever I do is fresh, and I'm just as surprised as the audience is. I prepare only the lines, for courtesy's sake, never the emotions."

REX HARRISON

Today, Sir Rex Harrison is best remembered for the London, Broadway, and movie role of Professor Henry Higgins in *My Fair Lady*. He debuted on Broadway in *Sweet Aloes*, running a scant twenty-four performances in March 1936, with famed director Tyrone Guthrie. But he became a star on the New York stage in *Anne of the Thousand Days*. By 1949, he'd starred on screen in *The Ghost and Mrs. Muir, Anna and the King of Siam,* and *Blithe Spirit*.

At the time he was married to Lilli Palmer, his second of six wives. One evening in March 1949, they dined with Charles Boyer, the suave French matinee idol, and were discussing the way they preferred to be shot on a movie screen.

"My left side is my bad one," said Boyer. "So's mine, and so is Rex's," said Palmer. "In fact, that's why Rex and I never can appear in a movie together. Our right sides are the good ones, and so we never could be photographed facing each other in profile."

Benny Goodman's wife was inspecting houses she wanted to rent in Hollywood. One was the home of Harrison and Palmer. She saw the bedrooms and the two dressing rooms. In one of them, she saw twenty photographs of Harrison in different roles. "This must be Miss Palmer's dressing room, right?" she asked. "No," she was told. "This one is Rex Harrison's."

When *My Fair Lady* opened on Broadway in 1956, it became a sensation—one of the greatest musicals in history, and one of Broadway's most famous performances. After a long run, Harrison finally took a vacation, and Edward Mulhare replaced him. On Mulhare's opening night, he found a telegram in his dressing room from Harrison: "It's a horrid feeling, isn't it? But it's better than being out of work. Good luck."

On the night of May 28, 1957, Harrison was out in front alone when he heard the set come tumbling down behind the curtains. He tried to give the cue to the orchestra conductor, who stood transfixed. Then he called for the clarinet, and the clarinetist obliged, enabling Harrison to "sing" "I Am a Most Forgiving Man." Then, briefly stepping out of character, he described the final setting to the audience, and then Julie Andrews joined him for the final number. Costar Stanley Holloway said: "Tonight the show didn't bring the house down. It brought the *scenery* down!"

Another night, the chandelier began descending above Harrison and suddenly lifted his toupee from his head. Harrison looked up at an actor's nightmare; the chandelier going up carrying the toupee. Somehow, he went on for Act II.

In the summer of 1957, Harrison and his subsequent wife Kay Kendall spent weekends on their boat cruising Long Island Sound. He'd sent to England for a British flag to be displayed on the yacht. When it arrived, his wife began to unfurl the flag, but Harrison asked her to put it away.

"It's odd," he explained, "but when we fly the Union Jack, nobody here ever waves at us."

Harrison said of his bride: "She *is* beautiful, but has to be reminded of that once in a while." Soon after that, she had her hair color changed almost to gray. When she returned to her hotel, the elevator man said, referring to her husband: "Your boy just went upstairs."

Harrison returned to Broadway in *The Fighting Cock*, wearing a suit of armor. His costar, Arthur Treacher, admired his costume and said: "Nice suit. Who's your blacksmith?"

The producer had ordered a large number of putty noses brought from England for Harrison, but discarded them. "What good is a good false nose if it makes the high-priced star of the show unrecognizable?" he wondered.

During his run of that play, Harrison had a painting of George Bernard Shaw on his dressing room wall. Shaw, then ninety, inscribed it to Harrison: "From the original, who is twenty years younger and considerably tidier."

Harrison costarred with Richard Burton and Elizabeth Taylor in the ill-fated, highly publicized *Cleopatra,* a disastrous movie that took months of location shooting in Rome and went far over budget. To make matters worse for 20th Century-Fox, Harrison sued the company for neglecting to give him the costar billing his contract required. Studio head Darryl F. Zanuck soothed him, then asked him to come to the New York office to inspect the new ad campaign that gave him full billing.

This satisfied Harrison, who then agreed to pose with a Fox executive holding opening night tickets to the world premiere. Just before the camera clicked, however, Harrison glanced at the tickets: Burton and Taylor's names were on them, but not his.

ERNEST HEMINGWAY

One of the earliest entries in "The Lyons Den" about Ernest Hemingway appeared on September 7, 1937, a year after my father first met him. It was during the height of the bloody Spanish Civil War. Hemingway was in Spain near the front lines, as a war correspondent, and my father chronicled his exploits from cables he received.

"During the recent shelling of Madrid," the item began, "Ernest Hemingway and a group of other Americans found protection in a hotel room. The conversation turned to boxing and one of the correspondents, a New York magazine editor, said he'd once been an amateur boxer. And so in that hotel room, with bombs bursting all over and above Madrid, Ernest Hemingway tested the truth of that statement, slugging it out with the editor, and knocking him out. When both bombardments were over—the one overhead and the other in the room—Hemingway wrote a letter of apology to his opponent, who was so proud that he showed the letter to every American he could find.

"But Hemingway felt he'd been exploited, so he found the editor and KO'd him again."

It was during the Spanish Civil War that Hemingway wrote the play called *The Fifth Column.* It was well received, even before it was staged. Broadway producers said they were interested in it, so they wired Hemingway, who by that time was annoyed at the previous efforts to present the play.

Hemingway's terse reply: "'Fifth Column.' Sixth draft. Seventh producer. Eighth refusal."

On July 30, 1940, he was back in New York for a short visit and revealed that he occasionally walked in his sleep. In his homes in Key West or Havana, where he slept in a ground-floor bedroom, this presented no

With Ernest Hemingway at the Stork Club on March 13, 1945. Hemingway's jacket label reads:
"War Correspondent."

problems. A New York hotel room, however, might be a different story. So Hemingway asked a friend: "If you ever catch me walking in my sleep, wake me immediately. Just yell: 'Dr. Hemmingstone, I presume.' That always wakes me up."

Later that summer, Hemingway returned to New York, and at the Stork Club, he saw old friend Dorothy Parker, the great writer. It had been two years since he'd seen the famous raconteur and wit and slapped her on the back.

"How ya doin', Dotty?" Hemingway asked. "What's new?" Parker turned and saw the imprint of Hemingway's hand on her reddened shoulder and replied curtly: "Nothing's new, Ernest. Except the way you're giving your autograph nowadays."

Late in 1940, Hemingway recalled that during his time in Spain covering the Civil War from the Loyalist side, he was in Guadalajara, the city were he'd seen Russian soldiers among the troops. But they were discouraged about their prospects for victory. Other journalists then reported that they'd seen Red Army soldiers fighting amongst themselves. Hemingway revealed that what those other reporters actually saw was the bearded Hemingway himself in a fur hat, boxing with a Russian soldier he'd befriended, to keep trim.

In the spring of 1941, Hemingway received an invitation to go aloft in a skywriting plane. "No thanks," he said. "You fliers get $20 a letter. Me? I don't get that much dough for a paragraph." In fact, by 1941, Hemingway's price had soared to about a dollar per word.

With the great sportswriter Jimmy Cannon, and an even greater writer, Ernest Hemingway, circa 1940. When Hemingway won the Nobel Prize for Literature in 1954, Cannon vowed to go home and beat up his typewriter.

In May of that year, he observed that New York newspapers always made too much out of brief fights in nightclubs. "Down in Key West," he said, "everyone there has at least three or four fights a night. We just call that 'exercise.'"

On January 15, 1941, the day King Alfonso XIII of Spain abdicated and went into exile in France, Hemingway witnessed his arrival in Biarritz, just over the border from Spain. As he and a friend sat at an outdoor café, Hemingway scribbled his impressions on a notepad, not realizing that that was the beginning of his inspiration for *For Whom the Bell Tolls*, one of the great novels of the twentieth century.

He received a handsome sum from Paramount for the movie rights to *For Whom the Bell Tolls*. "I wait one year before collecting my dough," he observed, "for a book which took me two years to write, after spending

three years getting shot at in some war collecting material. Then, I have to pay most of it to the government in four installments."

Hemingway didn't get to see the final movie version until three years later, in May 1944, but he'd attended two screenings. After sitting through an hour of the first showing, Hemingway had left, saying he was disappointed in the watered-down treatment of his strong anti-Fascist story. However, he liked Ingrid Bergman and his friend Gary Cooper. "But in the love scenes, Cooper keeps his jacket on," he said. "That's a helluva way for a guy to make love to a gal."

That same month, May 1944, Hemingway lunched in New York with a friend. A woman at a nearby table noticed that the other man had the beginnings of a beard. She approached the table and asked him about it. "Obviously an affectation," the other man replied. "The kind of thing writers like to do." It was future Nobel Prize winner John Steinbeck.

A few weeks later, Hemingway lunched with W. Somerset Maugham, author of *The Razor's Edge*, and Erich Maria Remarque, who wrote *All Quiet on the Western Front*. Hemingway invited a young, unknown writer to the table, saying: "I think this will be good for him, in case he ever writes his memoirs."

Hemingway had something in common with his friend Orson Welles. Both had been young reporters, and both had been caught skipping out on an assignment. Welles reviewed an opera he hadn't seen, and thus was not aware a different one was performed that night. Hemingway was assigned by the *Toronto Star* to cover the visit of British Prime Minister David Lloyd George to New York. The PM went to a Broadway show, and Hemingway waited outside, figuring he had two hours to kill. The reporters from the other papers, however, followed Lloyd George inside, and thus covered the noisy heckling by I R A supporters in the audience when the Prime Minister was introduced.

Hemingway, meanwhile, went off to attend a prizefight, certain he'd be back at the theater by the end of the show.

Paul Gallico, later to achieve fame by writing *The Snow Goose* and *The Poseidon Adventure*, was a fellow war correspondent and marveled at Hemingway's ability to cover the fighting. "Everywhere we went," said Gallico, "there was nothing at the front between us and the Germans. Except Ernest Hemingway."

Younger war correspondents near the front owed Hemingway a great debt. He would carry the wire service dispatches they filed back to the rear for delivery, and supplied them with tips on how to cable their stories. Hemingway explained that he was writing for a magazine, and thus enjoyed longer deadlines.

Just after D-Day, Hemingway had shaved his famous beard before encountering a young military policeman at a checkpoint. The clean-shaven Hemingway was wearing a white coat once owned by a Nazi officer on the Russian front. At gunpoint, the most famous writer of the century submitted his identification papers, including a photo of himself with his trademark beard.

The young MP pondered this for a moment, then said; "OK, you can pass. No spy would fake it that badly."

In March 1945, Hemingway arrived in Paris and headed straight for the studio of his friend Pablo Picasso, to make certain the artist was safe from Nazis still in the vicinity. Before he left, the soldier who'd accompanied Hemingway gave Picasso four grenades. Just in case.

Two months later, the fighting around Paris had finally subsided. Hemingway disappeared in the direction of the famed Abbey at Mont-Saint-Michel. He told his competitors from other media that he was off to do some historical research. Two week later, the correspondents found his trail.

On the walls of the liberated abbey they spotted the words: "Property of Ernest Hemingway."

On his way home to Cuba after the war, Hemingway sat with my father one night at Sardi's. Already at work on a new book, Hemingway said he was letting his hair go uncut again, to save time while working. He also wanted to be sure he looked unkempt, to avoid the temptation to hang out with his friends at the local bar.

Nevertheless, a few days later, a friend sailed his yacht into Havana harbor and invited Hemingway aboard for lunch. When told why Hemingway was letting his hair grow, the friend wondered: "What if my crew held you down while my barber cuts your hair? What would you do?" Hemingway drew his knife and calmly assured his friend: "I'd kill them."

Back in New York early the following year, Hemingway met a fan who told him she'd been unimpressed and disappointed with *To Have and Have Not*. "Did you buy it?" asked Hemingway, reaching into his pocket. "No, it was a gift," she replied.

"Too bad," he responded. "I was reaching to refund your money."

When he was finishing writing *Across the River and Into the Trees*, he explained it was then time to "use my personal junk detector. I spray it over the manuscript, and all the junk paragraphs and pages drop off. Whatever is left is published."

Hemingway wasn't concerned with what obituary writers might say about his place in American letters. But he did want one fact made clear for history: It could only be substantiated by George Brown, owner of Brown's gymnasium in New York. "He can attest to the fact that I had a quick left jab and a hard right cross," he explained.

This was in sharp contrast to the man who entertained the Duke and Duchess of Windsor the following April at his *finca*, his farm outside Havana in San Francisco de Paola. Hemingway solved the problem of protocol about how the Duchess should be addressed: Instead of referring to her as "Your Highness" or "Your Royal Highness," he simply called the former Wallis Warfield Simpson of Baltimore, Maryland, "Wallie."

When a magazine invited Hemingway to contribute an article, but said it would not pay a fee, he was assured he would be "writing for the cause of true art." "Sorry, pal," Hemingway replied; "I write for a living. I am not a 'true artist.'" When a young writer complained of high taxes on his books, Hemingway advised: "Accumulate your experiences now—and write about them later."

At the end of June 1949, *Esquire* magazine decided to republish a short story it had purchased from Hemingway in 1937. At that time, he'd promised the magazine he'd write the story, but had to finish another

My brothers and I (in the background) with Ernest and Mary Hemingway
and my father at Finca Vigía, San Francisco de Paola, Cuba, December 1952.

work first for *Cosmopolitan*. The day he finished that piece, Hemingway wrote *Esquire*: "Don't worry. I'll write you one tonight with the same African background."

The story for *Cosmopolitan* was the memorable *The Short, Happy Life of Francis Macomber*. But the story he wrote that night for *Esquire* was *The Snows of Kilimanjaro*, which some have praised as one of the finest stories ever written in English.

Hemingway said that 203 pounds was his "best writing weight." By 1949, he'd been receiving as much as $25 per word. A member of his household kept meticulous records of the number of words he wrote each day. A visitor studied the chart of his new book, which read: "July 18—77 words. July 19—1,272. July 20—573. July 21—nothing. My birthday."

My father, a friend of Marlene Dietrich, knew Hemingway was a great admirer of the famous actress, about whom he said: "Marlene is one of the few people who deserve the praise we usually give to people who don't deserve it."

Finally they met. It was in April 1950, and she told him a man was abusing women she knew. She of course was referring obliquely to herself. So, aware of this, Hemingway taught her how to hit a straight right cross, and she later used the technique to flatten the man.

At the Stork Club one night, Hemingway announced he'd sold the movie rights for one of his novels for $150,000. When the bill came, he asked for change. "It's still early," said proprietor Sherman Billingsley. "Wait until closing. We'll have enough in the till by then."

When *Across the River and Into the Trees* was published, John O'Hara, whose works include *Butterfield 8, A Rage to Live*, and *Pal Joey*, reviewed the book in the *New York Times*. He called Hemingway's novel "the loftiest piece of prose committed to paper since 1616." O'Hara was so respected, no editor was allowed to alter so much as one word of his writing. Nevertheless, the *Times*'s editors convinced him to explain "1616." So he added four words: "The year Shakespeare died."

On another visit to New York, Hemingway said he usually wrote three versions of a novel. Once the final version was completed, he burned the earlier ones. "Why should anybody be interested in the mistakes I've made?" he explained. "The writing in the finished manuscript is the best I know how to do. Anyway, people just care to look at the skin, not the meat and the bones."

He wrote in longhand or at a manual typewriter placed on a shelf, chest high, and worked standing up. A room at his home in Key West, now a museum, has just such a display. The rewriting for the second and third versions was done while he was seated at a desk.

"Dictating is not for me," he said. "I could dictate a novel a month if I had to, but it wouldn't be good enough."

His high school in Oak Park, Illinois, once invited Hemingway to return for a special day in his honor. That was because part of the planned ceremonies would be the display of his old high school football uniform and cleats. "I barely made the squad," he said, "and probably was the worst football player they ever had."

Concerning the frequent misstatements printed about him, Hemingway said: "If a writer thinks fiction is a necessary part of his autobiography, I think it would be simpler if he put fiction in italics."

He never wrote his own autobiography, though elements of his adventurous life were in his novels. But if he had written such a book, he'd surely remember the city editor of a Chicago newspaper who refused to hire the young reporter.

"He was right," Hemingway recalled. "Because I didn't even know where all the police precincts were."

"I never had to sell a share of stock I bought," he recalled on another occasion. "Never had to. I can ride out any depression, as long as they put me in a chair and give me a pen and paper."

On January 25, 1954, the world received the terrible news that Ernest and Mary Hemingway had reportedly been killed in an African plane crash. Soon afterward, however, came news that they'd survived. My father wrote: "Every writer will please step back. For the void has not yet opened at the top."

A few days later, Hemingway was back at his old haunts in New York and invited my father to accompany him the next morning to the basement shooting range of Abercrombie & Fitch, the famous sporting goods store. He was testing .577s, huge ammunition for an elephant gun he planned to use on safari.

My father, a self-described "street corner guy," neither knew nor cared about guns of any sort. What's more, he stood about 5 feet 9, so toting a hefty gun was no easy task. It would, furthermore, be a safe bet that he only used the word "recoil" in the sense of shying away from something repulsive, not reacting to the kick of a heavy hunting rifle.

Thus, acting on instinct alone, he lifted the gun and steadied himself against the back wall of the firing range. When he squeezed the trigger, the enormous recoil smashed my father against the concrete wall, dislocating his shoulder and nearly giving him a concussion, much to Hemingway's amusement.

In 1954, Hemingway won the Nobel Prize for Literature. Naturally he was inundated with congratulatory messages from all over the world. The lone operator at the Cuban telegraph office near his *finca* was swamped. He had but one telegraph key, one typewriter, and no assistant; thus he had to work without relief for hours. The main office in Havana could easily have forwarded the piles of messages to San Francisco de Paola by bus, which would've taken an hour. But rules were rules, and they had to be wired. It took four days.

"Carl Sandburg deserved it more than I," Hemingway said. When Sandburg heard that, he was pleased for several reasons. Years before in Chicago, he'd tutored a young reporter named Mary Welch, who would become Hemingway's fourth and last wife.

Soon afterward, Hemingway was back at work, saying: "No prize is worth interrupting work on a good book." He even rejected a lucrative fee to appear on television in New York. "Not until I begin to show some special talent," he explained.

Late in 1957, Hemingway had temporarily put aside his next big novel to concentrate on a newer, exciting project. The manager of the Ritz Hotel had found old trunks Hemingway had stored away in the basement in 1932 and forgotten about. They contained a treasure trove: his original manuscript for *A Farewell to Arms*, plus short stories not yet published, and notebooks he'd kept during those important years. He estimated it would take six secretaries, working year 'round, to transcribe the notebooks that covered his friendships and events of his years in Paris in the 'twenties.

One spring day, my father and Hemingway visited the Bronx Zoo, where Hemingway identified all the birds and animals, even the exotic ones. At the hippo area, he started making guttural, purring sounds saying, "I talk Hippo. But I need Miss Mary around for the grammar."

That night, they were joined at Toots Shor's by Jackie Gleason, who was kidded by Hemingway about his weight. Then Gleason opened a gold cigarette case, lit a cigarette with his gold lighter, flashed his gold cuff links, and displayed his gold ring and money clasp. Hemingway glanced at his own sleeves, which bore no cuff links, then showed Gleason his money clasp; a simple paper clip.

Gleason explained: "You've got talent and everybody knows it. But me? I need these gold things to prove to people I've got talent too."

They discussed the poor TV reception from Miami that Hemingway had to endure in Cuba. "I get four batters and four pitchers when I watch baseball," he said. "I'd settle for two apiece."

In January 1957, Hemingway invited my father to Paris to show him the city of his youth. When they arrived at the Left Bank, Hemingway recalled: "I used to hack around here after the First War. That's how you get to know a city: drive a cab." They stood for a moment on the bridge near the Place Dauphin. "A great spot to fish," he recalled, pointing to the riverbank. The wind was blowing off the Seine in whistling gusts. "After you get to a certain age," he observed, "it gets into your body and finds the places where it hurts."

While they walked, Hemingway maneuvered so that my father would be on his right side, because the hearing in his left ear was gone, a result of the African plane crash in 1954. A local doctor, assuring him that "Gin is good for you, inside and out," poured part of a bottle into the wound in his ear.

At the Cluny Museum they inspected ancient tapestries and the armor worn by Crusaders. "Those men were under five feet, mostly," Hemingway observed. "Bantamweights and featherweights, for maximum speed. Almost no good heavyweights. Nothing's changed."

Then my father had a surprise for him: a reunion with Ingrid Bergman, who'd starred in *For Whom the Bell Tolls*. Hemingway said he and my father would volunteer to be her "seconds," for what would surely be a duel with the press, when she returned to New York from her self-imposed exile after her scandalous divorce and marriage to director Roberto Rossellini.

When Hemingway had entered the room, she beamed and said: "It's wonderful to act the roles you create. Those words you write! An actress can digest them so easily. You don't have to use any salt and pepper."

Back in New York in April 1959, Hemingway was at his usual table at Toots Shor's restaurant. There he inscribed a copy of *The Old Man and the Sea* for Shor, the gruff restaurateur who was never mistaken for an intellectual. "Ruffle the pages a bit, Toots," Hemingway suggested. "That way, people will think you actually read it."

During his conversation with Shor, three women at a nearby table recognized him, and one ran out to a nearby bookstore and returned with an armload of books for him to inscribe. That often happened to him. On a drive from Venice to Monte Carlo, for instance, his car stopped at the mountain village of Cueno. The townspeople recognized him and brought out every Hemingway book in the small local bookstore, and requested that he inscribe them. Then, when they ran out of *his* books, they brought many he didn't write, and asked him to inscribe those, too.

"I was signing everything from Galileo to cookbooks," he recalled.

Nevertheless, at the French border, a Customs official ordered a thorough inspection of his car. Then he asked Hemingway his occupation. "I write books," said the most famous practitioner of that craft in the twentieth century. "I write books in stiff covers."

Back in New York soon after that, Hemingway was complimented by a confirmed bachelor who bragged he'd read all his books. "Sure," said Hemingway. "Any guy who sleeps alone must do lots of reading."

He recalled the time, years before in New Orleans, when he took his then-wife and her mother to the racetrack, armed with some good tips from friends. "I wanted to show her I could earn a livelihood," he said. Then he picked seven winners. His mother-in-law, watching him collect the large cash payoffs said: "I don't see why you waste your time with this other thing, this writing," she told the future Nobel Prize winner, "when you can do this!"

One night at a restaurant in New York, my father dined with Hemingway and his editor and adapter, A.E. Hotchner. Suddenly a stranger approached and interrupted the conversation. Then he asked: "Mind if I join you?" and before waiting for the answer he didn't want to hear, he sat down. Hemingway disdainfully referred to such people as "joiners." Mary Hemingway, at a Havana restaurant, once punched a joiner who insisted on staying at their table. He took the hint and left.

This particular joiner began: "My wife and I have read all your great novels: *All Quiet on the Western Front*, *The Bridge of San Luis Rey*, and your masterpiece, *The Grapes of Wrath*. You really captured the despair of the Depression in that one, Mr. Hemingway. Brilliant writing. Only you could've created those books."

To the astonishment of my father and Hotchner, Hemingway accepted the joiner's invitation to meet his wife at a nearby table, then returned.

"Ernest," asked Hotchner. "Didn't he ever hear of Erich Maria Remarque, Thornton Wilder, and John Steinbeck?"

"No, 'Hotch,'" replied Hemingway, patiently. "My way's better. He'll get the comeuppance he deserves tomorrow. He'll brag to all his friends about our conversation, and they'll correct him about the authors of those books, and then they won't believe it happened, that anyone could make such a mistake. Then if he persists, they'll tell him he's an idiot."

A few weeks before his sudden, shocking death, Hemingway told my father he was ready to leave his home in Ketchum, Idaho, having completed his new book. "He looks forward to returning to the Gritti Palace Hotel in Venice," my father wrote. "When he last stayed there, years ago, he and his friends held the world's first indoor Olympics in his large suite.

"They had sprints across the room, high-jump and pole vault competitions, hurdles over chairs and suitcases, and a soccer match using the hotel bars of soap. But the next day, when he checked out, the management refused his offer to pay for the damages. The manager said that the hotel had been the scene of many firsts since the fourteenth century. 'Yours was the first indoor Olympics. So that'll be 10 percent off your bill.'"

On Sunday, July 2, 1961, Mary Hemingway called the Beverly Hills Hotel in Los Angeles, where she knew my father was staying, and told him the terrible news. She asked him to make the announcement to the world.

The Hemingways had just returned from the Mayo Clinic, and Mary said they'd enjoyed a leisurely five-day drive by car. Ernest felt well enough to think of hunting again, and was cleaning his gun. "It went off, and he died," she said. That's how the story was released. Later it was revealed that Hemingway's father, an Oak Park, Illinois, physician, had taken his own life, and that he was suffering from cancer. And just shy by one day of the thirty-fifth anniversary of her grandfather's death, Margaux Hemingway, an actress and model, would follow suit.

In his tribute column to his old friend the next day, my father wrote: "Simplicity had a writing style so pure that another great writer, Ben Hecht, compared it to baby talk. I heard Somerset Maugham say that of all the storytellers, Hemingway was the giant."

The man who translated his books into

Russian said the hardest thing was duplicating his purity of style. Over the years, Hemingway never received even one ruble in royalties. Then, on a visit to Cuba, Russian Premier Anastas Mikoyan visited the *finca*, Hemingway's farm, and offered to pay at last. But Hemingway refused, saying: "I'll accept the royalties only when you pay all other American writers you've published in Russia too."

"He wrote of violence because he knew it," my father continued. "He still limped from his wounds from the First World War. I once saw him in a nightclub where he'd flattened a big-league ballplayer, trading punch for punch until the other man crumpled to the floor.

"'Me hurt?' he laughed. 'No. Spitting teeth is for suckers.'

"He never spat teeth, no matter the disappointments or tragedies, not even wars or bullfights or the plane crash in Africa. His was an adventurous life, full of violence but full of love, too. He was a man with five hometowns: Oak Park, Illinois; Paris; Key West; Havana; and Venice.

"Death came to Hemingway in none of those towns, nor on the battlefields nor on the hunts in Africa. It came to him on a peaceful Sunday morning in Ketchum, Idaho, in one brief, violent blast.

"Brendan Behan, the great Irish playwright and poet, who'd known him, called me from Dublin when he heard the tragic news:

"'Ernest Hemingway was the man all writers of my generation wanted to be. He was a way of life.'"

Three months after his death, Mary Hemingway wrote my father to update him on efforts to sort his huge collection of papers and books.

"We worked 12–14 hours a day sorting Papa's papers," she wrote. "You know he never threw away even magazine wrappers. He kept things in no sort of order at all—poems mixed in with garage bills and torn out clippings of baseball scores.

"There are 5,000 books in the *finca* in Cuba, books in four languages and covering varied branches of research from anthropology and oceanography to ecology and art.

"The original idea was to make a museum, but I want to make it a study center so that the books would be useful instead of merely ornamental, and they agreed. The *finca* as you saw it last and remember it remains as always."

She revealed that she'd burned letters he'd never sent, some written in anger, rather than let "strangers" get a look at them.

"Not any of these letters had anything whatsoever to do with literature or his or anyone else's biographies, or even with his literary style. They were hurtful to the people to whom he had written them, and since he did not send them I felt sure that he would not wish them to be available for reading. Ever."

AUDREY HEPBURN

Just as Marilyn Monroe is the enduring sex symbol of all time, so too Audrey Hepburn will always embody the height of sophistication and fashion, no matter what the era. She wasn't in New York often during her starring years, but when she was, she made good copy. She and my father became fast friends.

By early 1954, she'd become a star, after the movie *Roman Holiday* and on Broadway in *Ondine*, costarring with her future husband Mel Ferrer. When asked about her ascending career, the young actress said: "I'm both delighted and worried."

It was a London stage manager named Archie Thompson who'd discovered the Belgian-born beauty, the daughter of a wealthy English banker and a Dutch baroness. It was at a chorus call for *High Button Shoes*, the Jule Styne–Sammy Cahn musical. "She was pretty and looked American," Thompson said, perfect for a show set in New Brunswick, New Jersey. As the time for assembling the cast approached, however, she was nowhere to be found. Thompson had taken the precaution of getting her phone number, called her, and, to his amazement, was told she couldn't attend prerehearsal meetings because she had to perform at her ballet school.

"It's time to make a choice," he told the young dancer. "You're in the theater now. So is it ballet or theater?"

She thought a moment and said: "I'll stay with the theater." Thus was launched the career of one of the movies' enduring stars.

Later that year, she lunched at a midtown restaurant in Manhattan. Nearby sat Monte Proser who'd produced the London company of *High Button Shoes*. "Congratulations on your stardom," he began, then noticed her blank, inattentive stare. "Don't you remember me? I produced *High Button Shoes* in London. That gave you your start."

"I'll never forget you," she replied, now glaring at him. "You thought I was too skinny, and had to be convinced to hire me." She nodded curtly, then rose, and walked out.

There couldn't have been two more different types of movie stars than Hepburn and Gary Cooper, but at a meeting in New York, they compared the origins of their respective careers. "I began in the chorus," she told him. "Me too, sort of," replied Cooper. "I started out in the posse."

In June 1954, a Swedish newspaper ran a photo contest to select the girl who looked most like Audrey Hepburn. It published the pictures of those resembling her, and also a photo of the actress herself, just to see the reaction. The real Hepburn had entered the contest, and came in fourth in the voting.

When it was announced she'd be marrying her *Ondine* costar Mel Ferrer, she got lots of advice against marrying someone in the same profession. "I've learned this much," she replied. "An actress's best chance for a happy marriage is with someone in the same profession, with the same hopes, the same anxieties."

It was in the movie *Love in the Afternoon* that Maurice Chevalier, the elegant old French star, admitted to himself that finally he was no longer a young man. Director Billy Wilder stopped in the middle of a scene and said to the then-sixty-eight-year-old Chevalier: "Maurice, remember, in this movie you're not supposed to be in love with Audrey Hepburn. You're portraying her father."

Later Chevalier said: "I'm flattered to be portraying Audrey's father. Actually, I'm old enough to be her grandfather."

At a party in New York late in 1957, she sat with Rex Harrison and recalled how they'd met in Paris. "You told us that night about a new musical you'd signed on to do," she said, "and bemoaned the fact that you can't sing a note. Whatever happened to that little show?" That party, incidentally, marked Harrison's final performance in "that little show": *My Fair Lady*.

While filming the movie version of *My Fair Lady*, Hepburn wore dirty old clothes for her role as Eliza Doolittle, but, in between scenes, she squirted Givenchy perfume over herself. "I may look dirty," she laughed, "but I smell sweet."

ALFRED HITCHCOCK

Early in 1939, the New York Film Critics' Circle awarded its prize to Alfred Hitchcock for *The Lady Vanishes*. His American representative, Albert Margolies, immediately phoned Hitchcock in London with the good news. He forgot it was then 4 a.m. there.

"I'm too sleepy to take this in," responded Hitchcock. "Never wake someone with news like that."

Five hours later when it was then four in the morning in New York, Hitchcock called Margolies back and said: "Thanks."

A few weeks later, Hitchcock revealed to my father one of his favorite filming techniques. "One of my favorites," he said, "is to cut the sound of a woman's scream into a train whistle. But I'll never be able to do that here in America," he continued. "One of the first things I noticed is that American train whistles are several octaves lower."

Hitchcock once sailed for New York aboard the luxurious French liner S.S. *Normandie* (later to capsize at a Manhattan dock after a suspicious fire).

He was assured of the ship's exquisite cuisine. During the voyage he ordered every conceivable exotic dish, but never stumped the chef. On the third night out, Hitchcock ordered "Pompano."

"What's that?" asked the startled waiter. "That's a delicious fish, found in tropical waters," Hitchcock stated, almost triumphantly, no doubt.

"Just a moment" said the waiter, and rushed to the Captain's Table for a hurried conference. The captain's face reddened as he heard the exotic request. Finally he rose in his seat, made a sweeping gesture with his right hand, and ordered: "Turn south!"

The most famous quote attributed to Hitchcock was first reported in "The Lyons Den" on February 23, 1940. George Raft had

Jessica Tandy, Hume Cronyn, Alfred Hitchcock, and my father together in October 1955.

just completed costarring in *The House Across the Bay* and told Hitchcock what a pleasure it was watching the director at work. Uncredited, Hitchcock had shot a scene with costars Joan Bennett and Walter Pidgeon.

"Thanks," replied Hitchcock. "In my pictures," he kidded, "all actors are like cattle. I just take them and make them do what I want them to do."

Raft muttered, walked away, shook his head, and said: "Nobody's going to make me say 'Moo.'"

A few weeks later, Errol Flynn spotted Hitchcock in a restaurant and mentioned that quote to a friend, saying he'd read Hitchcock hates actors. "I'll ask him," offered the friend, who then went over to Hitchcock's table.

"No, I don't hate actors," said Hitchcock. "I merely loathe them."

Hitchcock was in New York in July 1940, and spoke about the kind of movie he likes to do: "It should be a story which can be told in a few paragraphs on one page of copy paper. From that is written the screen-play, in which the characters are delineated, their history and action explained, and then all the resources of the studio resolve it into film and sound track.

"Then, when a man sees it on the screen it should be the kind of story which he relates to his wife later in a few short paragraphs, which would be exactly like the original synopsis, and yet make her interested enough to want to see it."

On another occasion in July 1940, Hitchcock sighed. "Disney's got it right. He handles actors by drawing them."

At the end of July 1940, Hitchcock wanted to confer with a writer over lunch. The director showed up with four friends. The writer assumed Hitchcock would request a table for six, but instead Hitchcock said to the headwater: "Three tables for two, please."

In mid-May 1941, Hitchcock was shooting a film called *Before the Fact*, which later was changed to its now-famous title, *Suspicion*. His star, Joan Fontaine, called in sick one day, so Hitchcock, who always shot scenes in his head before rolling his cameras, decided to make use of what might've been a lost day of production and film another scene. At 9 a.m. he began to design a nightclub set and sent it to the Scenic Department for construction. He told the RKO casting director to hire an actor he'd used in an earlier movie, portraying a nightclub employee. In the afternoon, the director visited his set and ordered the nightclub wall repainted.

Finally at 3 p.m. they were ready to shoot. Hitchcock assumed his position, ordered the lights to be set, and the filming began. Then the nightclub employee lifted a phone and said: "Hogarth Club," and Hitchcock announced: "That's all, thank you. Now dismantle the set."

Hitchcock's trademark, besides tension, good performances, and fine directing, was always a cameo, usually at the beginning of his films. In *Suspicion,* he said he did a poor job of giving direction to himself in the cameo. He can be glimpsed in the background. But the camera was too far away to reveal what he was doing. He tries to deposit a letter in the mailbox. The envelope is too large, and so he shrugs, folds the envelope, then deposits it that way.

Hitchcock's first thriller was *Blackmail.* It starred the Czech actress Anny Ondra, whose embraces were crushing, powerful. "Take it easy," Hitchcock had to caution her. "This is a love scene, not a prizefight."

It became ironic, however, when Ondra married Max Schmeling, the reigning Heavyweight Champion.

When John Houseman, the writer-director-author-actor, was being investigated for a wartime government job, a federal agent visited Hitchcock to ask some routine background questions.

Hitchcock simply replied: "I know of three great Americans: Lincoln, Washington, and John Houseman."

John Houseman, incidentally, was born in Bucharest, Romania. He got the government job.

For civilians especially, any transatlantic travel during the war was hazardous. In December 1943, Hitchcock was going to return to England from Hollywood. He explained to a concerned friend: "First I go to Grand Central Station in New York. There I'll meet an old lady selling violets. I'll whisper to her 'M-42.' She'll give me a bouquet with a card reading: 'M-43.' This is a code telling me to take a certain train. At the end of the ride, I'll phone a 'Captain X,' who will answer: 'M-44.' Then I'll be blindfolded.

"When I hear the sound of either a throb or a whirr, I'll know whether I'm traveling by plane or by boat. Then, when my blindfold is removed, another old lady will hand me a card reading: 'You're in England! Welcome home.'"

During the filming of *Lifeboat,* a dispute broke out between Hitchcock and studio head Darryl F. Zanuck. He wanted music inserted at the most dramatic moments. "But it's set in a lifeboat in the middle of the ocean," Hitchcock protested. "People will wonder where the orchestra came from."

"The music," the music director replied, "will come from the movie director, from the same place the camera came from. There will be music in it."

While shooting, Hitchcock suddenly realized that Tallulah Bankhead, one of the people on the lifeboat, wasn't wearing underwear. So he stopped his cameras and asked her why.

"My dear boy," she growled in her deep Alabama drawl, "if a woman wants to be kissed, does she wear a veil?"

Hitchcock replied: "I'm not sure who to call first: wardrobe or makeup!"

When he returned to Hollywood from England in March 1944, Hitchcock brought back a souvenir for his fourteen-year-old daughter; a souvenir only Hitchcock would choose: a dud Nazi incendiary bomb.

In London, Hitchcock was conferring with his screenwriters and government officials when a young Women's Auxiliary Air Force private arrived. Hitchcock said to her: "Your hair needs doing." So he phoned the hotel hairstylist and arranged for the WAAF, "Gladys," to receive a permanent wave immediately. She thus kept the next customer, Princess Alexandra of Yugoslavia, waiting. The uniformed WAAF, "Gladys," was, in peacetime, the Hitchcocks' housekeeper.

Hitchcock wanted Salvador Dalí's visual genius for *Spellbound*, but he first had to hammer out a financial agreement. Dalí said he didn't speak English well enough to sign anything. So he brought his agent, Felix Ferry, to Hitchcock's house in Bel Air, where the director painstakingly described the plot. Ferry, a Romanian, translated it into French for Dalí, a Spaniard.

Then Hitchcock said he would discuss the amount of money Dalí would receive.

"Señor Hitchcock," said Dalí. "You speak about money, I understand English."

In October 1944, Dalí was in Hollywood to paint the dream sequences for *Spellbound*, and pretended he couldn't understand any of the languages in which he was addressed. A studio executive warned everyone: "There are twenty-six letters and ten numerals. The money-wise Dalí understands none of the letters—but all of the numerals."

Dalí had designed one scene showing three pianos suspended from the ceiling, upside down. But when he saw the completed set, he noticed that the pianos were not full-size as he'd planned, but were miniatures created to scale. He paced up and down muttering: "Not Dalí, not Dalí, not Dalí."

To which Hitchcock replied: "But Hitchcock. But Hitchcock. But Hitchcock."

Later, Hitchcock sent for a psychiatrist, Dr. Eileen Johnston, to get her approval of the sets and their proper psychiatric interpretation. Dalí watched her walk around the set studying his surrealistic touches. Finally he could stand it no longer. "Tell me," he asked. "Did Hitchcock hire you to examine the set—or me?"

When Dalí was on the set, *Vogue* asked him to pose for a photo with Hitchcock and Ingrid Bergman, the star of *Spellbound*. "I'll arrange the photo," said Dalí. Showing that he sometimes did not dwell in the surreal world, the photo he staged has Hitchcock and Bergman seated in low chairs, while Dalí, perched on a chair six feet high, had them looking up at him.

Spellbound is set in an asylum for psychopaths. Hitchcock arranged his opening scene and told his stars, Gregory Peck and Bergman, how he wanted them to play it. Then he turned to the twenty extras portraying patients and said: "The rest of you, behave just as you normally would."

In May 1947, Hitchcock was back in New York and reminisced about one of his early films, 1931's *Rich and Strange*. He showed a drunk weaving along the deck of an ocean liner, crashing into passengers. Then came a storm, and Hitchcock showed the same drunk walking as if on a straight line, while the sober passengers weaved and staggered along the deck of the storm-tossed ship.

Filming *Stage Fright* in England with Jane Wyman, Marlene Dietrich, and Richard Todd posed a problem. As production wore on, Hitchcock realized that the all-important 183rd day of his stay there was approaching. Any American taxpayer—which he'd become—who worked in England more than half a year, became subject to double taxation, paying both English and American income taxes. So Hitchcock flew to Switzerland where, by phone to the set in England, he rehearsed the last two days' work. Then he flew to Paris where his production associates showed him the results.

In March 1950, Hitchcock was back in

town and talked with my father about his favorite actresses. One was Alida Valli, who costarred with Gregory Peck for Hitchcock in *The Paradine Case*. He explained she was expert at crying real tears. To display this unusual ability, Valli once produced tears for him in thirty seconds.

Then, by way of encore, the actress said; "I'll now cry for you with the tears dropping only from one eye. Which eye do you want: left or right?"

He once was urged to try something different: a movie that was not a thriller. "How about a movie about baseball?" a friend suggested.

"The only baseball story moviegoers would accept from me," said the baseball-challenged Hitchcock, "would go like this: Bat meets ball. Then the ball explodes."

In early May 1951, Hitchcock, his wife, and actress daughter Patricia were touring Europe. In Venice, they came upon a line of gondolas in the Grand Canal, moving slowly into a procession. There in the lead gondola was a casket, and all the gondolas were draped in black bunting, in mourning. Hitchcock was intrigued; he'd never heard of a funeral by gondola and thought he might use that in an upcoming film sometime.

So he told his daughter to follow the gondolas and report the details of the procession to him. She did—including the Italian camera crew filming it for *their* movie!

During the filming of *The Man Who Knew Too Much*, Hitchcock revealed why, in *To Catch a Thief*, Cary Grant puts out his cigarette in an egg.

"I abhor eggs," he explained.

A short actor was hired by Hitchcock for *The Trouble with Harry*, but the trouble with the actor came when he was too short for a shot. So Hitchcock gave him a small bench, and then a box, to prop him up. That made him too tall. The director solved the problem by having him stand on a copy of the script.

When the scene was over the actor said: "This script is awful."

"You don't like your lines?" asked Hitchcock.

"No, the lines are fine. But my feet are, killing me," he replied.

Despite his international fame, Hitchcock was a shy, modest man. In January 1956, for example, he'd been reported missing on a flight to Hong Kong. It turned out to be the result of a reservation glitch. When he noticed the banner headlines about his being literally off the radar, he said: "Oh, I didn't think anybody cared."

Two of Hitchcock's stars got married the same week in 1956: One was Grace Kelly. The other was Vera Miles, who boasted: "Grace married a Prince. But I married a King; 'The King of the Jungle,' that is." Her new husband was Gordon Scott, the current Tarzan.

Hitchcock had an amazing ability to be prophetic in his films. In *Notorious,* for example, he showed Nazis hiding in Argentina, fourteen years before Adolf Eichmann was captured on a street in the outskirts of Buenos Aires. In *Foreign Correspondent,* a political leader was slain by a gun hidden in a camera, a year before a similar murder took place. In 1944, during the supersecret Manhattan Project research, Hitchcock and Ben Hecht, the great writer, were working on a movie about an atomic bomb. They asked a government scientist about uranium, and he responded: "You want to get arrested?"

"I'll never retire," said Hitchcock. "I'll work until the very end. And as they're lowering my casket into the earth, I'll sit up and say: 'Cut!'"

JUDY HOLLIDAY

Hers was a star that glittered all too briefly. Born Judith Tuvim, Judy Holliday was only forty-three when she died of breast cancer in early June 1965. By then she'd won a Tony Award and an Academy Award for *Born Yesterday*, recreating her stage role of the quintessential dumb-on-the-outside-but-wise-on-the inside character "Billie Dawn."

Born Yesterday was one of the first films I remember seeing. (*Kim*, one of Errol Flynn's lesser efforts, was the first, in 1949, for the record.) I saw it with my older brothers, and my mother was appalled when I kept repeating her signature line, complete with her accent: "Do me a fav-ah. Dwop dead!" Six-year-olds shouldn't talk that way.

Her other films of note were *It Should Happen to You*, with a debuting Jack Lemmon, *Phffft!*, one of the dumbest titles in movie history, and her other triumph, *Bells Are Ringing*, in 1960. Who knows what else she would've done had she lived a full life. Recently her memory was revived in an off-Broadway play about her called *Just in Time — The Judy Holliday Story*, with Marina Squerciati in the title role.

Holliday no doubt called upon her real-life experience in portraying the telephone answering-service operator in *Bells Are Ringing*, since she'd gotten her start in just that job. But she didn't answer the phone at some law firm or insurance company; no indeed, it was for Orson Welles's Mercury Theater.

Thirteen years before she created that role on Broadway, just after she opened on stage in *Born Yesterday*, Welles took credit for discovering her. "For a year and a half she was our phone operator," he recalled. "All day long she did nothing but answer the phones, and I never dreamed she could do anything else."

By June 1946, her Broadway stardom had led to several lucrative movie offers, but she said she would wait for "a big, important role." One was from Leo McCarey, director of movies like the Marx Brothers' classic *Duck Soup, Going My Way, The Bells of St. Mary's*, and *An Affair to Remember*, who offered her just such a role.

"It's a two-character movie to be called *Adam and Eve*," McCarey said.

"It could be a bigger and more important role," she replied, "if you call it *Eve and Adam*."

Her first big movie role was in *Adam's Rib* in 1949, billed third after Katharine Hepburn and Spencer Tracy. Every day after shooting a scene with Holliday, Hepburn would call all of Hollywood's columnists to tell them that the newcomer was so good she was stealing the movie.

In March 1951, she won the Best Actress Oscar for her 1950 role in *Born Yesterday*. For an actress so early in her career to beat out the likes of Bette Davis and Anne Baxter for *All About Eve*, and Gloria Swanson for *Sunset Boulevard*, was an achievement as remarkable as her performance itself.

Holding up her Oscar, she put the ceremonies and the very idea of comparing disparate performances into perfect perspective by saying simply: "It's crazy! The whole thing's crazy!"

In the movie *The Marrying Kind* in 1952, she had a scene requiring the shedding of real tears. Many actresses can do this, but they have different ways of getting to that point. Hers was simple: "I had to diet for this picture, so I just kept picturing buttered steak, mashed potatoes, and strawberry shortcake. And I cried."

She'd gotten her start in a performance group called "The Revuers," working for $50 a week in a tiny cellar club. Also in the troupe were Adolph Green and Betty Comden, the future composers/screenwriters of *Wonderful Town, Singin' in the Rain*, and *Bells Are Ringing*.

One day in June 1953, Holliday was filming

My father with Judy Holliday and Sydney Chaplin, then costarring in Bells Are Ringing, *on April 21, 1957 at El Morocco.*

The Marrying Kind in the middle of Columbus Circle, when Comden dropped by the set. Two directors' chairs were placed there for them, and there they sat, with police steering all the traffic and the onlookers away.

"Only Salvador Dalí is missing," said Holliday. "The two of us sitting here, now, with all we've accomplished. It's all so surreal."

Two years later she was rehearsing for a TV show called *Sunday in Town* and told Tallulah Bankhead, also appearing on the program, of her nervousness doing live TV. Bankhead often told other actors there was no need to be nervous, that their talent showed they deserved to be up there.

When Holliday told this to Ethel Barrymore, the great stage and screen star, she said: "Nonsense. You go back and tell Tallulah that after seventy-two years in the business, I still get nervous."

Harry Cohn, the ironfisted head of Co-

lumbia Pictures, was as well known for his temper as he was for the great films his studio turned out during his time. In November 1954, the phone rang at Holliday's home, and her mother answered. "I've got a great role for you in a picture called *The Solid Gold Cadillac*," the voice said. "You're not afraid of me, are you?"

"Mister," replied her mother, "I'm not afraid of anyone. Who is this, anyway?"

A few days later, the actress said that her two-year-old son didn't like to kiss or embrace her. "But I have a way to deal with that," she said. "I spin him around and he gets dizzy and holds his arms out for me to catch him. I know it's a dirty trick, but a mother should go to any extremes for her child's embrace."

In late April 1955, Holliday did her impression of Marilyn Monroe on a TV show. The next day, Monroe was walking with a friend down Fifth Avenue and passed Holliday. "I hear you do an impression of me," said Monroe. "I'd love to see it." They made a date, and the next day, over tea, Holliday showed it to her.

A few days later, Holliday had an important appointment and dressed carefully for it. "You look like a real woman," said a friend. "I thought I was a real woman," she replied, "until Marilyn Monroe came to my house for tea."

In late March 1956, Holliday was being interviewed by a reporter, and she showed him the pile of fan mail she'd been receiving; letters awaiting answers.

"Pick one, any one," she said. "See what it says."

The reporter picked a letter and read it aloud: "It's from a fan in Dubuque, Iowa," he said.

"'Dear Judy. I saw you in your new movie and love you. I'm leaving my wife to marry you. Name the date.'" The author was the superintendent of a pajama factory named Dick Bissell. He later wrote the hit Broadway musical *The Pajama Game*.

When he went to see her in *Bells Are Ringing* on Broadway, Noël Coward came backstage and told her: "What a treat it was for me—to sit there and, after the first five minutes, know that I wouldn't wince even once all evening."

When her name was called on Oscar night, fellow nominee Gloria Swanson, then fifty-two years old, said to the thirty-year-old actress: "Couldn't you have waited? You have so much time, so many years ahead of you. This was my only chance."

Gloria Swanson lived until 1983, seventeen years after Judy Holliday's death.

GRACE KELLY

In early May 1966, I was about to graduate from the University of Pennsylvania in Philadelphia. My parents' graduation gift was a trip accompanying my father on a press junket to Monaco to cover the filming of the movie *Grand Prix*. In those days, press junkets were special; studios would take journalists anywhere in the world to visit movies on location, sometimes during the filming. The year before, I'd accompanied my father to London to cover *Those Magnificent Men in Their Flying Machines*.

This year's trip was even more exciting. First, a return to London to visit the set of *The Dirty Dozen*, where I spent time with Ernest Borgnine, Lee Marvin, Robert Ryan (an actor whose work I especially admired), and an acting rookie named Jim Brown. He told me exclusively that he was retiring from the Cleveland Browns to devote his time to acting, and I broke that story by sending it to the *Jersey Journal*, where I was interning that summer. The editor was so pleased, he let me put it in my own column! It was my first exclusive.

Half the group of journalists on that set, including my father and me, was called away to visit the set of another film. I was crestfallen, wanting to hang out with Brown and the other actors. After all, who would ever hear of that other movie whose set we visited? Something called *2001: A Space Odyssey*.

Then it was on to Monte Carlo for *Grand Prix* with James Garner, Eva Marie Saint, and Yves Montand. The film had been completed, so the stars were there just for interviews. And there was the race, of course. I'd never heard such noise from engines, tearing through the winding, narrow streets of Monte Carlo.

The last night of the trip, we were guests at the palace of Prince Rainier and Princess Grace, the former Grace Kelly of

Philadelphia. Rivaled perhaps only by Catherine Deneuve, whom I interviewed in New York, and Sharon Tate, whom I met in London, Princess Grace was the most beautiful movie star I have ever met, or seen, for that matter.

I told her I was graduating in her hometown, two days later. "Send everyone my regards," she said.

My father first knew her in New York when she was modeling before turning to acting.

By 1954, she was already a star, shooting *Rear Window* for Hitchcock. "In a short time," he wrote, "she's won the best roles opposite the best leading men and is able to avoid the quota of poor scripts which usually beset all quickly rising stars. That's because Grace Kelly has a powerful alternative: She merely says she'll join her wealthy family in Philadelphia and wait for a good part."

Cary Grant and his wife taught her how to play craps before they visited a Las Vegas casino together. Later, when they were costarring in *To Catch a Thief*, she put what she'd learned to good use. She played one game of roulette at the casino in Cannes. She bet on number six and won.

Back in New York, she told my father she'd made an unusual discovery: her dentist had been married eleven times. "And now I suspect," she said "that I have gold from some old wedding rings in my teeth."

Her engagement to Prince Rainier of Monaco made worldwide headlines. He gave her a 12-carat diamond ring. Showing it to friends she beamed: "Isn't it sweet?"

She later used that ring in one of her last films, *High Society*, in the scene in which she studies it and rubs it gleefully against her dress.

Hitchcock was unconvinced she'd give up her career, however. "Given the choice between a good role and a royal scepter, I know what Grace would do. She's an actress. She'd go for the role."

Since it was while shooting a Hitchcock movie that she met her husband, the director was asked if he'd taken credit for putting Grace and Rainier together. "No," he said, "I just put Grace Kelly together."

Actually, fate played a hand, too. Hitchcock was about to film *Dial M for Murder* and wanted a leading lady with a British accent. Belgian-born Audrey Hepburn was his first choice, but she was committed to worldwide promotion for her movie *Gigi*. So the director signed Kelly but decided to give her a two-picture contract. The second film was *To Catch a Thief*, during which the fairytale romance was hatched.

This is, in fact how they met: Pierre Galante, of the magazine *Paris-Match* was asked by Rainier to kill a photo of him at the Cannes Film Festival, and the journalist agreed. So Rainier owed him a favor. Galante asked the Prince if he could bring the actress and a photographer to the palace, and Rainier agreed. Kelly was photographed sitting on the throne, and thus *Paris-Match* obtained the exclusive photo. The Prince arrived as they were leaving, and they were introduced. His first words to her, in fact, were: "You work for MGM? Isn't that the company with the lion? That's an old lion. Let me take you to the zoo, and I'll show you some young lions."

When she returned to America, Kelly wrote a thank-you letter to the Prince asking him to call her if he ever came to America. He did.

In May 1956, my father, who'd attended their wedding in Monaco with my mother the month before, was in Sardi's and introduced the Princess to Adlai Stevenson. He was then campaigning for his second nomination for president. My father noticed a blank expression on his face. "She was a movie star in films like *High Noon*, *The Bridges at Toko-Ri*, and *The Country Girl*. She won the Oscar for that one." Again, no recognition from Stevenson. "Her father is

John B. Kelly from Philadelphia," my father added.

"Oh, the Democrat?" replied Stevenson. "Why didn't you say this was his daughter?"

When Marilyn Monroe was asked how her husband, the bookish Arthur Miller, compared with Kelly's handsome Prince, she said: "Grace married a foreigner of no ability. I'm marrying a great American playwright."

Cary Grant said at the time he believed she'd never act again. "She'll bring to Monaco's throne the same strong determination to succeed that she brought to Hollywood. She sometimes was criticized for always being cool and composed. It was the composure born of confidence, application, concentration, and knowledge," he said.

"Grace reduced acting to its simplest form. Others," he said, "have to hide behind grimaces or narcotic roles, like amateurs who insisted on putting on lampshades when posing for a picture. Grace made acting look easy, the way Joe Louis made boxing look easy—so simple. Sometimes you see an artist work and you say, 'OK, I could do that.' It's only those who have worked the hardest and the longest, who can make it look that simple."

In September 1956, Princess Grace was back in New York and said that the one thing she wanted to show her husband was autumn weather. She said that her biggest problem adjusting to life in the palace was with the servants, who were accustomed to the old ways, not the new electric gadgets she brought from America.

Her father, a prominent Philadelphian, naturally carried pictures of his family to show friends. Several years after he became a grandfather, he was showing off the family pictures in his wallet. "And here's a picture of my daughter Grace and her husband. Keep it." It was the new one-franc postage stamp of Monaco.

Orson Welles was in Brussels during the 1958 World's Fair and was asked if he'd be in town when Prince Rainier and Princess Grace arrived the following week. "No," said Welles. "In fact, I've never met her. I'm the only person from Hollywood who knows him—but not her!"

One evening at the Palace in Monaco, José Iturbi, the great pianist, gave a concert. After the performance, the former Grace Kelly of Philadelphia approached him and said: "I used to come to your concerts at the Robin Hood Dell in Philadelphia, but I was always too shy to ask for your autograph. May I please have one now?"

Late in December 1965, Princess Grace made her last appearance in a movie. It was a United Nations film directed by Terence Young. Young, who directed the first James Bond film, *Dr. No,* and a sequel, *Thunderball,* was asked what it was like to direct Princess Grace. He shook his head and sighed: "What a waste. What a loss for the movies."

ROCKY MARCIANO

He was born Rocco Francis Marchegiano, and because of the grace and style with which he wore his crown he was one of the most beloved heavyweight champions in history.

Although he lost an amateur bout to Coley Wallace, "The Rock" from Brockton, Massachusetts, retired as the undefeated heavyweight champion, having won all his professional bouts. His 49-0 record included forty-three knockouts, a feat unimaginable today. He only reigned three and a half years, and by today's standards was undersized (5 foot 10), but he was incredibly brave and could absorb an incredible amount of punishment.

After he defeated "Jersey" Joe Walcott to win the title, he was given a party by the Grossinger family, since he'd trained at their Catskill resort. At the party he recalled the night of the fight. When it was over, he took a walk with his wife. "Then we went to bed," he recalled, "and I realized something was different. Then I remembered why: I was Champion."

A year later, he was training for a fight, and his sessions in the ring were filmed for a 3-D movie. The photographer asked Marciano to show the viewers what the Champ's opponent would face. So Rocky tossed a punch right at the camera. And shattered the lens.

In June 1953, forty sports stars visited the White House. To Marciano, and only to Rocky, President Eisenhower said: "I envy you."

That same week, Rocky spent several mornings at the Polo Grounds where his kid brother Lou was having a tryout with the New York Giants, as an infielder. Rocky had had a tryout in 1947 with the Chicago Cubs as a catcher, but had difficulty making strong throws to second base.

"No arm," read the scouting report on the young man who five years later would become heavyweight champion.

Lou Marciano would have preferred to become a fighter too, but Mama Marciano and the Champ opposed it.

"One fighter in the family is enough," said Mama Pasquelina Marciano.

Rocky added: "And I can't stand to see my kid brother in a fight. When you see something like that, my instinct is to get in there and help him. But of course I'd be helpless."

Marciano had the perfect temperament for a prizefighter. He enjoyed the physical contact, the rigid training, and had blocked from his view all things except keeping his heavyweight crown. When he told his manager Al Weill that he wanted to get married, he assured Weill it wouldn't interfere with his career.

The Marcianos spent their honeymoon at a beach resort, and one day Marciano disappeared for half an hour. It happened the next day and the next. His bride then discovered his mysterious whereabouts. He'd found a penny arcade and was practicing on a punching bag.

By September 1955, Marciano had become a household name. Even Maurice Chevalier, the suave, debonair French ladies' man, knew about him and his elegant demeanor. "Charm," said the French star, "is a quality of humility, indefinable warmth that goes to your heart. The American who has the most of it is Rocky Marciano."

Marciano was in Los Angeles in September 1955 and appeared on a radio show hosted by former heavyweight champ Max Baer. He had to stay overnight near the studio for the broadcast. On the air, Baer asked him a blunt question: "How do you think you'd have done against me in my prime? I think I'd have flattened you, Rocky."

"It would've been a good fight," replied the modest Marciano, "because I would've given it my all. But one night, I recall, you

My younger brother Douglas gets some pointers from heavyweight champ Rocky Marciano at Grossinger's, circa 1953.

didn't." He was referring to Baer's fourth-round knockout by Joe Louis in a nontitle fight seventeen years earlier.

In March 1956, Marciano went to the Cherry Lane Theater, to see an off-Broadway production of Shaw's *The Admirable Bashville*, a revival of his 1901 play. It concerns a society lady and a prizefighter, and ends with them in a fond embrace.

After the final curtain, Marciano said; "This fellow Shaw—he certainly was in our corner."

My father first met Marciano at Grossinger's where my younger brother Douglas, then nine, and my mother were in the same cottage as the Champ. He and my brother would take walks together. One day the house artist saw Marciano and asked to paint his portrait. When it was done, Marciano said: "You're the first man who's been able to put me on a canvas."

After he retired in 1956, Marciano befriended Abe Saperstein, who owned the Harlem Globetrotters. He asked Saperstein to supply the services of the team for a one-night benefit for a church in his hometown. "If you can do this," said Marciano, "I'd be a big man in Brockton."

He once was asked how it felt to knock Joe Louis through the ropes. It was long after Louis's prime, when he was out of shape and trying desperately to prolong his career.

"People all around you were weeping, seeing the sports idol like that." The questioner asked him: "So how'd you feel?"

"I was the happiest guy in the house," came the reply.

In September of that year, he was honored with a birthday party, and his wife Barbara wore the famous Vanderbilt diamond. The owner said it was worth $250,000. "I could get that for you," Marciano said to his wife. "I'd need to fight Archie Moore twice, though. The second fight would be to pay the taxes I'd earn on the first one."

Then he demonstrated that his decision to stay retired was permanent by ordering three portions of ice cream.

Marciano's last fight was against the light heavyweight champion Archie Moore, in late September 1955. It was in Yankee Stadium, and there was a chill in the fall air. Fans wore coats. "Weren't you cold?" he was asked.

"Not me," replied Marciano. "I had my gloves on."

One night in Toots Shor's restaurant he sat with Mickey Mantle, and they compared forearms. My father was the judge and said they looked the same, though he later wrote that Marciano's seemed slightly bigger. "But Mickey must be stronger," said Marciano. "I knocked out forty-three opponents in my whole career, but Mickey's already knocked out forty-seven this year, and the season's not over yet."

On another night in Shor's, a drunk stumbled by Marciano's table and said he'd appreciate it if the former champ would hit him. Of course Marciano declined, and the man asked again. "Earlier tonight," he explained, "I was hit by a guy I think was Rocky Graziano. I want to be able to say I'm the only man in the world flattened by both champs named 'Rocky' in one night."

In June 1957, Marciano met another former heavyweight champ, Gene Tunney, who urged Marciano to adhere to his retirement plans.

"The first two years are the toughest," said Tunney, who retired as champion in 1928. "You get the feeling you can lick the man who dared assume your title. Whenever that happened, I'd go to the New York Athletic Club and punch the heavy bags and box."

Later that month, Marciano brought his father Pierino to a dinner honoring Joe Louis, Ezzard Charles, and "Jersey" Joe Walcott, all of whom Marciano had fought and knocked out. Charles met the elder Marciano, surveyed his small frame (he weighed about 115 pounds at that time), and said: "Well, at least there's one Marciano in the house I can lick."

Marciano did flirt with a comeback. It was July 1959, right after Ingemar Johansson took the title away from Floyd Patterson. "They talk of a million dollar purse. I'd have to listen. At least listen," he said. He resumed some training, but remained retired. In August of that year, however, he went to Canada to spar with Archie Moore, the man who'd decked him in his last fight but whom he knocked out in the ninth round.

After their workout, nearly four years after their title bout, Moore told Marciano: "I still want no part of you."

In December 1957, Marciano had flown to Havana and went to visit Ernest Hemingway at the writer's *finca*—his farm at San Francisco de Paola. He arrived half an hour early, rang the doorbell, and Hemingway appeared bare-chested and wearing only trunks. "You're in great condition," Marciano said to his host.

"I wasn't showing off," Hemingway assured him. "If I'd expected you this early, I'd have worn a shirt, jacket, and tie."

Marciano was friends with Mario Lanza, the singer-actor, who'd built a small boxing ring in his gym. "The ring is shorter than regulation," he told Marciano. "That's the way you like it; less room for your opponent to run around; contact, contact all the time."

In December 1960, Marciano was asked how a prizefighter can tell when he's past his prime. "I retired at the height of my career," he said. "But other fighters who kept fighting tell me the symptoms are always the same: First a boxer's legs go. Then his arms. And then his friends."

ETHEL MERMAN

If a visitor from another planet came to Earth, with time-travel powers, and wanted to see one Broadway musical before returning home, I'd recommend anything with Ethel Merman, the greatest Broadway musical star of them all.

For decades she captivated audiences with her charisma, her untrained but incredibly powerful voice, and her unique way of performing. From her starring debut in *Anything Goes* in 1934, to *DuBarry Was a Lady, Panama Hattie, Annie Get Your Gun, Call Me Madam,* and *Gypsy,* she stood the American musical theater on its ear with electrifying performances. Even when she succeeded Carol Channing in *Hello, Dolly!* she made it her own. There never was, nor will there ever be, anyone like her.

She was a former secretary and shorthand champion from Queens, New York, for whose employer she had had to put through calls to the captain of his yacht, Captain Christianson. She always remembered this and was impressed by that yacht. So once she became a star, in 1940, she bought her own yacht. Complete with that captain's son at the helm.

She'd wanted to change her last name, "Zimmerman," when she began her show business career. "With a name that long up in lights, people below the marquee would die from the heat," she said.

Her father, however, opposed this. They compromised. She dropped the first three letters of her last name.

In January 1943, she opened in a musical called *Something for the Boys,* produced by Mike Todd. One night during the run the announcement was made that she'd taken ill and her understudy would go on. Of course, refunds would be available at the box office. But immediately after the announcement, Todd ordered the orchestra to play "The Star-Spangled Banner." The audience had to remain standing. The moment the words "of the brave" were heard, the curtain went up. No refunds.

Another night, when she was again ill, Todd himself made this announcement to the disappointed audience, many of whom were about to ask for refunds: "Ladies and gentlemen, for seven months a young understudy named Betty Garrett has been waiting for a chance. Tonight you'll see history—an understudy getting that chance to go on in place of Ethel Merman." Garrett also became a Broadway star.

One night in New Haven, Connecticut, in March 1946, Merman dined with friends. It was early in the evening, just before the opening tryout performance of *Annie Get Your Gun.*

"Aren't you nervous?" her friends asked her.

"No," replied Merman. "Why should I be nervous? The people in the audience— the ones who bought a ticket for an untried show—*they're* the ones who should be nervous."

In June 1947, she was wearing a bracelet that spelled out her name in diamonds and rubies. When a friend studied it admiringly, she explained: "I always wanted to see how my name looks in lights."

John Loder, a debonair English actor, heard Merman sing at a party in June 1949, admired her clear, ringing tones, and said: "Somehow, I feel that I could understand Greek, Arabic, or Chinese, so long as Ethel Merman was singing it."

In the play and movie versions of *Call Me Madam,* one of the standards she performed was a song called "I Hear Singing and There's No One There." In December 1952, Merman's son Bobby's teacher was writing on the blackboard and heard a child disobey her no-talking admonition. The teacher said; "I hear talking and there's someone there."

The young boy spoke up: "Hey, that's my

mother's song, and you've got the lyrics wrong."

In 1950, Merman met Perle Mesta, the diplomat she portrayed in *Call Me Madam*, who promised to try to be there opening night. "Will you come up and take a bow with me?" asked Merman.

"Let 'em try to stop me," replied Ambassador Mesta.

Later the two conferred on Merman's hairdo and jewelry, and the actress promised the diplomat to give her a "costumes by Perle Mesta" credit in the program.

In October 1956 at Le Pavillon restaurant, seated at separate tables were Aristotle Onassis, the Greek shipping magnate who owned the Monte Carlo Casino, Grace Kelly and Prince Rainier, and at a third table sat Merman. She was starring in the musical *Happy Hunting*, which, coincidentally, was set around the Kelly-Rainier wedding. The producer of that show, incidentally, had no understudy for Merman.

"That's a star," he explained. "If she can't play it, nobody else can."

Elaine Stritch understudied and then replaced Merman in *Call Me Madam*. She'd toured with the show, and in Los Angeles stayed at the Beverly Hills Hotel. One day while there, she received a complaint from another hotel guest, annoyed at the actress's rehearsing her songs on her terrace.

The complainant was Ethel Merman.

A few months later, actress Benay Venuta hired the most expensive babysitter in New York for her daughter Debbie. While the girl's mother went to see another show, she parked Debbie with Merman, who was performing *Happy Hunting* that night. Just before the curtain rose, the star parked the girl in the wings, stage-right. That's why, that night, she sang all her songs facing there.

Unlike other Broadway musical stars, she rebuffed offers to star onstage in dramas. "Only when my pipes give out," she said. "In my wheelchair days."

She did, however, later costar in the non-musical comedy films *It's a Mad Mad Mad Mad World* and *Airplane!*, among others.

In November 1957, Ginger Rogers was with Merman at the Harwyn Club in New York and mentioned that she was about to make her nightclub debut the following month.

"You'll find this out about working in nightclubs," Merman warned her. "There'll always be someone at a back table complaining he can't hear a word you're singing—while you hear every word he's complaining."

One night, just before she was supposed to make her first appearance onstage in *Happy Hunting*, she got word her husband, Bob Six, head of Continental Airlines, was calling from London. Then she heard her musical cue to go on. She paused for a moment, walked onstage, and performed. He called back later.

During the run of *Happy Hunting*, a cast member was fired for refusing to change back to his original hair color after he'd dyed it for a movie audition. He took to the radio and told stories of feuds between Merman and others.

Someone speculated that the final performance of the show might produce fireworks.

"You ought to know me better than that," said Merman. "On closing night, I'll give the same performance I gave on opening night. I always try to give an audience the best that's in me."

In September 1958, Merman's husband Bob Six gave a Western barbecue party at his Denver home. It was attended by TV Western actors who competed in a quick-draw contest. There was a dummy target and an electric timer ready.

When they were finished drawing and shooting, Merman's son Bobby was brought to the range. At the signal, he drew and fired—and beat the cowboy actors by

25/100th of a second. He was thirteen years old.

The most famous song from her hit show *Gypsy,* the most enduring, is "Everything's Coming Up Roses." Every night she performed it, it tore the house down. You could hear her for blocks. It seemed ironic, however, that Merman was allergic to roses.

Judy Garland attended the New Year's Eve performance of *Gypsy* in house seats provided by Merman. Garland had flown in from London to see Merman perform. But Garland didn't know that Merman makes an entrance from the back of the theater. Merman came bounding down the aisle, stopped at Garland's seat, embraced her, then went up onstage.

Well into the run of *Gypsy* in January 1961, she dined at the Stork Club on a Sunday night. "Isn't it monotonous, singing the same songs, night after night?" she was asked.

"Not at all," replied the star. "It's as monotonous as counting your money."

When she was on vacation from *Gypsy* in Venice in July 1960, Merman had an English-speaking gondolier. They compared notes about being the parents of teenagers, and found much in common.

"My Mario," said the gondolier, "comes home and says: 'Poppa, can I borrow the gondola tonight?'"

Merman was a Republican, and campaigned for Nixon and Lodge in 1960. Nevertheless, she was invited to sing "Everything's Coming Up Roses" at the inaugural gala.

"I guess the Kennedys aren't sore winners," she said, before accepting. Told the inaugural gala was to help pay off the campaign debt of the Democratic Party, Merman added, "Of course I'll be there. I helped cause that debt."

The afternoon of the gala, there was a snowstorm in Washington, and she was trapped in her car for five hours. She arrived at the ball just as the music started playing. Her assigned place backstage was between Anthony Quinn and Harry Belafonte, who'd been ready to start without her.

But as the show began, Merman realized she was still carrying her handbag. Then her professional reflexes kicked in. She tossed the purse behind her and yelled: "Hold this for me, someone," and went onstage, unruffled. This despite the fact that her handbag contained $250,000 in jewels. A stagehand returned it to her afterward.

In 1970, however, her jewels were stolen from her dressing room while she was onstage in *Hello, Dolly!* succeeding Carol Channing. Nevertheless, she refused to wear fake jewels at the next performance.

In February 1962, she began filming *It's a Mad Mad Mad Mad World*, the frantic comedy in which several groups of characters all chase a fortune. Since the action took place in one day, it meant she would have to wear the same dress—for eighteen weeks of filming!

During the filming of the movie, Phil Silvers told her how much he enjoyed her in *Gypsy*. "Thanks, Phil. I didn't know you'd seen it. Why didn't you come backstage?"

"Oh, I didn't see the show," he replied. "I just was passing by the theater and heard you."

In October 1936, she opened on Broadway in Cole Porter's *Red, Hot, and Blue*. Porter gave her a painting by a then-unknown primitive artist.

"All I remember," said Merman years later, "was that it had a lot of red chickens in it. Who needed a painting with a lot of chickens in it?" So she gave it to one of her relatives.

That painting by one Anna Mary Robertson Moses, better known as Grandma Moses, would be worth a fortune years later.

In February 1962, she told that story and sighed: "I can't even remember which relative got the painting."

In January 1963, Merman opened a charge account at a Manhattan department store. She wore sunglasses and went unrecognized. The clerk, filling out the form asked: "Where were you last employed?"

"Last night—on *The Perry Como Show*," she answered.

In November 1963, she was performing at the Persian Room in New York's Plaza Hotel. Guests at the swank hotel could hear her belting out songs from the lobby. Later, she was asked where she kept her concealed microphone.

"In my lungs," she huffed.

Her marriage to Ernest Borgnine lasted thirty-seven days. Thus, in her autobiography, the chapter called: "My Marriage to Ernest Borgnine" is a blank page.

In September 1965, Merman demonstrated the flaws of Soviet intelligence. On a visit to Moscow, she entered the dining room of her hotel where the string quartet began to play. Later, the leader asked her: "How did you like hearing your old songs?"

The songs they'd played were from *South Pacific* and *The Sound of Music*, Mary Martin's biggest Broadway hits.

In January 1966, she accompanied Van Johnson to Philadelphia to tape a TV show. At Penn Station, Johnson asked Merman if she'd brought her maid along.

"Maid? What maid?" replied Merman. "Oh yeah, here she is," she said, pulling out a steam iron.

Her fourth marriage, the short-lived one to Borgnine, would be her last. Still, in 1967, one of the men she was dating found a unique way to impress her. When he'd take her to the theater, he'd buy the two seats in front and in back of them as well. In front to guarantee an unobstructed view; in back so she didn't have to remove her hat.

In July 1968, she rented a house on Saint Maarten for a month's holiday with her two grandchildren. Their trip involved a change of planes in San Juan, but she refused to fly on a propeller-driven commuter plane. Their bags had gone on the flight, so that night she had to wash her and her grandchildren's underwear.

Their landlord on Saint Maarten had provided a huge Labrador retriever for security at the home. That night, under a full moon, the children asked to move into Grandma Merman's bed. "I was afraid myself," she said later.

But then the Labrador retriever, apparently also scared, climbed onto the bed as well. The next day, she packed up the children and returned home.

In February 1971, she revealed to my father her greatest thrill in her career. It came with her first show, *Girl Crazy*. She had been working at the Brooklyn Paramount Theater when she was invited to audition at George Gershwin's apartment. She sang the songs Gershwin handed her. Then came the greatest compliment she ever received, no doubt.

Gershwin said: "If there are any changes you'd want me to make in the melodies, I'll do them."

Another tribute came her way during the run of *Panama Hattie* in 1940. It was a matinee day, and that morning she went shopping at Gimbels department store, only to be stuck for several hours in an elevator. Six decades before cell phones, no one at the 49th Street Theater knew where she was.

Instead of starting the show with the understudy, the curtain was held until she was freed and arrived.

By early August 1971, Merman had seen the movie *Willard* several times, each with great glee. It was a horror movie in which the star was eaten by a huge pack of rats. The rodent's meal was played by Ernest Borgnine.

JAMES A. MICHENER

James A. Michener, the author of *Tales of the South Pacific*, *Sayonara*, *Hawaii*, and other best-sellers, was also a world traveler. That's how he found his source material. In September 1954, he returned from a trip around the world, and was in New York being treated for an injury incurred on his journey. After crossing the Himalayas and the Khyber Pass, enduring the heat and pestilence of Afghanistan, and visiting (for ideas) the dangerous opium joints and gin mills of Asia, he was relaxing in the steamroom of the Honolulu YMCA—where he fractured his toe.

In 1956, Michener visited the jungles around Angkor Wat in Cambodia. Suddenly he realized his wedding anniversary was the next day. Somehow he caught a flight for Rome where his wife Mari awaited him. When he told the concierge of the swank hotel he was checking into that his luggage would arrive the following day, he was asked what he'd wear in the meantime. "I'm joining my wife to celebrate our anniversary," said the normally shy Michener, "so on such an occasion, not having a change of clothing won't matter a bit."

One night in 1957 at El Morocco, Michener met one of his former students from the prestigious Hill School in Pottstown, Pennsylvania. The young man was Woolworth Donahue, whose cousin, Barbara Hutton, one of the world's richest women, had attended the school's prom. "That was the first time I got a real look at wealth," Michener recalled. "She pulled up in a private railroad car with a retinue of servants. And then she asked to dance with 'that new teacher, that Mr. Michener.'"

Michener attended all sorts of schools: grammar school, high school, Swarthmore College, even the University of Salamanca in Spain and Oxford. In no class was he ever less than the top student. He confided that this was never a triumph of superior intellect but only the result of his photographic memory.

In October 1957, Michener was flying across the Pacific on a C-47 Air Force cargo plane that crashed into the ocean near the island of Iwo Jima. After the rescue, he joined the pilot, a decorated Air Force colonel, in filling out endless forms, cables to relatives, and Air Force crash reports. "Well, it's over," Michener said to the pilot. "So let's celebrate by going for a drink."

"Not yet," replied the pilot. "I'm not quite finished yet. I've got one more report to file." He then went into the next room, knelt, and prayed.

Soon after all the postcrash forms were completed, Michener wrote to my father: "People who fly over water as often as you and I do naturally speculate on what might happen if . . . Now I know.

"If the pilot follows instructions worked out by the experience of military and commercial operators, the plane can withstand the shock. Passengers have about three to six minutes to get out, and at the time it seems like a comfortable half hour. The Mae West life preservers are wonderful and *do* keep you afloat and your head out of water. Also, they inflate the instant you pull the toggle. You can get sea-sicker in a life raft than in any other known object.

"A castaway who gets seasick and who throws up his stomach liquids will probably die two to four days sooner than the castaway who can control his seasickness. But who can? Waterproof watches with screw-in backs are really waterproof. Mine was immersed for nearly three hours and never lost a second."

He then quoted the famous saying: "Any landing that you can walk away from is a good one. But, I'd add that when you can *swim away* from it, it's glorious."

His wife Mari, a second-generation Japanese-American, had cabled him: "Thank Buddha you're safe. All waters that close to Asia are his responsibility." Then Michener added: "I figured I've been pretty good to the South Pacific, and there was no reason why it shouldn't be good to me."

When his wife arrived in Tokyo, she was told he was out playing golf. She knew he'd never played golf. Later he told her that when the engines conked out, he began to list the things he might never get to do; playing golf was on the list.

In 1959, over the course of twenty days, Michener sailed 3,000 miles across the Pacific with five friends. "I needed to know more about the ocean," he explained, "and I found out: It's cold, wet, bumpy, tremendously moving, and unforgivable of error."

When Michener was an enlisted man in the Navy, he was given a course in flag-code signaling, also known as semaphore. Veteran seamen taught the young sailors how to swing the flags quickly and in rhythm. But they couldn't concoct simple messages by code. So at the end of the course, the young Michener, asked to flash a message, signaled a phrase he'd no doubt heard repeatedly at bar mitzvahs of sons of Jewish friends: "Today I am a man."

During his naval service in the South Pacific, Michener met an Australian dentist, an officer who said he'd once capped a tooth for Errol Flynn before Flynn became a movie star. The bill was never paid. Eventually the dentist wrote Flynn, who remembered the incident and sent him his payment: an autographed photo. When a Flynn movie was shown to the servicemen in the jungle, the dentist turned to Michener and said: "Look at Flynn. Smiling at me with my own tooth!"

The Library of Congress began an unusual project decades ago. Five people a year were selected at random: a farmer, plumber, builder, lawyer, and writer. They agreed to give the library all of the papers relating to their work: bills, financial reports, correspondence, etc. The library's archives thus have files showing how typical Americans try to develop their businesses. Included in this group was a young, unknown writer named James A. Michener.

Just before the TV quiz show scandal broke in the mid-'fifties, Michener was watching such a program and saw an "expert" on Asia answer the obscure questions. Michener, a genuine expert on Asia, didn't know any of those answers, nor did the top Asia experts he later consulted. Confirmation of his suspicions came when one such show invited him to appear and assured him that he'd be "protected" for the first six weeks. He declined the offer.

In February 1960, Michener was the guest of honor at the PEN luncheon, the international organization of writers and editors. During the meal he needed a pen to inscribe one of his books. No one—not *one* of the sixty writers and editors had what he needed! He finally borrowed one from the bartender.

In March 1963, Michener sat in the lounge at the airport in New York awaiting a flight and noticed lots of relatives seeing loved ones off. "It's the same in Polynesia," he said. "I once saw an entire tribe come to see a man off, and he was only going to the next village!" He was seated in the El Al waiting area, and someone told him that in Hebrew "Shalom" means "hello" and also "farewell."

"That's just Hebrew for 'Aloha,'" said Michener.

MARILYN MONROE

On November 5, 1960, I turned sixteen. My father gave me a unique present: a phone call from Marilyn Monroe. This was a year-and-a-half before she would serenade President Kennedy on his birthday. I like to think she rehearsed with me.

Forty-eight years later, our son Ben was traveling in Hong Kong and came upon a museum dedicated to American pop culture. Intrigued, he went in and discovered a handwritten letter from Monroe to John Huston with the same date, thanking him for casting her in *The Misfits*, which turned out to be her last movie, as well as that of her costars Clark Gable and Montgomery Clift.

So now I know two things she did that day: call me and write that letter. When I interviewed Tilda Swinton, the willowy Oscar-winning actress, I told her this story without stating the specific date until the end. Because that same day, November 5, 1960, Swinton was busy—being born!

With all due respect to Swinton, an alluring, sensational actress, no star in the history of the movies, indeed in the history of American pop culture, has been as revered and adored as Marilyn Monroe. Her sudden, mysterious death in the summer of 1962 shocked the world and is still fodder for speculation and debate. To this day, her face adorns countless dorm-rooms, tacky sidewalk-schlock-dealers' pushcarts, movie posters, and billboards. And the cover of this book! The words "legendary," "awesome," and "iconic" are used so frequently they've lost their meaning. But think of her and you'll realize why she stood alone.

When you think of Marilyn Monroe, you think Hollywood, of course. But she spent lots of time in New York as well, before her marriage to Joe DiMaggio and while married to Arthur Miller. That's where she came to know my father.

One of the earliest entries about her in my father's column was in April 1952. By that time, she'd begun to amass memorable films like *Love Happy* (more famous today as the Marx Brothers' last movie), *The Asphalt Jungle,* and *All About Eve.* But superstardom, to use a contemporary word, was yet to come. Her now-iconic nude calendar, later to be published as the first centerfold in the fledgling magazine *Playboy,* titillated and shocked America. She was "Miss December, 1953."

She had only a bit part in *Love Happy,* but the studio sent her to New York to promote it anyway, paying her $100 a week. They first put her in a huge hotel suite for interviews, but that night she was quickly moved to a tiny room.

"I didn't care," she recalled. "They forgot to cancel room service, so I kept ordering caviar. Even caviar for breakfast. That's what I remember about New York that first time: caviar for breakfast." A few years later she returned, and every morning sat in a café in Grand Central Station, sipping coffee, alone.

On April 17, 1952, "The Lyons Den" had the following item: "PHOTO DEPT: 20th Century-Fox tried in vain to suppress the calendar which displayed the nude photo of MM. The studio now is trying to stop Miss Monroe from autographing the picture, which shows her lying nude, on her left side." Lucien Ballard, the cameraman who'd filmed Jane Russell's provocative movie *The Outlaw,* sent his copy of the calendar to the star for autographing.

She obliged and wrote: "This is *not* my best side."

By September 1952, she was dating Joe DiMaggio, and heard that he'd previously dated some other famous women including First Daughter Margaret Truman and Marlene Dietrich. She studied photos of those women and said: "I'd be afraid of only one of them, but I won't say which one."

This may have been a posed shot, since my mother adored Marilyn Monroe,
but it depicts the sentiments of every man everywhere, circa 1955.

One afternoon in the fall of 1954, a woman left her apartment on Manhattan's East Side and saw a crowd on East Sixty-First Street. She stopped to look, then joined some friends at lunch. "Guess what?" she exclaimed. "I saw Marilyn Monroe." The excited woman was Eleanor Roosevelt.

Several Hollywood press agents claimed credit for the publicity Monroe received on a visit to New York. The only one anyone believed said: "It was simple. I did the only thing any studio press agent for her has to do. When the photographers arrived, I got out of the way."

My father wrote a magazine article called "Never Marry an Actress." When he joined Monroe at a nightclub table soon afterward, she said: "I read your article. You're right. You're absolutely right!"

In March 1954, my family was invited to march in the opening procession of the Ringling Bros. and Barnum & Bailey Circus at Madison Square Garden. My mother was dressed in a black spangled jacket and carried a lion tamer's whip. My father, brothers, and I wore lion masks—get it?—as we marched.

Behind us, on an elephant painted white (you couldn't do that today, I'm sure) rode Monroe.

In December 1954, she was doing publicity for her latest movie, *The Seven Year Itch*, and was told she'd be on the cover of *Harper's Bazaar*. "At last!" she exclaimed. "I've always dreamed of being on the cover of a *women's* magazine for a change."

Marilyn accompanied Joe to Yankee spring training camp in Florida, and, in the batting cage, actually made contact with a ball, looping it into shallow left field. Knowing nothing about baseball, she asked what kind of a hit that would've been in a game. "A triple," said one of the players, "because who'd be looking at the ball?"

Back in New York shortly afterwards, she met with the playwright Sidney Kingsley to discuss possible stage work. They talked about her recent screen roles, and she said: "I now want to do movies which won't make me feel, after I drive away from the preview, that I ought to drive off a cliff."

There was the story going around, sometime in 1955, of a man who'd become weary of life and sought peace and solitude. "How will you know you've reached the place beyond which there is no civilization?" he was asked. "I plan to put a large photo of Marilyn Monroe on the front of my car's bumper, and as soon as someone asks: 'Who's that?' I'll know I've found such a place. That's where I'll stop and settle."

In early July 1955, the Actors Studio in New York had a noisy party celebrating the end of the theatrical season. It began at midnight, and by 3 a.m. neighbors had called the police. The cops asked who was giving the party and what the occasion was. They'd never heard of the Actors Studio but were told that among the guests was Marilyn Monroe.

"Really?" said one of the policemen. They decided that her presence was reason enough to celebrate and no complaint against such a party would stand up in court. Then they saw her and, starstruck, left.

The producer-director Josh Logan saw early scenes from *The Prince and the Showgirl*, which teamed Laurence Olivier with Monroe: the greatest actor and the most dazzling actress of their time. "It's the greatest teaming since black and white," he proclaimed.

It was the old-time actor Ben Lyon who suggested that young Norma Jean Baker change her name to "Marilyn Monroe," because she reminded him of a long-ago

My father with Marilyn Monroe circa 1960.

actress named Marilyn Miller. He never dreamed, of course, that someday Marilyn Monroe would become "Marilyn Miller" as well.

In the summer of 1956, my parents took me on my first trip to Europe, and while we were in Rome, they told me we'd be headed to London next. Somehow I'd heard Monroe would be there, so I asked if we could visit her. "She is *not* a historical monument," my mother said, over my objections. "Historical monuments don't move."

When Monroe was a child, shunted from foster home to orphanage and back, her mentally troubled mother suddenly appeared one day and took the girl to a newly purchased home. The furnishings were meager, but it was their home at last. Her mother then attended an auction of the actor Fredric March's household effects and bought a white piano for the new residence. But that brief time of tranquility in young Norma Jean's childhood soon ended when her mother collapsed and was taken away.

When Monroe became a movie actress and was able to save her first $1,000, she tracked down that white piano and bought it back: a symbol of one of the few happy times in her childhood. March never knew why she held him in high esteem.

When Arthur Miller was scheduled to testify before the House Committee on Un-American Activities, my father correctly predicted that Miller would state that he was a member of the Communist party. "Then he will demand his passport be returned so he can accompany his bride to England. After all, to deny a man a passport to honeymoon with Marilyn Monroe is highly un-American."

When Miller was elected to membership in the Institute of Arts and Letters, Monroe attended the investiture luncheon. She was seated between a writer who was hard of hearing on one side and another who'd never heard of her on the other. Alas, there is no record of any conversation.

Billy Wilder, director of *Some Like It Hot*, one of the great comedies of all time, asked Monroe to lose eight pounds for her

My father with Arthur Miller and wife at El Morocco circa 1958.

role. But she refused, explaining that her costars, Tony Curtis and Jack Lemmon, were dressed as women for eight reels of the movie. "Don't you want the audience to distinguish me from them? Besides, my husband likes me plump."

Wilder had criticized her for constant tardiness during the shooting, but after the healthy box-office receipts came in, had to admit: "I have an aunt in St. Louis who would've been on time, but of course she wouldn't have earned the movie a dime."

A Russian theater delegation visited New York and asked to visit the home of Lee Strasberg of the Actors Studio. The Russians also named the playwrights they wanted to meet: Tennessee Williams, Thornton Wilder, and Arthur Miller. Mrs. Strasberg called Miller to invite him, and he asked: "Do you think anyone would mind if I bring my wife?"

When Soviet Premier Khrushchev was visiting Hollywood, movie mogul Spyros Skouras introduced him to Monroe. With TV cameras looking on, Skouras said to Khrushchev: "Kiss her, kiss her!" But the interpreter refused to do his job, and Khrushchev moved on.

When Eli Wallach signed to costar with Monroe in *The Misfits*, his wife, actress Anne Jackson, ordered a series of low-cut gowns. "If you can't beat 'em, join 'em," she explained.

Wilder put it best: "Hers is the face that burns with more kilowatts than any other."

LAURENCE OLIVIER

He was considered the greatest actor of his time: the quintessential classic actor who commanded the stage and screen and influenced virtually every actor who saw him work. He began on the London stage and then came here for his American screen debut in *Wuthering Heights,* regarded today as one of the great romantic dramas of all time.

Laurence Olivier arrived here on the S.S. *Aquitania* in April 1939, the year that would come to be considered the greatest in movie history. He was not quite thirty-three. He paused before the ship's portrait of George Washington, turned to an American passenger, and asked: "Is that man still popular in your country?"

A week or so later, Helen Keller met Olivier and asked Katharine Cornell, the great Broadway star: "Is he handsome?" When told that he was, she clapped her hands gleefully.

By 1940, he was well entrenched in Hollywood, after *Wuthering Heights* brought the stage actor film stardom. That year, he would star in *Rebecca* and *Pride and Prejudice.*

In order for the actors to relax after a day's shooting, every night on the RKO lot in the projection room, old movies were shown to a select group of people.

One night in April 1940, the movie was *The Yellow Ticket,* a 1931 film. When the hero, named "Julian Rolfe," appeared, loud laughter was heard from a woman in the dark. Then a man seated nearby roared: "No, no! Take it off the screen! I'm terrible, simply terrible!" The projectionist stopped the film and brought up the lights. Vivien Leigh had been laughing, and her husband, Olivier, had begged for the film to be stopped.

When Olivier and Leigh decided to wed, they arranged the details with great secrecy. Their plans were last-minute, and the only people who shared the secret were the justice of the peace, the actor Ronald Colman and his wife, and their friend writer/director Garson Kanin. Neither their secretaries nor those who worked in their homes were aware of the wedding, and they didn't even tell anyone in their families.

They drove to Santa Barbara at night, and after the ceremony went to an appointed place where they'd switched their cars, to avoid recognition. Then, assured of complete freedom from detection, the newlyweds drove to their honeymoon cottage.

On the doorstep was a message that had just arrived. It was a congratulatory cable from London, sent twenty-four hours earlier, timed to arrive when they did. It expressed best wishes for a long and happy marriage. It was sent by Herbert Leigh Holman, the ex-husband of the bride.

The wedding party had been late in arriving, and the impatient justice of the peace didn't know that the couple, who had secured a marriage license under the names of "Laurence Olivier" and "Vivien Leigh-Holman," were the movie stars. But he recognized them and beamed.

"We want a very short ceremony," Olivier directed. The official agreed to give them "the shortest ceremony you ever saw." Then he proceeded to forget their names.

For several days after they were secretly wed, Olivier listened to the radio, which contained news of the war in Europe and the presidential campaign. Finally Olivier, who had successfully kept their nuptials secret, said: "Why don't they give the *real* news?"

In 1941, Olivier had joined the Fleet Air Arm, a branch of the British Navy. When news broke of the sinking of the *Bismarck*, Germany's fearsome battleship, Olivier came home and told his wife. She held her husband at arm's length, looked at him admiringly, and then said: "Well done, darling."

The year after the war ended, Olivier starred in the movie version of *Henry V*, filmed near London. He directed as well, with only one camera and limited Technicolor film. Aware that wartime shortages still existed, Olivier was so careful about preserving the film that he used a stopwatch on all takes. The chain mail worn by Olivier in the battle scene was painted string, knitted by blind nuns in Ireland. The armor that was to be used in the production was destroyed by Nazi bombs.

Before he began filming, Olivier gave copies of the script to all his friends, asking them to mark whatever words or lines they thought weren't quite clear. All the unclear words and lines were then eliminated.

Olivier's friends Garson Kanin and his wife Ruth Gordon would exchange frequent cables with Olivier, and all began with affectionate salutations: "Dearest Angel Hearts," "Dear Boy of Ours," etc. But when Olivier was knighted in 1947, their congratulatory cable began: "Dear Sir."

In the fall of that year, Olivier was starring in and directing himself in *Hamlet*. He also played the role of the Ghost. Director William Wyler visited the set and sighed: "It must be wonderful to go on the set in the morning and say to yourself: 'I'm starting today with a great big close-up of myself.'"

After he screened the rushes, Olivier eliminated himself as the Ghost and hired another actor to play the role.

"It just goes to show that I hate getting a part which is second fiddle, even to myself," he remarked.

His version of *Hamlet* became the first non-American film to win the Best Picture Oscar, and he became the first actor to direct himself to a Best Actor Oscar. Incidentally, the movie won Best Picture even though Rosencrantz and Gildenstern, two of its most famous characters, were eliminated from this version.

Olivier believed movies are a director's

medium, not an actor's. "It's natural for an actor to put himself in the hands of a director," he explained. "If he's not prepared to do that, then he shouldn't undertake the task."

Olivier called directing "the most exciting and the nearest that an interpretive craftsman, such as an actor (which I am), can possibly get to being a creator."

In an early acting job, Olivier embraced Greta Garbo, who pushed him away. He was then fired from the film and replaced by Garbo's lover John Gilbert. "She was absolutely right to do that," he said, looking back years later. "I was too light for her in those days, and too young for her. She had such blazing authority.

"It was the stage actor's time in the early 'thirties," he continued, "when they could make a life in films and become great stars. But for the most part, they depended on Garbo and Joan Crawford for the main grist of their mill. A lot of them had stage experience. Garbo certainly had. Chaplin was a stage star, wasn't he?"

Dame Sybil Thorndike, the great British stage actress, was once asked to assess Olivier's talent. "I saw Larry play Brutus when he was ten," she replied. "He was just as good then—electrifying. He knew it all." Jackie Gleason, who was within earshot, said: "'The Greatest.' Like me!"

OTTO PREMINGER

I first met Otto Preminger one night when I was making the rounds with my father. I knew who he was, of course, the great Austrian-born director of classics like *Laura, Daisy Kenyon, The Court-Martial of Billy Mitchell, Anatomy of a Murder, Advise and Consent,* and *The Cardinal*. And I liked his occasional acting roles, as in Billy Wilder's *Stalag 17* and directing himself in *Margin for Error*.

What I did *not* know at the time was that he was the father of one of my boyhood friends, Erik Lee Kirkland, the son of Gypsy Rose Lee. That didn't come out until just after her death in 1970, after which his father immediately adopted him.

Preminger came to America from Vienna in 1935 to escape the Nazis. On the ship coming over, he met producer Gilbert Miller. Miller was going to present a play called *Libel* on Broadway and, aware of Preminger's stage directing reputation, asked him to direct. The young Austrian had no idea of American pay scales, and asked Miller what he'd receive.

"Oh, I'll pay you what our top director, Guthrie McClintic, used to make," said Miller. And so he did. But it was only $1,200, the amount McClintic earned—as a stagehand!

Several years after his arrival here, Preminger was invited to the White House and wondered about the propriety of wearing a decoration at the reception to meet the President. He asked some diplomats who said there was no rule regarding decorations. By that time, his native Austria had been annexed by Nazi Germany, so Preminger felt it was OK to wear a decoration from a country "which no longer exists." And so he did, and never wore it again.

Preminger had met Albert Einstein in Vienna and Berlin before both came to America. In November 1939, Einstein attended a performance of *Margin for Error*, which

Preminger directed and in which he portrayed the Nazi Consul.

After the final curtain, Einstein was asked how he liked Preminger's work.

"Oh, I liked it very much," said Einstein, "but that actor who played the Consul was better than the play."

Margin for Error was an anti-Nazi play, and after it opened on Broadway, some German officials expressed their displeasure; America was still not officially at war with Germany.

Preminger had been doing eight performances a week as well as teaching at Yale four days a week. His voice became strained, and a friend noticed this.

"You're speaking softer," said the friend of his performance. "They can now hear you only as far as Buffalo."

"So long as they can still hear us in Berlin," he replied.

In February 1955, Preminger recalled the hours just before Hitler's *Anschluss*—annexation—of his native Austria in 1938. He and another man drove off from Vienna to freedom. They were, in fact, the last to cross the border before the Nazis took over. The other man in the car was Sam Spiegel, who sixteen years later produced *On the Waterfront*, which, like Preminger's 1954 movie *Carmen Jones*, was nominated for an Oscar that year. (Spiegel later produced *Bridge on the River Kwai*.)

One day one of his drama students at Yale asked him for a practical suggestion about directing a play.

"When you're directing on Broadway," said Preminger, "never take your star and producer to lunch. You'll always be stuck with the check."

When he moved into his apartment in mid-Manhattan, his wife, Marion Mill, said she'd rule the home. He objected. They settled it by playing two games of backgammon. She won both, and thus officially ran the household.

On a trip to Hollywood in May 1942, a beautiful woman spotted him at a restaurant, waved to her old friend until he noticed her, and came over. But she refused to give him her phone number. "I'll call *you*," she said. This didn't surprise Preminger; the woman was Greta Garbo.

Preminger had a role in a movie called *The Pied Piper*, and at the premiere he told a radio interviewer that the star of the film, Monty Woolley, had given one of the great performances of all time.

Woolley heard about the high praise and thanked Preminger the next day. "Oh, not at all," replied Preminger. "It was only a local station."

After the movie version of *Margin for Error* was released in 1942, Preminger said: "I had to reshoot some scenes with Milton Berle. The next day, the papers reported: 'Preminger having trouble with Berle.' The two other actors had difficulty with their lines, and the next day the report read: 'Preminger having trouble with those too.'

"Then came the scenes in which I directed myself, and the next day the report read: 'Preminger having trouble with Preminger.'"

In June 1946, Preminger was asked how he was able to teach drama at Yale when his English was a work in progress. "I assign the students to read a book or a play," he explained, "then I call on one of them to give an opinion. Then I call on another student to supply a contrary argument.

"All I have to do is listen."

Laura in 1944 earned Preminger an Oscar nomination for best director and solidified his place in Hollywood. A few years later he said he had no desire to direct on Broadway again.

"The theater," he said, "is a business where backers want their money back. Art should not be measured by profit. In Europe, I worked with Max Reinhardt. His backers never got a dime back."

Preminger directed *Daisy Kenyon*, starring Henry Fonda, Joan Crawford, and Dana Andrews. My father, playing himself in a scene set in the Stork Club, called writer Harry Kurnitz before the cameras rolled and asked him for a funny line, since my father had been given the OK to ad-lib.

Andrews, playing a lawyer, tells my father he's going to Washington the next day, but will return soon with some news.

"Thanks," replied my father. "Just for that, I'll let you handle all my libel business."

It was during the shooting of that movie that my father wrote that actors were no longer permitted to report for work dazed by drink, as in the days of John Barrymore. "The stakes are too high," he wrote. Then he reported that a young featured player had been warned to lay off the sauce (as they used to say back then), but came to the set drunk anyway. He assured Preminger his acting and appearance would be unaffected.

Preminger cured him of this idea by making the scheduled shots, including close-ups of the actor. Then he showed him the rushes—the rough prints of the scenes just filmed.

One look at himself under the bright lights, walking unsteadily, and he said: "If you destroy those takes and let me do a retake, I will never drink again."

Preminger tried to mention the Stork Club in all his movies, but when it came time to shoot a film called *The Fan* in 1948, he told Sherman Billingsley, the proprietor of the club, that this time it would be impossible. But Billingsley said there was a way to work in the name: "You can have a preface saying it takes place a few years before Sherman Billingsley, proprietor of the Stork Club, was born."

In October 1948, Preminger gave a party for my parents in Hollywood. One of the guests phoned my father in the afternoon and said he'd just learned he was expected to bring a dinner partner. My father named two unattached film actresses. But the man said he couldn't ask either at the last minute, and they surely had dates for that night anyway. So he invited someone else, and when he arrived, both actresses were there—alone.

By October 1953, Preminger had changed his mind about directing for the stage again and was back in New York directing a production of Franz Kafka's *The Trial* at the City Center. He assembled the cast and began: "I've just come back from Hollywood where I directed Marilyn Monroe in *River of No Return*. And frankly, from Monroe to Kafka is a jump so big, I need time to adjust."

In 1955, Preminger told my father his movie *The Man with the Golden Arm* was causing a problem for him with two unions. The Writers Guild objected to the billing: "A Film by Otto Preminger," saying his name was too prominent. The Directors Guild, however, complained that the phrase in the ads was written in letters too small.

William Holden loved to tell the story of Preminger directing him in his Oscar-winning performance in *Stalag 17*. "He had a small part in his film," Holden recalled, "and he'd set up the scene, then call: 'Action!' Then he'd walk out from behind the camera and into the scene, act in it, then walk back behind the camera and yell: 'Cut! Print! Excellent!'"

I went to a lecture he gave at the Lee Strasberg Theater Institute in 1972, and he said he always refused to use the word "industry" in discussing Hollywood.

"An 'industry,'" he explained, "manufactures shoes."

WILLIAM SAROYAN

There was never a more beloved American author than William Saroyan, the Pulitzer Prize–winning author, playwright, and short-story writer. His works often had themes related to his ethnic roots in the Armenian community of his birthplace, Fresno, California. I was old enough to appreciate his good friendship with my father and loved this loud, friendly man with a huge handlebar mustache.

When his 1937 book *Little Children* was released, my father revealed on July 30 of that year that the jacket carried this blurb: "The author unquestionably is one of the few first-rate writers of the day."

The blurb was unsigned, and for a very good reason: it had been written by William Saroyan.

In 1939, Saroyan was awarded the O. Henry Prize for short-story writing. However, when he received the $100 check for *The Daring Young Man on the Flying Trapeze*, he returned the money with the following message:

"When I was a young writer, I could've used five bucks, but nobody would stake me to it. I don't need this money now. So use it to encourage a promising young author who may be in the spot I was in when I first started."

Doubleday-Doran, the publishers who awarded the money, then sent it to a new writer they'd discovered. However, nothing was ever heard from that writer again, since he subsequently was executed for murder.

Besides Saroyan's obvious talent as a writer, what intrigued my father, I think, was the fact that Saroyan wasn't from Hollywood or Broadway, but was someone who never cut himself off from his roots in Fresno.

He could be objective about New York nightlife. Thus, when he returned to nearby San Francisco at the end of 1939, he wrote my father: "How can you hang around people who are busy all the time being great, without losing faith in humanity? Are they great? Sure. I know that. Sure they are. They're pathetic but great, too. You know what's the matter with them? They're broken up into surrealist fragments, each with a separate identity of its own. The hell with it."

Early in 1940, Saroyan wrote two letters to George Jean Nathan, then one of America's most prominent drama critics. The first letter ran 1,800 words. The second was more than 2,000 words.

Both were signed: "Yours in haste, Saroyan."

Famed director Harold Clurman of the Group Theater was responsible for starting novelist Saroyan on his dramatic career. When Clurman wrote Saroyan suggesting he compose a play, the reply came on a postcard, written in pencil: "Okay. I've never tried it. I'll write a great one, but I must direct it."

He did indeed direct his first play, *The Time of Your Life*, which ran just thirty-two performances, but it nevertheless won the Pulitzer Prize and the Drama Critics Circle award and solidified his reputation as a great playwright.

One of Saroyan's plays was criticized because the reviewers saw the influence of his contemporary Clifford Odets. Then Odets's play opened, and it too was criticized—for being too influenced by Saroyan!

Movie and TV producer Collier Young, who backed popular shows like *Ironside* and *Wild Wild West*, visited Saroyan, who explained to Young the writings of James Joyce and Gertrude Stein.

"I don't go for this doubletalk writing," said Young. "I like to see a subject, a predicate, and sometimes an adverb."

Saroyan glared at him and said: "That's what's been holding back literature for 5,000 years."

When Carl Sandburg met Saroyan, he asked him why he had refused the $1,000 that came with the Pulitzer Prize. "If I'd have known you would accept the money," replied Saroyan, "I would have, too."

In October 1940, Saroyan was on the dais of a dinner at New York's Commodore Hotel honoring exiled writers. Other literary giants were there as well. When it came time for Saroyan to speak, his chair was empty. He'd stepped outside to buy cigarettes, saw some bellboys playing craps, and joined in. Then he heard himself being introduced, raced back into the dinner, and hastily began his speech—starting on page 4.

The next month, Random House announced they would publish a collection of Saroyan's short stories and wired the author, requesting that he submit an introduction for the book. Two days later they received a 6,000-word introduction that began: "Is Saroyan a short-story writer? Yes. He won the O. Henry Prize. Is he a playwright? Yes. He won the Drama Critics Circle Award and Pulitzer Prize. Is he a genius? Decidedly. Did he write *Hamlet*? No. That was another *W.S.*"

In May 1941, Saroyan was due to come to New York. Just before his trip, he learned of the literature courses being given at the University of California. He secured a copy of the curriculum, then wrote to the college requesting entrance into the classes on English Modern Literature, Poetry, etc. The college officials never replied to his letters. So he took a streetcar to the campus, walked through all the rooms, and said: "Hell. Now I've been to college." Then he left for New York—to pick up his Pulitzer Prize.

During that visit to New York, Saroyan dined with Sinclair Lewis, the only other writer to reject the Pulitzer Prize. Lewis expressed admiration for Saroyan's play *The Beautiful People*.

"You're almost like a pulp writer," said Lewis. "You write about the poor to entertain the rich." Then Saroyan said that if he won another Pulitzer Prize, he'd again accept the prize but not the money, "but with a beautiful explanation."

In November 1941, Saroyan had received lucrative offers from studios to produce screen versions of some of his plays. He rejected them, to display his independence. While negotiating with MGM, he was invited to sit in Louis B. Mayer's box at a Hollywood racetrack. Mayer, one of Hollywood's most influential studio bosses, kept receiving tips on the races and passed them on to Saroyan, who ignored them.

"Just catch me going to L.B. for anything, especially racing tips," he said defiantly. All of Mayer's tips proved to be winners. Saroyan lost $2,000.

In June 1942, Saroyan learned that his play *Jim Dandy* might be produced simultaneously in thirty-five cities by the National Theater Conference. The audiences who'd already seen it were baffled. Saroyan had an answer: "When understood, things have neither quality nor dimension. A work of art which is not understood at the first crack is, if nothing else, a refreshment to the spirit and a challenge to the mind. For those who don't understand my play, it's probably because they do not as yet understand themselves."

Saroyan once tested his theory that people understand a play better after they've seen it a second time. His short play *Across the Board on Tomorrow Morning* was performed at the famed Pasadena Playhouse, and then after an intermission, was put on again.

Later the director said: "Bill, I had the feeling about the second play, that I'd seen it before."

Also in 1942 Saroyan wrote a song called "Of All the Things I Love," which Walter Huston sang in Saroyan's flop play *Love's Old Sweet Song*, which ran just forty-four performances. Only one copy of the sheet music for the song was purchased, so Saroyan received a royalty check of 1 cent. He'd been the lone buyer. And he'd bought it at a discount.

A young actress entered a cab in July 1942 and told the driver to take her to the Belasco Theater where Saroyan was casting his new play. The driver, on a whim, followed her into the theater. She didn't get hired. He did.

In September 1942, Saroyan was about to be inducted into the Army, so he gave his girlfriend a gold bracelet, lock, and key with a love message. "That's the first time I've ever done such a thing," Saroyan told my father. "The only presents I'd ever given girls were copies of my books. That wasn't only romantic, but it got me new readers."

Saroyan had a big fan in the hat-check girl at the Stork Club, so he gave her a part in one of his plays. But when it quickly closed, he was billed for her membership fee in Actors' Equity. Saroyan countered that "she said nothing" onstage and was therefore exempt. That was true in a way; she did have a one-word part; her one line was: "Nothing."

Some time before he entered the Army in 1943, Saroyan watched Orson Welles doing card tricks, in particular a seven of clubs trick. Saroyan tried repeatedly to do the trick but failed. Some days later, Welles needed a radio script within four hours and phoned Saroyan (who Welles knew wrote quickly), who said: "I'll meet you in half an hour. And I'll have the finished script."

Saroyan arrived, all right, five minutes late, but with a script, and he said: "This is *my* seven of clubs trick."

"But you were five minutes late," Welles reminded him.

"Oh, that's because I also wrote a song in that time," Saroyan explained, before singing the song. Welles never used the script, nor the song. Saroyan, meanwhile, collaborated with a fellow Armenian-American named Ross Bagdasarian, also from Fresno, California. He was "The Musician" across the alleyway from wheelchair-bound Jimmy Stewart in *Rear Window*, who later changed his professional name to David Seville and created the "Singing Chipmunks."

Incidentally, the song Saroyan and Bagdasarian wrote in five minutes? "Come On-a My House," which eight years later became a top Billboard hit when Rosemary Clooney, who reportedly hated the song, nevertheless recorded it. One of her biggest hits, it was later recorded by others, including Ella Fitzgerald.

In March 1943, the Army Signal Corps hired a Hollywood screenwriter for some special duties. He came to New York and was assigned to instruct soldiers in how to write a movie, probably for future Army training films.

One of the pupils in his class was surely the only Army private who'd already won the Pulitzer Prize and the Drama Critics Circle Award and had the current movie hit of that time, *The Human Comedy*: William Saroyan.

Saroyan is probably the only soldier who was drafted because he was kind. He was paid handsomely for writing *The Human Comedy* and gave his earnings to his cash-starved agent and to relatives. Since they were then not dependent on him, he was classified 1-A and drafted.

While he was in the Army, he was approached by several Broadway producers who wanted to put on a play Saroyan had written about studio boss L.B. Mayer, but they all wanted him to make some minor revisions, saying that would take less than an hour. Saroyan refused.

"When a man becomes a soldier," he wrote, "there's no spare time for private business."

To put it mildly, Saroyan was not a great soldier. He wondered why the Army, knowing he was a Pulitzer Prize–winning writer, kept trying to teach him how to take a machine gun apart, read military maps, and other difficult soldiering tasks. He couldn't pass any exams in these technical matters. Finally he was assigned to a course in wire splicing, but got the lowest marks on the skill test.

"You're going to learn how to do it, Private," Saroyan was told by his sergeant. "And if you learn, we'll give you a prize." He tried three times to splice a wire, and finally succeeded. The prize? The spliced wire.

During the war, many Hollywood figures were assigned to make movies for the Army, but still had to take periodic exams from career officers who considered them no different from other soldiers. Some studied for the exams, others cheated. Not Saroyan. He neither studied nor cheated, and failed every test. Except that one about splicing wires.

Saroyan spent New Year's Eve 1943 at a party in New York and gave a speech about the American theater. At 5 a.m. New Year's Day, he looked at his watch and said: "The first five hours of 1944 shot to hell. Not a play written to show for it yet."

In November 1944, Private Saroyan was on leave in London and spent three days in his hotel bed, reading books by several authors, including himself. He wore several layers of clothing and read under the covers, later explaining he wanted to recreate summer back home in Fresno.

Until the last week of her life, Saroyan's grandmother was never convinced of his success. He tried to reassure her by arriving by plane from New York carrying 100 silver dollars, which he placed in rows on her bed. That did the trick; the venerable Armenian lady considered it to be incontrovertible proof that he was indeed successful.

In April 1947, Saroyan was asked why he'd refused the Pulitzer Prize but accepted an Oscar for writing *The Human Comedy*. "I

turned down the Oscar as well, but one day it arrived at my house without a return address. So I had to keep it."

Saroyan didn't care where he was when writing. He'd write plays in a field in Fresno or in a suite in an expensive hotel in New York. At a restaurant in San Francisco, he was asked by the owner to write an introduction to a cookbook. "Sure," said Saroyan. "I'll do it here and now. Just bring me some paper. The mood and the setting are right for it."

Saroyan's amazing ability to write quickly was well known. At a party in October 1948, he began chatting with Frank Loesser, who wrote *Guys and Dolls*. They discussed an idea for a new show. Ten minutes later, someone called over to them: "How're you doing?"

"Fine," Loesser reported, "but we've got some problems with Act II."

In Saroyan's time, some European countries wouldn't permit author's royalties for works performed there to be taken out of the country. So he'd travel to Europe, collect his large fees, then ask a cab driver to take him to a "hopelessly expensive" hotel, to book a suite there until he'd spent the money.

When he visited George Bernard Shaw and told him he was an Armenian-American, Shaw said: "Armenian? I thought the Turks killed all of you."

"A few of us got away," replied Saroyan.

After his visit with Shaw, then ninety-two, Saroyan said: "I got the feeling I have a lot of time left."

As a young man, he'd seen a Shaw play from 25-cent balcony seats and couldn't hear the dialogue. He vowed then and there that his own plays would have action and dialogue comprehensible to the balcony-sitters.

In November 1955, Saroyan expressed his lack of enthusiasm for graduate studies in journalism and writing. "Schools can't help much in such fields," he said. "It's as if we were to start a school on how to be the Vice President or how to be a great figure, or how to be an Armenian. It just has to happen to you."

He then said he wished newspapers wrote about other Armenians. "We always have a look of loneliness and frustration. It comes from searching the newspapers every day, trying to read something about an Armenian, and never finding it."

Saroyan was a gambler. He'd wager on anything—cards, tennis matches, billiards, etc. He once offered to bet he could beat anyone swimming across the pool. The bets were placed, the swimmers leaped into the pool, but Saroyan couldn't even make it across.

"I guess," he said later, "that bet wasn't like poker: no bluffing."

Unlike most gamblers, however, he could afford losses, and it paid dividends. For example, he lost a fortune gambling at the dice tables in Las Vegas but didn't mind.

"Some of my best writing was the result of my needing money to make up for gambling losses. *The Human Comedy* [for which he won an Academy Award] was the result of my needing money to make up for gambling losses."

History, alas, does not have a Saroyan appearance on Edward R. Murrow's *Person to Person*, since the guests were never paid for appearing on the prestigious show.

"I've got enough prestige, whatever that means," said Saroyan in rejecting an invitation. "I want the loot."

In November 1957, my father wrote that Saroyan believed writers should only lease not sell their stories to movie studios. He also believed that every playwright should try acting in a play at least once. "After all," he explained, "isn't it natural for a person who writes a concerto for violin first to try playing the instrument himself?"

Oscar Levant, the famed pianist/actor/ raconteur/hypochondriac, criticized Saroyan's plays, telling the writer he only created sugary characters for children, and nobody ever dies. "Not true," replied Saroyan, who then listed characters in his plays who died.

"Maybe so," replied Levant. "But all your characters who die go to Heaven."

PHIL SILVERS

The recent release of DVD editions of *Sergeant Bilko* brought Phil Silvers back, in a sense, while also introducing his brash brand of humor to a new generation. So did his appearance on a 44-cent stamp, as his most famous character, in August 2009.

Born in Brownsville, Brooklyn, the youngest of eight children, his siblings would include a lawyer, businessman, architect, and, as his official bio page puts it, "one top banana," a reference to his other great role on Broadway and in a 1954 movie.

Silvers wasn't just another famous name my father knew and wrote about. He and his then-wife Evelyn, along with their five daughters ("my infield," he called them), lived in our building. They were regular guests at our Passover seders, and I remember Evelyn, who hadn't grown up attending seders, forgetting that the bitter herbs should be taken in very small doses every year. She fainted after trying a large portion.

An excessive gambling habit would cost him this marriage.

Silvers had three rules he taught his daughters: "One. Revere you mother always. Two: Drink lots of milk. And Three: Elope."

After years doing comedy in burlesque, he made his Broadway debut in *Yokel Boy*, billed fifty-eighth, incredibly. But his part was expanded, and when movie mogul Louis B. Mayer liked his performance and offered him a contract, he jumped at the chance.

On the opening night of *Yokel Boy*, Silvers told my father he'd been nervous. "So around 6 o'clock," he said, "I went over to the Gaiety Burlesque Theater, went onstage, and did a show. When I heard 'em laugh, I knew I was OK, so I went back and opened on Broadway."

On December 15, 1941, Silvers was at the Stork Club and had just completed work in the movie *All Through the Night*, which starred Humphrey Bogart. Featured in the cast, and sitting that night at Silvers's table, was the classic Australian actress Judith Anderson.

"This is democracy at work," said Silvers, "when Lady Macbeth sits at the same table as an ex-burlesque comic."

A week later, Silvers had a date with none other than Olivia De Havilland. She told him: "Don't wear those thick-lensed glasses of yours when you pick me up." Silvers, who could hardly see without those spectacles, showed up without them, all right, but with a Seeing Eye dog.

One of Silvers's older siblings was his brother Harry, who clipped every newspaper mention of the comic and pasted them in a scrapbook. When he looked at the clippings, however, Phil told Harry he was being overzealous, since the scrapbook contained clippings of every time the word "Silver" was mentioned, including the Lone Ranger's horse, articles about the stabilization of the silver market, and even department store sales of silverware.

No one knows which MGM executive ordered it, but Silvers auditioned for the role of Reverend Collins in the 1940 version of *Pride and Prejudice*, which starred Laurence Olivier and Greer Garson, two actors about as far away on the spectrum as could be from Phil Silvers.

Nevertheless, the Brooklyn-born comic learned his lines perfectly, and at the audition began: "There are many reasons why you two shouldn't be married. Foist—"

"Cut!" called the executive. "That's enough."

In November 1951, Silvers was starring in *Top Banana*, a show in which he was onstage for virtually every scene. The producers of the musical, aware of this problem, took unusual measures to be certain his voice would get its proper rest. They instructed him to spend every non-matinee afternoon at the movies, thus ensuring for at least two hours, he'd be silent.

After a performance a month later, Silvers greeted an unusual guest backstage—General Douglas MacArthur, who, introducing his wife to the comic said: "Mr. Silvers, this is *my* 'top banana.'"

In April 1954, Red Buttons joined Silvers at Sardi's just after Buttons came from performing on his own TV show. "Did you see the show?" asked Buttons. Silvers said he was watching the fights instead.

"But it went so well," said the disappointed Buttons.

"What would I have seen? Don't tell me," continued Silvers, who of course had indeed watched the show. "You'd have come out as this shy little boy, . . ." and then he recited every routine.

Silvers was a great baseball fan. He went to dozens of games, shared tables at Toots Shor's restaurant with home and visiting stars, swapped stories, and felt at ease with them. Then in May 1955, he made a startling discovery: "I came to my senses," he explained. "I recalled that neither Joe DiMaggio nor any of the other players I adore, players I consider close friends, ever sent me a wire on my opening nights."

That same month, Silvers began dating the model and TV personality Nancy Berg. She'd been late getting ready for their first date, which wasn't terribly unusual. But what was odd to Silvers when he picked her up was to see a smoking cigar in her ashtray. A man likes to think a lady's attention is exclusive, even if for just an evening. But that lit cigar had him thinking.

Then she picked up the cigar and continued smoking it.

By that time, he'd completed shooting the first thirteen episodes of his new CBS series, *You'll Never Get Rich*, better remembered as *Sergeant Bilko*. Even though the program wouldn't take to the air until the fall, two New York cab drivers who'd recognized him said: "Saw your new show, Phil. Loved it!"

Back when he was starring on Broadway in *Top Banana*, Jack Benny advised the then-young comic not to accept a TV offer. "Television will eat you up," he said. "Stay where you are."

Then, after *Sergeant Bilko* won eight Emmys, he wired Silvers: "You wouldn't listen to me, would you?"

In February 1956, Silvers was in Baltimore to receive an award from the Advertising Club. The dais included the governor of Maryland and one of its senators.

Silvers, noting their presence, told the audience: "I opened the Minsky Burlesque Theater here in 1932, where we were raided by the police and booked." Then he asked, "Where were you guys when I really needed you?"

By 1957, Silvers was living in the Hotel Fourteen, above the Copacabana, the famous nightclub. One night he realized that Martin and Lewis were performing their act downstairs, doing several shows a night. At 2:30 a.m., dressed in his pajamas, robe, and trademark oversized glasses, he came downstairs, marched onstage, put his index finger to his lips and said: "Shhhhh. I'm trying to sleep upstairs, guys. Keep it down, please."

One night Silvers performed at a testimonial dinner for Al Jolson in Hollywood. En route to the dinner, he met Conn McCreary, the jockey, who twice won the Kentucky Derby. Silvers decided to use McCreary, the tiniest jockey of them all, in his remarks that night.

His jokes, using the little jockey as his foil, were hilarious, but only Jolson, seated on the dais, laughed. That's because McCreary was so small, none of the guests could see him.

Phil and Evelyn Silvers and their daughters moved into our apartment building early in 1959. One of the first purchases for their new apartment was an old Steinway piano she'd picked up at a junk shop downtown, for $400.

But it wasn't just any old piano. It turned out to be one of the first five Steinway pianos ever made, around 1853, and when that fact came to light, the first offer they received was for $50,000.

In April 1960, Silvers spotted Ted Williams walking down Fifth Avenue the morning of a game against the Yankees.

"Hey, Ted," he called out to his friend.

Williams kept walking.

"Hey, 'Teddy Ballgame,' I hope you beat the Yankees tonight." The slugger kept walking.

Finally Silvers said: "Hey, Ted, I made more money than you did last year."

At that "the Greatest Hitter Who Ever Lived" finally turned around.

In January 1961, President Kennedy saw Silvers in *Do Re Mi* at the St. James Theater. Not surprisingly, the audience kept looking at JFK every time a joke came, to check his reaction.

Silvers decided to ease the tension. In one scene, he was auditioning actors and read from a list of aspirants. For that performance only, he added the name "Peter Lawford," the President's actor/brother-in-law, frowned, and tossed the list away.

One of the songs in the show, "All of My Life," included the word "goddamn."

For matinee audiences, however, Silvers changed it to "darn."

In December of that year, Maurice Chevalier, the great French star of stage and screen, saw Silvers's show, then went backstage. They were old friends, and Silvers owed Chevalier a debt. When he'd been a starving burlesque comic, he did a devastating Chevalier imitation that audiences loved.

Chevalier, then seventy-two, took note of the bevy of gorgeous showgirls backstage and sighed: "If only I were twenty years older."

"Don't you mean twenty years younger?" asked Silvers.

"No," replied the Frenchman. "If I were twenty years older, the girls wouldn't bother me the way they do."

Silvers often put in extra jokes or ad-libs in his Broadway shows, to keep them fresh night after night. One night, however, the playwright came backstage to complain.

"Listen," said Silvers, "if I do it just the way you wrote it, we'll all be in trouble."

One night in November 1963, Silvers was honored by a "roast." One of the speakers was the comedienne/actress Rose Marie, who said: "Phil is an exceptional man. Truly unique. In fact he constantly reminds me of St. Joseph. That's right. And everyone knows St. Joseph is one of the worst towns in Missouri."

FRANK SINATRA

Frank Sinatra was unquestionably the foremost singer and entertainer of the second half of the twentieth century. Born in Hoboken, New Jersey, he spent most of his adult life in California, but frequently returned to New York.

On June 5, 1943, my father printed the first item about the then-skinny young singer from Hoboken. Sinatra was introduced to Bing Crosby and complained to Crosby about the meager share he retained of his earnings.

"Tommy Dorsey [the leader of the band] gets a third of my earnings, his manager gets 10 percent, mine gets the same, and that's all before taxes."

"Only one thing to do," advised Crosby. He grabbed his own throat and then hoarsely suggested: "Tell 'em all those slices out of your salary have made you so nervous you just can't sing anymore."

That fall, he arrived in New York from Hollywood on a train with Danny Kaye and veteran actor Walter Pidgeon. A horde of wide-eyed, screaming Sinatra fans, "bobby-soxers" they were called, was waiting. They broke through the police lines and yelled for Sinatra's autograph. The young singer saw the wild mob, turned to Pidgeon and Kaye, and said: "You fellows are lucky you can't sing." Pidgeon admired the view and replied: "And you're lucky you can."

This is a measure of Sinatra's stardom: When he performed at New York's famous Waldorf-Astoria Hotel, the mailroom was swamped with a thousand songs a week from amateur composers hoping he would sing their song and bring them instant recognition.

A group of his fans squealed their delight at seeing Sinatra rush onstage to do a radio broadcast. They saw him place a wad of his chewing gum against the wall before he began to sing. The girls started hunting for the discarded gum. "That's terrible," an elderly man berated them. "What will you do with the gum if you find it? There are millions of germs in it."

"Germs?" replied one incredulous girl. "There just couldn't be. Not from our Frankie. Sinatra couldn't have germs."

His manager, Al Levy, was walking with him down a New York street when they passed a newsstand. Sinatra had just had a tiff with the press. Levy glanced at the headlines and gasped: "What have we done now?" He raced over, bought the paper, scanned the headline, and breathed a sigh of relief. "It's OK, Frankie. They don't mean us." The headlines screamed:

"ALLIES ATTACK SUMATRA!"

Before Jilly's and Patsy's restaurants became his New York haunts, Toots Shor's was a favorite for Sinatra. He always sat at the same table with the same waiter, who would receive generous tips. One night in 1944, the waiter shook his head sadly after Sinatra summoned him. Instead of coming over, he sent another waiter to the table. "What's the matter?" asked Sinatra. The waiter explained he'd "lost" Sinatra's patronage for a month in a craps game.

Sinatra first visited the White House on September 28, 1944. By this time he was the idol of millions of bobby-soxers. He politely waited his turn in the reception line, and approached the President. "Well, look who's here," said FDR, smiling broadly. "My doctor and I were talking about you." Sinatra wondered how on earth the President, running wars on several fronts all over the world, could take time to think of him.

"You have restored to the women of America something which they lost in the past fifty years," FDR explained: "The charm of knowing how to faint."

A few weeks later, Sinatra met with another patrician politician, W. Averill Harriman, future governor of New York, FDR's

With Frank Sinatra and Anne Jeffries at Toots Shor's circa 1958.

wartime ambassador to the Soviet Union, and one of the richest men in America. Harriman asked Sinatra about the singer's first participation in politics. It was in New Jersey's gubernatorial campaign. Jersey City Mayor Frank "I Am the Law" Hague invited Sinatra to appear at a rally for the Democratic candidate. He was told he'd sing and make his speech just before the candidate was to address the crowd.

"I know audiences," said Sinatra. "Put me on after the candidate." But Hague refused. Sure enough, Sinatra sang, then spoke. By the time the candidate took the stage, Sinatra's fans in the audience had left, and the hall was nearly empty.

With Bob Hope and Frank Sinatra at a Damon Runyon Cancer Fund celebrity golf tournament, circa 1954 in California. I guess I'll never know why my father and Hope are holding hands!

One day in March 1945, one of Bing Crosby's young sons was introduced to Sinatra. "I'd love to see your icebox," he said. "Because Dad says you took the bread and butter from us."

Sinatra was a painter. He'd spend long hours at his easel. Then he sent one of his oils to his manager, who was puzzled at seeing the canvas covered with black paint except for the upper left-hand corner. There it showed a light in a tiny window. "Frank, what's this supposed to be?" he asked. "That's a wartime blackout, but some dope's left his light on," the "artist" explained.

One day in April 1954, Sinatra was back in town and paid a sentimental visit to the Riobamba, the nightclub where he first rocketed to fame. Before and after Sinatra worked there the club was jinxed; other performers flopped. When, for example, Sinatra finished his engagement, they hired another young, unknown singer, who

flopped: a guy from Steubenville, Ohio, named Dean Martin.

In June 1954, Sinatra had an audience with Pope Pius XII, who asked him what he did and where he lived. "I live in Hollywood and I'm a singer," Sinatra replied. "What do you sing?" asked the Pontiff. Not expecting that question, Sinatra, for some reason, replied: "'Old Man River,' your Holiness."

In *The Man with the Golden Arm*, Sinatra's character was returning to Chicago after six months in a hospital for addicts. The script had him saying: "I gained ten pounds." Director Otto Preminger yelled "Cut!" He reshot the scene, changing the line to "I gained six pounds," and explained that "no moviegoer would believe Sinatra could ever gain ten pounds."

By the time Sinatra costarred with Cary Grant and young Sophia Loren in *The Pride and the Passion*, he'd won a Supporting Oscar for *From Here to Eternity*, which revived his acting career.

It was quite a journey for Sinatra, who as a young man refused a non-singing role, saying: "For me, doing straight parts is a good way to go hungry."

Sinatra refused to do publicity photos for the movie, saying he was too busy filming the role. Yet one night, he'd heard that Lionel Hampton, the great jazz vibraphone player, was performing in Madrid. Though he'd never met Hampton, Sinatra went to see the performance, leaped onstage, sang six songs, and made a speech.

When some scenes were filmed in the ancient city of Segovia, Sinatra described it as "that joint where Columbus did the egg bit for Isabella. You know. To get the loot."

Photographer Sam Shaw, best known for his iconic pictures of Marilyn Monroe, was living in Madrid then and was a friend of Sinatra. Shaw reminded Sinatra he'd have to readjust his hours to be ready for early morning shoots. This would be especially difficult, since Spaniards eat dinner around

9 p.m. and Sinatra was a night owl, used to staying up until the wee hours.

Shaw advised Sinatra to take a dull book to bed. So Sinatra obtained a book on meteorology. But he found it fascinating and became a weather buff. Then he was curious about acoustics, and became a bit of an expert on that subject, too.

In September 1957, Sinatra was in Monte Carlo and saw Sir Winston Churchill. "I've never done this before, Mr. Churchill," Sinatra began, introducing himself and shaking Sir Winston's hand. "And I am particularly pleased to meet you, Mr. Sinatra," replied Churchill, who'd once announced that he'd already met everyone he cared to meet. "My wife Clementine adores your records."

Sinatra was asked by a Broadway playwright to do a show. "On one condition," said Sinatra. "We'd get a good script from you, rehearse it well, make it right, take it on the road four weeks, open on Broadway, get great reviews, have a big party. Then close."

Sir Peter Ustinov and his wife lived next door to the Sinatras for a time. The English actor/playwright was at work writing his screenplay for *Romanoff and Juliet*, which he would direct and in which he would star. His wife didn't think he was working hard enough and wished he could concentrate on his writing the way Sinatra applied himself to his singing. Day and night they heard Sinatra practicing next door. Then one night, he heard Sinatra singing: "I Don't Want to Walk . . . to Walk . . . to Walk." It was a record and a stuck needle.

When he was part-owner of the Sands Hotel in Las Vegas, he was losing at the blackjack table. Then he exercised a privilege only an owner can enjoy. He had the dealer come upstairs to his suite to continue the game. He lost another $14,000.

Sinatra was once invited to a reception at the United Nations. He noticed a man there whose face looked familiar, but he couldn't place his name. He went over, slapped him on the back, and said: "How're ya doin' fella?" Slowly the man turned around. It was Andrei Gromyko, the stone-faced Soviet Foreign Minister, the coldest cold warrior of them all.

With Sophia Loren and Rossano Brazzi in Libya on the set of
Legend of the Lost. *Loren kept warm in the cold desert night*
by using my father's extra pair of woolen pajamas.

'60s

The Lyons Den

LEONARD LYONS

This was the most amazing decade of all, at least from my perspective. I finally was old enough to make the rounds with my father, as my two older brothers had done. I'd grown up seeing, in our home, the luminaries about whom my father wrote: Orson Welles, Marlene Dietrich, Joe DiMaggio, and the like. But sitting with them in their own element, in nightclubs and restaurants, gave me a whole new perspective.

In the summer of 1960, I got my first job in journalism, as a summer intern on the city desk of the *Jersey Journal*, a Newhouse newspaper in Jersey City. I remember one of the big stories concerned the international repercussions of the "U-2" incident, when the Soviets shot down a high-altitude U.S. spy plane and captured its pilot, Francis Gary Powers.

I got a close-up look at how a fairly large metropolitan newspaper worked, and would return to work there writing sports and other stories for two more summers.

In late June 1961, I returned to Spain to travel with Antonio Ordóñez, the great matador and a national hero in that country and in Mexico and Latin America. Ernest Hemingway had arranged it, and at fifteen I showed up on Antonio's doorstep,

fresh off the plane from Idlewild (now JFK) airport. I would spend six more summers crisscrossing Spain with him.

Then on July 2, 1961, came the terrible news that Hemingway had died. We were in the city of Jerez de la Frontera, and Ordóñez, appearing at a night bullfight, knelt on one knee in the middle of the arena and prayed.

In 1961, "The Twist" took New York by storm. It had not first been performed by Chubby Checker, who made it a worldwide sensation, but by Hank Ballard two years earlier, only to resurface and take off. The Peppermint Lounge, on West Forty-Fifth Street in Manhattan, became *the* place to see stars doing the new dance. Old mainstays like Toots Shor's were still popular, but the Stork Club would close in 1965 after thirty-six years. (Incidentally, when I looked up the Stork Club on Wikipedia, there was a photo taken by Alfred Eisenstaedt on a typical night in November 1944. At the left is Orson Welles; in the middle, sitting with owner Sherman Billingsley, is my father. I hope it wasn't taken November 5, 1944, because he should've been at the hospital, welcoming me into the world!)

Sardi's was still going strong, although

Sardi's East, on East Fifty-Fourth Street, never caught on; it was a Sardi's theater restaurant half a mile away from the theater district. It closed in 1968. But Downey's, the Irish pub, was in its heyday in the 'sixties. Jim Downey bought the establishment with money won on a horse, and it was the favorite place of Richard Burton and Elizabeth Taylor after he performed in *Hamlet* every night. I'd often take a date there and would meet up with my father for the rest of his rounds.

I got familiar with places like the Oak Room of the Plaza Hotel, Forum of the 12 Caesars, Voisin, the Four Seasons at lunchtime, Downey's, Sardi's of course, the Russian Tea Room, "21," and his last stop every night, P.J. Clarke's, where athletes not at Shor's would congregate, especially the Giant football stars. To this day, they still serve the best hamburgers and hot apple pie in town. The Giants were in the NFL championship games in 1961, 1962, and 1963, while the Yankees won it all in 1961 and 1962 before being swept by the LA Dodgers in 1963. The woeful NY Mets, formed in 1962, would become the Miracle Mets in 1969, nine months after the Jets won Super Bowl III. And the Knicks began what would be their first NBA championship season.

On Broadway, *Bye Bye Birdie, Hello, Dolly!, Camelot, How to Succeed in Business Without Really Trying, Stop the World I Want to Get Off, Cabaret*, and *Fiddler on the Roof* were big hits. I think my father must've seen *Fiddler*, with lyrics by his cousin Sheldon Harnick, fifty times, and probably wept at most of the performances. It was his favorite show of all time.

Barbra Streisand became a huge star in *Funny Girl* as Fanny Brice, while *Oh! Calcutta, Mame*, and *Hair!* drew thousands. My mother accompanied my father to the opening night of *Hair!* He asked her what she thought of the show, which featured naked men and women at the end of one number.

"There were naked women, too?" asked my mother.

Broadway also saw the astonishing success of a former writer for TV's *Your Show of Shows*, Neil Simon, whose fast-paced witty comedies kept New Yorkers and tourists alike in stitches. He had an incredible four shows running at once in 1966, an unparalleled achievement: *The Star Spangled Girl, The Odd Couple, Barefoot in the Park*, and *Sweet Charity*, the musical for which he wrote the book. All were hits, too. *Who's Afraid of Virginia Woolf?* was a revolutionary drama from Edward Albee. And as usual, my parents attended every opening night.

There was a 113-day newspaper strike, starting December 8, 1962, but "The Lyons Den" continued uninterrupted in syndication. It was the decade in which the *New York Post* began automation of its presses. From September 1966 until May 1967, the *World Journal Tribune* tried to continue the legacy of seven other newspapers, but the new creation failed to attract enough revenue and folded, leaving the *Post* New York's only afternoon paper.

The Burton-Taylor romance, which my father covered exclusively, captivated readers worldwide, and the arrival of the Beatles early in 1964 lifted New Yorkers still in shock and mourning after the Kennedy assassination.

My father's readership was changing, getting younger, so besides writing about established stars like Ethel Merman and Kirk Douglas, he wrote about Andy Warhol, the Beatles, and Streisand. He also added a few new places like Joe Allen to his nightly rounds, meeting younger actors like Dustin Hoffman and Jon Voight. He stayed current.

In May 1965, a year or so after her divorce from Richard Burton, his ex-wife Sybil, one of the most dynamic, charismatic people I have ever known, was determined to forge her own identity. She opened Arthur, which quickly became the hottest discotheque in New York. Her friends Julie Andrews, Roddy McDowall, and Stephen Sondheim were just a few of the celebrated investors in Arthur, the name the Beatles jokingly called their haircuts in *A Hard Day's Night*. For good measure, Sybil married Jordan Christopher, the handsome lead performer of *The Wild Ones,* the band at Arthur, and posed with them on their album cover.

Everyone from Princess Margaret to Warren Beatty, Julie Christie, and Truman Capote was seen there every night, ushered to the front of the long line outside. While it lasted, Arthur was a nightly stop for my father. Many nights he was probably there to check on me, since I was a young regular there, too. That is, until 1969, when Sybil sold it. Other places followed, but they were pale imitations of Arthur.

BRENDAN BEHAN

Of all the hundreds of friendships my father enjoyed in his lifetime, perhaps the most unusual and unlikely was the one with Brendan Behan, one of Ireland's greatest poets and playwrights. A shy, coffee-drinking New York Jew and a loud, gregarious Irish Roman Catholic—who would drink himself to death at age forty-seven.

Raised in different worlds, yet finding common ground and enjoying each other's company, they spent many unforgettable evenings together in New York. It was a time when hard drinking was often winked at, and certainly not looked at as it is today, a tragic, life-shortening disease in his case.

But there they were together, the New York journalist showing the Dublin man of letters the most exciting city in the world by night. Indeed, whenever a one-man show about Behan is produced, there is inevitably a portion in which the actor refers to this unlikely bond.

One of the things my father loved to do with Brendan (he insisted we call him by his first name—never "Mr. Behan") was take him to half-a-dozen Broadway plays in one hour. My father had the cachet to enter any theater, unannounced. He and Brendan would stand outside while my father looked at his wristwatch and said something like: "Okay, it's 9:15. Here's the premise of *Fiddler on the Roof*." Then he'd tell his colorful visitor what had happened so far in the show. They'd then walk in, watch one number, and leave during the thunderous applause, to move on to the theater next door.

Behan, who wrote *The Hostage* and *Borstal Boy,* came into our lives like a whirlwind. He would dance the hora at my brother's bar mitzvah and make a pass at my sister-in-law in a crowded elevator. And he'd call us on Yom Kippur, the holiest day in Judaism, and wish us well on the Day of Atonement, lacing his call with profanities straight from his large Irish heart.

The stormy playwright was born while his father was a prisoner of the British in an Irish rebel camp with Sean O'Kelly, later to become president of Ireland. Behan's cousin served as "substitute Mayor of Dublin," whatever that was. Behan, my father wrote in November 1958, deplored this. "Our new bourgeois have started to wear top hats, alas."

Behan described himself as "Ireland's Thirsty Young Man." "I'm addicted to drink," he said, sadly. "In the part of Dublin I come from, it's no disgrace to get drunk. It's an achievement."

Jackie Gleason, no stranger to the grape and proud of his own Irish heritage, wanted to star in the life story of Behan. "Can you imagine the opening scene?" "The Great One" mused. "I come rolling down the aisle, roaring drunk, while my play's being performed onstage."

Gleason in fact idolized Behan, and they finally met on September 6, 1960, in New York. "Any chance of your falling off the wagon?" Gleason asked Behan, then in the midst of one of his many futile attempts to give up drinking. "Oh, there's every chance," replied Behan. "I was given two rules in Dublin before I came here: Not to fall out of the plane coming over, and not to fall off the boat going back."

When his play *The Hostage* opened in New York, Behan did fifty-two interviews promoting it, but found time to paint the office of his producer, Leonard Field. Behan was a proud member of the Irish National House-painters' Union, and used his skills to slap a cream-colored first coat on the producer's walls.

"If the play is a hit," said Field, admiring his office walls, "I'm bound to get a second coat. Even if it flops, I'll get it, since Brendan will need the work. But a hit play will mean a free paint job."

On that same visit to New York, the Behans attended a party at the posh home of W. Averill Harriman. Mrs. Harriman showed them their famed art collection of Gauguins, Picassos, Renoirs, Van Goghs, and Matisses.

"I understand one of you paints," said Mrs. Harriman. "I paint," replied Beatrice Behan, whose father was also a noted artist. "Oh, I'm a painter too," her husband chimed in, pulling out his union membership card.

This was a time during the Cold War when Russia would invite well-known artists and people of letters to visit. But Behan received no such invitation. "They're snobs," he explained. "They think I'm too common." In his travels, Behan said he could quickly determine if a country is rich or poor: "The two sure signs of a poor country are good bread and young streetwalkers."

He often spoke proudly of his native city. "Dublin has two important theaters," he said. "There's The Gate Theater, which puts on avant-garde plays about Evil. And then there's The Abbey Theater, which features stuff for the peasants. They call these two theaters 'Sodom and Begorrah.'"

Behan was asked if he intended to continue to write his plays in Dublin, where the people tend to ridicule and demean anyone who found success elsewhere. "The Irish are snobs," he said, "but they'll not do that to me because I'm one of them. Joyce and O'Casey? They weren't from Dublin. The first farm I ever saw was owned by the king of England: It was a prison farm."

A psychiatrist once told Behan he could cure the writer of his neuroses. "I hope not," replied Behan. "That's the day I go back to painting houses."

Asked if it was important for a playwright to be represented on Broadway, Behan replied: "Any playwright without a play on Broadway is living in exile."

In April 1961, Behan was in Toronto to

receive the keys to the city one morning. The next day he called us from the police station where he'd been booked for public drunkenness. "They gave me the gold cuff links in the morning," he said wistfully, "and the steel ones at night. I wonder which one is more a credential for a writer." During his appearance in front of a magistrate, Behan whispered to his lawyer: "This is no time to talk to the judge about Socrates. He's anxious to get on to the next case and then, I'm certain, to go get a drink himself."

On his way out of the country, he said: "Canada is barbaric without being picturesque. It is banishment for naughty Irish authors. Ahhh but New York, on the other hand, is my Lourdes. I go there for spiritual replenishment. I'm so glad to leave Canada that even seeing the Howard Johnson sign in Buffalo cheers me up."

A few weeks later in San Francisco, he attended the opening of *The Hostage*. He acknowledged that his unkempt hair, broken nose, and missing teeth gave him the appearance of being drunk, even though at that time he'd been on the wagon for months. He recalled the time in Berlin when he'd gone to see a German production of his play *The Quare Fellow*, but since it was an all-German performance, Behan fell asleep.

A newspaper photographer, thinking Behan was drunk, took his picture, which appeared in the paper the next day above a caption that read: "Irish Barbarian."

When he saw that, Behan responded by citing the great eighteenth-century playwright David Garrick, who ordered drinks outside his own theater while it was burning, saying: "Can't a man have a drink at his own fireside?" Behan responded to the newspaper photo by asking: "Can't a playwright enjoy some sleep during his own play?"

Soon after that, Behan signed a contract to write the screen adaptation of his play *Borstal Boy,* based on his years in jail since joining the IRA when he was fifteen. But he had no experience writing a screenplay, so he bought a copy of one to learn the process. The movie script was *Hiroshima Mon Amour,* the complex story about an affair between a French film actress and a Japanese architect. Behan, of course, was bewildered. "What does a screenplay calling for a close-up of a woman's shoulder have to do with a teenager in prison?"

After months back home in Dublin, he wrote: "I miss New York. I miss the conversation you have there. London talks about people and who they are. Dubliners talk about people and what they're saying. But New Yorkers talk about people and what they're *doing!*"

Back in New York in February 1962, he attended the off-Broadway production of *The Hostage* and noticed some changes had been made in the script, with the jokes moved around. But he wasn't upset, surprisingly. "It's not as if I'd written Genesis," he explained.

Behan dropped into his publisher's office to discuss his sequel to *Borstal Boy,* called *Confessions of an Irish Rebel.* When the conference was over, Behan announced to the office: "Stop work, everybody!" Then he sang Irish songs to them, recited poetry, and encouraged them to join him in some dancing.

His love for New York was unaffected after he was mugged in March 1964, when his passport was stolen along with $250 in cash. He quickly applied for another passport at the Irish consulate. Ordinarily, an affidavit of Irish citizenship is required, but it was waived for Behan, *the* quintessential Irishman.

"With the compliments of the Republic of Ireland," the consulate said.

Behan's granduncle had been the Coachman in Joyce's *Ulysses,* and his uncle wrote

Ireland's national anthem. He thus was entitled to remain seated when it was played. "A definite advantage if you happen to be a drinking man," he said.

One night at the YMHA Poetry Center in New York, Behan gave a lecture and told his largely Jewish audience: "You Hebrews and we Gaels have much in common. Both are exotic enough to be interesting and not foreign enough to be alarming."

At a benefit performance for Hadassah, the Jewish women's charity, he saw a production of Paddy Chayefsky's *The Tenth Man*, about Jewish mysticism. Later, he said he couldn't get an objective reaction from the audience. "It was like seeing *National Velvet* with an audience of jockeys," he said.

Behan's entry in *Who's Who* listed his military service as "IRA, 1937–." Asked about the dash, he explained: "Does a leopard ever change his spots?"

Back in New York, Behan stepped out of his hotel, the famed Algonquin. It was a cold day and he'd forgotten his coat. Mrs. Ben Bodne, wife of the hotel's owner, noticed this, went upstairs, and brought him one of her husband's coats. "May you be the mother of a bishop," he replied in thanks. The Bodnes were en route to a family bar mitzvah.

On the night of a fierce snowstorm in New York, my father took the Behans to a coffeehouse in Greenwich Village where the folk singer and the waiter were the only others in the room. No one else in town could reach the restaurant. The singer decided to perform anyway.

When he finished his set, Behan said to the singer: "Smashin'. D'ye happen to know this one?" he asked and sang an Irish ditty. No, the singer hadn't heard that one. "Then this one," Behan began. This set off an all-night back-and-forth session of trading songs, while the storm raged outside.

RICHARD BURTON

In early July 1980, I interviewed Richard Burton in the bowels of the New York State Theater in Lincoln Center during the run of the revival of *Camelot*, which had made him a star twenty years earlier. In the middle of the interview, he stopped, looked at me, and asked: "Aren't you the brother who taught me how to bunt?"

Suddenly it came back to me. He and his then-wife Sybil were our neighbors. They lived in the same building, but around the corner on Central Park West, when I was growing up.

Every weekend, my father and three brothers and I would cross over to the park and play either baseball or football. One day during our four-man game of some version of baseball, he and Sybil walked by. The Welsh-born actor knew little of the game, but I remember teaching him the fine art—neglected in today's game—of moving the runner along with a bunt. How he recalled that remains one of life's mysteries.

He probably understood other aspects of baseball, however, because in a June 1961 game in the Broadway Show League, he came to bat for the first time in his life in the first inning, somehow hit a triple, and vowed never to play again. Claiming he'd read lots of books on the game, he said: "I know how it will look in the record books. I batted 1.000."

When he first came to New York in 1946, he brought along a trunk. A reporter sent to cover his arrival saw Burton lift the trunk with one hand and reported that here was an actor with amazing strength.

Actually, the trunk was empty. Britain was still under wartime rationing, and he'd brought the trunk to America intending to fill it with goods unavailable back home.

In May 1961, Burton was informed by his friend Laurence Olivier that he and his wife Joan Plowright would be having a baby. "I suppose he'll be named after me," Burton wrote them.

In early December that year, Burton received a brief message: "Dear Godfather," signed "Dickie Olivier."

Burton was at the height of his fame internationally, when during the long, often tortuous filming of *Cleopatra*, he would leave the beloved Sybil for Elizabeth Taylor. Multiply Brad/Angelina/Jennifer by ten, and you'd get some idea of the worldwide furor that was created.

When he was signed to star as Mark Antony in *Cleopatra*, Burton was still on Broadway in the original run of *Camelot* and had to be bought out of that contract. So Warner Bros. paid songwriters Alan Jay Lerner and Fritz Loewe $50,000 ($346,000 today) for Burton's services.

The movie was shot in and around Rome, and Burton sailed to Italy from New York. A week later, he asked the studio for a two-day postponement for reporting to the set to rest. No, he was told, he had to report immediately. So he flew to Rome, then waited to start shooting. For seventeen weeks!

By the time filming began, Burton had collected seven weeks of penalty overtime salary, and he would work on *Cleopatra* longer than his entire Broadway run in *Camelot*.

When Burton left *Camelot* on Broadway, his role of King Arthur was taken over by William Squire. After one performance, a fan said to him: "You sound just like Richard Burton."

"Considering," replied Squire, "that we come from the same village in Wales, and since I'm older, isn't it more appropriate to say that Burton sounds like *me?!*"

In early April 1962, "The Lyons Den" reported that the *Cleopatra* publicity involving delays, cost overruns, and the eventual romance between Burton and Taylor brought Burton to the top rank his talents and looks eventually would have given him. "Burton is such an attractive and articulate conver-

sationalist," my father observed, "that for the past few years Winston Churchill has invited him periodically for private talks."

One scene in the movie required Burton to run for several yards. He discovered his sandals seemed to be flapping as he ran, so he finally removed them. That's when the costar of a $25 million movie (that'd be $175 million in today's dollars) noticed he had been given a four-year-old pair of sandals with the name "Stephen Boyd" written inside. They'd been used by that actor in his portrayal of Messala in *Ben-Hur*.

Naturally, since Burton had waited seventeen weeks before the filming of his first scene in *Cleopatra*, he'd had more than enough time to memorize his lines. The first scene was with Rex Harrison as Julius Caesar and Elizabeth Taylor as Cleopatra. Harrison was to speak first and blew his lines again and again. A dozen takes. Then Taylor blew her lines.

At long last, both Harrison and Taylor recited their lines without error, and it was Burton's turn to begin. He started to speak, but his voice choked, spoiling the take. That's how the shooting of the fiasco would proceed.

And the insanity didn't end there. While pinching pennies by having Burton use sandals from an earlier movie, the studio spent $80,000 on Fiuggi bottled water for the non-Italian crew members. That's $175,000 should a crew get thirsty on a shoot today.

"Someone must have watered the water," my father observed on the set.

One day on the set, Burton put his head in an elephant's mouth, and the elephant lifted him in the air.

"I had to do it," he explained. "I couldn't resist. Besides, 6,000 extras were watching."

In December 1963, shortly before Burton's divorce from Sybil, she accompanied friends to the Players Club in New York's Gramercy Park. They told her that the club had once been home to Edwin Booth and pointed out the statue of the great nineteenth-century star in the park.

As they began to tell her the story of Booth, whose brother had assassinated Abraham Lincoln, the Welsh-born Sybil interrupted, saying: "Oh, I know about Booth. Richard played him in the movie *Prince of Players.*"

Burton said that Taylor transformed him as an actor. Then he was asked about his soon-to-be ex-wife Sybil.

"I had a great lady," he said of her.

The next time you see the movie *The Longest Day,* notice the odd-looking helmet Burton was assigned by the prop department. In portraying a downed RAF pilot, he was given a specially designed helmet to cover the curls he'd grown for his role in *Cleopatra,* being filmed simultaneously.

Although Burton's *Hamlet* received rave reviews and was the talk of the town and the hottest ticket of the 1964–65 season, the Tony went to Alec Guinness for his starring role in *Dylan.* The author of the play, Sidney Michaels, consoled Burton by saying: "Alec had a better play."

During the run of *Hamlet* on Broadway, Peter O'Toole cabled Burton from London: "I've spoken to people who've seen both our *Hamlets* and they say mine was better."

When he was filming *Becket,* Burton was visited on the set by his wife Elizabeth and her children, including her son Michael Wilding Jr. The boy had aspirations to become an actor, but Burton discouraged it and hoped that the tedium between scenes would do the trick. After a full day on the set, he asked the boy if he still wanted to act.

"Oh yes," said Wilding. "I want to be just like Peter O'Toole."

As is the case with many scenes in a film, the assassination of Becket had to be shot several times from various angles. Thus Burton, having to fall under repeated sword thrusts, looked up and said: "This proves it—a coward dies a thousand deaths."

Burton's *Hamlet* was directed by Sir John Gielgud, acknowledged to be the greatest Hamlet of them all. During the tryout, he'd written long pages of suggestions to the star at 5 p.m. By curtain time three hours later, Burton began performing them flawlessly.

"For all he's been through with the press," said Gielgud, "he shows no suffering onstage."

On July 20, 1969, Burton and Taylor were on their yacht, and he was watching the moon landing. Taylor was in the powder room as the historic moment approached.

"Come out, Elizabeth," he said. "He's about to land on the moon."

"Tell him to wait a minute," she replied. "I'm almost done."

Burton was that rare movie star who never forgot his stage roots, often returning to the theater. He once starred in *Othello* at the Old Vic at the same time another actor was doing the same play at Stratford. He asked a friend to scout the other production and assess their Iago.

Later, his friend returned and said: "It was worse than I ever dared hope for."

When he and Taylor returned to Rome for the first time after *Cleopatra,* a photographer approached him with a proposition: If Burton and Taylor would pose, kissing, he'd sell the photo for $8,000 and split it with Burton.

"The awful thing," said Burton later, "is that I hesitated a second before telling him, No."

Burton always avoided seeing his own films, except those he did with Taylor. He did watch *The Sandpiper,* but said of his own scenes, "I simply turned around when I came on the screen."

When Burton learned that Taylor would be doing a love scene with Warren Beatty in *The Only Game in Town,* he wired Beatty: "No rehearsals."

When she heard about that, Taylor said:

"Oh no need to worry about Richard. He's in Paris, kissing Rex Harrison in *Staircase*."

In February 1967, a persistent Italian producer sent Burton and Taylor a screenplay. Burton said: "I'll read it, but will somebody please tell him that just because Liz and I have made a few movies together, that doesn't make us Laurel and Hardy."

In March 1967, Burton and Taylor were in the Dorchester in London where they received a phone call from Hollywood. It was director Stanley Donen calling, hoping to speak to either one. Donen had codirected *Singin' in the Rain, The Pajama Game, Charade,* and many others.

"Never heard of him," said Burton. "You take it, Liz."

"I might as well take it," she replied, "I was once engaged to him."

As a token of their esteem and thanks for directing them in *Taming of the Shrew,* the Burtons sent their director Franco Zeffirelli a gold cigarette case inscribed: "With thanks from the Shrew and the Tamer."

Burton and Taylor were as famous for their extravagant lifestyle as for their acting. When, for example, he bought her a mink coat for $125,000, he explained: "In my particular case, and with my particular wife, she's just as excited over a gift that cost a million as one costing $3.75—both of which I've given her."

While he was filming *Villain*, Taylor visited the set. After a scene was shot, Burton lost track of her, and called to the crew: "Has anybody seen my wife?"

"What does she look like?" deadpanned a crew member.

During a fight scene in *Villain*, Burton accidentally hit his opponent. He stopped and muttered: "That's so unprofessional."

In November 1971, actor Victor Spinetti, who'd starred with the Beatles in *A Hard Day's Night* and *Help!* and with Burton in *Becket* (in an uncredited part), was applying for status as a resident alien in the United States. He needed a letter of recommendation from someone in his profession, so he asked his fellow Welshman Burton to write it.

Burton wrote: "Victor Spinetti is a man of good character. To my knowledge, the only thing he has ever stolen is a scene— from me!"

Burton was prone to surprising those around him. Once, for example, at New York's posh Four Seasons restaurant at dinner, he ordered a strange meal: French fries between two pieces of buttered bread. He explained that it was the kind of sandwich he used to enjoy when he was a boy back in Port Talbot, Wales.

While shooting *The Klansman* in Northern California in 1974, Burton asked his costar, Lee Marvin, if he'd like top billing. Marvin was understandably surprised and naturally agreed.

"You see," smiled Burton, "I'm getting more money."

TRUMAN CAPOTE

He was without a doubt the most colorful writer of his time, the subject of two excellent biographical films in consecutive years and a Broadway show. Even if he'd never written *In Cold Blood*, his masterpiece, Truman Capote would have been a celebrated personality of his time.

His first play, *The Grass Harp*, was written in Sicily, where he spent summers. Capote rented a house on a hill overlooking the sea and Mount Etna, a volcano. Friends would constantly drop by. Orson Welles was there on a day the volcano erupted. He accompanied Capote and other friends to the site for a close look, while locals were fleeing the vicinity.

Capote was asked what they did there. "What else was there to do," Capote replied, "but show our defiance by taking off our clothes and dancing."

When the play was in Boston tryouts, Capote was asked what he hoped to achieve with it. "When the curtain comes down," he said, "I'd like the audience to feel that they'd gone to some place and come back. That they've come back changed, if only a little bit changed, and for the better, even if this change lasts only twenty-four hours. That's what a playwright wants."

In June 1952, he returned to Sicily after his play opened. He went to Taormina, the city where he felt he worked best, but found that the house he'd always rented had been let to another tenant. Then he met a hotel owner who'd just completed building a hotel high on a mountain, overlooking the sea. Since he didn't plan to open until the following spring, he rented the entire building to Capote for the price of one room. So there Capote spent the summer, alone, master of a twenty-five-room hotel.

Capote was in Italy in 1953 working on the script for *Beat the Devil*, the bizarre movie cult classic that starred Humphrey Bogart, Gina Lollabrigida, Robert Morley, Jennifer Jones, and Peter Lorre. Bogie wanted to wrestle the diminutive Capote and taunted him until the delicate author finally accepted. What the screen tough guy didn't know was that Capote was a judo expert, and he easily flipped Bogart.

By March 1954, Capote and Harold Arlen were collaborating on a new musical, *House of Flowers*. Remarkably, they hadn't met. Capote was in Paris, Arlen in New York. The man who wrote "Somewhere Over the Rainbow" and "That Old Black Magic" wrote the music and collaborative lyrics with Capote by recording them and mailing this to Capote.

Then, when Capote returned to New York, Arlen was in Hollywood. They continued their odd long-distance collaboration by phone. Arlen would place the phone near his piano and play the songs for Capote in New York, decades before the Internet.

In December 1955, my father and Capote accompanied a theater troupe performing *Porgy and Bess* to Moscow. It was the height of the Cold War. Few Americans were allowed into the USSR. Capote was to return to New York a few days before my father, so he was given three columns of "The Lyons Den" to be delivered to the *New York Post*.

This was a time when the Russians searched hotel guests' baggage and probably bugged their rooms as well. Knowing this, Capote took the columns, then playfully looked up at the ceiling where he thought there might be a concealed microphone.

"Leonard Lyons has just given me an envelope full of columns to deliver in New York, to avoid censorship."

When Capote's plane reached Leningrad before the flight to New York, it was delayed ninety minutes while officials who'd stopped Capote read all three columns, cleared them, and allowed the plane to take off.

It was on that trip that as my father and Capote walked down Gorky Street, one of

My father with Truman Capote in a Moscow hotel room, December 1955.

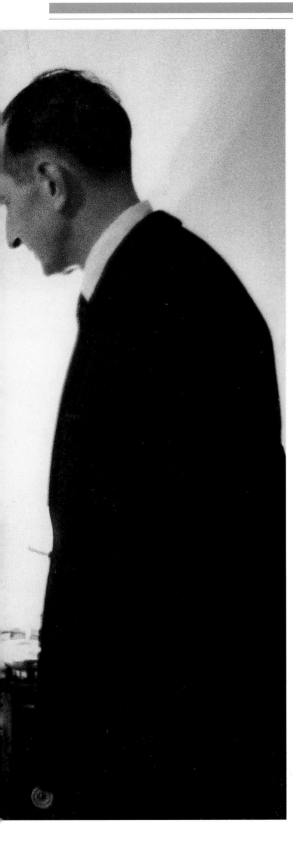

Moscow's prominent thoroughfares, several people took one look at the diminutive author and began to laugh. "Laugh, you dreary people, but what will you do for laughs next week when I've gone?" he commented.

All during the theatrical troupe's stay in Moscow, they were shown around the city by a guide from Intourist, the government travel and propaganda agency. No matter where they were taken, the guide extolled the virtues of the Communist system, always comparing it to what we had in the States. The guide said: "Moscow University has more dormitory beds than any school in New York." Finally, my father spoke up. "Wait a minute. You have all of yours in one place. If you add together the beds at NYU, Columbia, Fordham, Hunter, and CCNY, we have more." The guide ignored him, and moved on to the Moscow University Library. "This is the largest university library in the world—more than any in New York." Once again, my father spoke up. "Again, you have all your books in one library. If you add together the books at Columbia, NYU, Fordham, CCNY, and Hunter, we have more." Then he asked the guide, "What percentage of the faculty at Moscow University are members of the Communist Party?" The guide thought for a moment, then replied, "About 10 percent." My father said, "When I went to CCNY, we had more!"

When *In Cold Blood* was published, Capote's no-notes style of writing was derided by the author Dame Rebecca West: "That's not reportage. It's *Capoteage*."

On a winter vacation in Jamaica, Capote fascinated his friends with gossip from New York. "Yes, I gossip," he said, "but I gossip only about the interesting details of fairly well known facts."

My father wrote that *Life* magazine had a photo spread on Capote's masked ball and all the luminaries who attended, a follow-up to the list of invited guests that Capote had supplied. "But," added my father, "a dazzling list, too, is of those who declined."

In May 1958, *Harper's Bazaar* announced it was cancelling plans to devote its entire July issue to his newest short novel. Capote said: "Last week, I was asked to make certain word and phrase changes. I agreed to some, but not to those which would affect adversely the literary quality of my story." The magazine deemed his story "indecent."

Capote took consolation in the fact that it was later published and became one of the most iconic movies of the 'sixties: *Breakfast at Tiffany's.*

In April 1963, Capote went to Tiffany's with a friend who asked: "What did Tiffany's ever give you for having written *Breakfast at Tiffany's*?"

Capote said he had received nothing, not even a thank-you note from Tiffany board chairman Walter Hoving. He brooded about this neglect; after all, the publicity from the book and movie was incredible. He brooded while shopping there and buying a gold cigarette box for $1,000.

He charged it to his account, thinking that when Hoving noticed this, he'd never bill him for it. "He'll joke about it," Capote said. But he was assured that Hoving had no sense of humor about such things; so the next day, Capote returned the gold box to Tiffany's.

In February 1959, a woman sued Capote, claiming defamation of character. Her name was Bonnie Golightly. "Capote isn't a creative writer," she charged. "He's a biographical writer." But my father protested in his column: "I can attest that he *is* a creative writer. After all, I was a character in his book about our trip to Russia, *The Muses Are Heard.*

"My complaint is that Capote had too much fiction in his facts, and now Miss Golightly complains that Capote has too much fact in his fiction."

With that in mind, I remembered Capote's quote, used in both biographical movies, which he first said to my mother: "I have nearly total recall," he boasted. "Ninety percent recall."

When she heard that, my mother spit in her glass and said to him: "Here's a glass that is ninety percent clean. Drink up!"

On July 16, 1966, my father devoted a rare entire column to a living person other than a President: Capote. He severely chastised Capote's "total recall" form of novelized "journalism."

When Capote wrote about the *Porgy and Bess* tour to Russia in *The Muses Are Heard* in 1955, my father was portrayed as a sniveling capitalist, bragging about his tax bracket, and constantly telling the Soviet minders how much better we had it in the States. Of course, it wasn't true. "Only my brother Al knows my tax bracket," he wrote, "and he's my accountant."

When my father saw Capote at a restaurant shortly after the book was published, Capote told his companions: "Oh, Lennie is just upset that he wasn't mentioned in the *Saturday Review*'s story on *The Muses Are Heard.*"

My father, who never claimed to have total recall himself, took out his notebook, wrote down exactly what Capote had just said, and told all of Capote's dinner guests: "I'll send you all copies of the *Saturday Review* article tomorrow: My name is mentioned *three times* in the review! So much for 'total recall!'"

My father didn't like to carry a grudge. But he had a long memory, and he found an unusual way to retaliate against Capote: by writing frequently about his great rival Gore Vidal. One day, he wrote that Vidal's third play, *Visit to a Small Planet*, would be produced on Broadway—before Vidal's thirtieth birthday.

When my father got to his office at the *Post* the day that that item appeared, he said to his secretary, "I'm expecting a call from Mr. Capote today." He had just taken off his jacket and sat down at his desk when the phone rang, and his secretary said, "I have Mr. Capote on the line." When he picked up the phone, even at arm's length, he could hear that much-imitated whiny, nasal voice shouting: "HE'S THIRTY-TWOOOOOOO!"

Capote had his eccentricities, beyond eschewing note-taking. He had no idea how to change a typewriter ribbon, for example, so he always had six typewriters on hand. Then he bought a seventh. Just in case.

Another eccentricity: Whenever he visited the dentist, he'd insist on being blindfolded because he couldn't stand looking at the instruments.

Capote, citing his incessant curiosity, confessed to friends that he couldn't help nosing around their personal mail and diaries whenever in someone's house. He told this to his host, impresario/industrialist Billy Rose, who, to everyone's surprise, offered his diary for Capote's perusal. Capote declined, but Rose insisted. Capote then opened the diary—written in Rose's indecipherable shorthand.

In July 1961, Capote was working on a novel incognito on the Costa Brava in Spain. Local residents, however, thinking he was the son of the former president, insisted on calling him "Señor Truman" even though HST had only one child, daughter Margaret. Nevertheless, the locals refused to believe Capote wasn't part of the former First Family.

In December 1962, Capote lunched with the Queen Mother in London. Their talk ranged from Jane Austen, abstract painting, and the Brontë sisters, to tobacco, the sad first season of the NY Mets (though what Capote *or* the beloved Queen Mother knew about the Mets will, alas, forever remain a mystery!), to television.

Of TV, she told Capote: "There is so much to shudder over and so little to laugh at."

She mentioned that she had always wanted to attend a trial and even fancied the thought of serving as a member of the jury, although she probably would vote for acquittal, regardless of the crime. They discussed several recent British murder cases, and she said she sometimes thought of an easy way to commit a murder!

"It would be on a state occasion," she continued, "when the Royal Family is driven through cheering crowds." A murderer, she continued, could commit the crime by shoving the victim under her car. His defense could be that he merely was helping the victim to get a better view.

DUSTIN HOFFMAN

For a time, one of my favorite questions to ask actors was: "If every movie you've ever seen were placed in a huge vault and it caught fire, and you could save only one, which would it be?"

I got all sorts of answers, of course, but the best came from Chevy Chase, who said: "I'd save *To Sir, with Love,* then drive around the block, and toss it in again!"

That wouldn't be my answer. It would be *The Graduate,* a film that struck a chord in me when it opened late in December 1967 and went on to become one of the top grossing films of all time. Made for an estimated $3,000,000—of which a mere $17,000 went to its title player—*The Graduate* has since fallen way down the list of all-time box of-fice films, most of which are huge special-effects epics. But it'll always be Number One for me.

When I worked as a city desk clerk at the *New York Times* in the summer of 1967, under the legendary editor Arthur Gelb, I was offered the chance to write one story. My self-chosen assignment was a look at movies being filmed in New York City that summer. One was *Midnight Cowboy.* I visited a nighttime set and conducted my first interview with Dustin Hoffman, subsequently added to my list of movie heroes. There would be several more interviews with him over the years.

Hoffman's screen debut hadn't come in *The Graduate,* as many people think, but in a small indie film with Eli Wallach and Anne Jackson called *The Tiger Makes Out.* Mike

My father with Dustin Hoffman circa 1970.

Nichols accidentally spotted the young un-known, billed nineteenth, when Nichols visited an edit session and saw Hoffman's brief scene over the shoulder of someone looking at the rough cut on a Movieola ma-chine. It was a scene in which Hoffman's character was breaking up with a girl. (Eliz-abeth Wilson, also in that movie, appar-ently also caught Nichols's eye, for she later landed the part of Hoffman's mother in *The Graduate*.)

Although born in Los Angeles, Hoffman was a struggling actor in New York who'd performed in an off-Broadway play called *Eh,* and was billed tenth in the flop Broad-way play *A Cook for Mr. General*. Then he was the assistant stage manager for the noted play *The Subject Was Roses*.

He'd been signed for a role in that show, but an injury prevented him from act-ing. Nevertheless, his father advised him: "Don't be sad. Be glad for the actor who did get the part."

Later, Hoffman's parents came to New York to see the show anyway. The other actor who'd gotten the role, Walter Mc-Ginn, "coincidentally" took "ill" the very night Hoffman's parents were in the audi-ence, and they saw their son Dustin go on.

Summoned by Nichols to Los Ange-les for an audition for *The Graduate*, Hoff-man apparently was unimpressive. Several New York City subway tokens fell out of his pocket during his reading, and the stage-hands returned them to him, saying: "Here. You'll be needing these soon."

Hoffman said that when the movie opened, he received a gift from the stage-hands: framed tokens.

Incidentally, one of the other actors who auditioned for the role of Benjamin Brad-dock was one Charles Robert Redford.

On May 27, 1998, the morning of my twenty-fifth wedding anniversary, I ran into Art Garfunkel, who'd been my brother Warren's roommate at Columbia Univer-sity. Later, in another part of town, I met Paul Simon, whose songs adorn the movie. What were the odds? Then, confirming the karma *The Graduate* still has for me, my wife and I ran into Dustin Hoffman and his wife.

We spoke for about twenty minutes on the street, and he kidded me, saying: "I know, I know, *The Graduate* is your favor-ite film, but you haven't liked any of mine since," which he knew is untrue. He then asked where we were having our anniver-sary dinner. I told him.

When we arrived at the restaurant, there was a bottle of champagne, sent by him, awaiting us on our table.

I don't care if he and Warren Beatty re-team for *Ishtar II—The Story Continues*; I'll still try to find something redeeming about it.

When Joseph E. Levine, who was the ex-ecutive producer of *The Graduate*, brought Hoffman to the first preview of the movie, he turned to the young actor and correctly predicted: "This is the last time you'll be able to go anywhere without being recog-nized."

Soon after *The Graduate* made him a star, Hoffman returned to Broadway in *Jimmy Shine*. During one performance, he said the line: "I have to do one thing in my life that makes sense." Just then, a teenaged girl yelled out from the balcony: "Marry me!"

Hoffman knew he was a success after *The Graduate* when he was invited to a produc-er's party. It was the same producer of the play *Rhinoceros* where, at the Longacre The-ater, Hoffman had worked in the coat-check room.

In February 1969, Hoffman was appearing on Broadway at night while filming *John and Mary* with Mia Farrow in the daytime, when he had no matinee to perform. In one scene, he was chilled after playing tennis in Cen-tral Park. But that didn't make him ill. An-other scene involved his getting a shampoo. Nine retakes were needed, but that didn't make him sick either. But a third scene required him to eat two eggs. It had to be reshot twelve times. *That* made him sick.

In May of 1969, Hoffman told my father that for years, he suffered an inability to buy anything for himself without fear of some immediate punishment for his self-ishness. One day, he'd earned a good fee for a TV commercial and bought a new over-coat. Just as he stepped outside the store wearing the coat, New York City suddenly went dark. It was November 9, 1965, the first New York City blackout.

In December 1969, Hoffman met Dr. Christiaan Barnard, the pioneering heart transplant surgeon, who asked the actor if he was embarrassed filming a love scene in *John and Mary* in front of a large crew.

"Not at all," replied Hoffman. "It's like making love right in the middle of traffic."

In June 1971, he appeared on *The Mike Douglas Show* with lyricist Sammy Cahn. The host asked both to recite their Social Security numbers. Cahn, one of the great wordsmiths of all time, couldn't remember. But Hoffman, recalling the frequent bouts of unemployment every struggling actor must endure, quickly recited his.

LYNDON B. JOHNSON

One afternoon about ten years ago, I was in between screenings in Midtown Manhattan and ducked into a pizza joint. There at the next table was Lynda Bird Johnson and one of her daughters. I introduced myself, and she said: "Oh, Daddy knew your father." I smiled with pride, then wondered what they were doing in New York (but not what they were doing in a pizza joint). She explained they were in between Broadway shows.

"How'd you get your tickets?" I asked.

"Through Ticketmaster," she replied.

Channeling my father's voice, which I could hear in my head, I said: "My dear, the daughter of the thirty-sixth President of the United States does *not* get her tickets that way. You're not a tourist. From now on, contact me."

We've been friends ever since. In fact, in 2000, my brother Douglas and I were going to Washington, D.C., to lecture on base-ball trivia at the Smithsonian. She'd read about this in their newsletter and invited us to lunch at her home in Virginia, before giving us an insiders' tour of the U.S. Sen-ate, where her father had served as majority leader and her husband Charles Robb was a sitting senator. An incredible day, to say the least.

My parents first met LBJ when he was a congressman. It was at the home of Su-preme Court Justice William O. Douglas, a close family friend, after whom my younger brother is named. When Johnson won his congressional seat by just eighty-seven votes, he was called "Landslide Johnson," a prophetic name, because his win over Barry Goldwater in 1964 was one of the biggest landslides in American history.

Johnson was one of the most colorful presidents of modern times, a man born for the job. He was a Washington insider to a degree unmatched by anyone of his time.

On December 13, 1963, not one month in

office, for example, LBJ noticed that Washington columnist Drew Pearson was celebrating a birthday. So he phoned the famed newspaperman at home with a gift: several exclusive news items, as he explained, "Just so you don't have to work on your birthday."

He'd longed for the Presidency for years, but of course wound up initially as JFK's vice president. After he'd secured that position on the ticket, he said to Kennedy: "I'm just a soldier in the ranks now. Where do you want me to begin?"

Johnson was the only president who lived in Washington during the terms of five other presidents, starting with the Hoover administration when he was an aide to a Texas congressman.

Soon after he became president, he looked back on his time in Washington, saying: "I always dreamed of being a lawyer. But after twelve years in the House, then another twelve in the Senate, then as vice president, and now as president, well, I've had something to do with the laws of this land."

One evening in November 1964, Johnson hosted Milton Berle and his wife. Eddie Fisher sang, then Johnson gave a speech. Later he asked Berle why he didn't entertain the guests. "Mr. President," replied Berle, "because you were on too long." Another time Berle approached the receiving line at a White House dinner and said to the President: "I didn't catch your name."

A few months after he became president, LBJ had set rules for White House dinners where he'd share the dais with movie and TV stars. He spoke first. "I've spent too many dinners nervously studying my speech at the beginning of the dinner and missing the fun of hearing the stars," he explained.

Johnson was to have given a speech before JFK at the Dallas Trade Mart, where the ill-fated motorcade was headed. Dallas had been a hotbed of right-wing protestors before JFK's arrival, so Johnson's final words in the speech he would never give were: "And thank God, Mr. President, you came out of Dallas alive."

At a White House dinner in November 1965, Mrs. Kirk Douglas was dancing with LBJ when he asked if she realized that men often told her she was pretty.

"Yes, Mr. President," she replied, "but until now it never mattered."

In February 1966, LBJ was about to give a telecast from the East Room of the White House. Aides put some logs in the fireplace for a suitable background. But it started to smoke, and the smoke spread through the building. Johnson, in another wing, asked what had happened.

When told of the smoke-filled East Room, he said: "What are they using there—a British crew?"

On April 28, 1967, at the White House Correspondents' Dinner, Victor Borge, the great Danish concert pianist, was performing and doing his comedy *shtick*. Just as he approached the punch line of a joke, the orchestra struck up *Hail to the Chief*. LBJ entered, gave a twenty-minute speech, then left.

"As I was saying," resumed Borge.

In May 1967, the story was told of LBJ's visit to the troops in Vietnam. He was dressed in Army fatigues and mingled with the soldiers. "Hey, you look just like LBJ," said one.

"I *am* President Johnson," LBJ replied.

"Boy," replied the soldier, "does *your* draft board have guts!"

In June of that year, he addressed a function in New York at the President's Club and said: "It's difficult being in high political office; people picket you and call you dirty names, and your safety is threatened," he said. "But I'm not here to talk to you about Mayor Lindsay."

On September 1, 1967, my father broke

the story that LBJ's infant grandson, Patrick Lyndon Nugent, son of his younger daughter Luci, was spending time at the White House, and that the baby, a few weeks old, awakened mornings around 5 a.m. LBJ would carry the child into his bed and read to him.

And instead of reading an A-B-C book or any children's book, the President would read aloud the his top secret dispatches from overseas.

In September of that year, Robert Kintner, former president of NBC, was allowed to attend a Cabinet meeting and marveled at LBJ's ability to move from one cabinet secretary to another, showing familiarity with each of their areas of expertise.

"Amazing," said Kintner. "This man could run a big company."

One evening LBJ received reports from a bombing raid over Haiphong Harbor in North Vietnam. He dined alone, and couldn't sleep, worried about the rules of engagement he'd set, and the possibility of twenty American fliers not returning to home base.

Then Luci Johnson arrived and urged her father to accompany her to a nearby church, despite the late hour. He did, and they drove in a station wagon so as not to be recognized.

The priests were up, LBJ prayed and read some Scriptures, then returned to the White House. The next morning, he learned that all bombs were on target, no civilian homes were hit, and all U.S. planes returned safely to their harbor.

"This," said LBJ, "is just a few hours in the life of a President that nobody knows."

One day in February 1968, Joe DiMaggio was on the guest list at the White House. Jack Valenti, LBJ's special assistant—and later lobbyist for the movie industry—called the President and asked to be included in the meeting with the baseball immortal.

"He's always been one of my heroes," said Valenti.

"Confidentially, Jack," replied LBJ, "he was mine, too."

Johnson told an aide in May 1968 that he really felt the effects of his March 31 announcement that he would not seek reelection: "Journalists who'd been my harshest critics have begun referring to me as 'a statesman.'"

On vacation in July 1968, Johnson took some friends on a speedboat ride on Johnson Lake, Texas. He raced across the lake at a mile-a-minute clip. Then he startled them by calling to the Secret Service men: "Am I heading straight to that hidden reef, or is it off to the left?"

In September 1968, Lady Bird Johnson was entertaining 5,000 underprivileged youngsters on the White House lawn where a rock band performed a spirited number. Suddenly LBJ appeared on the White House balcony and simply said: "Cool it!" then returned inside to a Cabinet session.

In October 1968, the UN General Assembly was in session, and a visiting diplomat recalled why LBJ refused to wear formal attire to his Inaugural. He'd first met Johnson in 1962 at a state funeral in Europe, and asked how he liked being vice president.

"They got me wearing this," and pointed to his morning coat and striped trousers. "I'm an envoy to funerals." To LBJ that attire became a badge of his demeaning vice presidential role.

As his days in office became numbered, LBJ told the story of another president in that position, Herbert Hoover, who was said to have asked Andrew Mellon, his secretary of the Treasury, for a nickel to call a friend.

"Here's a dime, Mr. President," said Mellon. "Now you can call *all* your friends."

Soon after he left office, LBJ was given a farewell party in New York, which my father attended. My father reminded LBJ of a long-standing offer to make nightclub rounds with him one evening.

Lady Bird overheard them and said: "Hold him to it!"

Johnson replied that, after reading a *Holiday* magazine article in which the reporter followed my father to thirteen places one night, he thought he'd need a lot of time rocking on his porch to prepare for such a physical ordeal.

Like any president, LBJ had planned to write a book and told his friend John Kenneth Galbraith, the author, economist, and former ambassador to India, of the perils of writing a book. "I have a book which isn't even written yet," he said, "and already I've received seventeen unfavorable reviews."

On Inauguration Day 1969, an Air Force plane flew the Johnsons from Washington down to Texas, and, under orders from President Nixon, put their boxes and luggage on the runway, turned around, and immediately flew back to Washington.

Luci Johnson Nugent sighed: "Well, there goes the carriage. From now on, it's pumpkins again."

JOHN F. KENNEDY

Soon after Kennedy was elected, an actor with the same name refused to change it, saying: "I don't care if he's the President. I joined Actors' Equity first. And under the rules of the union, if he wants to get in *he*'ll have to change *his* name."

In mid-February 1961, JFK took some visitors on a tour of the Executive Mansion, and they studied the portrait of Chester A. Arthur, shown wearing a fur-lined coat. Kennedy looked at it and said: "He was always considered the best-dressed President. Until now, that is!"

And speaking of clothing, a friend hosted a Washington party for JFK that same month, and when the President arrived, he took Kennedy's coat. But the host couldn't resist the temptation to go through the pockets, searching for a souvenir, perhaps. He later reported: "Kennedy carries nothing in his pockets. Absolutely nothing."

Such was the loss of privacy that came with the office. For example, a Secret Service agent was assigned to turn on the faucet for the President before he shaved every morning, lest it be wired to a bomb.

On February 14, 1962, Jacqueline Kennedy gave America an unprecedented TV tour of the White House via CBS's Charles Collingwood. It became one of the most-watched shows in television history. Afterward, Pierre Salinger, the President's press secretary, called Mrs. Kennedy to say that reaction to the show was universally favorable. Then his expression grew serious, for JFK had come on the line. "Yes, sir," said Salinger. "You were good, too."

A longtime Kennedy aide and confidant, historian Arthur Schlesinger Jr., worked in the White House but had a side job reviewing movies for *Show* magazine. He was allowed to do so, but with the proviso that he would never knock any movie costarring Peter Lawford, the President's brother-in-law, lest it appear to be an official White House policy statement.

When Lawford and Kennedy's sister Pat had a daughter, Robin, JFK sent her a letter: "Welcome to the youngest member of the Kennedy clan. Your entrance is timely, as we need a new left end on the touch football team. Here's hoping you do not acquire the political assets of your parents, nor the prolific qualities of your godfather the Attorney General, nor the problems of your uncle."

In 1962, "The Lyons Den" reported that JFK had a button hidden under his desk in the Oval Office, near the President's knees. It was installed to allow him to press it without being observed. He used it to dismiss a visitor who'd been there too long. Pushing the button signaled for one of his aides to rush into the room and say the president of some country or other was waiting outside with urgent business.

Later that year, *Esquire* magazine ran a cartoon showing an old men's club member saying: "My daddy always said all Presidents were S.O.B.s but I never believed it until now." JFK requested the original.

JFK occasionally vacationed in Palm Beach, a favorite getaway. While there he wanted to speak to his father in Hyannis Port, but had misplaced the unlisted number. The operator recognized his voice and volunteered to give it to him, but Kennedy refused. "Don't give me his number," said the President. "I don't want you to break the rules. But it won't be breaking the rules for you to phone that number and tell Mr. Kennedy his son Jack would like to speak with him." She complied.

On another occasion, the Palm Beach bookstore reported that only one copy of Richard Nixon's *Six Crises* was sold. JFK came in and bought it.

One night at the White House, composer Fritz Loewe, who wrote the music for *Camelot,* JFK's favorite musical and song,

was a guest for dinner. The President was curious about how a melody is written. Loewe asked him to suggest a title, and JFK said: "It's a Passing Thing." So Loewe began composing a melody that night using those words.

Months later, Loewe learned that JFK had begun writing lyrics for that melody with a friend. But an end result never materialized, because when told of JFK's efforts at writing lyrics, he said: "The fact is, I've forgotten the melody I played that night."

One of the greatest political thrillers ever made was *Seven Days in May*, in which Fredric March portrayed the President. JFK even gave his friend, director John Frankenheimer, permission to film in the Oval Office. Thus when JFK stayed at a Hollywood hotel on a visit, March, in a suite on the same floor, was given security clearance to remain there. To show his gratitude, March sent roses to JFK's room. The two met in the lobby when JFK was leaving, after which March returned to the floor. He peeked into the newly empty room, noticed ice buckets and half-filled glasses, and a vase containing a dozen roses—his roses. So he picked them up and that night presented them to friends saying: "These are from the President."

On another visit to Los Angeles, in June 1963, JFK attended a party at the President's Club in Beverly Hills. At each table, an empty chair was left so that the President could circulate and visit everyone. When he reached Jack Benny's table, he spoke to each guest except Benny. Finally, he turned to the comedian and asked him to accompany him downstairs to a high school prom.

"Of course," said Benny, "but on one condition. First you say 'hello' to me." JFK did, and they dropped in at the prom.

That same month, the owner of a chain of Southern restaurants, who'd stood with a shotgun in the doorway of one of his places when hundreds of nonviolent antisegregationists knelt on his lawn, announced he would henceforth accept black patrons. J F K had phoned the man, who explained: "I'm following the orders of the President of the United States."

That same year, J F K spoke at the dedication of O'Hare Field in Chicago, but the banquet room at the airport had been booked long in advance. Instead, the President lunched in a hangar. The banquet room was occupied—by a cat show.

In June 1961, J F K sat for a portrait by René Bouché for a *Time* magazine cover. The President worked through the two scheduled sittings reading reports, answering calls, and talking with aides.

"Have you ever had a worse sitter?" the artist was asked. He said he hadn't, but did say that J F K became his first male subject to say: "Please don't give me too much hair." When she saw that cover, Caroline Kennedy said: "Daddy, where did you get those spooky eyes?"

Six months into his term, J F K met Jerry Lewis, and the comic referred to him as "Jack." "Don't worry," said the President when Lewis began to correct himself. "'Mr. President' still sounds new to me, too."

Frank Sinatra was producing and starring in *The Manchurian Candidate*, the superb Cold War thriller that at first was rejected by United Artists. They thought the film, which involved a North Korean spy and a planted vice presidential candidate, would be a disservice to the White House. Undaunted, Sinatra sailed off the coast of Hyannis on the presidential yacht with J F K, who told Sinatra he was a fan of Richard Condon's books, including that one. When he told that to the heads of United Artists, they quickly gave the movie the green light, and it came to be regarded as a classic of the genre, although it was suppressed for years after the assassination.

In April 1961, word came of the existence of a cousin of J F K in Ireland with the same name. He nevertheless declined an offer to lead a country parade celebrating J F K's inauguration.

"The only parade I ever led," he explained, "was when I was let out of jail during The Troubles. We now have some good land, and, I understand, in America that other Kennedy is doing well, too."

Luther Hodges, the former governor of North Carolina, served as J F K's Commerce secretary. One morning he came to the Oval Office for a short meeting with J F K and was told the President had only fifteen minutes available. It was a minor matter, and Hodges began talking, only to be interrupted by Caroline Kennedy, who entered and said she and the First Lady were leaving. Hodges began again. Another knock. Caroline returned, saying she'd forgotten to kiss her father goodbye. Hodges glanced at his watch, then began a third time.

Another knock. Caroline yet again, asking when J F K would be joining them. She left happily when told he'd be with them soon. Hodges then glanced at his watch, saw that fourteen minutes had gone by, thanked the President, and left.

In March 1963, the Harvard College class of 1938 held its twenty-fifth reunion at the Harvard Club in New York. Just before the welcoming address from President Nathan Pusey, an announcement was made, requesting that the brother of a class member who'd died defending his country be remembered. It was a wire from J F K, whose older brother, Joseph P. Kennedy Jr., was killed on a dangerous mission in August 1944.

Just after J F K named him ambassador to India, John Kenneth Galbraith decided to begin keeping a detailed diary. That's because when he was named to the post, J F K asked: "Just what does an ambassador do all day?"

J F K was never photographed with his advisors. Except once, by accident. Arnold

Newman, the White House photographer, assembled the advisors for a photo for *Holiday* magazine. JFK, true to form, refused to join the shot, saying it would distract viewers from the men around him. At the last minute, however, he walked in to say something to the advisors, and the camera clicked. The photo was withdrawn from the story, which ran after the assassination.

JFK was the first president to appear on live television. Young people of my generation watched his every appearance. I even went to a press conference, which my father arranged through Pierre Salinger. I noticed and emulated Kennedy's habit of walking with his hands in his jacket pockets, or at least pretending to delve into the pockets. That was his way of resisting the temptation to reach for a cigarette.

Speaking of young people, on a trip to California, a group of teenagers met JFK, and one asked: "How'd you get to be a war hero?"

"It was absolutely involuntary," he replied. "They sank my boat."

Frank Sinatra Jr. was kidnapped in 1963–64, and, after his release, recalled that he'd spoken with his kidnappers about the Kennedy assassination. "They must've been out of their minds," said the kidnappers.

JFK's military aide, General Ted Clifton, was on duty the day the Hot Line was first installed from the White House to 10 Downing Street, residence of the British prime minister, and to the residence of President Charles de Gaulle in Paris. JFK's Air Force aide, General Godfrey McHugh, was the first to try it out. He began: *"Ici est General McHugh, a la Maison Blanche."*

De Gaulle's aide had him repeat it, then roared back: *"'La Maison Blanche?'* We've been calling it 'The White House' for fifty years."

JFK appointed William Benton U.S. ambassador to UNESCO, and Benton thought it ideal. "After all," he explained, "I only have to work two or three months a year in Paris, where every man's wife wants to go, and I have the rest of the time off. No ceremonies, no cocktail parties, perfect."

JFK beamed: "Thank God. At last a man who's not complaining."

This is how Robert F. Kennedy became attorney general: Few people know that JFK originally offered the post to Connecticut Senator Abe Ribicoff, who turned it down, saying he preferred to be secretary of Health, Education, and Welfare. Then he suggested to the President that RFK would make a great attorney general.

"During the campaign," he told the President, "I noticed that when a major problem arose, you would always consult Bobby. You'll be calling on Bobby more and more. Let him come through the front door, not the back."

One day in 1969, Chief Justice Earl Warren, who was Thomas E. Dewey's running mate in 1948, remembered a White House luncheon he had attended with LBJ. President Kennedy said: "Three of us wanted to be President, and one made it." Then JFK bowed. Then Kennedy said: "Three of us wanted to be Vice President, and one of us made it," he said, pointing to LBJ.

Finally Kennedy said: "And three of us wanted lifetime security," and bowed to Warren, "and one of us made it."

Years after the assassination, Senator Margaret Chase Smith, the Maine Republican who'd been the only woman senator of that time, recalled that back then a senator's wife was always included in a White House dinner invitation, but she was never invited to bring an escort. Except by the Kennedy administration, the only one to afford her that courtesy.

Before he was named to the Supreme Court, Arthur Goldberg served as JFK's secretary of Labor. Cabinet members were instructed by JFK to keep their remarks brief at Cabinet meetings. So when Goldberg drafted legislation covering equal rights for working women, he presented it to JFK.

The President asked what it was.

"You like women, don't you? Mr. President?" asked Goldberg. When JFK nodded, all Goldberg said was: "So sign."

Frank Sinatra wasn't awed by anyone. Except JFK, we know this because at his estate in Palm Springs Sinatra erected a plaque that read: "JFK slept here."

Before Cliff Robertson was cast as JFK in *PT 109*, Warren Beatty was being considered for the role. He was urged to go to Washington for a week or so and study the President. "Let him study me instead," Beatty was reported to have said.

Only Beatty never said that, and felt terrible about it. Ironically, he did fly to Washington and sought help in rectifying that misquote from Pierre Salinger. Salinger picked up the phone and said: "Get me Leonard Lyons!"

SOPHIA LOREN

In July 1956, my parents took me to Spain for the first time. We stayed in the recently completed Castellana Hilton. Orson Welles and his then-fiancée Italian actress Paola Mori had stayed there, and when Welles plugged in his electric razor, the elevators short-circuited. But I didn't care. I was in Europe for the first time!

Next door were two young women: the Sicclione sisters. The older one was Sophia, who had become a star in Italy but was in Madrid to film her first English-language movie, *The Pride and the Passion*, costarring with Cary Grant and Frank Sinatra. Stanley Kramer was the director. Somehow we struck up a conversation, and the next evening a spaghetti dinner, cooked just for me, came over the adjoining terrace.

I saw her nine years later at the opening of *Doctor Zhivago*, produced by her husband Carlo Ponti. "How was the spaghetti I cooked for you in Spain?" she asked.

In his column of July 19, 1956, my father reported that I asked him to type quietly, lest we wake up the sleeping beauty in the adjoining room. My father's retort: "I assured him that to a working actress, the sound of sweet words being typed about her is as sweet and lulling as an orchestra of violins."

In June 1958, he shared with readers that I'd formed a Sophia Loren fan club at my high school, Fieldston. "That's some progressive school," my father wrote. "They now have a built-in Sophia Loren fan club."

"I decided to be an actress when I was born," she said. "I *had* to be an actress." She eschewed formal training, but learned the craft from the great director Vittorio De Sica. She never dieted as a young actress. "I am false thin," she explained. "I look thin, but I'm not."

"As a child I dreamed that Hollywood is a big stage with musicals in each corner."

With Sophia Loren in 1957.

When asked if she wanted to have a family, she said: "Yes, it's important for an actress to be a woman."

When she came to America, MGM, then in its last years of glory, offered her a role in a musical, but she wanted to spend at least six months in America before deciding on anything. "You have to get the feel of a nation before you can do a musical," she said.

She studied English by reading books and underlining unfamiliar words. Her manager explained: "When she reads a book and there's a woman in the story, she wants to play the movie version, even though it's already been filmed."

She even read her Paramount contract this way, but only after signing it. She pored all through the seventy-six pages of legalese. Her manager described it: "They give you the feeling they're making a contract against you instead of with you."

The actress, then twenty-one, quickly picked up American phrases, most of which were taught her by Sinatra. But I taught her my favorite phrase, courtesy of Art Carney on *The Honeymooners*, then at the height of its popularity: "Va va va voom."

In *Boy on a Dolphin*, which was filmed in Greece, Loren had a scene with windmills. A sudden gust of wind made the sails spin much faster than they were supposed to, forcing her to scamper off quickly to a safe spot. "Mama mía," she said. "Those things have more arms than some of the directors I've known."

In Libya, on the set of *Legend of the Lost*, my father trained her for two hours for her imminent trip to America, and how to face the intrusive questions the press might ask her about her romance with Ponti, a man half her height and twice her age. "Her trepidations proved needless," my father reported. "She had a ready response to all inquiries." She handled all such questions easily.

Thinking the desert in Libya would be steamy, even at night, she hadn't brought any warm clothing, and fainted in the cold. My father had come prepared with woolen pajamas, and after Loren hinted she could use such garments, he presented them to her in a mock ceremony his last morning on the set.

Loren told my father she'd be there for forty-eight more nights. Seven weeks later, she returned his pajamas in New York.

In 1961, she was back in Spain filming *El Cid*, and after finishing the day's shooting of that medieval epic, Loren would always turn on Dave Brubeck and Dizzy Gillespie records. "It's the best way to snap back to the twentieth century," she explained.

Early in her career, her great rival was Anna Magnani, the original choice to portray "Cesira," the mother in *Two Women*, but Magnani thought she was too young for the role. So it went to Loren, twenty-six years younger, who won the award for best actress at the Cannes Film Festival, Italy's Silver Ribbon, and the Academy Award, the first by an actress in a foreign language film.

When reminded that she was voted the Oscar by fellow members of the Screen Actors' Guild, she quoted the Bible: "Thee, Shall Thy Brethren Praise."

In *Five Miles to Midnight*, Loren had to punch her costar, Tony Perkins. After the film opened, Sophia sent him a memento: diamond-studded cuff links, shaped like boxing gloves.

In *Yesterday, Today and Tomorrow*, Marcello Mastroianni, probably Italy's most dashing leading man, patronized a prostitute. He was asked how he could convince his fans his character needed a prostitute. "Easy," he replied, "when she's played by Sophia Loren."

When he announced that he had hired the two stars for his next movie, *Marriage, Italian Style*, producer Joseph E. Levine called them, "The most successful Italian twosome since Romulus and Remus."

Early in 1965, she was told her movie

Operation Crossbow would play at New York's famous Radio City Music Hall. She was overjoyed. "When I was a girl, I dreamed of getting into Radio City Music Hall," she recalled. "But in my dreams it wasn't as a movie star, but as a Rockette."

PAUL NEWMAN

I'm certain that if Paul Newman could have made the decision, he'd want to be remembered first as a humanitarian and then as an Oscar-winning actor. He was a reluctant movie star and not the easiest one to interview. When I did so for *Road to Perdition* in 2002, he was quiet, not terribly giving, and almost shy. He obviously didn't like being interviewed. So I turned to my father's anecdotes to spark his interest.

In July 1957, Newman was completing *The Helen Morgan Story* with an October release. One scene had title player Ann Blyth being hit in the face by Newman's character. At a rough-cut screening, studio executives decided that Newman hadn't hit her hard enough to be realistic. Thus the scene had to be reshot.

Newman, in New York by then, had to be flown back to Hollywood. At the airport a friend asked him where he was going. Newman replied: "I've got to go back to Hollywood just to belt a broad."

In another scene, Newman's character is killed by a submachine gun. Without the director's knowledge, Newman had prepared for that scene by going to the LAPD to inquire about how a victim of such a weapon dies. Two detectives explained that the victim usually is lifted, then drops. So Newman did it that way, but veteran director Michael Curtiz yelled "Cut!"

"You asked cops?" he asked Newman. "Listen," said Curtiz. "I've 'killed' George Raft five times, Jimmy Cagney six, and Edward G. Robinson in seven movies. Do it my way."

In 1959, he was on Broadway in Tennessee Williams's *Sweet Bird of Youth*. During the run, members of the cast noticed that he gave his most moving performances on Wednesday and Saturday matinees.

"How do you get to cry so easily at those performances?" he was asked. "I just think of the sunshine outside the theater, and think I could be in Hollywood, poolside. That always brings tears to my eyes," he explained.

Newman never had much interest in what we critics said or wrote of his work. He needn't have, since his was a résumé of quality. When he received raves for *Sweet Bird of Youth*, he explained: "I'll tell you how an actor remembers his reviews. If a critic were to say that my performance was the greatest on Broadway, ranking with Booth's and Barrymore's, I'd only remember it if he misspelled or mispronounced my name."

In November 1959, between acts of the matinee performance of *Sweet Bird of Youth*, Newman ordered a steak dinner from a restaurant across the street. A delivery man brought the meal backstage at the Martin Beck Theater and asked the stage manager where Newman was. He was directed to the stage where Newman was in the middle of the hotel scene. The delivery man, without hesitation, walked onstage, put the tray down, then realized where he was. Undaunted, he finished setting out the meal and calmly walked off.

The following year, Newman was filming *Exodus* in Israel. His wife, Joanne Woodward, accompanied him to the location, but not before taking Hebrew lessons for weeks. While there, her agent called, offering her a role in a French film called *Kilometer 65*. She turned it down, explaining: "I make no other commitment when Paul is working. My commitment is to my husband." The film was never made.

Later that year, Newman was in Paris starring in *Paris Blues* as a jazz musician. He wanted to buy a German car but director Martin Ritt told him: "Nothing doing. You're playing a Frenchman. So think like a Frenchman. Buy a French car." Newman used his friend Conrad Janis's trombone in the movie and practiced for weeks, so often that it gave him visible muscle lines near his lips—the way a real musician would have looked.

Late in the winter of 1963, Newman, an avid skier, had the urge to drive to Vermont for a weekend. Then he remembered his small car had no ski rack on top. He couldn't buy a rack, so went to the dealer, saw another car with a rack, and bought it on the spot. Such are the perks of stardom.

"I'm two people," he told me in our interview. "A human being and an actor. The first one is not for sale. Not ever. Ahh, but the second one sure is!"

In 1961, Newman honored his friend Gore Vidal by naming him the godfather of his daughter. It was Vidal's fourth godchild, about which he said to Newman: "Always a godfather. Never a god."

BARBRA STREISAND

I remember it as if it were yesterday: the weekend of the Kennedy assassination. We all thought the world was coming to an end, especially when news came that President Johnson's plane took a zigzag course back to Washington to evade possible Soviet attack.

My brother Warren, an off-Broadway producer, decided to come down to Philadelphia to visit me. I was a sophomore at the University of Pennsylvania. One of my big brothers! On campus! It really calmed me down and gave some stability to things.

I remember taking him to the neighborhood Italian restaurant, and he asked for iced tea. Told they didn't serve iced tea, he asked: "Got any ice? Good. Any tea? Great. Bring 'em both, please."

A semblance of normalcy had returned; my brother was being witty.

He'd come down to get a preview of a show in out-of-town tryouts; something called *Funny Girl,* starring a vaguely familiar young singer/actress named Barbra Streisand. She'd had a memorable part in the musical *I Can Get It for You Wholesale,* had an album released, and was a guest on *The Tonight Show* and other shows, but the performance we saw, portraying the great comedienne/singer Fanny Brice, would help catapult her to the pantheon of show business. It was a role she alone was born to play.

She was quoted in an item in "The Lyons Den" on March 29, 1964, saying that an item on April 18, 1962, started her career off. My father had quoted the showman Billy Rose, an ex-husband of Fanny Brice, who said: "of all the comediennes he's seen, the one whose comic qualities most clearly approach Miss Brice's is Barbra Streisand."

When she was fourteen and already working in a summer theater, two of her baby teeth had to come out. "So I made my own false teeth," she recalled, "out of chewing gum. I stuck them in to cover the gaps. For two years, I didn't smile, for fear my chewing gum teeth would fall out."

When she met Rose after her performance in *Funny Girl,* he said: "You know, I was married to you for ten years."

"How was it?" Streisand asked Rose.

"Very good. For the first eight years."

When young Streisand opened at the Blue Angel, then one of New York's hottest nightclubs, her manager, Marty Erlichman, booked her for $200 a week. He also represented the headliners, The Clancy Brothers, the Irish folk music group, by then earning $250,000 a year. The group protested that Erlichman had been devoting more time and effort to the newcomer, Streisand, than to them. He thus had to choose between clients.

Erlichman went to his father for advice. He told his father he was giving up 10 percent of $250,000 a year to take his chances with 10 percent of a $200-a-week singer. "My feeling," he told his father, "is that Barbra Streisand will make as much in one week as the Clancys do in a month," he said.

"Then do it," said his father. "Every person should have one big shot in life."

No doubt Streisand often made that amount in one night.

Erlichman, incidentally, once placed a fortune cookie in the elevator of the apartment of a woman he was dating. He'd planted the following message inside the cookie: "If you are proposed to today, accept." Then he knocked on the door, and later, when the couple left, she found the cookie in the elevator, opened it, and looked at him. He proposed. She accepted.

By May 1965, Streisand was an enormous star. Proof of that came in the mail. One letter was addressed simply: "Barbra—New York City" and the other had only a cutout photo of her on the envelope. She received both within twenty-four hours.

In March 1965, Burt Lancaster bought tickets to see her in *Funny Girl*, but she took ill before curtain time and couldn't go on. Her understudy did the performance. Six months later, Lancaster again had tickets, and again she was ill and missed the Saturday matinee. At 6 p.m. she learned that he'd be in the audience that night; so sick or not, she rushed to the theater and performed.

In December 1965, Streisand was in London on a royal receiving line. As she approached Princess Margaret, she was suddenly at a loss for words, so she turned to fellow actor Tommy Steele, an Englishman, and said to the Princess: "You two must know each other—from London."

In March of 1966, she had two then-unheard-of luxuries installed in her Bentley: a television set and a refrigerator.

"Watching TV is no fun," she explained, "unless you've got something to nosh."

Later that month, Streisand left JFK for London to prepare for the West End production of *Funny Girl*. The passenger ramp at that time was at eye level with the pilot's cabin. Just before departure, her press agent, Lee Solters, rapped on the glass window of the cockpit and yelled to the pilot: "Please drive carefully."

In June 1966, she gave a concert at the U.S. Embassy in London and invited British officials to her closing-night party after the July 16 performance of *Funny Girl*.

"I'm going to serve hot dogs," she said, "Nathan's Famous hot dogs from Coney Island."

When asked by one official where Coney Island was, she said: "Just go to Cornwall, then keep going West until you hit Brooklyn."

When she gave a concert in New York in Central Park's Sheep Meadow, few of the 130,000 fans could hear Streisand correct them while taking her bows.

"It's not 'Bravo!'" she yelled back. "It's 'Brava!'"

In all her concerts, Streisand sings an obscure song called "I'm in Love with Harold Mongart." She sings it out of a determination to make it a hit, justifying her early faith in it. The song is from a flop review called *Another Evening with Harry Stoones*, her first show.

In May 1968, the ads for the movie version of *Funny Girl* began to appear with only the names "Barbra" and "Omar." Last names weren't needed.

In November of that year, Streisand received the "Star of the Year" award from the nation's film exhibitors. She approached the podium and began: "Is the owner of the Albemarle Theater in Brooklyn here?" Somewhere in the vast audience, a man raised his hand. She spotted him and then said: "You didn't put enough butter in the popcorn."

PETER USTINOV

Sir Peter Ustinov had several careers: an actor (and two-time Oscar-winner), playwright, author, raconteur, and lead voice in the marvelous *Babar* animated television series. He was one of those international people who was part Russian, German, Ethiopian, Dutch, Slav, Italian, and French. His wife was born in Canada, their first child in America, and their second in London.

"I feel at home nowhere," he said, "but more at home everywhere than anyone else does."

I interviewed him several times, and it was a joy to be in his presence. As with Danny Kaye before him and Robin Williams after him, you never knew which voice would come out of him, besides his upper-class Oxonian English. I adored him.

He first went to Hollywood in June 1947, and upon returning to London said of the movie capital: "Hollywood reminds me of the remnants of a huge wedding cake, prepared for more guests than came."

During World War II he worked for the esteemed British director Sir Carol Reed, making war films. Reed spotted Ustinov's talent and put him in an important position. One day this involved his sitting in on a meeting with high-ranking officers. So rather than have Private Ustinov stand meekly in the corner, Reed let him don a Russian general's uniform and convince the British officers that Russia routinely promoted young men, and that he was indeed a general.

In 1951, he was perfectly cast as Nero, the decadent Roman emperor who, legend has it, fiddled while Rome burned. (Who knows if they had violins back then?) During the shooting of the film, *Quo Vadis*, he made a startling discovery; if he fed the lions that were positioned near him, they would become docile and enjoy being petted. The producers disliked this practice, since the lions no longer seemed ferocious.

Incidentally, two extras in the crowd scenes urging the lions to devour the Christians were a young Sophia Loren and her mother.

In the movie *Hotel Sahara*, Ustinov portrayed Yvonne De Carlo's amusing fiancé.

"He's the sort of guy," said Ustinov, "Nero would've thrown to the lions."

Although he was a brilliant speaker, especially extemporaneously, Ustinov hated to make after-dinner speeches. He said it inevitably spoiled his dinner. He cited history as proof.

"In ancient Rome," he said, "a man thrown to the lions walked up to one hungry cat, whispered into its ear, and the lion fled to the other side of the arena. The man's life was saved.

"Later, Nero asked him what he said to the lion to make it run away.

"'I just told the lion,' said the man, 'that after his dinner, he'd be expected to make a few remarks.'"

He portrayed the Prince of Wales in the movie *Beau Brummell* and was assured that the plot was based on a true incident, but some liberties had been taken. Unconvinced, Ustinov did a bit of research and found out that when the events in the movie took place, Beau Brummell was six years old.

Ustinov once explained the frequent habit of the British to stammer, and cited Winston Churchill and Rex Harrison as examples.

"That's because the English language is so rich," he said. "You have to search for a long time, even to use the wrong word."

He once was invited to play tennis with a man from the Soviet Embassy in London. The Russian diplomat, named "Romanoff," thought this appropriate, since Ustinov had written and acted in the popular play *Romanoff and Juliet*.

The match took place on the embassy

grounds' tennis court with a Russian umpire. Ustinov thought it was just a game between friends, with nothing at stake. Then, when he was a point away from winning the first game, he heard the umpire call out in a thick Russian accent, "Ad-wantage Great Bree-ton."

Ustinov once explained the roles he preferred to play as: "I never touched a hero without a weakness nor a villain without a heart."

Ustinov stood about 5 feet 9 and was heavyset. One night he met Carl Sandburg, who complimented him on his roles. "Thank you," replied Ustinov. "But if you're thinking of having me portray Abe Lincoln in Illinois, you'd have to surround me with tiny, fat actors, to make me look tall and lean."

During the 1957 Christmas season, Ustinov, then performing on Broadway, took his young daughter for a walk along Fifth Avenue to see the department store windows. Then they came upon three sidewalk Santas, so naturally the little girl asked about this.

"Simple," replied her father. "This is America. Here they have more of everything."

While he'd found success in movies and TV, he had always preferred the theater. "You step onto the stage and face 1,000 strangers every night," he said. "They come from everywhere, strangers to each other, too. That's the challenge you face with every performance. And before the night's over, they're all linked, through you. It's uniquely satisfying."

In August 1961, Ustinov was producing, directing, writing, and starring in the movie version of *Romanoff and Juliet*. When Ustinov and his cast left Hollywood by train for a shooting location, they discovered that one

trunk with important equipment had been left behind. The train pulled into the Reno, Nevada, station and was held a few minutes while he got off to phone the Los Angeles stationmaster about the trunk.

On his way back to board the train, he dropped a dime into a slot machine—and won the jackpot.

When I interviewed Sir Peter, I reminded him of an incident during his performance in Ibsen's five-hour marathon, *Peer Gynt*. He laughed at the memory.

"It's a tall mountain to climb," he recalled. "There's one character—the buttonmolder—who doesn't come onstage until just before the end of the show. The old actor in the role came towards me and froze. I realized he'd forgotten his one line. So I just looked at him and said: 'Are you not the buttonmolder?' 'Thanks,' he said, and walked away."

He then recalled a soccer game he'd attended in Turkey, which was decided in a most unusual way.

"One player kicked the ball into the goal, but it rolled out, just as time ran out. It was an earthquake!"

I wondered about the ceremony of a knighthood investiture. "What happens is they ring you up from Buckingham Palace with the good news, then send you a form. One of the questions is: 'I can kneel/I cannot kneel,' because many of the recipients are elderly.

"So I had to call them back and say: 'I can kneel, but then I can't get up again.'

"Then, as I walked down the aisle at Westminster Abbey, the band played, of all things, 'I'm Gonna Wash That Man Right Out of My Hair' from *South Pacific*! But it being a military band, I wasn't quite sure that's what they were playing."

BILLY WILDER

A Billy Wilder–directed film, such as *The Apartment, Sunset Boulevard,* or *Some Like It Hot,* always had a whimsical sense of humor about it, and Wilder's movies are among the finest films ever made. After fleeing his Austro-Hungarian homeland when Hitler rose to power (his mother and stepfather would die at Auschwitz), he came to America via Paris and began writing screenplays in Hollywood. He'd arrived speaking no English, but roomed with his countryman Peter Lorre, then one of the most successful character actors in films.

At first Wilder couldn't get a job, but he'd send his mother all the clippings, books, and stories by and about Thornton Wilder, explaining that he had to change his first name. When he finally got a job at Paramount, he wrote his mother confessing the hoax, saying he did it so she wouldn't worry about him.

"I'm relieved," she wrote back. "I never liked those books you sent anyway."

One of his first mentions in "The Lyons Den" came on June 17, 1942, when he finally got the chance to direct his first American film. It was *The Major and the Minor* with Ginger Rogers. Wilder was complimented on his promotion from writer to director.

"That's not a promotion," he insisted. "I'd rather be known as a writer who also can direct than a director who also can write."

In the fall of 1944, Wilder and his writing partner Charles Brackett were at work on the screenplay of Charles Jackson's *The Lost Weekend,* the first important Hollywood movie dealing with alcoholism. Just as a joke, they wired Jackson that they'd decided to change the locale of the movie from New York. "It'll all take place on a battleship."

Late in the war, Wilder worked in the Office of War Information's Film Division in Germany. When it came time to come home, he had to fill out answers to nearly sixty questionnaires concerning his work for the government. On V-E Day he went to the Office of War Information headquarters in New York to see if the paperwork had gone through, but no one could find the forms. They'd been torn into confetti and tossed out the window as part of the V-E Day celebration.

While on assignment for the OWI in Germany, Wilder attended a conference with Russian representatives about films to be shown in postwar Germany. The Russians heard his name, and sent two secret service agents back to headquarters for a background check. They returned and made their report to the Soviet film officials.

Wilder feared they'd discover he'd written *Ninotchka,* which lampooned the Soviets, and that might disrupt the conference. "Wilder?" he heard them say: "*Mrs. Miniver?*" Wilder nodded and smiled. "*The Little Foxes?*" they continued. Again Wilder smiled, for this was the first and only time Wilder was glad he'd been mistaken for fellow director William Wyler.

The confusion between Wilder and Wyler continued after that. It became more involved when Billy Wilder's brother, William Wilder, gave up his banking business to become a producer for Republic Pictures. When William Wilder's new job was announced, William Wyler wired Billy Wilder: "Just read about your brother William Wilder. Doesn't he mean 'Wildest?'"

When Bing Crosby was told he'd be making *The Emperor Waltz* with Wilder, he received a phone call from the director, who asked: "How would you like Joan Fontaine for your leading lady?" Crosby had such faith in Wilder and Brackett's talent, he answered: "It doesn't matter. Just tell me when and where I'm to show up and if you want me fat or skinny."

When he completed *Sunset Boulevard* early in 1950, he was asked if the movie about Hollywood and the movie industry was a documentary. "Only a semi-documentary," he replied. "Only half the people in it are heels."

Cecil B. DeMille, the great epic producer and director, played himself in *Sunset Boulevard*, which Wilder cowrote and directed. It's the scene in which Gloria Swanson returns to a movie set after years away, still treated like the movie star she'd been in silent pictures. When DeMille arrived on the set for the scene, he asked Wilder for instructions. Wilder was a child in Vienna when he first saw DeMille's films and said: "Play the scene your own way. You are the master."

"No, I'll play it your way. After all, I'll be acting out ideas which are yours. Frankly, between us, there are very few directors who can act," he said. Wilder replied: "And just between us, there are very few directors who can direct."

In October 1952, there was a report that Wilder would make a movie with Yul Brynner, and Wilder was asked if Brynner's contract with Paramount allowed him the right to direct, too.

"Even though he's directed for television, I don't believe Yul wants to become a director," said Wilder. "Actors study direction for the day when they lose their hair. Yul's already lost his."

Wilder met with Sam Goldwyn in 1953 to interest the producer in a movie on the life of Russian dancer Vaslav Nijinsky. Wilder told Goldwyn the Nijinsky story—about the world's greatest dancer whose mind was beset by strange illusions and who ended up in a sanitarium. Goldwyn shook his head, and said he wanted no part of a movie that ended on such a tragic note.

"Gregory Peck should wind up in a Swiss madhouse, thinking he's a racehorse? Never," said Goldwyn.

"Oh, it's not a downbeat ending," replied Wilder. "He winds up winning the Kentucky Derby."

In June 1954, Wilder was in New York working on *Spirit of St. Louis*, the great film in which Jimmy Stewart played Charles Lindbergh. He was conducting screen tests in a Midtown studio, taking close-ups of the performers and concentrating on their eyes.

"The movie camera is a thing of magic," he explained. He mentioned the way the cameras used to shoot close-ups of Garbo's eyes, making moviegoers feel the emotional storms raging inside her.

"And all the time," said Wilder, "don't you know what was going through Garbo's mind? *Nothing*! Absolutely nothing!"

Some of the early scenes in *Spirit of St. Louis* showed barnstorming wing-walkers in the early days of aviation. Wilder scoffed at the idea that the stunt of standing on the wings of a plane in flight was really dangerous. He made a bet with producer Leland Hayward that he too could do it. Wilder stood atop the wing of an old Standard J-I barnstorming plane. It flew at 1,000 feet at 65 miles per hour, over a ranch near the Santa Anita racetrack. Hayward took movies of the flight, then paid Wilder the bet.

In *Love in the Afternoon*, Audrey Hepburn played a cellist. The film was shot in Paris, and one night the cast and Wilder went to the Sorbonne to listen to Pablo Casals on the cello. The next day, when the filming resumed, Wilder told his star: "Audrey, you're a combination of Garbo and Casals. You act like Casals and play the cello like Garbo."

SHELLEY WINTERS

Born in 1920 in St. Louis to a men's clothing designer and a singer, Shirley Schrift came to New York as a child and went on to a fifty-year career in movies, winning two Oscars. She eschewed "dumb blonde" roles, then in vogue, and insisted on portraying characters with substance, which is why she has an enduring legacy.

One of her first important movie roles was in *A Double Life,* one of Ronald Colman's last big films. A friend of Winters, an extra in the movie, was being paid a mere $75 a day, so Winters kept flubbing her own lines to ensure that her friend would get additional days of work.

By 1955, she'd appeared in more than forty films. The evening her film *Night of the Hunter* premiered, she was taking a limousine full of friends to the theater. Suddenly Winters asked the chauffeur to drive around the block where the theater was a second time.

"I just wanted to show everyone in the car where I worked as a salesgirl not so long before I became a star." It was a Woolworth next door.

At a publicity event for one of her films in New York, a sailor shook the star's hand and said: "When I get back to my ship and tell the boys I got a handshake from Shelley Winters, they'll never believe it."

"As long as you're going to be accused of telling a lie, let's make it a bigger one," she said. Then Winters grabbed the young sailor and kissed him hard on the lips.

On one of her visits to the Cannes Film Festival, a Frenchman gave Winters what he called an antique diamond brooch and said Napoleon once gave it to Josephine. She showed it to Customs agents on her return to New York, saying that since it was an antique it was duty-free. "It even has a lock of Napoleon's hair," she insisted. The expert studied the "antique," then said:

"Miss Winters, do you always believe what Frenchmen tell you?" She paid the duty on the piece of glass.

Her father Jonas Schrift was a huge fan of Al Jolson, one of the great entertainers of the twentieth century. He admired Jolson so much, in fact, that he bought the cemetery plot adjoining Jolson's in Forest Lawn, where he lies today.

On August 20, 1962, Winters had a birthday party at a Manhattan bar where the large crowd of guests quickly overflowed onto the street. The bouncer was forced to turn people away, including one man the bouncer later said "didn't look important." It was Tennessee Williams.

In April 1962, Winters had appeared in Williams's *The Night of the Iguana.* It was her first week in the role of Maxine Faul, succeeding Bette Davis. She hadn't quite memorized the part, so when asked if she was enjoying the role, she joked: "Yes, in fact, I like it so much, I sometimes make the same speech twice."

During her days off from her Broadway show, Winters flew to Los Angeles and appeared on the Academy Awards show as a presenter, sold her house, received a sapphire ring from a beau, and, for good measure, she won a Twist contest. All in two days.

In June 1962, news came that the movie *Something's Got to Give* was cancelled due to the continual tardiness of Marilyn Monroe. Winters, who once roomed with Monroe, sighed: "The studio doesn't understand one elementary thing: Marilyn is one of the Night People. So is Sinatra. So are several others. It's a mistake to ask them to start acting early in the morning. Even with overtime rates, it's cheaper and surer to work with them at night."

Marilyn Monroe died six weeks later.

Winters described her role as the mother in *Lolita* as: "a story about a mother who couldn't get a babysitter." Then, reflecting on the suggestive story, she said: "If I had realized how shocking this movie was, I'd have asked for more money."

She was certain she'd be Oscar-nominated as the overbearing mother for *Lolita* and went to California to begin campaigning for the honor, saying: "If nominated, I will accept. And if elected, I will grab it!" She wasn't nominated.

Lee Strasberg and his wife used to give huge New Year's Eve parties. All the great stars in New York attended. Winters went to the 1961 party, and Strasberg praised her development as an actress. "From now on," Winters said, "I plan to take on the great roles—Camille, Anna Karenina, and Juliet. Yes, the fourteen-year-old Juliet. Mind you, I may have to marry a rich backer for that one first."

She was invited by Uta Hagen and her husband Herbert Berghof, the legendary acting couple, to lecture at their drama school. She told them: "All the acting hopefuls want to know from me is how to get a job. I'll tell them how: First, find an Actors' Equity member who will look at the bulletin board at the union about new plays being cast. Then, I'll tell them to steal a copy of the script. And never depend on the imagination of the producer or director; come to the audition dressed as the character they hope to portray."

She lectured at Harvard in March 1962, and prepared as thoroughly as she'd ever done for a play or movie role. Her conception of the lecture was as a three-act play: Act One, the comments she wrote out and then memorized; Act Two, some notes on which she would elaborate; and Act Three, a question-and-answer period.

She received a mere $300 for the lecture. "I'm going to break Harvard's bookkeeping system," she said, "because I've framed that check. I'll never cash it."

Her first job in Hollywood had been in an obscure movie called *There's Something about Hollywood*. Her first payment was $110, paid in cash. An assistant director drove her and her sister from the set back to their apartment. They invited him to stay for dinner, until she discovered that a $20 bill was missing from her purse. The man left, brazenly saying: "Whoever took that $20 bill will have no luck with it."

Indeed he had no luck. Nearly twenty years later, he was a codefendant in a California murder trial.

In July 1963, Winters was appearing on the New York stage in *Cages*. Then she flew to Russia for the Moscow film festival, where she saw five movies, toured the Kremlin and the Stanislavsky Museum, attended six parties, made eight speeches, ate curry, caviar, and drank vodka, and her stomach was pumped by three Soviet doctors before she returned to the stage in New York—all in three days.

In the movie *The Balcony*, Winters wore one dress opening a door, and another one closing it—a rare oversight by the continuity director on the set. She was puzzled by the reaction to this from French critics who saw this as some sort of symbolism.

"It was just a mistake," she said. "No 'symbolism.'"

In September 1966, Winters appeared in an episode of *Batman*, as "Ma Parker," an obvious parody of the infamous criminal mother Ma Barker. The director chided the great Method actress for laughing.

"Of course I was laughing," she said later. "There I was, machine gun in hand, facing two guys strapped in an electric chair, grenades hanging in my hair, wearing a bulletproof girdle, while all the time I'm thinking: 'What's my motivation?'"

One night while making his nightclub and restaurant rounds, my father, accompanied by my oldest brother George, sat with Winters, who gave him some news items about her latest film. She wore a dress with designs of stock quotations of IBM, AT&T,

and General Motors embroidered into a pattern. My brother, a stock broker, noticed the prices and correctly told her the dress was three years old.

A few months later, she was on Broadway in a short-lived Saul Bellow play called *Under the Weather*. One morning, she suddenly flew to Los Angeles to visit her mother, who'd been taken to the hospital. The actress was permitted to nap in a nearby room that was air-conditioned, unlike her mother's. When she learned that the room where she'd slept was reserved for a patient who'd be coming in a week late for elective surgery, she moved her mother into the air-conditioned room.

The head nurse objected. "You can't do that," she told Winters.

"Oh yes, I can," she replied. "I've done fifty-one benefits for this hospital."

In October 1963, Winters was in a fender-bender with a truck and later was asked why she insists on driving around Midtown Manhattan when there are 12,000 cabs in New York City.

"Because," she explained, "every driver has a play for me to read."

Early in 1964, she received a message from a British newspaperman she knew asking her to host four young men around town. "Take them to a political meeting," he suggested, "then to a session at the Actors Studio. That way they won't be bored in New York. They call themselves 'The Beatles.'"

Producer Joseph E. Levine promised Winters a diamond bracelet if she'd lose thirty pounds. While publicizing the movie *A House Is Not a Home,* she calculated that for every pound she lost, she'd gain a carat on that promised bracelet.

In November 1964, Winters went to a doctor for a checkup. As instructed, she took off her clothes and donned a gown, then listened as the doctor in the office outside instructed the nurse to send a donation to the Goldwater campaign. She quickly got dressed and walked out.

In December 1964, she was having trouble with her apartment because of New York's rent control laws. Her daughter was living with her, and soon her stepdaughter by Vittorio Gassman, the Italian star, would be moving in. So would Gassman, who would be coming to New York to study for the theater.

"We need just one more person to keep the apartment out of the luxury-apartment class and under rent control," said the actress. "I need a husband."

Wendy Condon was once introduced to Winters. The daughter of Richard Condon, author of *The Manchurian Candidate* and later *Prizzi's Honor,* said she was an aspiring actress.

Winters surveyed the nineteen-year-old beauty and said: "I've got enough trouble without you."

She once introduced her mother to Porfirio Rubirosa, the playboy whose only "job" was marrying rich women. The Dominican diplomat and polo player had been linked to, among others, Eva Peron, Veronica Lake, Ava Gardner, Joan Crawford, Marilyn Monroe, Eartha Kitt, and Zsa Zsa Gabor. He married both Doris Duke and Barbara Hutton.

Winters's mother was, nevertheless, unimpressed. After meeting him, she said to her daughter: "Shelley, what's so special about him?"

Rubirosa overheard that remark and said: "Madam, the day I don't make love, I consider wasted."

"By you that's special?" Winters's mother replied. "Why don't you work?"

Late in 1967, Winters was asked about her conflicts with scenic designers, and explained: "Their job is to build sets whose purpose is to divert the customers' attention from the stars."

In December 1967, the actress announced

she would be taking a six-month vacation. "After all," she explained, "I've just come off of two years of steady work—thank God!"

In February 1968, news came of the death of Stan Berman, the New York cab driver and notorious gate crasher, infamous for sneaking into the Kennedy box at the Inaugural Ball. Winters confessed: "I was a presenter at the Oscars, and when he walked onstage, I thought he was a winner, so I handed him the award for best black-and-white photography."

In December 1968, she was performing a scene in an acting workshop and was being directed by the great Harold Clurman. He became exasperated by her interruptions, so he shouted: "Not a word out of you from now on, unless it's in the script. Not even 'Good Morning.'" She obeyed, and the next day said to Clurman: "My analyst says you're handling me the right way."

Two years later, she was starring in the movie *Bloody Mama* as gangster mother Ma Barker, while on Broadway in *Minnie's Boys*, as the mother of the Marx Brothers. "One group of my sons steals money for laughs," she said, "while the other steals laughs for money."

While this was going on she still had time to write a play called *One Night Stands of a Noisy Passenger,* which was performed in a workshop production at the Actors Studio. During one scene, the costume of costar Salome Jens caught fire, and Winters jumped out of the audience, grabbed a nearby pitcher full of water, and doused it. The other actor, then a rising star, was upset she'd interrupted the scene. It was Robert De Niro.

That same month she said: "An actress knows she's ready for marriage when she can turn down a part and mean it. When you're young and in love, the worst thing is not to have the phone ring.

"But now that I'm mature, I feel if the phone doesn't ring today, it'll ring tomorrow."

Late in 1972, she assessed some of her famous roles. "In *Place in the Sun* I was with Montgomery Clift in a rowboat which overturned and I was drowned. In *Night of the Hunter* Robert Mitchum stalked my children, tied me up, put me in a boat and sunk it in a river, where my character drowned. In *He Ran All the Way,* John Garfield first saw me in a swimming pool. And in *The Poseidon Adventure,* I rescued Gene Hackman from an ocean liner which has turned upside down after a tsunami, and then I suffered a fatal heart attack.

"As Esther Williams said about her own career, 'Wet I'm a star. Dry I'm not.'"

On the back lot at M G M with Clint Eastwood and Don Rickles in Los Angeles, August 1969. Notice my father wearing a tie in Southern California; ever the New York newspaperman.

THE NEXT GENERATION

The first person I interviewed professionally was Debbie Reynolds. I didn't have a sense of carrying on the family tradition or anything like that. It was just an opportunity that came along, thanks to the well-known NBC producer Lucy Jarvis. My father had instilled in me the need to prepare for interviews better than anyone else. It was the equivalent of a ballplayer who gets to the batting cage early, before any teammates, every day. And prepares, and prepares, and prepares.

There were no DVDs, no VHS cassettes, nor the resources on the Internet. But I had magazine articles and newspaper clippings as sources back then, as well as having seen thousands of films.

When I got my chance, it was a radio interview for *Monitor,* NBC Radio's wonderful weekend network marathon that ran from 1955 to 1975. It was 1969, the year before I began my television career.

I had no idea where this would lead, but I felt ready. I'd grown up with larger-than-life people who were family friends. Those were different times. Perhaps they cultivated friendships with my father because of the column; I'll never know. But I do know that they often evolved into lifelong asso-

ciations filled with affection for my father, and my mother as well.

None more so than with Ernest Hemingway. It was our family friendship with him that helped me be at ease among such personalities.

Of all my parents' hundreds of friends all over the world, none influenced my life as much as Hemingway. Arguably the greatest novelist of the twentieth century, he'd been a close friend of my father's since the early days of "The Lyons Den" in the 1930s. By then, Hemingway had already published *A Farewell to Arms* and *Death in the Afternoon.*

My father had a special relationship with the great writer, forged over years of sharing a table at Toots Shor's or El Morocco or other New York nightspots, plus visits to the Hemingway home in Cuba and frequent correspondence. The famous author trusted my father as he did no other journalist.

In December 1952, when I first met Hemingway, I was eight. We were houseguests at his *finca,* outside Havana in San Francisco de Paola. We'd flown to Havana in a rickety, gray Cubana Airlines DC-3 for the short hop from Miami. Fulgencio Batista ruled Cuba with an iron fist, but left Hemingway alone.

The Hotel Naćional in Havana had European-like wooden shutters on the windows, which seemed out of place in the steamy Caribbean. It had a beautiful view of the harbor and a rock-lined swimming pool. When you're a child, you remember such details.

The next day we were driven to the Hemingway home to spend what would be one of the most memorable days of my young life.

In the spring of 1996, there was an off-Broadway play called *Papa*, starring Len Cariou, in which the gruff Canadian actor portrayed Hemingway. It was set in the living room of the *finca*, reproduced exactly as I remembered it. There was a lion-head rug in the middle of the book-lined den. I took my son Ben backstage, with a family photo of us shot outside the house (page 207), to greet Cariou, an old acquaintance from the Broadway Show League, telling him this was the next best thing to taking Ben to that enchanted place. I remembered the Hemingways' large black poodle named "Blackie," who was blind in one eye but greeted us warmly. Hemingway would bathe that dog's eyes every day. He always used the same soap, so Blackie could follow him by scent.

I also remembered the hordes of six-toed cats, whose descendants still live in the Hemingways' other home, in Key West, Florida. Mary and Ernest were gracious hosts. He'd heard about my brothers and me from my parents and often referred in his letters to us four boys as "The Infield," so he didn't mind us exploring the house. In fact, he encouraged it.

Outside stood the remains of a brick wall riddled with bullet holes. Atop it, at the end of the yard, stood a line of mostly blue and red wine bottles.

"Target practice," Hemingway explained. "From time to time, we have 'visitors.' Bandits and rustlers come down from the hills, so we have to practice with our *escopetas*, our rifles."

Later that afternoon, he and his wife lined up my brothers and me and gave each of us a .22 rifle, inviting us to shatter the colored wine bottles.

We followed Hemingway to a field near the house, and he showed my oldest brother George how to hold his gun. George fired and missed. "You've got to shoot as if whatever is coming toward you is going to kill you if you don't kill it first," the great hunter told George. My brother fired and smashed the bottle, dead center.

Then he told Warren how to aim. "Try and get calm first," he said. "Calm inside, as if you're in a church. When that lion is coming toward you, get something to believe in. Then shoot the sonofabitch."

Warren fired, and he too smashed the distant blue bottle. After lunch we walked outside again in the warm Cuban sun, and Hemingway asked us members of "The Infield" to punch him in his stomach. I took my turn and remember it was like hitting a brick wall. "You have to keep your stomach muscles relaxed in a fight," he said, "but hard and prepared for a surprise blow."

Later that afternoon, George asked the ultimate question: "Mr. Hemingway, how do you write a novel?" As my parents looked on in disbelief, the greatest novelist of the twentieth century began: "You just put everything you've ever known about people into your characters. Then write the sentences as if they're being tattooed on your back." When he saw we didn't quite understand the analogy, he continued: "That'll keep your sentences short and to the point."

A few nights later, the Hemingways took us to a jai alai game, the Cuban indoor sport imported from the Basque region of Spain. It's been called "the fastest sport in the world." With large wicker gloves, a little white ball is whipped around a four-walled court as hard as any baseball I'd ever seen hit. Hemingway wrote something on a piece of paper, wadded it up, and stuffed it into a tennis ball that had one side cut away. Then he tossed it down to the court. "You can bet on the next part of the game," he explained. "I usually lose."

Over the next three years, I read *Death in the Afternoon* and *The Sun Also Rises*, books that would change my life. Then in the summer of 1956, my parents took me on my first trip to Europe. The first stop was Spain.

Francisco Franco was in power, and his *Guardia Civil* roamed the streets and highways toting light machine guns and wearing bandoliers of bullets. Taxis were old Ford sedans from the 1920s, looking like props from a gangster movie. The average cab fare was 15 cents, and Americans were strongly urged not to drink the tap water. In those days, couples on the street just even holding hands were often admonished by policemen.

The day after we arrived, we went to Toledo, the ancient city near Madrid, for sightseeing and a bullfight. My life was about to take a dramatic turn.

The old arena in Toledo is dusty and unbearably hot in July, especially late in the afternoon. I learned that day, and would never forget, that a *corrida*, a bullfight, a spectacle so revered by Hemingway in his writings, is the only thing in Spain that begins on time. At exactly 5 p.m., the bugles sounded, the gates swung open, the *toreros* marched in for the *paseillo*, the opening parade, and the pageant had begun. I remember that two of the matadors were Antonio Bienvenida and Gregorio Sánchez, both of whom, I would later learn, were among the best of their era.

Bullfighting is uniquely Spanish. Americans hate the concept and are right to do so. It *is* cruel. It can be awful. But you cannot know the Spanish psyche without understanding it. Boxing, horse racing, dog rac-

ing, hunting, and, for that matter, fishing are also cruel, but they don't have a direct connection to our culture or our outlook on life the way "the bulls" do in Spain. Those sports don't touch our collective soul. Baseball does, of course, being the quintessential American game. But the art of bullfighting—and, like it or not, it is an art when done well—has always had a connection to the hearts of people in Spain, Mexico, Colombia, Venezuela, Ecuador, and Peru. Top matadors are national heroes.

This is by no means an attempt to justify the ancient ritual. It is indefensible. When performed poorly, it is inexcusable. But it does have an enduring place in those societies.

The next day, Richard Condon, who'd guided us through the intricacies of the *corrida* in Toledo, drove us up to Pamplona, that fabled city in northern Spain made famous by Hemingway's *The Sun Also Rises*. Condon would later write *The Manchurian Candidate* and *Prizzi's Honor,* and all through the drive, he continued to explain "the bulls," as the Spaniards call it. I was fascinated.

It was the first day of the *Féria de San Fermín,* the weeklong festival made world famous by Hemingway, who is honored by a huge bust in the middle of town. The daily *encierro* is the running of that day's bulls through the streets toward the arena. They are moved along by the *cabestros,* the "Judas" steers, so named for leading the bulls to their inevitable death in the afternoon. Thousands of men run alongside them (at that time it was only men), dressed in white shorts, pants, and shoes, with traditional red bandannas around their necks and waists. Most know nothing about how fighting bulls behave, and many are tossed. Many are tourists on a dangerous lark, and a few have gotten killed in the melee. Every July 8, American TV shows the insanity. ESPN used to have blanket coverage.

Big American movies were being filmed

in Spain in those days and afterward. We'd visited Cary Grant and a young Neapolitan starlet named Sophia Loren near Madrid on the set of *The Pride and the Passion,* directed by Stanley Kramer. And later, movies like *King of Kings* and the Clint Eastwood "spaghetti Westerns" would be filmed near Madrid and Almería.

Up in Pamplona, 20th Century-Fox producer Darryl F. Zanuck was shooting the movie version of *The Sun Also Rises.* Ava Gardner, Errol Flynn, Eddie Albert, Tyrone Power, and Mel Ferrer were in town, along with a handsome, young, inexperienced actor portraying "Romero," the matador. His name was Robert Evans, and his wooden acting had been so despised by his costars that he'd nearly been kicked off the picture in the early filming in Morelia, Mexico. That's when Zanuck came down to the set, picked up a bullhorn, and bellowed the six words that, forty-seven years later, would become the title of Evans's memoir and acclaimed documentary: *"The Kid Stays in the Picture."*

That summer, I was still a grade-schooler smitten with my first crush: Alice, Evans's kid sister. We're still friends. Her brother Robert would later become Hollywood's most powerful producer, head of production at Paramount, with hits like *Love Story, Marathon Man,* and *The Godfather,* movies that helped save the studio from being dissolved by its corporate parent, Gulf+Western.

Zanuck's first day of shooting was a disaster since he accidentally shot right into the sun, forgetting that the *encierro* was in the early morning, not late afternoon. But I was forever hooked on Hemingway and bullfighting. Little did I know that five years later I'd spend the first of seven summers touring Spain with Antonio Ordoñez, whose father Cayetano had been the model for Hemingway's matador "Romero."

(Incidentally, the family "business" con-tinues with Ordoñez's grandsons Francisco and Cayetano Rivera Ordoñez, the subjects of a recent *Sixty Minutes* one-hour special called *Blood Brothers.*)

As for Hemingway and Evans, the two met a little over a year later. It was in Yankee Stadium, just before the first pitch of the 1957 World Series. Hemingway was seated in restaurateur Toots Shor's box along the third base line, next to the visiting dugout. It was that magical moment, just before the first pitch. Whitey Ford, the Yankees' ace, was about to toe the rubber and look in to Yogi Berra for the sign. The stadium fell silent in anticipation.

Suddenly a perfectly manicured hand in front of a tailored cuff in front of a tailored arm of a tailored suit reached out in front of Hemingway, obscuring the writer's view. As he shook that hand, the young man on the other end said: "Mr. Hemingway. I'm Robert Evans. I played the matador in *The Sun Also Rises.*"

Hemingway, who'd seen the rough cut of the film, which included Evans's wooden performance, replied: "No, you didn't!"

Two summers later, I returned to Spain, determined to quickly learn Spanish, to facilitate my understanding of bullfighting. My parents found a Madrid family with boys a year older and younger, and I spent the summers of 1958 and 1959 living on their farm in nearby Alcalá de Hanares, one of several Spanish *pueblos* in which Miguel de Cervantes, Spain's greatest writer, was reportedly born.

As the summer of 1961 approached, my father had reminded the Hemingways of my enduring interest in "the bulls." Mary Hemingway called in early June and told us she'd asked the great *matador* Antonio Ordoñez to allow me to travel with him, thus beginning one of the most amazing journeys of my life. It was akin to being a roadie for the Beatles or a batboy for the Red Sox.

It was July 1961. I'd spent two weeks

traveling up and down the Iberian Peninsula with Ordóñez and his *cuadrilla*, his entourage of assistants, when we arrived in Jerez de la Frontera, way down in southern Spain. Ordóñez was at the pinnacle of his fame, adored all across Europe. But at this point, I was just a kid following along; our friendship was just developing.

There was to be a rare nighttime *corrida*, for charity. The *toreros* weren't wearing the traditional *traje de luces,* "the suit of lights," but instead the *traje corto,* the chaps, boots, and short bolero jacket, with a straight broad-brimmed hat and chin strap.

That very day, in Ketchum, Idaho, Mary Hemingway had found her husband's body after his apparent suicide. But not wanting to be the one to inform the world of Hemingway's death, she phoned my father at the Beverly Hills Hotel to ask him to reveal the awful news that the greatest novelist of our time had died.

When we got the news in Spain, Ordóñez was about to face his first bull. He headed to the middle of the arena, ignoring the huge animal off to the side, and knelt on one knee. Then he rose, held aloft his large-brimmed hat, and dedicated the death of the bull to his fallen friend and godfather: Ernest Hemingway, who two years earlier had written *The Dangerous Summer* about the *mano a mano* competition between Ordóñez and his brother-in-law, the suave, handsome Luis Miguel Dominguín. Hemingway, one of the few Americans whose opinion on bullfighting was respected by Spaniards, had anointed Ordóñez the greatest *matador* of them all.

Today, five decades later, Hemingway is considered by some to be a chauvinistic anachronism, a product of his day. But in that time, there was no more charismatic, fascinating presence on earth, a man truly larger than life. And I'll carry our friendship forever.

It was that incredible experience and the subsequent summers in Spain that gave me the confidence to face the challenge of meeting actors, interviewing them, and having them come away impressed with my preparation and eventually eager to return.

I began interviewing on TV several years after I joined WPIX-TV in 1970. They had a midday network show, and several times a week, stars pushing movies came by. Glenda Jackson, Dudley Moore, Milton Berle, Julie Andrews, Liv Ullman, Robert Mitchum, and Sylvester Stallone were some of those interviewed. Then when I joined WNBC, others began coming by, culminating with weekly interviews for *Reel Talk,* my nationally syndicated movie-review show that ran for four seasons and may soon return. I was determined to be the best prepared, thoroughly researched interviewer any actor would ever encounter. Anywhere. Word got around among press agents. The stars came.

The following are compilations of some of the best interviews from the NBC years. The Michael Caine interview combines the half a dozen times he came by over the years.

My son Ben Lyons continues the family tradition, conducting interviews several times a week on the E! Channel's *E! News. Now* I allow myself to think the family tradition is continuing into a third generation.

ANTONIO BANDERAS

Back when I was still doing hotel-room press junket interviews, I was scheduled to be the last one of the day for Antonio Banderas. He must've done forty interviews publicizing *Spy Kids*. I had to find a way to stand out. Realizing I was surely the only journalist there who'd spent many summer afternoons prowling the very bullring in Málaga, Spain, where Banderas had worked as an usher, I came in humming the *pasodoble* played in that old arena, "*Pan y Toros*," or "Bread and Bulls." As I came out of the blinding light, his eyes were open in shock. Then I did the public address announcement from that arena: "*Quinto Toro. Cerveza Victoria. Malagueña y Esquisita.*" The fifth bull. Victoria Beer. Made in Málaga and exquisite. As would be the case with his countrywoman Penélope Cruz, I had a friend for life.

After that, he always came to my set. One interview was in relation to the release of *The Legend of Zorro*, in which he proudly told me he's the first Spanish actor to portray the iconic Latino hero of Old Mexico. I asked him about doing stunts and sword fights. He was forty-five when the movie was made and confided that after a rough day on the set: "I feel pain in the morning, at night, and in the afternoon. I didn't feel that when I was younger. Normally, a sword fight isn't explained in the script. It becomes a longer physical challenge when you shoot it because of the retakes from different angles."

He was careful to prepare for the role by watching the work of previous Zorros, Tyrone Power in 1940's *The Mark of Zorro* and Guy Williams, who starred on the popular TV version in 1957.

"I did that to understand the character," he explained, aware of the extra pressure he faced, being the first Spaniard in the role.

"We had one scene in which my horse had to lean against a wall, like the horse in *Cat Ballou*," he continued, "but we couldn't get it to do that, so they just tipped the camera. My horse, by the way, was really nine horses, so establishing a relationship with each one was difficult."

He began acting on TV in Spain and in movies, most of which weren't seen here. One TV series, in fact, cast him as, of all people, Benito Mussolini. When he came here, he learned his lines phonetically for *The Mambo Kings*. Roles in big, important American films followed. *Assassins, Philadelphia*, and singing superbly as Che Guevara in *Evita* solidified his stardom.

Nevertheless he said he still has "doubts about tomorrow; doubts I had ten years ago. It's always an adventure. You fight for it every day. Nothing changes. I love the fight of this profession and the fight of life itself.

"After sixteen years in America, my happiest time was not in front of a camera, but on Broadway doing *Nine*. If I'd been twenty years old, the possibility of a Spanish actor working in America wouldn't have existed.

Antonio Banderas, who visited Reel Talk *four times, came in to promote* The Legend of Zorro *(2005). At once a throwback to the old swashbuckler type or suave matinee idol, he also happens to be a terrific actor, having honed his craft on the Spanish stage.*

I was absolutely overwhelmed when I came here.

"I remember doing Bertolt Brecht in Spain, and I was arrested because it was so provocative." It helped that his father was a policeman in the early post-Franco years in Málaga and couldn't believe it when young Antonio was brought to his desk. "What're you doing here?" was all he could say. "But he gave me the chance to be an actor, once I realized that my dreams of playing professional *fútbol*—you call it 'soccer'—didn't succeed.

"So after doing street theater in tiny *pueblos* around Málaga, I went up to Madrid with my father's blessings. I was paid five dollars a day and lived in eleven houses. I thought I was going to last fifteen days in Madrid before having to go home."

I interrupted him and asked if he'd ever performed in towns like Ejica, Campillos, or Arriate, where I'd spent parts of the summers with Ordoñez. Banderas doubled over with laughter and nearly fell off the sofa. "It's just that I've never heard any American mention those tiny, tiny *pueblos*," he said.

This onetime street performer, who would look under parked cars for spare change, would come to be honored by King Juan Carlos. His wife, Queen Sofia, noticed Banderas's wife Melanie Griffith's tattoo with his name on her arm. "The Queen turned to the King and said: 'Juanni, why don't you get one of those?'" He laughed. "I'd never seen the King in person before. Only on the money. Now we dine with them every year in Majorca because my brother is a competitive sailor who bought the King's boat.

"Then another time I came into a room and my wife was on the phone. She covered the receiver and said: 'I'm talking to the King!' Can you imagine!?"

Although he's an international movie star with half a dozen films completed, in production, or "announced," he remains true to the roots of his craft.

"My roots are in the theater," he told me. "When I was a young actor, I learned quickly that sometimes the audience applauds, and other times they want to stone you. I remember being in the wings the opening night of *Nine* thinking: 'Oh my God. This is in *English*! And it's a *musical*! On *Broadway*!'

"Theater is a dialogue with the audience. It's the only thing that will remain years from now that's really pure."

Banderas and his wife divide their time between New York and Los Angeles and often visit Spain, of course. Adjusting to life in America came easily, but it wasn't overnight. "Everything in LA is masks, metaphors, unreality," he said. "Everyone's so concerned with image here. But America is many Americas." He showed just how much he understands about other parts of the country with his intelligent direction of *Crazy in Alabama* in 1999.

"I do miss the culture of Spain when I'm here," he said. "The flamenco, the rest of the culture. But the combination of living in both countries is very important in my life."

Director Robert Rodriguez put him in starring roles in his popular films like *Desperado* and the *Spy Kids* franchise. Like Penélope Cruz's relationship with Pedro Almodóvar, Banderas would probably drop everything to work in another Rodriguez-directed project.

"One thing I learned doing the *Spy Kids* movies," he recalled "was from Ricardo Montalbán. Not from anything he said, but just by observing how he handled his stardom. He was in pain and in a wheelchair, but he always had a beautiful smile for actors like me who'd complain about the heat or whatever. I never forgot that."

JAVIER BARDEM

I interviewed Javier Bardem several times, including on his promotion tour for the superb *The Sea Inside* and the routine *Goya's Ghost*.

Born in the Canary Islands, he liked it that I spoke Spanish, and with his every visit to my set, I noted a vast improvement to his English.

Once he became an actor, Bardem used what is surely the most unusual method of learning English: he played recordings of the heavy metal groups AC/DC and Metallica, along with the Rolling Stones and Pearl Jam. He also subscribes to a unique religion: "I don't believe in God, I believe in Al Pacino," he explained.

"When I close my eyes, I pray to Al Pacino," he continued. "He's the best actor in the world. I had the chance to meet him, and when you adore someone so much you're scared of being disappointed, but he's a great person. I could barely speak. I was shaking. He didn't know my work. Of course not." It's fair to say, however, that since Bardem's Oscar-winning performance in *No Country for Old Men*, that's changed. Pacino knows Bardem's work now.

Bardem, now married to Penélope Cruz, divides his time between Madrid and Los Angeles, but he has a bit of a problem when living here. "I don't know how to drive," he confessed. "I walk. I get stopped walking around in LA.

"I like directors who work quickly," he said. "I once worked with a director who did something like thirty takes of every scene. I had to open a door thirty times. But I'm like a fourth- or fifth-take actor. Certainly not a one-take actor like Sinatra."

The actor is meticulous in describing his profession. "Don't call me an actor," he said. "Call me a worker." In *The Sea Inside*, Bardem portrayed Ramón Sampedro, a quadriplegic confined for decades to a hospital bed, who waged a fight to legalize euthanasia. "I had to spend most of three months in that bed," he recalled. "I couldn't sleep much of the time. You never get used to it."

The makeup for the role, in which he looked twenty years older, took almost six hours a day. Then there was the problem of Sampedro's Galician accent, different from the Spanish the Canary Island–born actor speaks.

"Every country has an accent people make fun of. I had to learn that Galician accent." To prepare for the role, he watched documentaries about the real man. "I wanted to go beyond imitation to try to grab the essence, the soul of the man."

Bardem comes from a family of actors, but he doesn't take his success for granted. "One day you're up, next day you're not," he said. "You cannot manage the consequences of your work."

CATE BLANCHETT

It doesn't happen often, but sometimes a big star you hadn't interviewed before has such charisma and radiates such charm that you're instantly put at ease, as if you're about to chat with an old friend and don't have to prove yourself. Such was the case with Cate Blanchett, who came to my set to promote *Elizabeth, The Golden Age,* a historical sequel to *Elizabeth,* which she'd filmed nine years earlier. She is extremely down-to-earth, unpretentious, and outgoing—rare qualities for an Oscar winner.

"The culture of England was really crystallized under her reign," she began, showing that she'd done research before learning her lines. "She never married, which was important, since it allowed her to concentrate on her role as Queen. She stabilized her reign. And what a time it was! The age of exploration and Shakespeare."

I reminded her of several scenes in the movie in which she had no dialogue but was on camera a lot. "I love scenes with no dialogue," she laughed. "A screenplay is a malleable sort of thing. You can think about dialogue that's been cut."

I asked her about picking up a portrayal of the same historical figure nine years later. "You don't want to go in the opposite direction just because you did it in an earlier role," she explained. "Where do you begin the second time is the most difficult part of such a challenge." In the role she had to wear some uncomfortable wigs. "Celine Dion has ninety wigs for her Las Vegas act," she laughed. "I think I can manage. Mutton dressed as lamb, as the old saying goes."

Then I asked her about doing an American accent, albeit such a curious one as Katharine Hepburn's, in *The Aviator,* which won her a supporting actress Oscar. "I grew up in Australia," she said. "That's about halfway between American and English.

Growing up, Alan Alda was sort of my substitute father. I watched him on *M*A*S*H* every week. Then we got to work together in *The Aviator.*"

Just before our interview, the story broke about an extra who'd been fired for revealing plot developments in *Indiana Jones and the Kingdom of the Crystal Skull,* in which she costarred. "The franchise is so loved, so the curiosity is understandable," she said diplomatically. "It felt strange, almost *Zelig*-like being on the set that first day. It's such a great franchise, you sense a responsibility to the fans."

Our talk returned to her portrayal of Elizabeth. "You have to be technical at the beginning and at the end. No one wants to see your homework at the end of the day. You can do so much research on Elizabeth I: what she achieved, who she was, but in the end you have to inhabit the character as depicted in the script. I'd seen earlier Elizabeths by Bette Davis, Glenda Jackson, and Flora Robson, and pictures of Sarah Bernhardt."

An underappreciated Blanchett movie is *Veronica Guerin,* as the real-life Irish journalist who was murdered after exposing drug dealers. In one scene, she gets the stuffing beaten out of her by one of the gangsters, and I asked her about the morning that scene was filmed.

"Gerard McSorley was the actor," she recalled, "and he can be terrifying. I thought I could dodge his punch, so I told him just to fire away; and somehow he hit me sooner than I thought and caught me right in the nose. I went flying, and they used that take. Doing that scene I learned you can't pre-empt emotions. You have to be in a neutral space, in comedy or drama. If you're too tense, you'll close down."

I asked if she's still in touch with her old drama coach. "Yes, and we talk about other things, too," she said. "You become a peer as you evolve."

Sir Michael Caine, in town to promote Secondhand Lions *(2003), gives you the sense that he can't wait to tell you wonderful stories. Besides acting, he should give lessons to actors on how to be interviewed.*

MICHAEL CAINE

I first interviewed Michael Caine in 1984 when he was still wearing those thick, black-frame glasses he made popular in *The Ipcress File* as gumshoe Harry Palmer. I've since interviewed him about ten times, more than any other actor. The incredible thing about him is that he always makes you think you're his first and only interview. No two stories are alike, and every time we've met, he manages to come up with some anecdote, some incident or observation, he's never made before.

He is one of those rare people you'd want to sit next to on a transatlantic flight, staying awake and talking all through the night. Caine is the litmus test against which all other actors' skills in interviews should be judged.

Michael Caine was born Maurice Joseph Micklewhite, Jr. in the impoverished area of East London. His father was a porter in a fish market, and young Maurice, named after his father, left school at fifteen, with no skills, but bearing the Cockney accent. That would become his trademark all through his rise to international fame, eventually landing him the nickname: "The Cockney Cary Grant." But first came service

in the British Army, in the Royal Fusiliers, where at eighteen he saw combat in the Korean War.

He hasn't often spoken about his war experiences, but he did with me.

"We were shipped out," he recalled, "and didn't know where we were headed. We ran into some French troops in a bar in Colombo, Ceylon. It was on a stopover, and they didn't know where they were going, either. Then someone said: 'Korea,' and we still didn't know where that was." His unit survived an ambush.

When he returned to London, he got a job as an assistant stage manager before getting a small role, billed tenth, in *Morning Departure*, which starred John Mills.

An early film was *A Hill in Korea*. "They didn't like me as an actor," he recalled. "They thought I'd make a good technical advisor. They paid me a lousy wage and never took any notice of what I said. And the battle scenes are terrible."

Eventually it was *Zulu*, in 1964, that began his starring career. By that time, he'd accumulated a long résumé of work on television and in the theater. "I appeared in 125 TV shows in seven years in the UK. All live," he recalled. "I played the lead in a three-hour ten-minute play. British actors take pride in memorizing, even for TV. No cue cards. When we had to do a retake, I asked how long my speech was, and I was told seven minutes twenty-eight seconds. So I knew I could still memorize my lines.

"My job is to hide the machinery of the acting," he told me. "Acting is the only thing I can do." In *Zulu*, billed fifth, he portrayed Lieutenant Gonville Bromhead, an aristocratic army officer.

"The challenge," he recalled, "was to portray an upper-crust chap. I'm very good at observing people and noticed that powerful people, like Prince Charles, for example, don't gesticulate. They don't wave their hands when they speak, because they're used to being the center of attention and don't need to wave about to get you to listen to them. Another thing is how people hold their hands.

"Actors often don't know what to do with their hands. They put them on their hips. They fold their arms. They hold the lapels on their coat or jacket. I noticed that rich people often walked with their hands behind their back, since they're used to having doors opened for them. So that's what I did in *Zulu*. There I was, walking about the army camp under siege, with my hands behind my back, as if I'm waiting for a door to be opened for me!"

During the filming of the movie, a cable arrived from the studio. It was from one of the producers: "Get rid of actor playing 'Lieutenant Bromhead.' Doesn't know what to do with his hands."

That part propelled him past other young actors of the so-called "Angry Young Man" generation, who arose after the war. He could now begin to afford some of life's luxuries.

"I could never afford driving lessons, much less a car," he recalled. "I was broke in my twenties and making about thirty pounds a week. My mates were making good money. They were factory workers and printers and worked only two or three nights a week. But it was steady. They ignored me because I couldn't buy a drink in the pub. But I was a millionaire by the time I was thirty-two.

"I didn't learn to drive until I was fifty, but I wanted to show off my success. So I bought a Rolls-Royce when I was thirty-two, even though I couldn't drive it. I walked into the showroom, and the snooty salesman didn't believe this guy with a Cockney accent could afford any car, much less one of theirs. So I told him: 'This time next week, I'm going to ride by your showroom in my new Rolls-Royce that I'm buying from someone else down the street and

I'm going to give you the finger.' And that's just what I did!"

By this time, he'd gotten roles on British television and with repertory stage companies and, just as important, changed his name. His agent had booked him for an audition with an hour's notice to come up with his acting name. So Maurice Micklewhite sat at a sidewalk café near a movie theater showing *The Caine Mutiny*, and the name "Caine" appealed to him. "If I'd had a different table," he joked to me, "my name might've become 'Michael Mutiny.'"

Years later, he would be knighted under his real name, to honor his father, just to hear the Queen say: "Arise, Sir Maurice Micklewhite."

When he was knighted, the band played the theme song of his old outfit, The Royal Fusiliers. We know it as "The Colonel Bogey March," the music first made popular when it was whistled in *The Bridge on the River Kwai*. The words, however, make scatological fun of Hitler, Himmler, Goering, and Goebbels, so only the music became famous. It was considered too raunchy for 1957 audiences. As for the Queen, known for unintentional gaffes at such ceremonies, she said to him: "I understand you've been doing this for quite some time."

Caine told me he merely said: "Yes, Ma'am," resisting the temptation, lest she withdraw the honor, to say: "And so have *you*!" He is certain that if he had said that, he'd have been tossed into the Tower of London.

"What you notice about the Queen," he recalled, "is that the lowlier the person being honored, the more time she spends with them. That day I saw a woman who'd been cleaning Buckingham Palace for years get an Order of the British Empire from her. The Queen spent lots of time talking with her. The people getting knighted? She just told them to rise, shook their hands, and kind of quickly pushed them away. She called me 'Mr. Caine,' and I thought that would be the last time I was called 'Mr. Caine.'"

Caine loves to talk about his profession, and has written and taped a definitive book and DVD on the craft, *Michael Caine on Acting*. "No serious actor goes into the profession hoping to be a movie star," said this movie star who's made more than 100 films and who, along with Gene Hackman, was the most prolific star of his time. "Doing Ibsen in Poughkeepsie in plus fours? That's a real actor. And working with great actors makes you great." Caine's father had given him good advice: "'Never take a job where you can be replaced by a machine.' But now," he laughed at the irony, "we have computerized animated movies."

It was *Alfie*, the rake's rake, that made him an international star in 1966. "She was in beautiful condition," he would say in the movie, about his costar Shelley Winters. It became a bit of a watchword after that, in one of the revered films of the sexual revolution.

Away from the cameras, he continued to wear his now-trademark Harry Palmer glasses, and this attracted the attention of a giant of Hollywood's Golden Age of silent films, Harold Lloyd. "He saw me in *The Ipcress File*," Caine recalled, "and when he came to London, we had dinner together at The White Elephant and became great friends. He told me I was the first leading man since him to wear glasses. He liked that."

Caine mentors younger actors. You can see that in his DVD. Each twenty-something actor assumes the role of "Alfie Elkins," then he steps in and shows why he created a sensation back in 1966. "I try to inhabit a role," he said. "You have to make a decision at the beginning of the film. Am I going to be Michael Caine or the character?"

In his instructional video, he explains how an actor should focus on the outside eye of the person opposite him, i.e., the one closer to the camera, and not to blink excessively, lest one convey a sense of weakness. "Unless you're Hugh Grant," he laughed. "His panicky delivery is perfect for him."

Caine is also keenly aware of how far he has come. He once returned to his old slum neighborhood in East London, for he'd heard that the house where he was born was being torn down, or as the British say: "Pulled down."

"As I was standing there, a little old man walked by, looking for his house for the same reason. He told me he was born nearby. Then I realized it was Charlie Chaplin. I came back a few weeks later, and there he was again. I don't know if he recognized me, but all he said was: 'This street was filled with Irishmen.'

"My worst fear as a young actor was having one line in a big scene and blowing it," he joked. "Every prop, every extra, all the stars are in place in some war picture, for example," he joked. "The director calls 'Action!' and you get your close-up and blurt out: 'The Germans are *clombing*'! I was terrified of doing that."

Unlike many stars, whenever Caine begins a new movie he's careful to introduce himself to young actors. "I once was a young actor," he explained. "And everyone treated me like dirt."

To young actors he advises: "Know what you're thinking when you're not thinking. Work by instinct. Don't think and your lines will come to you. I once was onstage as a young actor and sulked in the corner with no dialogue for ten minutes. The director spotted that and asked me what I was doing. 'You've got nothing to say in the scene?' he asked, knowing full well I didn't have any lines. 'You've got wonderful things to say but have decided not to say them. Sit there and do that.'"

Caine went to Hollywood to make his first American movie, *Gambit*, with Shirley

MacLaine, who'd chosen him. She showed him around, and introduced the young star to everyone. Then, a day or so before he was to return home, he was standing with a friend in the lobby of his hotel in Beverly Hills when a tourist approached him.

"Michael Caine!" she gasped. "I'm so glad I got to meet you. We're from Iowa, and my husband and I have been here a week and we're leaving today and we didn't get to see one movie star until now. What a thrill!"

She then turned to Caine's friend and said: "Isn't it amazing how you can try for a week to see a movie star and have no luck, then when you least expect it, you run into Michael Caine!"

"Yes, quite amazing," smiled the other man: Cary Grant.

For two decades, Caine vied with Gene Hackman for the most screen roles. "Except for Gérard Depardieu," he laughed. "I haven't seen a French film in the last twenty-five years he wasn't in."

After reaching the pinnacle of his profession and winning Oscars for *Hannah and Her Sisters* and *The Cider House Rules*, Caine still has great enthusiasm for his work. "Whenever I get a script I like, I scream: 'I got it!'" he said, with all the enthusiasm of a young leading man who's just landed his first big role.

Caine recalled the time he was working in a small theater in London with only twenty-two people in the audience. "But one of them was Orson Welles," he said. "I knew that laugh. Sure enough, he came backstage and we decided to do the movie version of *The Dresser*. But Albert Finney and Tom Courtenay already had signed on for it by then. That became the best movie I never got to make."

For years, Caine was also in the restau-rant business in London. "I'm the customer from hell," he recalled. "I'll get someone fired only for one thing: If I ever see a waiter looking at his watch in front of customers."

When he needed to do a Texas accent in *Secondhand Lions* and a New England accent in *The Cider House Rules*, he was asked if he could affect the appropriate accents. "Ask an actor if he can fly a plane for a role and he'll say yes and then rush to take flying lessons," said Caine, who won an Oscar for the latter role. "Vivien Leigh taught me the key to speaking American English: Keep repeating 'Four door Ford. Four door Ford.'"

He's keenly aware of the difference between acting here and in England. "British actors make talking pictures," he explained. "American actors make moving pictures. We have the theater and films in the same city. You're always getting playwrights writing movies and you get loads and loads of dialogue. Here in America, the theater is in New York and films in Los Angeles so you get more action films here."

When Caine began to get starring roles, his mother, who'd been a charwoman all her life, said she'd been on a bus and sat next to "a real lady." Her son, by that time a millionaire, asked: "How'd you know that?"

"She spoke with a fancy accent and had lots of jewelry," replied Mrs. Micklewhite.

"Mom, I know a lot of ladies who talk like that and believe me they're not real ladies," he replied. "You're a real lady." Then he told me: "I bought her a lot of jewelry the next day. Oh, and a house." His mother, flabbergasted, asked him how much he made for each film. "A million pounds," he replied. "How much is that?" she asked.

John Wayne once told Caine to "talk low and **don't** say much." "So I spent the next ten years talking in a high voice and speaking quickly."

GEORGE CARLIN

I miss George Carlin. I really do. Though he was seventy-one when he died in June 2008, he had so much more to give us; so much more laughter, so many pompous people to deride, so many challenges to throw out at us. The best cure for these feelings of loss is simply to go to YouTube, and there he is, anytime, to make you laugh and get you to think. And one last book, an autobiography called *Last Words,* was published in 2009.

"Nothing scares me," he said in one of the four interviews I conducted with him. "I root for the end of everything. I enjoy watching this society, this culture, destroy itself. It's circling in a drain, and it's fun to watch the circles get smaller and faster. So I view it from a safe emotional distance.

"A long time ago, I detached myself out beyond the Kuiper Belt, beyond Neptune and the other planets, looking at all of this and saying 'Aren't they interesting!'

"When you're born, you're given a ticket to the freak show. When you're born in America, you're given a front-row seat. I love watching the show and commenting on it. The last thing we should be doing is sending our grotesquely disfigured DNA out beyond this biosphere to another environment. It's bad enough. Keep it here. The solar system has already been selected."

Carlin hosted the first *Saturday Night Live* in 1975. "They knew SNL was breaking new ground," he recalled, "even though it had been shunted off to after the news hour. It was irreverent sketch humor on a network. But it was a good time for it, for it gave it a feeling of being outside the boundaries.

"There were two turning points for me. One was a major thing which was very visible to people. I grew up as a kid fighting regulation, authority, religion, and structure. I was kind of like a little outlaw. And I got kicked out of everything; I didn't quit. I wanted to be like Danny Kaye, but I didn't realize that to be like him you had to be mainstream and please people. And that's what the culture was structured for, in the late 'fifties.

"The first half of the 'sixties I was out there in a suit and tie, and the culture changed beneath my feet, and I suddenly realized I was in the wrong place.

"I was thirty, the kids were twenty, their fathers were forty. The fathers were in the nightclubs. I was entertaining their fathers. I belonged entertaining the kids. That was a big switch in 1970. I once performed to no people at a Baltimore nightclub. It was called The Blue 'something.' On July 4th in the early 'sixties. It was a brand-new nightclub. Some animal that was blue. Eight-thirty came around, and there was no one there.

"The manager said 'Show time.' But if somebody comes, I want him or her to think there's a show going on. So the waitresses and the bartender enjoyed it. The band knows what's funny. Especially the jazz guys.

"My father was given his hat early in the relationship. He was the national ad manager of the *New York Sun,* the *New York Post,* and the *Philadelphia Bulletin.* He won the 1935

George Carlin, who came to my Reel Talk *set to plug one of his hilarious books, was one of the most brilliant monologists of our time. He pointed out the absurdities of everyday life. His books are among the funniest ever written.*

Dale Carnegie public speaking prize at the Waldorf-Astoria Hotel. My mother could tell you a story that occurred on her trip on the Broadway bus. She could do all the voices and come up with a punch line. She said she belonged on the stage.

"'Inner city,' 'Urban.' Those euphemisms are an ugly way to avoid the truth. Things like 'Thank you for not smoking,' instead of 'No smoking.' We're thanking people for not giving us a tumor by using a euphemism. 'Do not disturb' became 'privacy please.' Room service became 'in room dining.' You collect them and group them. It's a way for us not to recognize the ugliness we have created. 'Final destination' is another one. All destinations are 'final.' That's where the word 'destiny' comes from."

I concluded every interview with Carlin by asking him to retell the story of his days as a morning disc jockey at KJOA, in Shreveport, Louisiana. "I was the morning DJ, the drive-time guy," he recalled, beginning to smile at the recollection.

"But one morning, I overslept, and didn't get behind the mike until about eight. I knew the boss was listening, so I flicked the switch and said: '. . . tly cloudy and high in the seventies. We've been having some technical problems all morning, friends, but I think we've cleared them up.'"

GEORGE CLOONEY

People often compare stars of different eras. I think it's mostly a waste of time; different movies, mores, demands on an actor, whatever. With two exceptions: Penélope Cruz is the Sophia Loren of our time, and if there is a Clark Gable of our time, for my money it's George Clooney. He exudes charisma so effortlessly that if you'd never heard of him, or if there were no such thing as movies or television, you'd nevertheless come away knowing you'd met someone special.

I've interviewed him twice. The first time was in 1996 for that preposterous Batman movie, but much more important was the day in 2005 when he came to my set promoting *Good Night, and Good Luck*, one of the most important films of the decade.

It depicted how, in the early days of television, Edward R. Murrow stood up to the vicious attacks by reactionary Senator Joseph McCarthy (R-Wisc.) and helped bring him down. Clooney portrayed Murrow's executive producer Fred Friendly, fighting not only McCarthy but his CBS network boss, William S. Paley.

"When I started working on it, there was a lot of revisionist history about that

George Clooney came in to Reel Talk *to promote* Good Night, and Good Luck *(2005) and is one of the nicest, most intelligent actors I've ever known. His dream job was the play center field for his Cincinnati Reds.*

episode. People were saying McCarthy was right. I decided it was time to recalibrate. First of all, McCarthy wasn't right.

"It wasn't what he was saying," he continued. "It was his methods, which didn't let you face your accuser. That was a huge chip away at the Constitution."

Clooney was careful to double source as much of the dialogue and events depicted as possible, and I asked him whether, if he ever does another historical drama, this is the standard to which he'll adhere.

"Right now, it's a popular thing to marginalize the entire piece. This one required great responsibility. I wanted this movie to remind us about the debate. It's almost a newsreel, and we decided to use real footage of McCarthy rather than an actor. Sure he's way over the top, but that's how he really was.

"Look, I'm a fairly outspoken liberal, but I'm also a good friend of conservatives. Remember, it was conservatives who brought him down. The struggle between McCarthy and Murrow was a long war between two gladiators, and both men atrophied in their own places."

David Strathairn, the respected actor, portrayed Murrow, but on the first day of shooting announced he not only wasn't a chain-smoker like Murrow, but hated smoking.

"Hearing that scared the hell out of me," Clooney recalled. "But once we got rolling, he smoked fifty cigarettes a day. We filmed it in color, because it's easier to light than black-and-white, and then we took the color out. I wanted the words to get the job done, not the camera."

Clooney once said he didn't want to be sixty-five and worrying what some casting director thinks of him.

"It's more fun to do other things," is the way he explained his desire to direct movies as well as star in them.

Right before he hit it big as "Dr. Doug Ross" on ER, someone wrote that he could be headed to "Jack Scalia-ville," a reference to a "B" actor. Clooney said that "if ER had been on Friday or Saturday nights instead of Thursday nights, I wouldn't have become a movie star. That may not be true of other actors, but that show made me a star. We had 40 million people watching us back then, just before the explosion of added stations."

We spoke of his late uncle George, who drank hard, piloted a B-17 in World War II, and dated a Miss America. His last words about his own life were: "What a waste." I wondered if there was a movie about his life worth considering.

Clooney's illustrious family includes his famous aunt, Rosemary Clooney, and her ex-husband, Oscar-winning actor José Ferrer.

"I was cutting tobacco for a living in a factory in Kentucky and didn't know my uncle José nor [his cousin] Miguel very well. Then in 1982, they were making a movie down by where we lived, and they thought I should drop everything, move out to LA, and try acting. So I did."

By the way, that movie was called *And They're Off*, but the producers were convicted of embezzlement and went to jail.

Success didn't come easily, and Clooney made a string of pilots that never panned out before he began to get work in shows like *Sisters* and then *ER*. He even auditioned five times for *Thelma & Louise*.

"Pretty boy Brad Pitt got that role, and I sulked a few years before I watched it. And you know what? They were right."

He also auditioned for a two-line role in *Guarding Tess*, which starred Nicolas Cage and, as a widowed former First Lady, Shirley MacLaine.

"There was this great chasm between TV and movies," he recalled. "Years after Mc-Queen and Eastwood had bridged it, it was still there to an extent. I couldn't get in to auditions," he said. "I was under contract to Les Moonves, and I got a role on a show called *Sunset Beat*. My character was an undercover cop masquerading as a biker named 'Chic Chesbro,'" he laughed.

Clooney's father Nick was a popular anchorman in Cincinnati, but George knew it wouldn't be his calling. He did have a tryout with the Cincinnati Reds as an outfielder, and quickly got the same message there as well.

"You can teach hitting," he explained. "You can teach fielding; how to catch a ball and get a good route to it. But you can't teach speed. If you're hoping to be signed as a center fielder, you can't bounce the throw to the cutoff man."

I asked him which he'd rather hear: "From NBC News World Headquarters in New York, this is NBC Nightly News with George Clooney." Or: "And the Oscar goes to George Clooney" (which he did hear the following year). Or: "Fly ball left field, *home run*! George Clooney hit the first pitch out of the park, and the Reds win the World Series!"

"I only lacked talent for being a baseball player or a broadcasting job. A 'walk-off' homer is a great feeling."

And he left it there.

PENÉLOPE CRUZ

I'll never forget the first time I met Penélope Cruz. Who could? She was and is astonishingly beautiful in a unique way; sort of a reincarnation of Sophia Loren, only a Spanish version, with the same fiery charisma that could light up a room. And that smile! She was just twenty-four and had completed her first American movie.

The film was *The Hi-Lo Country*, one of those movies trying desperately to be compelling. But you sensed it would quickly find a comfortable spot in the back of film anthologies and be seen only by critics and a few others. There was no buzz at all about it. I still have the message pad with the logo of the movie on it, knowing that when such items are included in the press materials, the film is usually a dud.

That insight proved correct, but her bit role stood out. We all know where it's led: an Oscar, several nominations, and international superstardom in several languages.

She walked into my studio at WNBC, looking nervous. She had a small role in the movie, the tempestuous girlfriend (they knew even then how to cast her) of Billy Crudup's character. But unlike countless other young starlets I'd interviewed, there was a special aura about Cruz.

I sensed her fear at doing an interview in English, and I thought of my father, the first American journalist to meet Sophia Loren forty-two years earlier. It was in Spain where Loren, then twenty-three and also acting in English for the first time, was filming *The Pride and the Passion* with Cary Grant and Frank Sinatra. My father warned her about the intrusive questioning she'd face in America: questions about her marriage to producer Carlo Ponti, half her height and more than twice her age.

I suddenly began speaking to Cruz in her own dialect, Castilian Spanish, and her eyes—now so famous and the envy of

Penélope Cruz dropped by Reel Talk *to promote the American release of* Volver *(2006), the fourth time she'd come to my set. Her beauty and grace are matched only by her dignity. She makes acting look effortless.*

women everywhere—opened almost to the size of doorknobs. I'd made a friend for life. We got through that interview, and, to reassure her, I interviewed her in Spanish for Telemundo. Since then each time we've met, her English has improved at an astonishing rate. Although she still has a Spanish accent—purring her Rs is its signature—she has an amazing English vocabulary, and her syntax is perfect.

At this point in her career, if Cruz were somehow able to speak with no accent, it wouldn't be the actress the world now adores. It would be a contrivance. That's part of her unmatched allure. Nevertheless, she told me she keeps working on it. "The more I work on it, the more I can find English names for things that are diverse. I learned my lines for my first English-language movie phonetically, so I missed information during the filming.

"I always try to pick up things around the set, and I couldn't do that on that movie. I always like to hear what people are saying about how I'm doing. I remember hiding in the bathroom and crying at the frustration of not understanding what they were saying."

Her mentor, Pedro Almodóvar, spoke with me about his movies with Cruz. "My movies couldn't have been made during the Franco regime. I afforded her the chance to expand her craft before different demands of English-language movie roles came her way."

"Pedro Almodóvar is the reason I decided to become an actress," she told me. "He's my priority. I'd begun studying to be a dancer like my sister. I know Pedro better than almost anyone. I even knew his mother. I think of her when I'm working in his movies. She was an amazing woman I adored.

"I remember when Pedro received a medal from King Juan Carlos, she was crying, remembering how worried she was when he quit his job at the telephone company because she thought it was safe and steady. She was terrified."

Away from the cameras, she knows how to live the proper life of a movie star: dignified, private, out of the tabloids, not often photographed, especially with her husband, Javier Bardem. Just doing some of the finest screen work of any actress of her generation.

JUDI DENCH

Of all the actresses ever to be "damed" by the Queen, none has worn the title with more grace and elegance than Judi Dench. At the same time, she exudes humility. She quickly put me at ease, in the first of what would be three in-depth interviews. The movie that brought her to New York was *Shakespeare in Love,* for which she won the Oscar for supporting actress, portraying Queen Elizabeth I. This was 1998, when I was still doing "junket" interviews, waiting for hours with other journalists for a few minutes with the star. It doesn't matter to the studio publicists how big your TV station is, how many more viewers you have than smaller market journalists; everyone gets the same amount of time. In and out.

After the usual questions about the movie, I ended the interview with a question that would solidify our acquaintance for years, for it was something no one had ever asked her. I reminded her about her debut on TV in a long-forgotten English series called *Hilda Lessways,* and I wondered about acting under the steamy lights of that era of television.

Her eyes lit up, and she said: "Do we have time for a story about that show?" Without looking at the young woman with the clipboard, walkie-talkie, and stopwatch, I of course said that we had *plenty* of time.

"It was 1959," she said, "and it was live TV. There was one moment when I had to run across the studio and appear on the stairs, and the camera came right up to me. Just then, my skirt fastener broke, and all I was wearing was a blouse! Luckily the camera didn't catch that. Then one character named George Gannon, asks me to marry him. 'I'll think about it' was my reply.

"After we went off the air, my father, a doctor, rang me up from York and said: 'Mummy and I are thrilled, of course. Now, we know it's just a story, but that George

Gannon character is a cad. Be careful of him!'"

On her subsequent visits to New York, I'd leave a message for her with her press agent: "*Hilda Lessways'* biggest New York fan eagerly awaits you on my set at NBC." And she would indeed come to my set on several occasions. Then my son Ben, the film critic/interviewer for the E! Channel, interviewed her in November 2009 for her role in the movie version of *Nine,* and as his last question, brought up her part on *Hilda Lessways.* Not having made the association between me and another journalist named "Lyons," she nearly shot out of her chair, turned, and saw me in the back of the room mouthing "That's my son," and burst out laughing.

I picked her 2005 movie, *Mrs. Henderson Presents,* as the best film of the year. She played a previously little-known, real-life London theatrical producer, a rich, feisty widow, who bought a run-down theater called The Windmill, renovated it, and re-opened it. She kept her theater going despite the Blitz during the Battle of Britain. Then, to boost the box office and attract the young soldiers, she put on nude reviews to great acclaim.

"Everyone knew about the theater, of course, but not about her. Only about her producer, Vivian Van Damm, played so well by Bob Hoskins," she said. Dame Judi spent years on the London stage and in British TV before 1995's *GoldenEye,* in which she played the new "M," propelled her to international screen stardom. When I asked her about portraying Laura Henderson, who initially exudes boredom over a montage with no dialogue, she said she relied on her stage acting.

"Lena Olin, that wonderful actress, put it best. 'You can always recognize a stage actor because they're unspoiled about their approach to the work. They just do the work with no fuss.' I'd like that on my tomb-

In her third interview with me, Dame Judi Dench came by in November 2005 to talk about the delightful Mrs. Henderson Presents. *She commands a screen, as she did for decades on the London stage.*

stone, along with the words, 'and laughed a lot as well.'

"I didn't have a hankering to do much movie acting until Harvey Weinstein [the producer] suggested we do *Mrs. Brown* as a movie, not on TV as originally planned. So there I was on the big screen after thirty-eight years of mostly doing stage work."

She won an Olivier Award, the English equivalent of the Tony Award, for *Absolute Hell,* a drama, as well as for the musical *A Little Night Music,* in the same year. "It was satisfying," she recalled, "but you'll always meet someone who didn't care for one or the other. When that happens, it's always a shock, but I say: 'Sorry, I'll try harder next time.'"

As for her years doing Shakespeare, she mused: "I just wish he'd written more roles for seventy-year-old women."

I wondered about her most embarrassing moment in the theater. It came when she wasn't onstage but in the audience, at a production of an old comedy called *Cuckoo in the Nest.* "I laughed so hard Mummy had to take me out of the theater after the first act, and I had to come back later to see the rest of it."

As I do for every actor knighted, or in her case "damed," I asked what her memories were of that great day. "I was in a room with a sergeant at arms and seven men about to be honored as well. One asked if he could smoke.

"'No,' I said. 'You may not. But you may play the piano if you like.'"

CLINT EASTWOOD

One afternoon when Clint Eastwood was growing up in Northern California during the Depression, a man came by the family's back door. He offered to chop wood in exchange for a meal. The boy never forgot that. That memory is part of what propelled him to his incredible success; a determination never to have to chop wood for a sandwich.

When Eastwood enters a room, he fills it with a unique presence. Suddenly, it's cooler.

He came to my set in 2008 to appear on *Reel Talk* promoting *Gran Torino, Changeling,* which he directed, and *Invictus,* then in pre-production. Tall, with a slightly high waist and a gait that's part of his trademark persona, he still has a boyish grin. If you knew nothing of his stature as a living American movie icon, or if you'd lived in some unimaginable corner of the earth where he was unknown, you'd know "someone" had just walked in, even if it was *The Man with No Name.* He has that effect.

The most surprising thing about Eastwood is his self-effacing nature. "I can ham it up as much as the next person," he said, "but on screen, less can be more." It's no accident that the first movie he saw as a child was *Sergeant York* starring Gary Cooper, an actor he would come to idolize. As with the stoic Cooper, many of his roles were the strong, silent type. Inevitable comparisons to John Wayne are frequent.

"His performance in *The Searchers* is sensational," Eastwood said. "We talked about working together. I knew him socially and used to play tennis with his wife. I was a young guy, and he thought that maybe I'd come along in his boots, because I also came up in the same genre, the Western."

But Wayne had just seen an Eastwood movie, 1973's *High Plains Drifter,* and didn't care for it. "I told him it's an allegory.

Every Western doesn't have to be a pioneer story." Wayne disagreed, and they never worked together.

After a stint in the Army in the early 1950s, the San Francisco native worked as a swimming instructor, a lumberjack, and drove a truck bringing supplies to the Universal lot. "I was going to Los Angeles Community College after I'd gotten out of the Army and a buddy was going to acting classes downtown," he recalled.

"He convinced me to go, saying there were great-looking girls there. It's surprising what kind of motivation will get you into a career. The class had thirty girls and four guys, and I thought: 'This class needs *me!*'"

He got a contract at Universal and paid his dues in small roles in "B" pictures for eighteen months—movies like *Revenge of the Creature* and *Tarantula.* Yet he always lived according to his acting teacher's mantra: "Don't just do something! Stand there!" He also quickly learned another important acting lesson: Sometimes an actor can say a lot without any dialogue.

It would stand him in good stead in those Spaghetti Westerns like *A Fistful of Dollars* and *For a Few Dollars More,* which would propel him to stardom in the late 'sixties.

"I started getting big roles on TV with *Rawhide,*" he recalled with a smile. I reminded him that at the time, 1959, there were forty Westerns on television, decades before cable. "We were a late season replacement," he remembered, "and I wasn't sure we'd be a hit. The *LA Times* critic said: 'Just what we need! Another Western.' But we were good and lasted eight seasons."

When his role as Rowdy Yates, trail boss Gil Favor's second in command, began getting him noticed, Sophia Loren appeared on *The Tonight Show.* She told host Jack Paar she was "dying to meet America's next great actor, Clint Eastwood." Paar stared at her and asked: "Who's that?" So Eastwood

In 2008 Clint Eastwood appeared on Reel Talk *to promote* Gran Torino *and his directing work in* The Changeling *and the then-forthcoming* Invictus. *Eastwood doesn't walk—he strides in a cool, smooth gait evoking the laconic aura of Gary Cooper.*

had a way to go before becoming a household name.

Today the actor is comfortable with his iconic status. When I told him I often see pictures of screen immortals painted on the walls of large movie theaters, I wondered what it was like being up there, literally, with Gable, Newman, Stewart, Fonda, Wayne, and Bogart. "I'm just glad I'm the one who's still alive," he laughed.

If Eastwood had never become an Oscar-winning director, his movie roles would've still made him an immortal. But directing brought out new sides to his talent. When I met a producer of his movie *Gran Torino*, she beamed at the memory of a director who brought his film in on time, under budget, and with good feedback from cast and crew alike. "I learned that from Don Siegel and other directors, too," he explained.

"Orson Welles and De Sica, with whom I worked, made their movies that way. I treat the actors and crew as part of a family. Sometimes circumstances can get in the way of a smooth production," he explained. "But if someone is dumb enough to finance my movie, I can at least respect that and be prepared."

I told him that Welles once said that "raising money for a movie is 95 percent hustle and 5 percent luck." "It's pretty much the same for me," said Eastwood, not mentioning the fact that, unlike Welles, he never had trouble raising money and knew how to handle it. "He went down a lot of different avenues, making movies on a shoestring. I never did that."

Eastwood did, however, direct and star in *Gran Torino* over just a few weeks the previous summer. He filmed in Michigan during a hiatus in post-production of *Changeling* while the special effects for that film, with incredible backdrops of Los Angeles eighty years ago, were still in the computers. There had been talk that this would be his last time in front of the cameras. "You muse out loud in front of journalists," he said.

"Sometimes they put it down as an absolute. I'm just saying that at my age they don't write roles for senior actors so much. Not that many, anyway."

There'd also been some Oscar buzz for his portrayal in *Gran Torino* of a grizzled Korean War veteran whose ideas on minorities eventually evolved. "The more he growled, the more I liked him," said Eastwood. "I just kept going straight ahead, not being afraid to attack the man's character.

"In this 'PC' generation, we've been inundated with that over the last few decades. Everybody's sick of it, and people like seeing a guy like this. And we've learned tolerance, which he learns at a late age."

One wonders how someone so famous can live a semblance of a normal life. "You can't complain about it, because what good's it going to do? You got into this business, and had a little bit of luck, and that's just circumstances. You don't sit there and groan about it. You chose this life."

But he didn't choose to be Charlton Heston's last-minute stand-in cohosting the Oscars in 1973. "Chuck had a flat tire on the freeway," Eastwood recalled, the hint of a cringe in his face.

"They picked me out of the audience and told me just to read the introductions. But they'd been written for Heston as a parody of Moses in *The Ten Commandments*. So with millions of people tuned in, I gave it a try, even though nobody knew why it was me up there doing this! Heston came in halfway through, and he started all the way back from the beginning! He didn't realize I'd been reading his lines for ten pages. So I went to the producer, Howard Koch, and said: 'Don't *ever* invite me back on this show again.'"

But he came back, of course, to pick up Oscars for directing *Unforgiven* and *Million Dollar Baby*. He has five, including the honorary Irving Thalberg award.

The former mayor of Carmel, California, had some praise for New York's billionaire mayor Michael Bloomberg. "There aren't enough people who go into politics nowadays, and one thing's certain: he's made so much money he's not going to embezzle anyone!"

Eastwood never directs the same sort of movie twice. "No two films are alike. The genre is always different. That's important to me, especially at this stage in my life. I'm too old to be doing sequels. I just kind of move on with something new," he said.

Clint Eastwood was an eleven pound baby, the largest recorded at the local county hospital. He hasn't stopped growing since.

RALPH FIENNES

The first time I remember seeing Ralph Fiennes's work on screen was in *Schindler's List*, as the venal commander of the concentration camp known as Paszow in Poland. The role, which he portrayed with an icy disdain for any form of humanity, won him an Oscar nomination and international fame. I've interviewed him three times to date and always found him intense, cordial, and eager to talk of his career and craft.

Incredibly, Fiennes is the only actor to date to win a Tony Award for portraying Hamlet.

"A role like that lingers in your system after you leave it," he said. I asked him about the time when, as a young actor, he met Sir John Gielgud, generally acknowledged to be the greatest Hamlet of the twentieth century. "I was late for lunch," he laughed. "I took the local train, which stopped at all the villages. You don't arrive late for lunch with Gielgud. He was about ninety-five then, but still feisty, and I was about to play one of his other famous roles, *Richard II*.

"Some actors can portray versions of themselves and be brilliant," he said, "but I pretend to be somebody completely different. All acting is reacting. I'm drawn to people who are confused in their lives, projecting one side of themselves, but another comes out. The process of making movies can be frustrating for an actor. You have to prepare for that, knowing you have long times of waiting between scenes. The days change, the weather doesn't cooperate. None of that is onstage. My agents know I love the theater, even though it's for less money and a longer commitment sometimes."

Fiennes struck me as a stage actor who does movies, in the footsteps of Laurence Olivier and Albert Finney, rather than a movie actor who occasionally returns to stage work. His mother supported his pen-

Ralph Fiennes, here promoting The Reader *(2008), struck me with his combination of laid-back intensity. A classical actor, he was surprisingly forthright and eager to talk about his work.*

chant for playing alone at kids' parties. While still a child, she gave him records of Olivier's *Hamlet* and *Henry V*.

"A bit odd, isn't that?" I asked.

"There was magic in it," he told me, delighting in the long-ago memory. His mother also gave him a replica of a Victorian theater. She knew even then he'd be an actor, especially when he wouldn't let anyone else play any of the parts. She may have been certain of his destiny, but Fiennes, so memorable in *The Reader*, wanted to be a soldier. But just for one day. When he visited a nearby barracks, that's all it took to end his desire to don a uniform.

Fiennes has an interesting family. I mentioned his cousin, an explorer and daredevil who trekked across Antarctica alone several times. The actor found a movie about his cousin's exploits intriguing, though the brutal weather conditions didn't appeal to him.

Another of his memorable performances came in *Quiz Show*, directed by Robert Redford. Fiennes, playing the patrician contestant Charles Van Doren, who was given answers in advance on a TV quiz show, drove to Cornwall, Connecticut, where the family lives.

"On a very hot summer day, I saw him sitting there, but decided we didn't have to meet," he recalled. "It would've been an invasion of his privacy. So I drove up and asked him directions to the village. I saw a vulnerable human being. That visit reminded me of his humanity."

I asked him about Redford as a director. Fiennes mentioned his "unnerving generosity. He kept asking me if I was happy. Very few directors ask that. But I was happy. I need to act. I don't know why, but I do. I'm lucky to get asked to work."

DENNIS HOPPER

When Dennis Hopper died in May 2010, he was described as a rebel, an icon, an anti-hero. All those descriptions swirled through my mind the day he came by the studio in 2008, promoting three films: *Swing Vote*, *Elegy*, and *Hell Ride*. I felt an immediate connection to him and to Hollywood of the 'fifties. For here was a living member of that era of classic movies like *Rebel Without a Cause*, *Gunfight at the O.K. Corral*, and *Giant*.

Hopper's movie and TV credits span an amazing 199 roles. Not to mention *Easy Rider*, *the* iconic film of the late 'sixties, which affected an entire generation of Americans and still resonates today.

"You were born in Dodge City, Kansas," I began. "I was born and raised on the Upper West Side of Manhattan. Do you mind if I borrow your birthplace just for today? It's so cool to be from Dodge City," I said. He laughed at that.

Two of his earliest roles, now lost in the mist of the early days of TV, were as a Civil War amputee in 1954 in a show called *Cavalcade of America* and in *Medic*. Hollywood studios didn't know what they had on their hands. They would find out soon enough.

"I thought I was the best actor I'd ever seen. Until I saw James Dean," he told me. "I came out of the old Globe Theater in San Diego when I was thirteen. I was a Warner Brothers contract player. I'd never seen anyone improvise. I had line readings, gestures, everything preconceived. 'What is *he* doing here?' I thought, watching Dean in *Giant*. 'It's not on the page.' I was amazed."

Though born in Fairmont, Indiana, Dean had come out of stage and television work in New York at the Actors Studio. In his brief career, he revolutionized modern acting, just as Brando was doing in a similar fashion.

"I came in to meet Columbia's head Harry Cohn, who told me he'd try to get rid of that

Dennis Hopper was on Reel Talk *to promote three films. He was one of the last links to the great postwar era of the antiheroes like Brando and Dean. But he evolved and endured, enjoying a 56-year career.*

'Shakespeare stuff,' as he called it. Cohn stood in front of a long shelf with a long line of Oscars. I'd never been in a studio and had never seen an Oscar. I'd read a book called *Minutes of the Last Meeting*, which got me interested in acting and directing. Directing changes your perspective. Every actor should demand of himself to understand the responsibilities. As young actors, you can't grasp everything that goes into a film.

"*Easy Rider* is a movie which still holds up. At the time we were shooting, I'd hear songs by the Byrds and Hendrix and put it into the riding sequences. The words from their songs tell more about the story than the screenplay," he explained. "As for those bikes, they were later stolen, and many believe chopped up. They belonged in the Smithsonian. We could've been gunfighters riding into town on horses."

Hopper has been described as "America's most dangerous hero, the missing link between the sinner and the saint." He reveled in that appraisal of his screen persona. But he also remembered the other side of life for a young actor: "At the time we hated being contract players. But looking back, it was a great time. We had a great pool of actors, writers, and directors. There were no film schools in the mid-'fifties. To be able to see them score a film or see Holden and Brando working was amazing. That was our school, hanging around the sets at the studio."

One thing he didn't learn quickly, however, was to follow a director's direction. He clashed famously with Henry Hathaway on a set. Take after take they shot, with Hopper refusing to do the scene Hathaway's way. Soon word spread around town about the epic confrontation. Executives from other studios reportedly came by to watch the continuing standoff. Such stubbornness cost Hopper several years of not getting a crack at top roles.

Until I began researching his career, I never knew Hopper dreamed of becoming a painter. He might've been, well, another Hopper. He studied art, and one of his teachers was the great muralist Thomas Hart Benton. Benton looked at the young Hopper's painting in class one day and said: "Kid, you won't understand this, but if you want to be a painter, get tight and paint loose."

Samuel L. Jackson certainly has his own walk—a charismatic swagger which goes with his incredible screen persona, commanding a role without overwhelming his costars.

SAMUEL L. JACKSON

I've interviewed Samuel L. Jackson, perhaps the most prolific film star of his generation, four times. He'd often arrive with a trademark peak cap worn backwards, as if headed to the next hole on a golf course, his favorite activity. He has a familiar bounce to his step. Like John Wayne, or more recently Christopher Walken, his way of walking is part of his screen persona. One interview came in conjunction with his movie *Resurrecting the Champ* in 2007.

"I love golf," he began, even though he hadn't yet been asked a question, "and I'd love to be out there playing, but I love being on a movie set more. I get up and go to work like people in my house did when I was growing up. Vacation for me sometimes is having three days off on location to explore the place I'm filming." By that he means looking for the best place to use his clubs.

"I always tell actors one of the most important lessons learned was knowing where you came from and where you're going. If you have that information, all the stuff that falls in between kind of gets filled in, in the right way, all the right information. You try and achieve your goal of moving on towards where you're going."

Jackson reads seven scripts a week, and is in the enviable position of rejecting most of them. He's looking for the type of characters you'd talk about after seeing the movie. His first role was as the Sugar Plum Fairy in grade school. Unfortunately, no footage is extant.

"Film acting is tougher than stage acting," he believes, and he's done both. "There is no energy, no feedback like you get when you're onstage. In that way, it's draining. In the theater, there's a healthy sharing of energy, and you give something to the audience, and they return the favor. In movies, you give, give, give to a machine. Meanwhile, the crew is often thinking of the next setup."

Jackson's favorite all-time actor is Jack Elam, the longtime character actor who specialized in Westerns. Look him up and you'll surely recognize him, although he was never a star. "He had an agenda and looked different from other people. That's what attracted me to him.

"I longed for the time I knew I could carry a film," he recalled. It came after *Pulp Fiction*.

"After I starred with Bruce Willis in *Die Hard: With a Vengeance*, in 1995, he told me it would change my career.

"I knew that if I had the right character I could make it interesting enough and compelling enough and become engaged. And that's how it happened."

Jackson and I share a love for *Sea Hunt*, the cult-favorite TV show that starred Lloyd Bridges. We even swapped plotlines to prove our devotion. "I wanted to be an oceanographer because of that show," he laughed.

"And now, when I'm playing golf with friends and someone in our group hits one into the drink, I'll hum the theme song from *Sea Hunt*. Half the time they don't know what I'm doing." I did, and hummed along.

Speaking of music, Jackson has an issue with rappers trying their hand at acting in his movies. He says they haven't earned credibility as actors. "When you take someone from another venue," he explained, "and put them in my venue, I can't validate their career before they've done anything. I heard 'no' forever. I pounded the pavement, honing my craft. If they're put in the movie to bring in fans of their music, it goes against me and all the young actors sacrificing so much to get to that point."

BEN KINGSLEY

Born Krishna Pandit Bhanji in London in 1943, Sir Ben Kingsley first came to my studio in September 1983, during his brief run on Broadway in *Edmund Kean*, a one-man show in which he played the famous British actor. He dominated the stage with one of the most powerful performances of the season. By contrast, in the studio, he was almost shy, self-effacing, but very informative. Since then, I've interviewed him five times and noticed a surprising sense of humor from someone prone to portray serious types, as in *Gandhi*, or Simon Wiesenthal in *Murderers Among Us*, or Itzhak Stern in *Schindler's List*. But he remains a classical actor, equally at home on stage or on the big screen.

When I first interviewed Sir Ben Kingsley, I thought he'd be standoffish, but he's a closet comedian who, no matter how sinister or serious his roles were, always injected a joke in the interviews we did.

"I'm getting better at reading scripts," he told me in 2007. "I did theater work when I was younger, and it teaches you to explore the text, the language, and find the rhythm of each character. Then you find how the chemistry plays together."

When he was still deciding his future in 1964, he went to see a production of *Richard III* with Ian Holm.

It was at Stratford-Upon-Avon, the Bard's birthplace. "It was a very hot day," Kingsley recalled. "I was unable to get a seat, so I stood in the back of the theater, pacing back and forth. I was so moved by what I saw. But I passed out from the heat and the intensity of the situation. That convinced me to be an actor. It was a unique combination: The heat, no seats available, the powerful performances on stage—all of it. I knew then I couldn't live without it."

Kingsley, who was actually reading a biography of Gandhi when actor-director Sir Richard Attenborough called him about the movie, understands the thought process that brings him to the character he's playing. "What goes through my mind," he told me, "is the effort I make to get as close to nothing as possible. An empty slate. I try not to bring my agenda to interfere with the character's agenda. If I'm playing a real character, I'll trust the director before studying the real person.

"When I was portraying Nazi-hunter Simon Wiesenthal [in *Murderers Among Us*, in 1989], he came to the set in Budapest. I saw him sitting nearby, crying. To get his trust was amazing."

Kingsley has a propensity to portray historical figures; Gandhi, Wiesenthal, composer Dmitri Shostakovich, gangster Meyer Lansky, Lenin, and Otto Frank come to mind.

"They all came as surprises to me," he recalled. "I remember Wiesenthal calling me and I remember standing at attention because he's one of the greatest men in the world. But had I won the Oscar for portraying Dan Logan [a sadistic London gangster in *Sexy Beast*], audiences would've treated me differently.

"We make it difficult for the audience to divide the character from the actor. Because that's our skill. It's a bit unfair to respond to a fan by saying: 'It's only acting.' The more I'm fascinated by the tiny line between acting and being, the audience has a right to say you were that person. This is particularly true in cinema."

Sheridan Morley, the late, respected critic and son of the wonderful character actor Robert Morley, once wrote: "Ben Kingsley is from the Gielgud/Scofield tradition rather than from the Burton tradition." Kingsley addressed that: "I have a great admiration for Sir John Gielgud but I really adored Sir Ralph Richardson. The roles he and I have played have some kind of resonance. I can take from him safely."

Kingsley explained the different demands between stage and screen acting: "It's like a painter going from landscapes to portraits; it's a different technique with different demands. I love the interaction with the audience. On a set, however, there may be just fifty people watching you. And supporting you."

In *Gandhi*, his portrayal spanned fifty-six years of the great man's life. "Some of the historical journeys I've been on in movies have been bizarre. Had they been fiction, they wouldn't be that strange. You need some spine to the character, some se-cret message in the back of your head that makes every scene come from the same animal sense of that character, especially since you don't shoot movies in sequence. Fact, furthermore, is stranger than fiction."

Whereas Olivier could never quite handle an American accent, Kingsley is in that select group of British actors who can master American speech perfectly. "I like to think I have a musical ear with perfect pitch," he explained. "Luck of the draw to get a good ear. My childhood treat was impersonating someone when they left the room. I could replicate them quickly, like a caricature."

When he was knighted, he too experienced the Queen's firm handshake and the sense after that of being quickly pushed away. "She asked me what lay in the future," he recalled. "I replied: 'Ma'am, I'm going to the Oscars, but I hope the Academy understands that that somewhat pales compared to what I'm going through today.' Her amazing command of the situation is that the way she takes your hand and shakes it, and punctuates it, it makes you feel safe."

JAY LENO

I've always been a fan of Jay Leno. I first saw him on TV in the early 'seventies, and his humor had an edge to it I liked. We were both influenced by Robert Klein, who is adept at calling attention to the hilarious absurdities of everyday life. I began recording Leno's appearances on *The Tonight Show* and *The Late Show* on my black-and-white reel-to-reel videotape machine in 1977, and haven't been able to break the habit. "Headlines" and "Jaywalking" are among my favorites, along with his topical monologue.

One day in 2005, I'd heard he was in town to do *The Today Show*, plugging his book *How to Be the Funniest Kid in the Whole Wide World*, and I wouldn't take "No" to my request that he come across the street to my set.

Unlike a movie star, here was someone millions have welcomed into our living rooms and bedrooms for nearly two decades. It was a bit surreal at first. Also, unlike a movie star, he came alone.

I reminded him that when he was starting out he worked at a joint in Massachusetts called Lennie's on the Turnpike. "They really don't have places like that anymore," he recalled. "Lennie's was a jazz club, the first place I appeared where people really listened.

"Then there was a place called The Beachcomber in Revere. And the owner told me to wear old clothes, because people would smoke in the front row and flick their ashes at you. My jacket started to burn one night!"

Early in his career, he appeared on *The Midnight Special*, a weekly network variety show. "They'd tape it in the afternoon," he recalled, "and they'd give people on the street waiting to sit in the audience a box lunch with an apple. Most of them were homeless. It was 1977, and I was onstage and put my hand out to shake hands with a man in the audience, and he began screaming. 'He thinks you're trying to take his apple,' the producer said in the overhead speaker. It was that kind of a gig."

It was about that time that he was performing at a joint called La Stella Dora, opening for the great troubadour Muddy Waters. One night, a patron, impatient for the main act to begin, tossed a ketchup bottle at the stage during young Leno's performance. But the missile was intercepted and Leno was saved from serious injury by one of the strippers onstage. A woman named "Anita Mann," appropriately.

Then our talk got serious. "The first five minutes of an act are the most important," Leno said about doing stand-up. "If you're well known, you get those first five or ten minutes free. I used to open for Tom Jones and knew I'd have to come out punching, really. Hit them with my best stuff right away.

"I remember when I came to LA and was just starting out. It was 1976 when *Rocky* was opening. I called my Mom and told her Sylvester Stallone got 10 million dollars a week. She said: 'What about the *other* weeks of the year? He's not getting that money in *those* weeks.'"

Jay Leno never comes East, but when I heard he'd be in the building that morning, I insisted on a half hour with him. I wouldn't take no for an answer.

Then I showed Leno the Al Hirschfeld caricature of him that appeared on the cover of *Time* magazine.

"I called my mother in Andover, Massachusetts, where I grew up, to tell her the good news. I told her to call Aunt Eydie and Uncle Mike to tell everybody to pick up *Time*. But she didn't get the concept. She thought my picture was only on the cover of the Andover edition of *Time*, certainly not in other places.

"Never perform for your family," he advised. "On audition night at The Bitter End, in New York, I got the chance to appear instead of the regular guy. I made the mistake of calling my parents with the good news, and they called my Uncle Lou who was at the racetrack. He came and brought my grandmother, who spoke no English. At that time they served only herb tea, so Uncle Lou let them know in a loud voice he wanted liquor and he wanted it now! *Never* perform for your family."

I told him I have probably the largest collection of his monologues, "Headlines," "Jaywalking," and other segments in private hands and wondered if he'd saved any of those classic routines.

"Comedy is disposable," he replied. "So I don't have any of those." Though he rarely takes vacations and performs in Las Vegas several times a year when he's given time off from *The Tonight Show*, he said you "have to keep your distance from show business.

"It's like falling in love with a hooker. Enjoy it, have fun with it, but it'll kill you. Comedy is just doing it. I enjoy making love. I just don't want to be a gynecologist."

WILLIAM SHATNER

Like his fellow Canadian Leslie Nielsen, William Shatner reinvented his screen persona. He evolved from the serious, forceful Captain James Tiberius Kirk of the *Enterprise* on *Star Trek* and the policeman *T.J. Hooker* into a wry, sometimes sardonic, humorous actor on *Boston Legal* and in films as well. He loves telling stories, especially since I warmed him up by reciting lines from his performance in the 1970 TV version of Saul Levitt's masterful Broadway play, *The Andersonville Trial*.

George C. Scott had directed that production, having previously starred in the same role of the prosecuting attorney Lt. Colonel N.P. Chipman. The play recreated the post–Civil War trial of Captain Henry Wirz, the brutal commander of the infamous Confederate prisoner of war camp. In fact every time I see him, I recite, to his astonishment:

"That was more than just a military line.
Men crossed that line to get where the water was
  drinkable.
And counsel dares call it 'a proper military line.'"

Once his shock at that abated, I reminded him of the time he was on Broadway in 1958 in *The World of Suzie Wong*.

"France Nuyen was the title player, and she had a problem with our director, Josh Logan," Shatner recalled. "In fact it got so bad, she refused to utter any dialogue to me if she spotted Logan anywhere in the theater. And she did one night and just stopped talking in the middle of a sentence," he continued, suddenly stopping and staring at me until I got the joke.

Star Trek has made him an enduring international star, as have his low airfare commercials, TV work in *Boston Legal*, the many movie versions of *Star Trek*, and appearing solo at the closing of the 2010 Winter Olympics in Vancouver. But the short-lived TV series *Star Trek* has had an afterlife longer than any cancelled show in television history. He told me he never knows where he'll meet a fan.

One night, for example, Shatner was at an event in Hollywood and got into a limousine. The driver turned around and thanked Shatner for saving his life. "I was a POW in Vietnam," he explained. "We were in those tiger cages they showed in *The Deer Hunter*, and we were going mad. Water up to our necks, dangling in those horrible cages for hours on end. But then my buddies and I began telling each other episodes of *Star Trek*, and that kept us going and kept us sane. We began reciting the dialogue from the episodes we all knew by heart. I was you in several of them!"

EPILOGUE

A few days after my father retired, Pete Hamill, the great New York journalist, wrote a column in the space opposite the *Post*'s editorials. My father's column called that important space home for four decades to the day, May 20, 1934, to May 20, 1974.

Among his observations in tribute:

"'You gotta work at it, kid,' Lyons said to me one smoky midnight. 'You gotta work at it.' He was right, of course, and he followed his own advice for forty years, six days a week, pounding millions of words. . . . The beat was Sardi's and '21' and Basin Street East, the Embers, Danny's Hideaway, Toots Shor's, The Blue Angel, and the Stage.

"There were lots of other places, too; dinner parties, elegant openings, the lobbies of theaters, places where they would not let a photographer and a kid reporter through the door, but always had a welcome for Leonard Lyons.

"And Lyons worked at it so hard and for so long that there were some people around this town who took him and 'The Lyons Den' for granted. His column . . . was some elaborate, wonderful, very dependable bulletin board of the city. We knew from Lyons when Hemingway was in town, and what Saroyan was doing, and whether Behan was still off the sauce.

"We learned who was publishing books, who had landed a role on Broadway, and who had gone to Hollywood, and what all of them had to say about such things. Lyons . . . never succumbed to what finally destroyed Winchell: the instinct to punish and maim in the name of America. Leonard Lyons was not a mean man.

"At the end of those forty years, Shor had closed three joints, the Stork was turned into a park, Lindy's became a Steak 'n' Brew, Ruben's was shut down. The town shifted; nightclubs closed, and singles joints opened. TV kept people home. The Broadway theater was shrinking and started to become a museum.

"But Lyons kept going. When everybody was giving up on New York, Lyons stayed around and looked for the diamonds. He found them more often than anyone could have expected.

"Leonard Lyons did not engage in lurid feuds; he was an ornament to the profession. I cherish his continuing friendship and salute forty years and thank him for being kind to a kid reporter in some smoky saloon, years ago, when just about everybody I knew was young."

The city and our society have changed. Not necessarily improved, but clearly changed. Nightclubs, fancy dinner places—mostly gone. Want to learn about your favorite newsworthy person? Go online, or watch TV. Even the most mundane events—a starlet out on the town pretends to avoid the horde of flashbulbs, privately reveling in the free publicity. "Who cares?" is no longer a watchword.

My father worked in a world without cell phones, without texting, without e-mail, and without faxes. He got his news the old-fashioned way: he went out and spoke to people. And they spoke to him. As has been said, he probably knew more newsworthy people than anybody. And he wrote about them, 1,000 words a day, six days a week, for forty years.

I've often wondered what it would be like if he were alive and working today. Sure,

he'd carry a cell phone—but probably have trouble using it. (He couldn't make coffee for himself, although he drank it constantly.) Sardi's is still there. Broadway is still there. But the exclusivity, the pride in breaking a story, is largely gone today because of all the new media.

But my father knew how to change with the times. When Arthur, the discotheque, became a popular nightspot in 1964, he became a regular, meeting people there who were twenty-five years younger than many of the other people he wrote about. When Andy Warhol came along, they became friends. He even sent me to "The Factory" to deliver something. Newsworthy and interesting, that's what he was drawn to.

In his farewell column, after recapping his incredible career and life and family, he concluded by writing: "I know that when I will hear a good story or new item, I will, out of instinct, reach for my notebook and jot it down, then call the paper that has been so loyal to me and my family for forty years."

Ever the journalist. Probably still so.

INDEX

Page numbers in *italics* refer to illustrations. Page numbers in **BOLD** refer to showcased personalities.